MARKETING ISSUES IN TRANSITIONAL ECONOMIES

MARKETING ISSUES IN TRANSITIONAL ECONOMIES

edited by
Rajeev Batra

a volume in
The William Davidson Institute Series on Transitional and Emerging Economies

Kluwer Academic Publishers
Boston/Dordrecht/London

Distributors for North, Central and South America:
Kluwer Academic Publishers
101 Philip Drive
Assinippi Park
Norwell, Massachusetts 02061 USA
Telephone (781) 871-6600
Fax (781) 871-6528
E-Mail <kluwer@wkap.com>

Distributors for all other countries:
Kluwer Academic Publishers Group
Distribution Centre
Post Office Box 322
3300 AH Dordrecht, THE NETHERLANDS
Telephone 31 78 6392 392
Fax 31 78 6546 474
E-Mail <orderdept@wkap.nl>

Electronic Services <http://www.wkap.nl>

Library of Congress Cataloging-in-Publication Data

Marketing issues in transitional economies / edited by Rajeev Batra.
p. cm. -- (The William Davidson Institute series on transitional and emerging economies)
Papers presented at a conference organized by the Davidson Institute in Ann Arbor, Mich., on July 24-26, 1998.
ISBN 0-7923-8498-9
1. Marketing--Developing countries--Congresses. 2. Mixed economy--Developing countries--Congresses. 3. Developing countries--Economic conditions--Congresses. I. Batra, Rajeev. II. William Davidson Institute. III. Series.
HF5415.M29954 1999
658.8'009172'4--dc21 99-35795
CIP

Printed on acid-free paper.

Printed in the United States of America

TABLE OF CONTENTS

INTRODUCTION AND ACKNOWLEDGMENTS

This book examines issues facing marketing managers and scholars as the markets in the "transitional economies," or TEs (China, the Czech Republic, Hungary, Poland, Romania, Russia, Slovakia, Vietnam and others), become more deregulated and open. The issues examined include changes in consumer behavior; challenges to making firms in these countries more "market-oriented"; issues in creating and managing distribution channels; and issues in competitive strategy and tactics, including market entry and brand-building.

The sixteen chapters in this book are organized into five sections. We have, first, a chapter that "sets the stage" by reviewing recent changes in the marketing environment in these countries, and then draws managerial implications for marketing managers in multinational companies operating in these economies, as well as local firms. This chapter is based both on the literature as well as a set of very valuable reports written by student teams from the William Davidson Institute.

This is followed by a section on The Changing Consumer. In his chapter, Russ Belk draws on his research in China, Romania and Russia to help us understand why the presumably-poor consumers of TEs seem to place such a high value on luxury and status goods. The resulting insights into the feelings of "deservingness" and "yearning for respectability" that exist have major implications for all students of consumer behavior. David Tse and colleagues then present a very interesting study of intergenerational differences in conflict resolution among Chinese women, alerting us to subtle changes in consumer values in China. This theme continues into the next chapter, where Bernd Schmitt presents his data on the nature of consumer segments in China (Beijing and Shanghai), showing how acceptance of (and responses to) marketing institutions and practices varies among these segments as China undergoes its "Consumer Revolution." Finally in this section, Steven Burgess and Jan-Benedict Steenkamp take us to a very different part of the world—South Africa—to analyze the structure and consequences of consumer value priorities, including their impact on consumer openness-to-change.

The third section moves us to the other main set of actors, the firms. Here, the three chapters examine challenges relating to the measurement and creation of a market orientation among firms. Patricia Huddleston and Linda Good begin by presenting data from the Polish retail sector: they find that most of the relevant constructs developed by Kohli and Jaworski can in fact be reliably measured. The chapter by Rohit Deshpandé and John Farley reports a broader investigation, from more countries and of more constructs and scales—but they, too, report that measurement issues should no longer be considered a hurdle. The remaining challenge (and the more important one!) is of finding ways to make firms more market-oriented. This is the topic of Ron

Savitt's chapter, who reports field data from the Czech Republic to conclude that the firm-level restructuring to date has mostly been "shallow," and that deeper changes are still necessary.

Distribution issues are the focus of section four. We begin with a review of recent changes in the Distribution sector in Romania, by Carmen Balan, who offers her perspective on how and why these changes occurred, and how the sector may evolve in the future. Debra Dahab and Jim Gentry then look at Hungary, focusing on one particular phenomenon, changes in the importance of personal relationships ("embeddedness") and in the role played by branded products as a "governance mechanism." Louisa Ha, Mrinal Ghosh and colleagues then present exploratory data from China, showing both the distribution challenges facing firms and the manner in which firms are coping, using a transactions cost perspective to help explain their data.

The section on Strategy and Tactics follows. We first see how multinationals and local firms differ in the strategies and tactics they use in the Romanian market, through exploratory field data collected by Lalita and Ajay Manrai and Dana-Nicoleta Lascu. Yigang Pan and Xiaolian Li then discuss empirical results from several different large studies on the timing and mode of entry into the Chinese market—and conclude that it is indeed better to enter early, using equity joint venture arrangements. These results challenge conventional wisdom and are worthy of much reflection. The last three chapters address marketing challenges facing local (TE) firms as they fight global entrants. Drawing on their wealth of case data from China, India, Russia and other countries, Dawar and Ramachandran lay out strategies for local firms to exploit their "local-ness," pre-empt brand positions and distribution channels, leverage cost advantages and compete on speed of market responsiveness. Erich Joachimsthaler and colleagues address the brand-building challenges facing TE firms in more detail, and provide evidence that it will be necessary for these local brands to develop stronger personal and cultural connections with local consumers, than their global adversaries. Finally, Batra and Yi examine challenges facing TE companies as they try to market in developed overseas markets, using the example of South Korea. Their conclusion is that it is better to position TE brands as having high quality, instead of just superior value-for-money, if the country of origin image is poor. They offer several suggestions on how such high quality might be communicated.

Together, these chapters present data and frameworks on a wide range of topics concerning marketing issues in transitional economies. To our knowledge, no previous volume has brought together this quality of scholarship on these important topics, and this volume should, thus, make a valuable contribution to the literature. Most of these papers were originally presented at a Conference organized by The Davidson Institute in Ann Arbor, Michigan, on July 24–26, 1998. The Davidson Institute also funded many of the projects reported in this book, and we are all grateful to it for this support. Interested researchers are invited to learn more about the Institute and its programs through its web page, http://wdi.bus.umich.edu.

The authors of these chapters are obviously the first people I need to thank for their role in this book, but there are many others. Martha Lee, Heather Martinson and Amy Moored of The Davidson Institute helped put the original conference together, and Sharon Nakpairat and Karen Eisenhauer cheerfully helped bring this book to fruition.

Mary Ceccanese of the University of Michigan Business School was indispensable in copyediting and proofreading these chapters. Jan Svejnar and Hans Brechbuhl, present and former Directors of the Institute, provided the financial support we needed. Elizabeth Murry of Kluwer accepted and encouraged this book proposal. To you all, and to the others I may have missed, my thanks.

Rajeev Batra
Area Director for Marketing, The Davidson Institute

Overview

1 MARKETING ISSUES AND CHALLENGES IN TRANSITIONAL ECONOMIES*

Rajeev Batra
University of Michigan
and William Davidson Institute

Introduction

The movement towards freer markets in China, Vietnam, the former Soviet Union, Poland, Hungary, the Czech and Slovak Republics and others (the so-called "Transitional Economies," or TEs), has led to great interest in the marketing challenges and issues unique to these economies. Some of this interest comes from multinational corporations (MNCs), who see the growth and leadership potential in these emerging markets and have hastened to expand their operations in them (Nakata and Sivakumar 1995). Others are interested in these newly-opened TE markets because of the potential threat they represent to local TE corporations (TECs), as new MNC competitors flood in and take away market demand from these TECs. Some of these observers wish to strengthen these TECs, because strengthening them should contribute to the overall health of these TE economies and thus to the likelihood of success of the fragile economic transition process.

The interest of MNCs in TE markets is easy to understand, because of the attractiveness of these new markets. For example, the household penetration of durables in most of these countries is growing rapidly from very low base levels, and households are rapidly moving up their shopping lists of motorized two-wheelers, TVs, VCRs, air coolers, washing machines and clothes dryers, electric ranges, air-conditioners and cars. These increases in demand are fueled by rising incomes, increased availability of credit, the "demonstration effects" of expanding television reach and an increased demand for convenience from two-earner households (Jain 1993, p. 140). China reportedly now accounts for more refrigerator sales every year than the United States, and global appliance manufacturers such as Whirlpool, Bosch-Siemens and Electrolux have all recently expanded their operations there (*Appliance Manufacturer* 1995). According to *Business Week* (1994), the rate of growth in automobile demand in these economies is twice that in the industrialized countries; Czechs already buy more cars every year than the Swedes.

As mentioned, another reason for this interest in marketing challenges in TEs is the activity of organizations and individuals who wish to promote the commercial and market success of local (domestic) enterprises in TEs, operating in their own domestic markets and/or in overseas (export) markets. One such organization is The Davidson Institute at the University of Michigan Business School, established in 1992 to understand and facilitate the transition of TEs from command to free-market economies. As part of its mission, The Davidson Institute has for the past five years sent students and faculty to selected enterprises in TEs (both MNCs and TECs) to assist them in improving aspects of their management and marketing operations.

This chapter summarizes some of the recent marketing developments in TEs, drawing implications for both locally-based firms (the TECs), as well as MNCs operating in these TE marketing environments. It draws not only on published literature on these issues but also on a series of unique reports on the marketing issues facing particular firms (both TECs and MNCs), written by the students and faculty teams working for The Davidson Institute. Over the last five years, these teams have performed in-depth field studies of the existing marketing operations and environments of several firms operating in TEs, and their reports on these firms provide a rich source of information and insight into marketing issues and challenges facing them. (Background information on these the William Davidson Institute affiliated firms is provided in the Appendix.)

Note that our discussion and review concerning TEs will in some cases extend into issues that pertain to "emerging markets" and "less-developed countries" (LDCs) more generally. TEs were defined in the beginning of this chapter as economies moving from planned or command economies to free-market ones. LDCs have, in turn, been characterized as typically having agrarian economies, low incomes and income growth, poor infrastructures and low capital availability, high illiteracy, high infant mortality and low life expectancy, among other characteristics (Samli and Kaynak 1984). "Emerging Markets," by one definition, have some momentum and acceleration in their economic growth rates; while they have relatively low levels of per capita incomes, they are moving from a lower to a higher stage of economic development with some degree of success (Nakata and Sivakumar 1995).

Using these characterizations, it would seem that many TEs (like China or Poland) are clearly emerging markets, because of their high-growth rates, while some (like Russia) are probably not. Many TEs (such as China and Vietnam) are LDCs, while others (like the Czech Republic, Hungary or Poland) are probably not. Clearly, many emerging market LDCs (such as Brazil, or India) are not TEs in the sense that they are not just beginning to move from planned or command economies into free-markets, but have already had mostly-free market structures for many years.

Thus while there is substantial overlap among the countries called "transitional economies," LDCs and "emerging markets," it is clearly not complete. We will, therefore, wherever possible, point out whether a set of comments applies to all TEs, or just to the LDC TEs. Nonetheless, because of the overlap in TEs and emerging markets/LDCs, many aspects of our discussion will apply not only to TEs but to emerging markets/LDCs more generally.

TE MARKETING ENVIRONMENT: "BASELINE CONDITIONS"

Any characterization of the marketing environments of TEs must be preceded with two caveats. The first is simply that these economies are changing so rapidly that any description of what their markets look like is very likely to be out-of-date by the time it appears in print. The second, as just discussed above, is that there is obviously great variance across the many markets that are here collectively being called the TEs. It goes without saying that some of these markets are more "advanced" than others in terms of consumer incomes, average education levels, transportation and logistics infrastructure, the availability of high quality marketing data and human resources and many other very important market dimensions.

Nevertheless, several common conditions seem to characterize most of these TEs, though the extent to which any particular condition applies to any particular TE market may vary. Since these often change rapidly as a result of recent market and other reforms, these may usefully be thought of as "baseline conditions;" changes in these are discussed separately below. Other authors (e.g., Kaynak 1982; Samli and Kaynak 1984) have characterized such conditions along seven dimensions: economic, market, level of technology, general structure of distribution, social, competitive and legal/political. We prefer a more fine-grained description, and suggest that these "baseline conditions" for TEs include:

1. Consumer incomes, on a per-capita basis, that are low by Western standards. In "raw" (unadjusted) terms, per-capita incomes are approximately US$500 per annum (p.a.) in China, US$2–4,000 in the Central/East European countries, compared to US$26,000 in the United States. When adjusted for "purchasing power parity," they are about US$5–8,000 in Central/Eastern Europe and about US$2,500 in China (see Table 1).
2. Economies that typically have high rates of inflation (10–30 percent p.a., sometimes even more), foreign trade deficits, high unemployment rates (especially "hidden unemployment, or under-employment), high costs of capital, but low labor costs.
3. The presence of what has often been called a "dual economy" structure (Mahmoud and Rice 1984), with a relatively small elite urban high-income market amidst a relatively much larger subsistence- and low-income market (e.g. China's coastal vs. inland income gap), reflecting a relatively high degree of inequality in the distribution of income and wealth. In some of these countries (such as India), the top 10 percent of the population earns 30–40 percent of the income (Jain 1993, p. 74), and this is usually the market segment targeted by MNCs, especially since most of this segment tends to concentrate in major metropolitan areas (Gillespie and Alden 1989).
4. A traditional reliance on high levels of indirect taxation (such as sales and excise duties) for public finance, especially on "luxury" goods, in view of the relatively small amount of tax revenue generated by direct income taxes. This is often accompanied by high import duties and strict foreign exchange controls and non-convertibility (Mahmoud and Rice 1984). Other bureaucratic "hurdles" usually include investment controls, policy reversals, bureaucratic graft, a lack of coordination across government ministries and customs/import problems.

5. Major differences across metro and non-metro markets, or other geographical disparities. In China, for example, a major income gap exists between the coastal and the inland areas. Some larger TEs, such as the former Soviet Union (FSU) countries, also have a large number of cultural/religious/linguistic segments.
6. A historic tendency for markets to be "sellers markets" (Frazier, Gill and Kale 1989; Shama 1992), with demand exceeding supply, a consequent "price-control" orientation among governments and a "shortage psychology" among consumers and distribution channel members, with a tendency to buy, hoard or take advantage of scarce supplies of in-demand goods. TE consumers have frequently received goods through a "lottery-like" system in which scarce goods were distributed to buyers willing to either stand in line or participate in raffles after having prepaid for the item. This was frequently accompanied by the presence of a "black market," in which goods were available at prices much higher than the official ones (Zurawicki and Becker 1994). Black markets in all kinds of goods and services exist when a shortage of supply combines with government price controls, so that unscrupulous traders hoard the scarce good. This behavior often leads to price controls that prompts even more forward-buying behaviors by distributors and retailers (Samiee 1993).

   As will be commented on below, this is rapidly changing at present, with supply quickly catching up with (and in some cases even exceeding) demand. Some researchers claim that, because of this "shortage economy," TE consumers in countries such as Russia have little experience with variations in pricing, and thus do not quite know how to factor that into their choice processes (Golden *et al.* 1995).
7. A historic tendency among local marketers, often protected from foreign and even local competition by various governmental barriers and regulations, is to simply take advantage of market shortages and growth, instead of focusing on competing for market share through the development of products and services of higher quality and value. Since production from government-owned manufacturers was guaranteed to find buyers, who had to take whatever little they could get, producers were under no pressure to respond to buyer needs (Kaynak 1982).
8. Limited availability of marketing information, both secondary and primary (Kaynak 1984). Primary data collection is hampered by high non-response rates, a reluctance among consumers to be interviewed, high "yea-saying," very limited telephone access (and thus incomplete sampling frames) and a shortage of trained personnel. Secondary data are limited because of insufficient government budgets, but several government departments do put out key statistics, such as those on foreign trade, demographics and industrial production by sector (cf. Demidoff 1993). Walle and Ryans (1992) point out that Western companies can sometimes use World Bank "SIA" data, but these are usually qualitative, not timely, and not detailed enough.
9. The great importance of distribution intensity (and a "push" strategy) to any marketing program. This is due particularly to the low levels of literacy and incomes and the consequent inadequate development of channels of mass communication, as well as either the necessity to use existing "fragmented" and "long" distribution channels, or the near-absence of pre-existing distribution channels.

In those markets where distribution channels already exist (as in India), the reasons why they tend to be of this long and fragmented form is both very complex and very important (Bauer 1968; Samiee 1993; Mueller, Wenthe and Baron 1993). Consumers in these markets tend to live in geographically dispersed areas, tend not to own cars (and, often, refrigerators, which have a penetration in China of about 50 percent) and to have small homes and small incomes. These factors combine to lead to daily, instead of weekly, food shopping trips, and the shopping outlets therefore need to be located very close to where consumers live. In addition, because of their low incomes and therefore high-price orientation, consumers tend to comparison shop across many retail stores before actually buying. Furthermore, the retail sector tends to be an easy avenue of self-employment in these job-scarce economies, leading to more retail outlets than are needed.

Another important reason why these economies have this fragmented and very large distribution network is that these retail outlets typically rely for their inventory financing not on formal banking institutions but instead on distribution intermediaries such as wholesalers and semi-wholesalers, who in turn rely on the marketers themselves for such financing. The length of these channels is thus partly a consequence of the need for each level of the channel to provide financing to the next-lower level, and the inability of any level to finance a greater number of large retailers at that lower level. These dispersed and small retail outlets require frequent product deliveries, given their low capital base, and frequent sales force calls. In India, for instance, Hindustan Lever has a company sales force of 400 people directly calling on 220,000 retailers in 3,600 markets, with an additional coverage of 60,000 outlets in 6,500 smaller markets being provided by the sales force of their wholesale stockists (Varadarajan 1984). The lack of capital and of formal credit mechanisms means that these outlets operate on rapid turnover at low margins (often as low as 3–5 percent at wholesale and 5–10 percent at retail). Transactions are usually on a cash or consignment basis.

All of these factors lead to the existence of a very large number of independently-owned, small-sized and geographically-dispersed retail outlets, sometimes called "micro-retailing" (Simon-Miller 1984). These retailers are often 20–30 percent the size of Western retail outlets (Mueller, Wenthe and Baron 1993). There are about 3,000,000 retail outlets in India (Varadarajan 1984). Wedel, a chocolate and candy company in Poland, has over 180,000 "points of retail sale" and about 1000 wholesalers (Wedel Team Report 1995). Poland has an estimated total of 529,000 retailers and 20,000 wholesalers, according to *Business Central Europe* (1995). While Western countries often have 50–80 percent of sales occurring through large chains, such chains typically account for under 10 percent of retail sales in countries such as Poland (*Business Central Europe* 1995).

Clearly, these features do lead to system inefficiency, and an inadequate/difficult channel communication infrastructure. The length and fragmentation of these channels—as well as the fact that in supply-scarce economies such as these distributors do not need the manufacturers to create demand—makes it hard for manufacturers to exercise much control, and to get merchandising support and "push."

Many TEs do not have the kind of distribution structure just described. In China and some of the Central/East European countries, for instance, both domestic and MNC marketers are confronted with a near-absence of existing distribution channels. This is the result of the abandonment of the historical distribution system—in which state-owned manufacturers shipped goods to central distribution facilities owned by the Ministry of Commerce or Trade, and then on to its local/specialized distribution centers—without the compensating growth of new private channels. In China, until 1986, 80 percent of all goods were covered by the State Planning Commission, which gave companies production goals and allocated raw materials (the so-called *fenpei* system). Once produced, goods were shipped to the three major distribution Centers of the Ministry of Trade (after 1993, called the Ministry of Domestic Trade) at Tianjin, Shanghai and Guangzhou, from which they flowed to local centers that specialized by product. Such systems were often supplemented by other public sector or state-trading companies, and/or by cooperative distribution networks belonging to semi-governmental organizations. All imports were usually channeled through state foreign trade organizations, often specialized by product category. A few large distributors also existed that owed their historical origin to colonial trading companies (Reinganum and Helsell 1994).

An example of the "old" distribution system can be seen in Figure 1, which shows the way in which Dong Feng Motors (DFM), China's biggest truck manufacturer, used to distribute its trucks until recently (DFM Team Report 1994). Obviously, a company compelled to selling exclusively to a Ministry (such as DFM, or any importer) had no need at that time for its own distribution network—and found itself without one when the Ministry network disappeared. An alternative, or supplement, to such Ministry-run channels was the cooperative retail network in some countries.

10. Many of these markets have inadequate physical distribution and logistics infrastructures (Byrne and Jozefowski 1994; *Business Central Europe* 1995; Reinganum and Helsell 1994). It is especially hard to get to rural and semi-urban areas, which have poor transportation coverage. The roadway network is often inadequate in reach and size, and heavily congested with traffic, leading to extremely long shipping times. It has been reported that the maximum de-facto speed on China's highways is 40 kmph (25 mph), and that 20 percent of China's agricultural produce spoils by delivery. This is compounded by the presence of bottlenecks at various internal or external border and customs checkpoints, where graft and inspections slow traffic even further (often by 2-3 days). In China, these difficulties are made worse by the difficulty of shipping goods across provincial borders, which often have incompatible rail and other systems. Freight rates are often high, and there are very limited cold storage transportation facilities. Railway car availability is also often very poor, and rail shipment times long. DFM, for example, frequently found its trucks piled up at its railhead of Shiyan because no rail cars were available to ship them out (DFM Team Report 1994). Port shipping facilities are often primitive, with inadequate container shipping facilities.

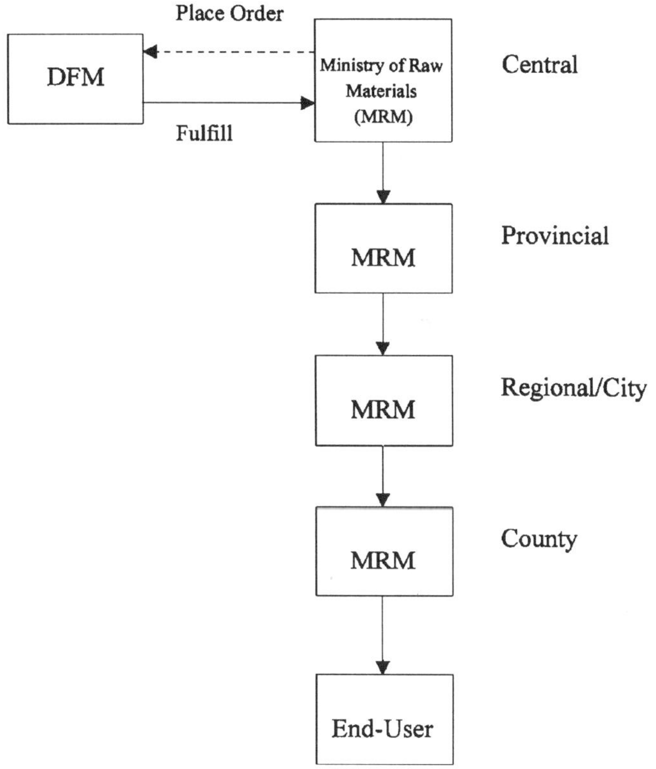

Source: Dong Feng Motors Corporation Team Report 1994

Figure 1. DFM's Distribution System Under the Planned Economy

There are reports of high crime in every transportation modality: highjackings of trucks on roadways and of railcars on the railroads, in addition to port crime. There is usually a shortage of quality warehousing space at important commercial centers, as well as a shortage of telecom facilities that are needed to coordinate and track product shipments. Some Western companies are attempting to use satellite-based cargo and truck-tracking systems to get around this problem. All of these problems suggest the need for products that have packaging that creates high shelf life and minimizes breakages (Samiee 1993).

11. A "gray market" often exists in imported and scarce commodities. Gray markets in imports exist when goods enter the country illegally without the payment of import or other tariffs (such as China's 17 percent VAT). Mechanisms include misuse of the right to ship duty free, or without customs inspection (often with the connivance of corrupt border officials), or false declarations on customs documents of product quantity, value or duty categories). Such practices obviously undermine the local sales of legitimately imported or locally-produced or as-

sembled versions of these imported products, and can even harm quality reputations if issues such as product freshness, or after-sales service, are important in that product category (China Hewlett-Packard Team Report 1996).

12. Such TE economies are also often characterized by labor disputes and strong trade unions, as well as labor laws that make it difficult to lay-off workers (*Business Week* 1994). Parts and supplies of satisfactory quality are often hard to obtain, and suppliers hard to locate. In one celebrated example, Nestlé had to set up its own system in China to buy milk from farmers and physically transport it from the farms to factory collection points (*Fortune* 1994). Local content legislation is often quite restrictive. These and other factors often profoundly alter manufacturing, sourcing and site location decisions.
13. The local political and regulatory environment can often be stifling and subject to corruption and/or the importance of personal relationships. China is famous for its "guanxi" system, in which the extent of one's "connections" can determine the success or failure of ventures. Having local partners is thus almost always essential to building the necessary contacts and providing "insider access." Regulatory and non-tariff barriers are often used to protect various markets from foreign competition: in the insurance market, it took AIG seventeen years to set up operations in China. The legal system is often underdeveloped and/or inefficient, and investment protection and other laws are often not in place (Zurawicki and Becker 1994). Laws regarding intellectual property (such as patents and trademarks), in particular, are sometimes not adequately enforced; this has recently led to trade tensions between the United States and many countries, notably China (Nakata and Sivakumar 1995).

TE MARKETING ENVIRONMENT: RECENT TRENDS

Economic and Regulatory Environment

The key transformation in most TE economies (such as the Czech Republic, Hungary and Poland) has been substantial enterprise privatization, with majority shares of GDP now coming from the private sector (see Table 1). Inflation rates are mostly down (to 10–20 percent, or even less), and unemployment is down and stable, though it still remains between 10–15 percent in some TEs such as Slovakia and Poland. While the reliance on heavy indirect taxation reported earlier has not changed, the import duty and foreign exchange regimes often have. Import duties are coming down because of the GATT/Uruguay Round agreements, while foreign exchange controls are being relaxed as part of market-opening measures mandated by institutions such as the World Bank. Companies that previously could only import goods via State Trading Organizations can now often do so directly.

Market Size

The rapid annual growth of incomes (in the 9–11 percent range in China, and the 5–8 percent range in the Central/East European countries—see Table 1) has led in many cases to very high rates of category demand growth, often 10–30 percent (Jain 1993,

p. 140). This is often even greater than the percentage increase in incomes, because the relevant growth rate is not that in average incomes, but in the number of households that exceed a certain threshold income.

A major source of growth in many TEs is the great increase in the number of households and of the ratio of consumers falling into younger age groups. In Vietnam, for instance, 36 percent of the population in 1994 was under 15 years of age (see Table 1). However, purchasing power is usually significant only in the 30+ age bracket, with the 18-25 age group usually not having significant income (*Business Week* 1994). In some economies, a second source of growth is rising incomes in the rural or non-metro areas, as consumers in these segments switch from non-branded (bulk) or traditional products to modern or branded ones (Jain 1993, pp. 62-63). This has implications both for MNCs and for TECs, which are discussed later. A third source of growth is the replacement or retro-fitting of older products that are now seen as technologically or stylistically obsolete. This process is sometimes hastened by regulatory change: in Poland, for instance, new environmental regulations (to take full effect by January 1997) have led to many existing owners of boilers deciding to replace or retrofit older, less environmentally-friendly boilers, thus creating a huge marketing opportunity for Ahlstrom-Fakop (now Foster-Wheeler Fakop), which uses a "clean-burning" technology (Ahlstrom-Fakop Team Report 1995).

In contrast to this increase in market sizes, however, companies that historically sold to the old FSU have often seen their entire markets wiped out, given the inability of FSU customers to pay in convertible currency (or to pay at all). For instance, the LET aircraft manufacturing company of the Czech Republic, which used to sell eighty 19-seater L410 turbo-prop aircraft annually to the FSU (mostly to Aeroflot), saw 90 percent of its its annual demand disappear, and its well-developed reputation for quality and durable products in the FSU become meaningless virtually overnight, when the FSU broke up (LET Team Report 1994). Similarly, Tatra, which makes durable off-road trucks with air-cooled engines, saw a 73 percent decline in sales from 1989 to 1993, with the collapse of the FSU (Tatra Team Report 1994).

Consumers

Consumer incomes have been growing rapidly for at least an urban group of middle-class consumers, leading to increased economic mobility. In addition, the increased exposure of consumers to global media, and depictions of Western lifestyles in local media, have increased their desires for quality branded goods and services. Several observers have claimed a great increase in the degree of consumer materialism, as consumers in TEs (such as Romania) feel a great need to keep up with the spending habits of neighbors (Belk and Ger 1994). There also appears to be an increased sensitivity to branding and status needs. Simon-Miller (1984, p. 123) points out that because of the scarcity of many kinds of goods in TEs, even functional goods can become seen as status goods, since their ownership and public display communicates power and prestige.

There has also been an escalation in the expectations of TE consumers regarding the level of quality in the products they buy. Shama (1992) found that Russian consumers were doing more comparative shopping and purchasing better quality and more

Table 1. Selected Marketing Statistics on Transitional and Other Economies

	China	Vietnam	Czech Republic	Poland	Hungary	Slovakia	Romania	Russia	India	Brazil	United States
# Households (1994, in thousands)[a]	285,135	15,524	3,338	11,450	3,955	1,832	7,610	5,210	182,496	37,565	97,312
Growth in # of households (1994/1993)[a]	1.08%	1.57%	0.06%	0.78%	1.15%	1.05%	1.01%	–0.04%	2.23%	1.79%	0.86%
Population growth rate (1995/1994)[b]	1.04%	1.71%	0.26%	0.36%	.02%(est)	0.54%	0.09%	0.20%	1.77%(est)	1.22%	1.02% (est)
Population distribution[b]:											
% <15 years	26%	36%	19%	23%	18%	23%	21%	22%	35%	31%	22%
% age 15–64	67%	59%	68%	66%	68%	66%	67%	66%	61%	64%	65%
% age 65 or older	7%	5%	13%	11%	14%	11%	12%	12%	4%	5%	13%
% Households with TVs[a] (1993)	80%[1994]	14%[1994]	98%	98%	99%	99%	95%	98%	19%[1994]	89.9%[1992]	97%[1994]

[a]*European Marketing Data and Statistics 1996* (1996).
International Marketing Data and Statistics 1996 (1996).
[b]*World Fact Book 1995* (1995).

durable products. Technology and feature/functionality expectations are also rising. In Whirlpool's experience, Chinese consumers buying washing machines, for instance, tend to prefer not the old twin-tub technology but the newer fully-automatic machines. Similarly, consumers in most TEs buying refrigerators have shown a willingness to pay for more expensive no-frost refrigerators instead of the older technology (Whirlpool Tatramat/Whirlpool Polska Team Reports 1995) . Obviously, different consumer segments exist, but there are signs that many TEs are evolving from a situation where one, low-priced, basic brand was all that was necessary, to situations where two, and even three, levels of quality and price might be warranted in many product markets.

Consumers are also at a formative stage regarding the formation of brand loyalty, as many of the old traditional local brands are dying out, and many new brands are being launched in the marketplace. In addition, many of the product categories that consumers are buying are new to them, and their low levels of knowledge about these product categories lead them to rely on brand name cues. Many consumers in TEs associate new, foreign products with superior quality (Shama 1992). One study found that buyers of TV sets in Russia, Poland and Hungary perceived sets made by U.S., Western European and Japanese companies, regardless of brand name and place of assembly, to be of higher quality and preferable to locally-made sets (Ettenson 1993). However, consumers in many cases also appear to have discovered that not all brands with Western brand names have high quality (this sometimes happened because the gray market goods they bought were old, etc.), and there have in some cases been reports of a backlash return to local-branded goods. Finally, there are reports of resurgent economic nationalism or chauvinism in some countries, such as Poland (Whirlpool Polska Team Report, 1995).

Competition

Most domestic competitors (formerly, or currently, state-owned enterprises) in TEs tend to be smaller in size, technically backward, overly integrated, and very high-cost manufacturers, operating in fragmented industries. Their manufacturing emphasis is usually on low-cost production of small levels of output, rather than scale economies (Nakata and Sivakumar 1995). They do tend to have high brand awareness, though not always a reputation for high-quality brands. Many traditional local TE manufacturers tend not to be marketing-driven companies, either because they have historically been able to sell whatever they can produce, or because they fatalistically believe that the market is beyond their control (Kaynak 1982). Small entrepreneurial businesses are another type of TE competitor; these tend to cater to small "niche" markets, and tend to be more consumer-oriented. However, they are usually small in size and impact, and are normally displaced by larger domestic or MNC enterprises after a market develops (Zurawicki and Becker 1994).

In most product categories, there has been a recent influx of MNC competition, from global or regional brands. This influx has been hastened by the usual lowering of tariff barriers, and these brands are either imported, assembled locally from knocked-down components, or manufactured locally (often in joint-venture arrangements). These new competitors usually tend to have much larger global volumes, and thus economies of global scale, as well as higher technical quality standards and more advanced product features. Their larger unit volumes tend to give them lower unit costs, especially in the case of South Korean competitors such as Samsung, Daewoo, Hyundai and Lucky-Goldstar. What these new competitors tend to lack in most TE markets, however, are distribution and/or service networks, as well as price levels low enough for the mass market (various Team Reports).

This has led, in many TE markets, to an increasing number of joint ventures or strategic alliances between global and local players, in which the global player provides technology and financial resources, while the local player provides distribution and service networks, and low-cost local manufacturing capacity. The global players, in many cases, are interested in local manufacturing capacity both to serve the local market and as a low-cost manufacturing source for other markets. They need the local players to speed-up their access to such low-cost local manufacturing capacity, as well as for local market knowledge and political access. The local players, in turn, need the global players for technology and quality improvements, as well as for superior marketing "know-how," to better compete in local markets and to gain market access to foreign markets.

The great increase in the number of foreign competitors (and manufacturing capacity), along with market maturation and increasing consumer expectations, is setting the stage in many markets for a "shake-out" and consolidation among competitors. Those local TECs who fail to hook-up with sophisticated global or regional competitors are under particular danger, unless they alter their business and marketing strategies rapidly. (Some options facing these TECs are discussed later in this chapter.)

As noted before, in some cases MNCs end up also competing with gray market versions of their own (and/or competitive) products, sometimes of lower quality but always of lower price, and a strategy to compete with such goods is also often necessary. China Hewlett-Packard, for instance, has decided to manufacture only those products in China which it does not produce anywhere else in the world, so that it does not have to compete in China with its own gray market products from other manufacturing locations (China Hewlett-Packard Team Report 1996).

Product

Given the influx of new competitors into TE markets, these markets have recently seen a ramping up of technical, quality and feature standards. Low quality goods/services are historically common in TEs due to low-grade inputs, antiquated production methods and equipment, poor managerial and human capital skills, captive markets offering no incentives to upgrade quality and the lack of enforced quality standards within industry and by government bodies (Nakata and Sivakumar 1995). The entry by regional and MNC suppliers usually leads to the introduction of global-quality products and services into TE markets, and raises quality standards throughout.

At the same time, the creation of new manufacturing capacity by these new competitors has led to a change in the old supply/demand imbalance discussed earlier. Where once demand exceeded supply, the situation today is (or will soon be) frequently the reverse, despite the great increase in demand (fueled by increasing incomes, discussed earlier). Some of this increase in supply has come from small entrepreneurs, who have rushed to take advantage of market shortages (Johnson and Loveman 1995).

Price

TE markets appear to have gone through two price phases. In the first phase, when the markets opened up and Western goods flooded in, consumers suddenly saw much higher prices in stores for the Western brands than for their local brands, usually much higher than what local purchasing power levels would warrant (Zurawicki and Becker 1994). Nevertheless, these Western higher-priced brands did still sell (in many cases), because of their perceived higher quality, their import cachet, their appeal to an upper-end elite consumer segment, etc.

In the second, more recent phase, however, the increase in supply capacity just discussed has, in many cases, led to a price shakeout. For instance, in the telephone switching market in China, Siemen's production facility in Beijing was only able to operate one of their three production lines available, because of insufficient demand, and offered customers their switching equipment for hundreds of thousands of dollars less than the price set by AT&T (AT&T of China Team Report 1994). The price of such equipment in China has dropped by 20–30 percent over the last two years.

Despite such shake-outs, however, the prices of Western-branded goods still tend to be much higher than the mass-market level, and still tend to be suitable only for the upper-end of most markets. Most smart MNCs, as a consequence, are performing "value-engineering" exercises, trying to squeeze out all costs for product/service features that are not highly valued by local consumers, whose tastes and wants are often different from those of the "home" consumers for these brands, in an attempt to "set-costs-based-on-price" rather than "price-up-from-cost" (Interbrands Team Reports 1995). Attempts also need to be made to make sourcing and procurement decisions in the most cost-effective manner.

There is also still a major shortage of easily available credit/installment financing facilities in most TEs. Consumers thus often have to save up the entire purchase amount (often several months' salary, for appliances or cars) before they can buy. Some Western banks like Citibank have made the provision of consumer credit in TEs a very profitable part of their business (*Forbes* 1996), and manufacturers like Whirlpool have also begun to expand the TE operations of their consumer finance subsidiaries (Whirlpool Tatramat/Whirlpool Polska Team Reports 1995). Clearly, the provision of such consumer credit can be a major competitive tool in such TEs.

Finally, there are some indications that TE consumers have begun to learn that initial product prices (and/or brand name, or country-of-origin) may not be an adequate decision-making criterion. In some cases, consumers have had performance problems with imported products, such as certain durables (Whirlpool Tatramat Team Report 1995). This has led to the consumer realization that after-sales networks, and warranties, are also important, in addition to initial price.

Distribution

In those TE markets where almost no private distribution systems existed, such systems are now growing rapidly. In China, those outlets that previously served as local distribution centers of the Ministry of Trade or Commerce have evolved into independent distributors or retailers, with their own warehouses, trucks, etc., contracting independently with manufacturers or other wholesalers. Factories that previously could only distribute through the Ministry distribution networks are now usually free to distribute their goods directly through any channel they choose, with possibly only a small portion reserved for government use or distribution, especially in the case of products with a national security need (DFM Team Report 1994). Large department stores (such as Beijing's People's Central Store #1) have begun to act as distribution centers for various suppliers, in addition to acting as retailers for them (Reinganum and Helsell 1994).

The retail sector in China now consists of about 9.2 million very small (one-and-two person) retail shops, of which about 7.8 million are privately owned; about 290,000 state-owned retail enterprises, mainly department stores, accounting for 41 percent of retail sales; and about 1.2 million collectively-owned enterprises, averaging six persons per venture and accounting for 28 percent of retail sales (Harvard Business School Case 1995). The wholesale distribution system in China is still predominantly government-run, however, and consists essentially of warehouses segmented into regional, county and township units, each level supplying the ones below according to decisions made at the top. Foreign companies are not allowed to enter the wholesale sector. Imports can now usually be made directly by authorized importers, instead of having to go through state-trading firms. Trade fairs are often an important venue for buyers and sellers to meet each other.

In those markets where private distribution systems did exist, in the long-and-fragmented form described earlier, there are signs of consolidation at both the retail and wholesale levels. This is leading to increases in average size of retailer and of distributor, in the degree of concentration, in specialization, and in efficiency and a decrease in channel length (Samiee 1993). Retailers are getting better training, are offering more retail services, including retail credit, and doing better merchandising (Dannhaeuser 1987). Larger stores now often compete on assortment and price, using their economies of scale, while smaller ones—often part of the "informal sector," such as open-air stalls—compete on convenience (Mueller, Wenthe and Baron 1993). There is a limit to how big these large stores can get in TEs, however. Retail historians have argued that for self-service supermarkets to grow, there needs to be an increase in average per-store volume, in consumer literacy, in labor costs, in the acceptance of fixed prices (instead of the traditional haggling) and in the growth of packaged (instead of bulk) goods. These factors are quite likely to emerge sometime in TEs, but not very soon.

As an example of such consolidation, Mueller, Wenthe and Baron (1993) have reported on the changes occurring in Hungary in the food industry distribution system. The "old" distribution system consisted of a geographic monopoly—one vertically-integrated wholesaler in each of eleven geographical regions—each selling to many retailers, including state-owned retail chains and cooperative networks. The "new" system is vastly different. There are now thirty independent wholesalers, each covering the entire country. New "cash-and-carry" and discount wholesaling channels have also emerged, to service smaller retailers who do not have to order quantities large enough to justify direct delivery. The state-owned retail chains are being broken up and sold as individual stores. There are many more private food retailers than before, including retail chains with 100+ stores in Budapest, that offer better customer service than smaller stores, including longer hours. These obviously have tremendous buying power with manufacturers, and deal directly with them, bypassing wholesalers.

There are also signs of international consolidation: retail giants such as Carrefour and Walmart are expanding into TEs (in South America and in China), and global marketers such as P&G and Whirlpool increasingly have to offer them products at similar prices and terms in all their locations. Not surprisingly, such global retail consolidation is moving negotiating power into the retailers' hands.

As these distribution channels evolve, both MNCs and TECs are modifying their own distribution systems to take advantage of these opportunities, and these company systems are therefore often in a state of transition and flux, with new channels sometimes grafted on to older ones in an ad hoc manner. In China, for instance, the truck manufacturer Dong Feng Motors now has the distribution system shown in Figure 2, in which portions of its output are distributed through 13 subsidiaries, 53 partially-owned exclusive dealers, 1147 non-exclusive dealers and 327 service stations. DFM has 30 non-exclusive dealers in its "factory town" of Shiyan itself (population 400,000), leading to inevitable price warfare among retailers (DFM Team Report 1994). Importantly, the growth in TEC distribution networks is apparently much more pronounced in consumer goods businesses than in industrial goods and certain specialized sectors (Avrora Team Report 1995).

MNCs have often been at the vanguard of creating or improving distribution networks. P&G, for example, has set up van sales representative visits to smaller retail outlets, as well as initiated cash-and-carry availability in Romania (Interbrands Team Report 1995). Coca-Cola has reportedly invested huge sums to set up direct weekly truck distribution to 20-25,000 stores and kiosks in numerous TE countries, including Romania, with new fleets of trucks and drivers making deliveries to them once or twice a week (*International Herald Tribune* 1995). Some other MNCs (such as the clothing company Bennetton) have chosen to set up their own retail stores, but this is obviously only feasible where only the geographically-concentrated urban/metro market is being targeted.

The options facing MNCs usually include:

1. Going via one, or very few, national distributors (such as Polbita in Poland, which has 22 warehouses and reaches 25,000 retail outlets, and makes money by demanding 90-day credit from manufacturers while extending only 14-day credit to its retail customers) (Mueller and Broderick 1995);
2. Selling to many (e.g., 200–400) wholesalers, on a cash or other basis;
3. Setting up exclusive distributors/wholesalers on a regional basis;
4. Direct distribution (as in the case of Coca-Cola and some snack and candy/confectionery companies); or
5. Owning or franchising own retail stores (such as Benetton).

Any company seeking to create or expand a distribution network is faced with difficulties in locating and evaluating distributors (usually on the basis of capital, expertise, location and talent), and in controlling and motivating them (given the uncertain legal enforceability of distribution contracts/agreements). Given the difficulty of ob-

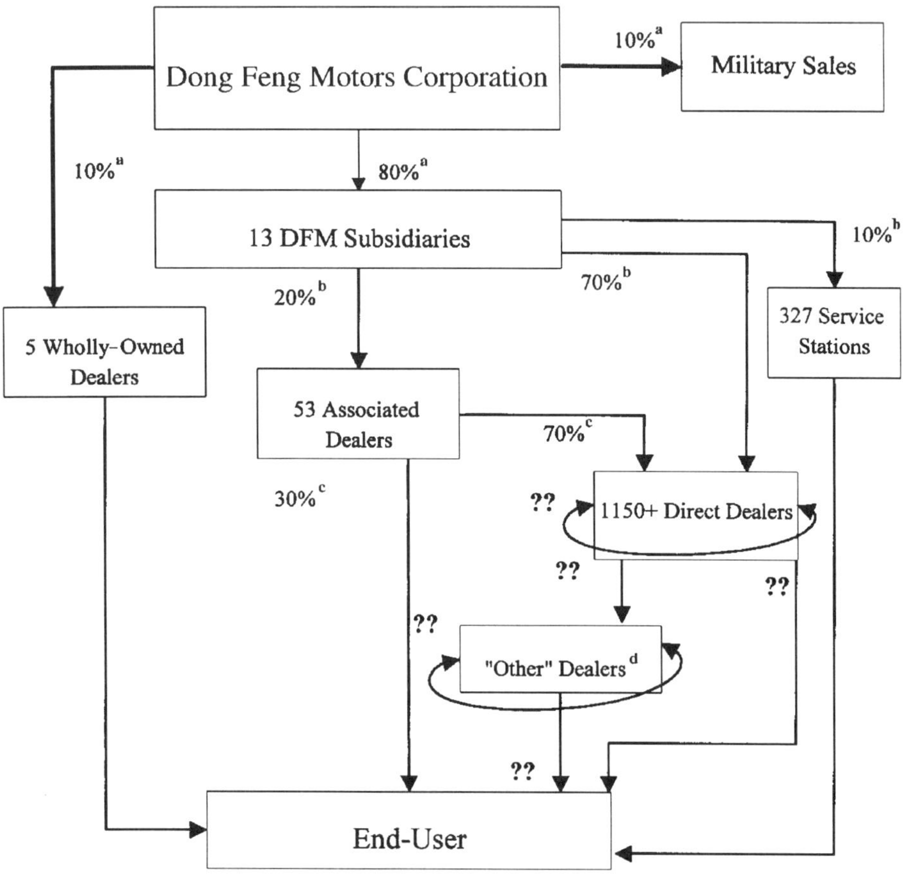

[a]Portion of DFM vehicles through each channel.
[b]Portion of DFM subsidiaries's vehicles through each channel.
[c]Portion of DFM associated dealers' vehicles to end-users or other dealers.
[d]An estimate of the total number of "Other Dealers" may be as high as 10,000. Intradealer trading occurs in both the Direct Dealers and "Other" Dealers level.

Source: Dong Feng Motors Corporation Team Report 1994.

Figure 2. Dong Feng Motors Corporation New Distribution System

taining market information and of locating suitable distributors (in terms of capital, expertise, entrepreneurial flair and good location), MNCs have not surprisingly made some poor selection decisions (Zurawicki and Becker 1994). Most MNCs still have limited distribution; this is one area where local firms still have an advantage. In some cases, such as China, MNCs are prohibited from entering the wholesale distribution business.

Clearly, these still-evolving distribution systems in TEs can be inefficient in various ways, and various problems and bottlenecks remain. Thus, substantial potential exists for improving them. These include the growth of institutions to provide credit and liquidity to retailers and consumers, as well as dismantling barriers to the free trade of goods across provincial borders, notably in China. Payment liquidity is also a major issue in China that needs resolution, with the existence of "triangular debt," in which firm A owes firm B, which owes firm C, which owes firm A, with none of these having the liquidity to pay its creditors (or suppliers). As a result of such problems, goods are often sold on a 20 percent down, 80 percent consignment basis, or on very long (such as 50 days) extended payment terms (Reinganum and Helsell 1994). In Russia, distribution networks often have strong links to organized crime (*Wall Street Journal* 1995).

Infrastructure

Most of the TEs have reported plans to improve their transportation infrastructure (railroads, roadways, port shipping, etc.), as well as their telecommunication facilities. Poland, for instance, intends to invest almost $8 billion in a 2,600 km network of toll motorways (*Business Central Europe* 1995). China's goal is to develop an integrated system of highways within the next 10 years; this may be unrealistic, however, and provincial protectionism still remains a barrier to free movement of goods in that country (Reinganum and Helsell 1994).

Improvements are also occurring in marketing infrastructure. While shortages still persist in the availability of high-quality information and managerial talent, many Western suppliers have now started operations in TEs, often with local partners, and Western-affiliated advertising and market research agencies are usually available (Shipley *et al.* 1995). Both Gallup and the Survey Research Group, for instance, now conduct research in China (*Marketing News* 1994). Nevertheless, this is limited in extent, and these services are usually unaffordable for smaller domestic enterprises. Substantial gaps still remain, such as in the case of direct marketing information and skills.

Promotions

The amount of advertising spending in TEs has skyrocketed from very low initial levels, though reliable figures are hard to come by (Terpstra and Sarathy 1994). The growth in spending is fueled mostly by MNCs, which have a resource advantage of "deep pockets," but local firms have also greatly increased their spending in an attempt to keep up and be competitive. Such high levels of advertising spending are especially important at a time when markets are growing so fast, and so many new consumers are entering the market.

In terms of media reach, there has been a great increase in TV viewership, including satellite-based and cable-fed global, regional and local channels. Ninety-one percent of urban Chinese households now own television sets (Harvard Business School Case 1995). Illiteracy and limited media reach are still problems in rural areas, however, and point-of-sale, cinema and outdoor media are thus still very important in many markets, as are sponsorships (e.g. of sports events), and trade fairs. Public relations can be especially important in building low-cost awareness, and in establishing local credibility for MNCs. Cost-efficient media placement is still a problem in many TEs, however, because of the scarcity of reliable audience data.

Enterprises in TEs have little experience with planned sales promotions, and frequently slash prices very deeply when inventories pile up (Zurawicki and Becker 1994). Couponing and sample promotion are rarely practiced, and are even legally prohibited in some TE markets. However, MNCs are often the sources of innovative practices in this area. Whirlpool, for example, uses discounts, co-op advertising and lotteries (sweepstakes) to increase trade partner motivation in Slovakia, as well as consumer promotions such as free installation offers and lotteries (including one targeting newlyweds who can win furniture for their apartments if they purchase a refrigerator) (Whirlpool Tatramat Team Report 1995).

MANAGERIAL IMPLICATIONS: MNCS

Product

In their rush to expand and grow their TE businesses, most MNCs have thus far aimed at the higher-end segment of consumers. However, to truly take advantage of the demand in TE markets, MNCs need to also compete in the mid-range segment, if not the low-end. This calls for product development and modification that strips out of their existing higher-end models those features—with corresponding costs—that are not highly valued by this middle segment. The key imperative for MNCs on the product end, therefore, is to adapt their products to better meet basic needs in TEs. For instance, cars meant for TE markets need to be designed with heavier suspensions, in smaller sizes, without fancy features and with the ability to use gasohol or leaded gasoline (*Business Week* 1994). As an example, the 5-ton trucks made in China by Dong Feng Motors are very successful there simply because they exceed local market expectations on a most vital "low-end" feature—they were actually capable of carrying more than a 5-ton payload, which cargo-carrying customers found very useful (DFM Team Report 1994).

The William Davidson Institute field research brought to light various examples of MNCs that had not, at least initially, done this "stripping-down." AT&T, for example, found that its world-class 5ESS-2000 telephone switching equipment in China was over-priced in the Chinese market, largely because of a software component that was far too sophisticated for local buyer needs, but one that the parent company had sunk huge costs into and therefore wished to recover through pricing (AT&T of China Team Report 1994). A boiler company in Poland, Ahlstrom-Fakop, found that its environmentally-superior circulating fluidized boilers were too expensive for local utilities, which did not at that time feel compelled to pay the extra amount for that feature (Ahlstrom-Fakop Team Report 1994). Whirlpool's microwave ovens, when first sold in Hungary and Poland, were chock-full of little-used features that raised the price above levels affordable to the local market, especially given low-end South Korean entries. Whirlpool eventually moved to a cheaper production source in China for its Central/East European microwave supplies (Whirlpool Polska Team Report 1995). Such product re-design is often done more easily in non-U.S., "third world" locations. MNCs (and TECs as well) often find local market research facilities and organizations to be inadequate, however, and have to develop internal procedures for obtaining reliable consumer feedback on new product concepts, etc.

A second product imperative for MNCs is that products sold in TEs must be those that are exceedingly reliable and need less servicing (Simon-Miller 1984, p. 123). Two William Davidson Institute companies that had high local market demand, at least initially, were LET aircraft and Tatra trucks, both of the Czech Republic, that had carved out market niches in the FSU with aircraft and trucks, respectively, that were very suitable for rugged operating and climatic conditions. LET's L-410 aircraft could take off from and land on short and unpaved runways, and withstand very high and very cool temperatures, require low maintenance and provide low operating costs (LET Team Report 1993). Tatra's air-cooled trucks could operate better than water-cooled ones at extreme temperatures, and the absence of a radiator system made the engine less prone to damage during rugged off-road use, making Tatra trucks renowned for their performance in severe climatic regions such as desert and Arctic areas (Tatra Team Report 1994). MNCs therefore need to design their products with TE operating conditions in mind. Appliance manufacturers, for instance, would do well to design their products with an ability to withstand voltage fluctuations and to be very energy-efficient.

The need to design "stripped down" and "tough" products for TEs should not be taken to mean that MNCs need to compromise on basic quality standards. Indeed, a key opportunity for MNCs is to gain "first mover" advantages by being the first to offer high-quality products and services that stand out in a sea of low-grade offerings, and that meet market needs for consistency and reliability (Nakata and Sivakumar 1995). Finally, where the MNC products are being assembled in TE markets from components imported from outside manufacturing sources, the parts should be designed to be assembled easily, in conditions where a high degree of quality control and high productivity may not be possible, though efforts to get them are obviously necessary (*Business Week* 1994). As noted earlier, strict local content regulations may also apply. Such local assembly might, however, diminish the product's "manufactured overseas" cachet, and thus lower the price premium that can be commanded in the local market. AT&T found this to be the case in the Chinese telephone switching market. (AT&T of China Team Report 1994.)

One other product-related issue facing many MNCs (and TECs) is the inability to forecast production volumes accurately in such fast-growing markets, leading to very low forecast accuracy and consequently frequent out-of-stock or excess-inventory situations. Whirlpool recently found its "3-month-out" forecasts in the Central/East European region were not accurate enough (Whirlpool Polska Team Report 1995).

Price

The fact that average consumer incomes in TEs are relatively low has already been mentioned. Not surprisingly, this leads to a great degree of price-sensitivity (Simon-Miller 1984, p. 124), and demand for lower-priced products is consequently very high (Vachani 1990). MNCs thus need to create value-priced versions of their products that allow them to better meet these lower price points, through stripping out features and "value-engineering" their products and services to cut out costs that are unnecessary for local consumers (such as high-tech gadgets in cars). The exception to the need to launch more price-competitive products is for cases where a "status" good is involved (Simon-Miller 1984).

AT&T, for example, found that it could sell its telephone switching equipment better if it took out its high-cost software component that was not adding enough locally-perceived value. Whirlpool found that it had to come out with a lower-features and lower-cost Ignis brand in Central/Eastern Europe, priced below its initial Whirlpool-branded launch, to be adequately competitive at mass-market price points. Obviously, one way for MNCs to be able to price their TE models/products low is to take advantage of economies-of-global-scale, by designing and marketing these products on a global basis, using modular designs where feasible (Henley 1968). In addition, all kinds of costs need to be cut, including distribution and overhead.

Besides lowering the unit prices of their products, MNCs also need to increase the affordability of their products by making possible installment financing and leasing arrangements, to lower the amount of money needed by consumers at the time of purchase. As mentioned, the existing banking systems in TEs do not at this time (in many cases) provide such facilities or, where they do, do not sometimes consider some MNC customers to be good credit risks. The appliance manufacturer Whirlpool, therefore, is greatly expanding the global reach of its Whirlpool Finance Corporation consumer financing operations. The scarcity of local credit information can often be overcome by using innovative tactics, such as by offering credit to employees of reputed companies (Whirlpool Tatramat/Whirlpool Polska Team Reports 1995). AT&T has found that it needs to provide customers with financing facilities in order to sell its telephone switching equipment in China.

In the consumer packaged goods area, one way to reduce the amount of cash needed by a consumer at the point-of-purchase is to reduce the size of the package, to lower the per-unit price. Many low-income consumers in these countries, a large number of whom are paid daily wages and thus have very high "cash flow" needs, often cannot afford the unit prices of standard (in the West) pack sizes. P&G (and Lever Brothers) have both been very successful in increasing the sales of their shampoos in India and China by marketing them in single-use sachets, with each sachet priced at a very affordable unit price. This followed the realization that the source of future growth was going to be not an increase in market share but rather in market size, by attracting new users to the shampoo category from those lower income and more rural consumers who would otherwise have used more traditional, and cheaper, hair care products. By making available low-unit-price single-use shampoo sachets, both companies succeeded in getting these consumers to use modern shampoos once or twice a year, on special occasions (such as weddings), hopefully on the way to using shampoos more regularly. This strategy of marketing single-use packets, it should be noted, was followed earlier in these TE markets by companies marketing tea, coffee and similar products.

It should be remembered that the way to market price-competitive products in TEs is not only to lower unit prices, but also to add "perceived value" in other ways. For example, MNCs might find it possible to offer highly-valued warranties or extended service arrangements as part of their product offerings, thus adding to their perceived value and compensating, to some degree, for higher prices. Such warranties might be highly valued by local consumers who have experienced poor quality in previously-purchased local goods—buyers in TEs have traditionally had to deal with manufacturers who intentionally shortchange on volume, dilute product or violate other quality standards (Nakata and Sivakumar 1995). In addition, such warranties are crucial in "signaling" reliability in cases where the local after-sales networks of the MNCs might be small and thus a cause for concern to local consumers. In other cases, raising "perceived value" might require an educational effort, where consumers are told how a brand's "extra" features raise revenue and/or lower lifetime system cost. AT&T found the need to do this in China, for the software component of its telephone switching equipment (AT&T of China Team Report 1994).

Having said that, however, it should be repeated that lowering unit prices should really be the first priority for MNCs, and "unbundling" features and services is probably the more successful approach. Thus, if extended warranties are offered, they should probably be offered as extra-cost options, rather than as part of the basic unit's price.

Communications

High levels of mass communication are very important in TEs. Markets are growing rapidly, and the level of competition is intense. Many new consumers are becoming first-time purchasers in many product categories and are seeking basic product information, and long-lasting brand loyalties are being formed. Research has shown that pioneering brands often become "de facto standards" in their product categories, and become very hard to dislodge because of their "reputational advantages" (Carpenter and Nakamoto 1989). Thus spending levels for mass communications (as a percent of sales) need to be higher in TEs than in more mature and slower-growing Western markets. The low level of advertising clutter in most of these TEs presents an opportunity to MNCs to build long-lasting reputational effects (Nakata and Sivakumar 1995).

Since the individual brands being marketed may be starting from very low-awareness positions, and since the marketing MNC may wish to introduce additional brands down the road, it might be advisable (or more efficient) to supplement the building-up of individual brands with the building-up of the corporate brand as well. Procter and Gamble (P&G), for instance, found the need in Romania to make customers aware that it was the company behind the individual brands, through advertising and P-O-S communications (Interbrands Team Report 1995). This is something the company does not do in the United States.

In creating mass communications for their TE markets, MNCs obviously need to be conscious of local variations in what benefits are desired, as well as of cultural, social, political and religious sensitivities (which might even vary across cultural/ethnic segments within a country). These might call for adaptation in advertising, packaging and brand names. P&G, for example, found that consumers in some Eastern European markets laughed at the "shampoo-and-conditioning" benefits of its "Wash and Go" shampoo, because few consumers used (and were thus seeking) conditioners after their shampoo use. Further, P&G found that consumers in Romania found the candid discussion of feminine hygiene needs in their TV commercials for Always products to be disconcerting and offensive (Interbrands Team Report 1995). Other companies have found that it is sometimes better to downplay the foreign origin of their products, because local consumers may prefer to buy locally-sourced products, out of a sense of national pride (this was the case for Ahlstrom-Fakop boilers in Poland). The public visibility of local chief executives, as well as other public relations and advertising programs, can help to create such a "local image," when necessary.

Companies also need to be aware of differences in family decision-making roles and customs: communications aimed at females in one culture ought to be aimed at males in more traditional male-dominated cultures; old age might be more respected than youth; the role of children in decision-making or shopping might be minimal. Some TEs (such as China, or India, or Vietnam) also have non-Western religions and cultures, which may require a special level of sensitivity (Mahmoud and Rice 1984).

Of particular importance is the difference in product category penetration, and thus in consumer knowledge levels, across Western and TE markets. Since consumers in TEs typically are more consciously shopping for quality goods (having had poor experiences in the past with low-quality domestic goods), and since they are in most cases unfamiliar with product category attributes and benefits, as well as with the plethora of new brands, they may well be more responsive to factual, informative communication campaigns than to the image-intensive advertising suitable to more developed parity markets in the West (Simon-Miller 1984). Indeed, such consumer desires for product information also lends itself to influence tactics at the point-of-purchase, such as by retail salespeople.

Low literacy levels in some TEs—adult female literacy is only about 38 percent in China, 50 percent in India, though much higher in Eastern/Central Europe—create the need for less text, and more pictorial content, on product packages and in print mass communications, as well as requiring the use of broadcast media (with their audio-visual content) in preference to print media. Print media might also be preferable if the advertising strategy is to give substantial category and brand information, as just discussed. Direct mail and telemarketing infrastructures are often poor in many TEs, limiting their use.

The choice of media, in fact, is much more complicated in TEs. Not only is there much less reliable media/audience data, but many of the most appropriate media are non-traditional or fragmented, such as transit and city posters, point-of-sale, movie theater commercials, rural vans and even the press (Mahmoud and Rice 1984). Public relations and publicity are often much cheaper and more effective ways to create brand awareness and credible quality reputations, as are attempts to harness and generate positive word-of-mouth from visible opinion leaders (Simon-Miller 1984, p. 124).

Trade and consumer promotions might be especially valuable in TEs, given that consumers traditionally are used to bargaining and haggling behaviors at retailers, instead of buying at fixed prices. Trade promotions might help overcome reluctance by space-constrained distributors and retailers to carry new products (Samiee 1993). They might also be very useful in incentivizing trade channel members, especially if the stores are personally-owned. They are often vital to getting merchandising support, such as window displays. Incentives for retail sales people, for instance, might be especially helpful in "closing" sales, while consumer promotions might help consumers feel like "smart shoppers." Some of the sales promotions practices of Whirlpool in Slovakia were described earlier. It should be noted, however, that the sales promotion infrastructure in TEs is often very limited, and that their use is often restricted by government regulations.

Channels and Dealers

MNCs need, first of all, to expand the reach of their distribution channels in TEs to go beyond the major metro areas. As mentioned, many MNCs are pioneering in the creation of such channels, mostly in the consumer packaged goods area. In Romania, for instance, P&G is investing in establishing many more sub-distributors to reach the counties where it did not have a significant distribution presence with its existing distributors, as well as in building up its "cash-and-carry" and "van distribution" methods of operation, designed to serve smaller and more remote retail outlets (Interbrands Team Report 1995).

There needs to be a parallel effort, however, to make distribution systems in TEs far more cost efficient, because wringing excess costs out of distribution is one way in which MNCs can bring down the unit prices of their products and services. Many companies are thus investigating ways of increasing the cost efficiency of their channels. Wedel, Poland's major chocolate and candy company, is investigating ways to cut down its number of dealers, concentrating on those dealers that are more important to its business (Wedel Team Report 1995). P&G, in Romania, as well as other markets, is developing ways to lower the costs of its van sales and cash-and-carry sales operations that service lower-volume dealers.

Such cost-efficient channels can be one source of cost advantage for MNCs who are competing with local competitors with more traditional channels. In some TEs, such as India, the traditional distribution channels used by TECs and existing MNCs are already very "lean-and-mean," operating on very low levels of overhead and margins. Nevertheless, the huge numbers of outlets and channels, combined with the high fragmentation and low levels of concentration, mean that economies of scale are not used to lower costs, a situation made worse by the virtual non-use of information technology. Thus great potential exists for cost reduction.

In addition to expanding the effectiveness (reach) and cost-efficiency of their distribution channels, MNCs must often innovate in ways to provide credit and inventory financing for their distribution channels, since traditional banking institutions often do not exist to meet this need. The credit terms necessary in TEs often need to be more liberal and flexible than in the MNCs home markets.

MNCs (and TECs as well) also need to design ways to make distribution channels work more effectively in terms of providing better and timely market information to the manufacturer, including better quality sales forecasts. Incentives for such information should supplement the usual ones for higher sales quantities. These are necessary because few manufacturers in TECs treat their distribution channels as partners; instead, an adversarial relationship often exists between manufacturers and distributors/retailers. Mechanisms need to be implemented to create true partnership between manufacturers and dealers, including better joint promotion planning (Centertel Team Report 1995). In addition to incentive systems, partnership-building mechanisms include dealer contests and conferences, as well as basic relationship-building (especially important in China). Depending on the nature of the product category, MNCs may also need to invest more in dealer training, especially if after-sales service is involved, as in the appliance business.

A very important issue facing many MNCs is that of creating a single sales and distribution system to service the multiple joint ventures (JVs) or manufacturing units that may exist in one TE market. In China, for example, AT&T and Whirlpool both have multiple JVs, for different product lines, that nonetheless sell to the same customer (dealer or end-user). These different JVs naturally each start out with their own sales and distribution infrastructures, as created by the original local partner before the JV was created. It is clearly better to unify these disparate organizations into one, so that the dealer or end-customer has to deal with just one company sales person, one ordering and invoicing system, etc. The many implementation issues in such integration include working out mutually satisfactory cost-sharing arrangements, information technology issues, etc. (AT&T of China Team Report 1994; Whirlpool Greater China, Inc. Team Report 1995).

MANAGERIAL IMPLICATIONS: TECS

Start/Improve Distribution

Paradoxically, TECs are often in even greater need of assistance in creating distribution systems in TEs than are MNCs, because while the MNCs often have great experience with creating and managing such systems, TECs have none. Such TECs have historically simply sold their goods to government Ministry channels, which have now totally evaporated, leaving the TECs to start distribution systems from scratch. Many TECs (such as Glasunion and DFM) simply expect customers to pick up their goods from the factory (Glasunion and DFM Team Reports 1994). TECs thus need to locate potential distributors, evaluate them, contract with them, and motivate, manage and control them, once a relationship starts.

For some TECs (such as LET) the issue is more one of starting an export business and reaching overseas markets, with the consequent complication of finding the resources to be able to set up foreign distribution networks and conduct foreign sales trips (LET Team Report 1993).

It should be noted that the markets most suitable for TEC penetration might in many cases not be Western markets, where high quality and high technology are often market norms, but instead be markets in other developing countries, where low price and a lower level of technology and quality are most desirable to consumers. Since TECs often possess relatively low technology capabilities, but also have relatively low manufacturing costs, the markets most suitable for TEC penetration might in many cases be markets in other developing countries, where low price and a lower level of technology and quality are most desirable to consumers. LET, for example, is finding some success marketing its rugged L410 aircraft in countries such as Bolivia, India, South Africa, etc. These and similar markets are suitable because the L410 aircraft can operate in extreme climates and unpaved, short runways; because it is cheap; and because such markets do not require FAA certification, which LET is still in the process of acquiring (LET Team Report 1993).

In some cases, the "market" needed by these cash-strapped and nearly-bankrupt TECs is not one for finished products, but for sub-contracting work. The Czech LET aircraft company, for instance, now gets 30 percent of its revenue from sub-contracting contracts with various companies. Some of these are not paid for in cash, but in parts for LET's own aircraft. Identifying opportunities for such sub-contracting work is done in mostly "ad hoc" ways, such as prospecting sales visits and meetings, rather through a systematic communications program (LET Team Report 1994).

Fighting "Global Brands"

Given the recent entry of MNC brands into TE markets, clearly the most important challenge facing many TECs is to successfully fight these global competitors. While the global brands have advantages of global scale and therefore lower production and marketing costs and often more advanced technology, they can potentially be "out-localized" by local competitors who design their products and communications to better suit local conditions and needs.

MNCs usually tend to minimize the number of product changes to "home country" products before launching them in LDCs (Hill and Still 1984). Local TE consumers, especially those in non-metro areas or non-elite segments, may have attribute or benefit needs different from those emphasized by MNCs in their globally-standardized products, and may have communication and packaging preferences to which MNCs are inadequately sensitive. In consumer packaged goods, for instance, there often exist consumer segments desiring more "local" or "traditional" (e.g., herbal) ingredients and formulations. TECs therefore need to find ways to "out-localize" their global competitors in these and other ways. This may, but need not, mean identifying market niches or segments where TECs possess some kind of competitive advantage over MNCs, either in distribution, after-sales networks, technology, consumer insight or some other kind—such as aiming at rural or more "basic" markets. TECs might then be able to target these markets with products designed with more "basic" or "localized" formulations or functionalities, at lower prices, taking advantage of regulatory advantages wherever possible (e.g., lower excise tax rates for smaller enterprises). In India, for example, many TEC successful brands (such as Nirma washing powder) have successfully used such strategies to defend market share from MNCs (cf. Vachani 1990).

In addition, TECs need to find ways to compete with the global players in technology, quality and cost, through product and process improvements and through greater scale. Many of these local competitors have competed historically in many diverse businesses, to take advantage of local market opportunities, but this has often led to low-scale production in each of these many businesses. They thus need to withdraw from some of them, competing in only a few, where they can expand their volume of production and take advantage of economies of scale and scope.

Another area in which TECs need to invest is branding investments: in advertising, packaging, product design and other areas that will give their brands the same quality reputations, awareness levels and preference-forming brand associations that will enable them to compete with the global brands that often come with such strong brand reputations. One accompaniment of opening markets in TEs is a consumer preference for brands that symbolize new and Western values and lifestyles, not the old lifestyle regimes of the past. Old local brands that fail to contemporize their brand imagery risk losing out over time to brands that appear fresher and more exciting. Obviously, such branding investments take time to pay off, and TECs need to find both the cash and the patience to make such long-term investments. Since such branding investments are expensive, TECs need to prune their brands, concentrating their investments on those few brands that have the potential to become the "mega-brands" of the future, extendible and leverageable into other product categories.

Pruning stockkeeping units (SKUs) in product lines may also be also necessary, for it allows management time and resources to be devoted to only the more important items, providing efficiencies in manufacturing, inventories, and field selling. Wedel, for example, embarked on a program to cut its SKUs by 50 percent, after finding that keeping minor and slow-selling SKUs on its books led to manufacturing and inventory problems (Wedel Team Report 1995).

Improve Marketing Competencies

Perhaps the most fundamental challenge facing TECs, however, is simply improving their basic marketing competencies in terms of structure, systems and processes, organizational culture and human resources. Organizations such as the William Davidson Institute training managers from TECs need to focus on these issues in designing their education programs. The William Davidson Institute field research has identified the following frequently occurring skill improvement areas for TEC managers:

1. Fundamental skills at formulating marketing strategy. Research and analysis to identify customer segments, and their own strengths and weaknesses versus the competition, leading to the identification of which customer segments to pursue, with what value-propositions.
2. Knowledge of overseas markets. TECs that exported goods previously used to do so through state trading companies (such as OMNIPOL in the case of LET Aero), which were responsible for procuring orders and passing them on to the TEC. As a result, the TEC usually gained no direct experience in marketing its goods overseas. Today, therefore, with the state trading companies playing a diminished role (or none at all), TECs are often in a position where they desperately need to get orders from overseas markets, but lack the skills and confidence to do so.
3. Barter and countertrade, and in leasing and long-term customer financing, as TECs build markets among cash-strapped third-world and FSU companies. LET, for instance, has found itself trading oil, bearings, cotton, aluminum and caviar—as well as parts such as batteries, oxygen bottles and bearings—for spare parts for its L410 aircraft. Since dealing through specialized barter companies means giving up 3–7 percent of the exchange price as commission, LET attempts to arrange these barter deals in-house (LET Team Reports 1993, 1994).
4. Creating, managing, motivating, and controlling distribution channels and sales forces. This issue has been dealt with at length earlier: TECs often face problems identifying and setting up distributors because of their lack of local market knowledge, their inexperience, their lack of local market reputation (and hence low "consumer pull"). Related to this is a lack of managizing sales forces.
5. Sales forecasting systems and skills. This is necessary because TECs previously simply produced to Ministry requirements and schedules, and now face the need

to forecast accurately and often, frequently with poor market information and poor information systems. TECs often determine their production schedules for individual products without much market information, and the manufactured product mix is therefore often out of sync with market demand. This can lead to very low "fill rates", and very high "out-of-stocks" rates (Wedel Team Report 1995). Such TECs apparently need to invest in better information systems and in better current market information, and in building in more accountability for forecasts, among sales personnel and distributors. In addition, more coordination is often called for within the company (between marketing, sales and logistics departments) and between the company and its distributors, which often do not meet frequently enough (DFM, for instance, apparently meets just once a year with its distributors, and never updates forecasts made at these annual meetings).

6. Improved cost accounting systems, to allow for more accurate pricing and bidding. This is a common need, especially for TECs that previously manufactured bulk, standardized orders, but now have to produce much smaller, customized lots (Zurawicki and Becker 1994). LET, for instance, previously supplied most of its 80 annually produced aircraft to Russia's Aeroflot in one configuration, but now needs to customize aircraft configurations, in much smaller quantities, to its new customers (LET Team Report 1994). Improved cost accounting systems are also of great importance in situations where capacity utilization is low, requiring a careful application of overhead cost allocations. In the case of the Polish Ahlstrom-Fakop firm, for example, the majority of its costs were fixed, so that overhead rates would fall dramatically as output rose. Because the company was operating under full capacity, however, the overhead rate used in pricing its competitive bids was high, leading to overpriced bids (Ahlstrom-Fakop Team Report 1994).

   In many cases, overhead expenses are applied to product costs primarily on the basis of direct labor costs as a proportion of total direct labor hours. When plants are underutilized, this leads to the few individual products that get produced receiving a very heavy overhead allocation, leading to the setting of non-competitive prices under the frequently-followed "cost-plus" pricing guidelines. TECs in such situations often need basic training in the need to break down costs into fixed and variable costs, and need to be trained in the principle that any contribution to meeting fixed costs, via low prices that exceed variable costs but not full costs, is preferable to a situation where high full-cost based prices lead to no sales at all (Avrora and Ahlstrom-Fakop Team Reports 1995). Further, raw material costs often have no or unrealistically low provisions for wastage.

7. Improved systems and skills are needed in customer satisfaction measurement and diagnosis, including a willingness to put long-term customer satisfaction needs above short-term sales and profit goals (Centertel Team Report 1995).
8. TECs need assistance in setting up of appropriate marketing organizational structures, marketing information systems and a marketing culture that promotes cooperation across sales, marketing, production, logistics and other divisions. "Marketing Orientation" has been conceptualized by Narver and Slater (1990) as a combination of customer orientation, competitive orientation and interfunctional

coordination. Research has shown that while many TECs have official marketing departments, and claim to be both customer and competitor oriented (Golden *et al.* 1995), they often do not display adequate communication across departments such as marketing, sales, production and logistics (Shipley *et al.* 1995). This has been borne out in the William Davidson Institute's experiences with several companies.

9. TECs need training in communications planning and implementation, and brand-building, including the creation of brochures, promotions, advertising, public relations and database marketing. Some of the needs facing these TECs are very basic: Avrora, for example, needed a dedicated phone line for an English-speaking sales representative, "open" during Western business hours, as well as basic skills in producing press releases, catalogs and trade journal advertisements (Avrora Team Report 1995). Training in public relations skills is especially valuable for TECs, given their extremely low marketing communication budgets. Glasunion, for instance, because of its severe cash crunch, had to reduce its marketing expenditures and activities to almost zero, and was unable to revise its leaflets and brochures for over six years (Glasunion Team Report 1995).

   Avrora, along with other TECs like LET, also needed training in the creation and management of customer and prospect databases, to allow for databased marketing efforts using direct mail, etc. These databased marketing efforts are especially important for companies where after-market sales opportunities are significant, such as Dong Feng Motors, or appliance manufacturer Whirlpool (various Team Reports). Direct mail is especially useful for TECs because it typically requires low "fixed cost" investments (unlike media advertising). Such TECs obviously also need to be exposed to affordable and accessible sources of market, competitive and prospect information that could then be input into the database.
10. New product development and value-engineering. Historically, most product development at TECs has occurred without adequate consumer input. For example, Russia's Avrora developed its ozone-producing "ozonizer" device (for use in factory environments where it seems necessary to clean the air that workers breathe) with very little feedback from the market, leading to poor subsequent sales (Avrora Team Report 1995).
11. Low-cost or "guerrilla" marketing. The budget constraints facing most TECs has been mentioned earlier, and this naturally requires that they innovate in low-cost ways of out-competing their marketing adversaries. For example, companies like Glasunion have been unable to allocate any money to formal market research, but instead have been forced to rely on informal methods, such as its conversations with wholesalers for information about market and competitive conditions (Glasunion Team Report 1994).

SUGGESTIONS FOR FUTURE RESEARCH

While there are undoubtedly numerous topics on the subject of marketing in transitional economies that require research attention—such as the creation and management of distribution channels, or the appropriate strategies and tactics for global versus local brands—one issue appears to be especially deserving of further research. This is the issue of the likely evolutionary path of these TE markets. How can the different TE markets, as they exist today, be placed on one (or more) dimensions of market evolution? How are they likely to evolve in the future? Will the TE markets necessarily grow as today's developed markets have historically done, or will they develop in some unique ways, blending traditional characteristics with "modern" ones, and leapfrogging some of the "traditional" stages of development? Answers to these questions can be of use not only to theory-builders in marketing but also to practitioners, as they plan marketing strategies for the exciting years ahead.

CONCLUSION

The "opening up" of fast-growing TE markets presents great challenges and opportunities to both domestic TE enterprises as well as newly-entering MNC competitors. Faced with consumers who are rapidly changing in their expectations, incomes and levels of knowledge, as well as business conditions that are difficult to operate in but also provide opportunities for market-winning innovation, these competitors are "pioneers" in the true sense of the word. How these markets will evolve, and which kinds of marketing strategies and tactics will prove to be the most appropriate as they grow, is consequently of great interest today. This chapter has attempted to document the nature of this evolution-in-progress, and discuss some of the consequent marketing strategic and tactical issues as gleaned not only from the existing literature but also from the field research of the William Davidson Institute. It is hoped that the perspective provided by this chapter will be of use to both the scholarly and managerial communities in marketing.

Notes

I gratefully acknowledge the contribution to this paper by the numerous companies that have partnered with the William Davidson Institute and have allowed it to learn about the marketing challenges facing them, as well as the William Davidson Institute Internship Fellow Teams that documented these challenges in their Team Reports. Thanks also to Martha Lee, Heather Martinson and Amy Moored of the William Davidson Institute for their assistance in preparing this paper, and to Hans Brechbuhl, Susanne Heike and Ted Snyder for comments. The views expressed in this paper are those of the author and do not necessarily reflect official views of the William Davidson Institute.

*A shorter version of this chapter originally appeared in the *Journal of International Marketing* 5, no. 4 (1997): 95–114. Reproduced by permission.

References

Appliance Manufacturer (February 1995): W21.

Bauer, P. T. "Some Aspects and Problems of Trade in Africa." In *Markets and Marketing in Developing Economies*, edited by Reed Moyer and Stanley C. Hollander, 48–69. Homewood, IL: Richard D. Irwin, Inc., 1968.

Belk, Russell W. and Güliz Ger. "Problems of Marketization in Romania and Turkey." In *Research in Consumer Behavior*, Vol. 7, 123–155. Greenwich, CT: JAI Press, 1994.

"Ben and Jerry's Is Trying to Smooth Out Distribution in Russia As It Expands." *Wall Street Journal* (September 19, 1995): A18.

Byrne, Patrick M. and Stephen Jozefowski. "Global Logistics: Plan for the Challenges of Eastern Europe." *Transportation and Distribution* 35, no. 8 (August 1994): 49–54.

Carpenter, Gregory and Kent Nakamoto. "Consumer Preference Formation and Pioneering Advantage." *Journal of Marketing Research* 26, no. 3 (August 1989): 285–298.

Central Intelligence Agency. *World Fact Book 1995*. Washington, DC: Central Intelligence Agency, 1995.

"China Emerges as Latest Battleground for Marketing Researchers." *Marketing News* (February 14, 1994): 1–2.

"Citibank Blitzes Asia." *Forbes* (May 6, 1996): 44.

Dannhaeuser, Norbert. "Marketing Systems and Rural Development: A Review of Consumer Goods Distribution." *Human Organization* 46, no. 2 (Summer 1987): 177–185.

Demidoff, Michel. "New Marketing Opportunities in the Russian Federation." *International Trade FORUM,* no. 4 (October–December 1993): 18–21, 31.

Euromonitor. *European Marketing Data and Statistics 1996*. Euromonitor, 1996.

Euromonitor. *International Marketing Data and Statistics 1996*. Euromonitor, 1996.

Ettenson, Richard. "Brand Name and Country of Origin Effects in the Emerging Marketing Economies of Russia, Poland, and Hungary." *International Marketing Review* 10, no. 5 (December 1993): 14–36.

Frazier, Gary, James D. Gill and Sudhir H. Kale. "Dealer Dependence Levels and Reciprocal Actions in a Channel of Distribution in a Developing Country." *Journal of Marketing* 53, no. 1 (January 1989): 50–69.

Gillespie, Kate and Dana Alden. "Consumer Product Export Opportunities to Liberalizing LDCs: A Life-Cycle Approach." *Journal of International Business* 20, no. 1 (Spring, 1989): 65–74.

Golden, Peggy A., Patricia M. Doney, Denise M. Johnson and Jerald R. Smith. "The Dynamics of a Marketing Orientation in Transition Economies: A Study of Russian Firms." *Journal of International Marketing* 3, no. 2 (1995): 29–49.

Henley, Donald S. "Marketing and Economic Integration in Developing Countries." In *Markets and Marketing in Developing Economies*, edited by Reed Moyer and Stanley C. Hollander, 70–86. Homewood, IL: Richard D. Irwin, Inc., 1968.

Hill, John and Richard Still. "Adapting Products to LDC Tastes." *Harvard Business Review* 62, no. 2 (March–April 1984): 92–101.

Jain, Subhash C. *Market Evolution in Developing Countries: The Unfolding of the Indian Market.* New York: International Business Press (Haworth Press), 1993.

Johnson, Simon and Gary Loveman. *Starting Over in Eastern Europe: Entrepreneurship and Economic Renewal.* Boston: Harvard Business School Press, 1995.

Kaynak, Erdener. *Marketing in the Third World.* New York: Praeger Publishing, 1982.

_____. "Marketing Research Techniques and Approaches for LDCs." In *Marketing in Developing Countries*, edited by G. S. Kindra, 238–252. New York: St. Martin's Press, 1984.

Mahmoud, Essam and Gillian Rice. "Marketing Problems in LDCs: The Case of Egypt." In *Marketing in Developing Countries*, edited by G. S. Kindra, 76–94. New York: St. Martin's Press, 1984.

Mueller, Rene D. and Amanda J. Broderick. "Quantitative Analysis of East European Retailing." *International Journal of Retail and Distribution Management* 23, no. 1 (January 1995): 32–44.

Mueller, Rene D., James Wenthe and Peter Baron. "Case Note: The Evolution of Distribution Systems." *International Marketing Review* 10, no. 4 (1993): 36–52.

Nakata, Cheryl and K. Sivakumar. *Factors in Emerging Markets and their Impact on First Mover Advantages.* Working Paper No. 95-110. Cambridge, MA: Marketing Science Institute, 1995.

Narver, John C. and Stanley F. Slater. "The Effect of Marketing Orientation on Business Profitability." *Journal of Marketing* 54, no. 4 (1990): 20–35.

"Nestlé's Brand-Building Machine." *Fortune* (September 19, 1994): 130, 147–156.

"New Worlds to Conquer." *Business Week* (February 28, 1994): 50–52.

Reinganum, Julie and Tina Helsell. "To Market, To Market." *China Business Review* 21, no. 1 (January–February 1994): 30–34.

"Romanians Welcome a Conquering Soft Drink: Investing in Eastern Europe, The Cola Wars." *International Herald Tribune* (March 1, 1995).

Samiee, Saeed. "Retailing and Channel Considerations in Developing Countries: A Review and Research Propositions." *Journal of Business Research* 27, no. 2 (June 1993): 103–130.

Samli, A. Coskun and Erdener Kaynak. "Marketing Practices in Less-Developed Countries." *Journal of Business Research* 12, no. 1 (1984): 5–18.

Shama, Avraham. "Transforming the Consumer in Russia and Eastern Europe." *International Marketing Review* 9, no. 2 (June 1992): 43–59.

Shipley, David, Graham Hooley, Jozsef Beracs, Krzysztof Fonfara and Kristina Kolos. "Marketing Organizations in Hungarian and Polish Firms: Part 1." *Journal of Marketing Practice: Applied Marketing Science* 1, no. 2 (1995): 39–54.

Simon-Miller, Francoise. "African Marketing: The Next Frontier." In *Marketing in Developing Countries*, edited by G. S. Kindra, 115–129. New York: St. Martin's Press, 1984.

Terpstra, Vern and Ravi Sarathy. *International Marketing.* 6th ed. Fort Worth, TX: Dryden Press, 1994.

"Transitory Problems." Transport and Distribution Survey. *Business Central Europe* (May 1995): 37–50.

Vachani, Sushil. "Strategic Responses of Multinationals to Competition from Developing Country Cottage Firms." *International Marketing Review* 7, no. 3 (1990): 31–47.

Varadarajan, P. Rajan. "Marketing in Developing Countries: The New Frontier." *Long-Range Planning* 17, no. 6 (December 1984): 118–126.

Walle, Alf and John K. Ryans. "SIA, Developing Countries and Marketing Opportunities: A Primer." *Management Decision* 30, no. 7 (1992): 25–29.

William Davidson Institute. *Ahlstrom-Fakop Ltd. Team Report* by Luis A. Colon, Rafal Golebiowski and Nell Tracy. University of Michigan Business School, Ann Arbor, MI, 1994.

_____. *Ahlstrom-Fakop Ltd. Team Report* by Peter Andrews, Arek Dorynek, Mikolaj Kokot and Jeffrey McDaniel. University of Michigan Business School, Ann Arbor, MI, 1995.

_____. *AT&T of China Team Report* by Lee Boyd, Brian Jeffries and Kaja Sehrt University of Michigan Business School, Ann Arbor, MI, 1994.

_____. *Avrora Team Report* by Thomas Savage and John Seasholtz. University of Michigan Business School, Ann Arbor, MI, 1995.

_____. *Centertel Team Report* by Tucker Holland, Lela Panagides, Tomasz Pietka and Iwona Okon. University of Michigan Business School, Ann Arbor, MI, 1995.

_____. *China Hewlett-Packard Team Report* by David Kujawa, Patrick Piscatelli and Peter Staples. University of Michigan Business School, Ann Arbor, MI, 1996.

_____. *Dong Feng Motors Team Report* by Ben Chu, Jim Fralick, Mike Jung and Eric Rotzoll. University of Michigan Business School, Ann Arbor, MI, 1994.

_____. *Glasunion Kft. Team Report* by Amy Downs, Reka Fodor, Melissa Quesnory and Kathryn Rado. University of Michigan Business School, Ann Arbor, MI, 1994.

_____. *Glasunion Kft. Team Report* by Eniko Racz, Theresa Sigillito and Kristin Smallwood. University of Michigan Business School, Ann Arbor, MI, 1995.

_____. *Interbrands Team Report* by Jeff Bernicke, Scott Cooper, Darius Gazinschi and Edi Ioan. University of Michigan Business School, Ann Arbor, MI, 1995.

_____. *LET Team Report* by Phil Barta, Lee Berger and Will Colston. University of Michigan Business School, Ann Arbor, MI, 1993.

_____. *LET Team Report* by Elizabeth Dimling, Mike Donahue, Lawrence Signes and Katrina Urikova. University of Michigan Business School, Ann Arbor, MI, 1994.

_____. *Tatra a.s. Team Report* by Jim Adox, Ryan Hudson, Kyle Karnes, Patrik Matlak and Michael Staiti. University of Michigan Business School, Ann Arbor, MI, 1994.

_____. *Wedel S.A. Team Report* by Monique Adair, Piotr Kulagowski, Melissa Laske and Eric McCloskey. University of Michigan Business School, Ann Arbor, MI, 1995.

_____. *Whirlpool Greater China, Inc. Team Report* by Judy Lew, Patrick Piscatelli and Dale Simonson. University of Michigan Business School, Ann Arbor, MI, 1995.

_____. *Whirlpool Tatramat/Whirlpool Polska Ltd. Team Report* by Mona Gohla, Ludovit Jambrich, Alicia Nelson, Janek Pawlik, Anna Pysz and Ewa Wampuszyc. University of Michigan Business School, Ann Arbor, MI, 1995.

Yoffie, David B. and Richard Seet. "Internationalizing the Cola Wars (A): The Battle for China and Asian Markets." Harvard Business School Case No. 9-795-186. Cambridge, MA: Harvard Business School, July 1995.

Zurawicki, Leon and Kip Becker. "Marketing Issues and Strategies for Change in Central/Eastern European and CIS Countries." *Journal of Euromarketing* 3, no. 2 (1994): 61–90.

APPENDIX

Company Backgrounds of the William Davidson Institute-*Affiliated Firms*

AT&T Qingdao (AT&T QD) is a joint venture with several Chinese partners, and was set up in 1993 as a semi-knockdown (SKD) operation to sell and install telephone network switched in China. A full complete knockdown (CKD) production facility should be in operation by the end of 1996. Its 5ESS network switch is technically complex, and consists of numerous pieces of hardware and complex software that send and administer data and voice information. Such products are sold to provincial Post and Telecommunications Bureaus, which select vendors through a competitive bidding process (although relationships— "guanxi"— also matter a great deal). Nine vendors with market shares between 1 percent and 50 percent currently compete; AT&T is one of the smaller players.

Avrora is a manufacturer of piezoceramic products based in Volgograd, Russia. Its product line includes piezoceramic elements, buzzers, ignitors and filters. It is a privatized company with the majority of outstanding shares owned by Russian investors. Prior to market reforms, Avrora only operated within the borders of the USSR and the Eastern bloc. Today, the company desperately needs new markets, is operating at very low capacity, is heavily in debt and faces a cash flow crisis every month (despite having laid off 75 percent of its workforce over the last three years).

Centertel is a joint venture between TP S.A. (51 percent ownership), a state-owned Polish telecommunications company, Ameritech (24.5 percent), and France Telecom (24.5 percent). Centertel is the first mobile phone operator in Poland. Since its inception in 1991, Centertel has made great inroads to provide communications service throughout the country. Currently with 80 percent coverage (excluding remote areas), the company hopes to achieve 100 percent coverage by the end of 1996 and expects to have over 100,000 subscribers by the end of July. The Customer Service Department is critical in creating and maintaining the company's image within the competitive environment. As a result of the increase in competition in the Polish telecommunications industry, the company views a high standard of customer care as a strategic priority.

China Hewlett-Packard is responsible for overall sales and support for Hewlett-Packard products in China. Hewlett-Packard Company (HP), the third largest computer manufacturer in the United States, first opened operations in China in 1985. Since then it has invested more than US$100 million in the country. It has joint-manufacturing sites in Shenzhen, Beijing, Qingdao, and Shanghai. China Hewlett-Packard was formed in 1985 as a joint venture with China Electronics Import and Export Corp., China Great Wall Computer Group and Beijing Computer Industry Company. HP established another joint venture in 1991 in Qingdao for medical-equipment manufacturing (HP Medical Product Co., Ltd.), and another in Beijing for sales and marketing systems integration (Puritan Integration Co., Ltd.).

Dong Feng Motors (DFM) is the largest producer of medium-sized trucks in China. In 1994, the company was 100 percent state-owned. They produce mainly medium-duty five-ton trucks for the Chinese market. DFM is diversifying its product line to include buses, an 8-ton truck and a passenger car to adapt to the changing market.

Foster-Wheeler Energy Fakop was formed in 1995 when Foster-Wheeler Energy International, Inc. purchased Ahlstrom-Fakop Ltd., the oldest boiler manufacturer in Poland, from the Ahlstrom Corporation. Foster-Wheeler Energy Fakop manufactures large industrial boiler components and heat exchangers in Katowice, Poland, and is working to establish itself as the low cost supplier of large industrial boilers in the Central European market.

Glasunion Kft. is a glass processing company located in Salgótarján, Hungary. The company used to produce three types of processed glass (laminated, double glazed and tempered), but has shut down its flat glass production. The company is a designated supplier to the Suzuki automotive plant in Hungary.

Interbrands is the sole distributor of Procter & Gamble products in Romania and Bulgaria. Interbrands also distributes MARS and Kellogg's products, although P&G makes up more than half of its business.

LET a.s., the largest aircraft manufacturer in the Czech Republic, is headquartered in Kunovice. In the fall of 1995, LET a.s. became the first company in the Czech Republic to have its debt restructured. This was made possible by a change in restructuring policies at Komerπnò Bank, a privatized Czech bank, and has given the company a new opportunity to revive its lagging sales and profitability. They recently won an order for 21 L410's (a small aircraft) and discussions are underway with an American computer-aided design company regarding a possible joint venture to develop CAD/CAM products.

Tatra is the Czech Republic's oldest truck company and is located in Koprivnice, which is 150 miles east of Prague. They chiefly manufacture off-road trucks over 12 tons with air cooled engines. Tatra trucks are known for their performance in severe climactic regions and are mainly used for oil and gas production, construction, power stations, mining operations and military uses.

E. Wedel S.A., located in Warsaw, is a famous brand name in the Polish confectionery business, established over 150 years ago. It produces high-quality chocolates, cakes, and snacks. In 1991, Pepsico Foods and Beverages International acquired 65 percent of E. Wedel S.A. shares.

Whirlpool Corporation is the world's leading manufacturer and marketer of major home appliances. With over 45,000 employees, manufacturing facilities in 12 countries and products for sale in approximately 140 nations, the corporation is aggressively pursuing the goal of becoming the dominant force in the global major home appliance industry. In accordance with this strategy, Whirlpool Europe BV (WEBV), one of the four major divisions of the Whirlpool Corporation, is quickly moving into Central and Eastern Europe. One of the National Organizations (NSOs) is headquartered in Budapest, and is spearheading the development of two new NSOs in Romania and Bulgaria. In Slovakia, Whirlpool Tatramat, a manufacturer of both washing machines and water heaters, was incorporated as a joint venture company in May 1992. WEBV purchased a minority interest in Tatramat a.s. from the government during the first round of coupon privatization. In early 1995, Whirlpool Corporation joined forces with Beijing Whirlpool Snowflake Electric Appliance Company, Ltd., a refrigerator manufacturer; SMC Microwave Products Company in Shunde, a microwave manufacturer; and Shanghai Narcissus, a washer and compressor manufacturer.

The Changing Consumer

2 LEAPING LUXURIES AND TRANSITIONAL CONSUMERS

Russell W. Belk
University of Utah

Introduction

According to Abraham Maslow's (1954) well-known hierarchy of needs, as humans we satisfy our lower-order bodily needs for food, shelter, clothing, and some measure of safety before we become concerned with the more symbolic social and psychological needs for love, esteem, and self actualization. Although Nevis (1983) has suggested that a somewhat different hierarchy applies in the East, it still shares with Maslow a hierarchical prioritizing of lower order needs over higher order needs. This logic would suggest that the least likely place to find luxuries in the world is in a society where the majority of people must struggle to meet basic needs and where extravagance in consumption is likely to reduce the thin accumulations that allow any margin of security in providing for the health and well being of family members. Yet this logical premise is countered by early human propensities for making art, assembling collections, and burying our dead with ornaments, armaments, and floral bouquets (Belk 1995). Cave paintings, sculptures, and grave goods can be traced back at least 30,000 years, while collections of curious pebbles have been found in caves inhabited 80,000 years ago. Such objects seem clearly to be luxuries appealing to "higher order" needs rather than necessities that address "lower order" needs. Ger (1997) argues that the desire for the beautiful is, in fact, a basic human need. I will attempt to demonstrate and explain how this long-standing lure of luxuries has become even stronger in our contemporary and increasingly global society, **especially** among consumers in transitional economies. Besides attempting to explicate and understand this phenomenon, I wish to assess whether the leap to luxuries is laudable or lamentable. Based on this assessment, I will then consider what, if anything, responsible global marketers and their local counterparts in transitional economies should do about this luxury-loving contradiction of Maslow's hierarchy.

LUXURIES IN THE LEAST LIKELY PLACES

My interest was initially drawn to this anomaly from a historical content analysis of U.S. magazine advertising in which Rick Pollay and I found that status appeals curriously peaked during the heart of the 1930s Great Depression (Belk and Pollay 1985). In addition, motion picture depictions of luxurious living were especially common at this time, which also seems curious in light of high unemployment levels and other forms of impoverishment during the 1930s. As an initial result of noticing this anomaly, I investigated the seemingly inexplicable presence of luxuries in the Third World (Belk 1988), finding ironic consumption practices such as people putting up unconnected television antennas on huts lacking both electricity and televisions, and families forgoing needed food in order to afford a refrigerator which subsequently remained empty. Ger (1992) cites the example of selling nutritious cow's milk in order to buy candy for Turkish children who have seen it advertised on television. But the presence of luxuries in transitional economies was driven home for me during a sabbatical year in Romania during 1991–92. After a decade of severe consumer deprivations during which the best food, clothing, shoes, tools, beverages, and other consumer goods were shipped abroad to repay a massive foreign debt, retail availability began to change suddenly. Goods that were long absent from store shelves, as well as never before seen consumption items, had rapidly begun to enter the Romanian market. The trigger for this avalanche of consumer goods was the execution of the *Ceausescus* during the 1989 Christmas season revolution. But the goods that most quickly and prominently appeared in new retail kiosks, established state stores, and in the streets and markets, were not the desperately needed and still rationed goods such as sugar, petrol, meat, flour, and bread. Instead they were luxury items such as imported candies, liquors, perfumes, cigarettes, televisions, VCRs, cameras, cosmetics, and high-end automobiles such as Mercedes and BMW which had quickly established Romanian franchises. Even during the revolution itself, one of the first broadcasts by the revolutionaries who captured the state television network was not a political message or news of the revolution, but a showing of a copy of the American film, "E.T. The Extraterrestrial."

These impressions of rampant desire for luxury in Romania were confirmed by some quantitative results obtained measuring materialism in a dozen countries (Ger and Belk 1996a). These data confirmed that Romanians were the most materialistic of these consumers and that Ukrainians were fourth and reunified Germans fifth (the USA and New Zealand were numbers two and three respectively, while India, United Kingdom, France, and Sweden were the least materialistic nations). We had also measured Germans before reunification and found their former level of materialism to be much lower, like that of the other Western European nations in the sample. The high levels of materialism (defined as the belief that material possessions are the greatest source of happiness and unhappiness in life) in Eastern and Central Europe provide further suggestive evidence of the important role of luxuries for consumers in transitional economies. But these data do not explain why this should be the case. There are implications of pursuing status, prestige, material achievement, and aesthetic desires that seem quite different from those of pursuing desires for adequate nutrition, comfort, and safety (Ger 1992). Are those who pursue luxuries, even at the expense of necessities, better off because of it? How does this differ between rich and poor consumers? How is this phenomenon different in affluent and transitional economies? Why does it occur at all?

In the following analysis I more thoroughly consider the popularity of luxuries in transitional economies. I begin by exploring what constitutes a luxury and then briefly consider the history of luxuries and attitudes toward luxuries, primarily in China and Russia. Historical analysis helps to frame the current fascination with luxuries in these countries and raises the very basic questions of whether luxuries are good or bad for individuals and societies as well as why luxuries are especially appealing to consumers in transitional economies. I draw upon diverse evidence to help enlighten the role of luxury in transitional economies today and discuss how this may be impacted by yesterday's patterns of consumption in these same countries.

WHAT IS A LUXURY?

The classification of a product or service as a luxury is a fluid one. Often, though not always, yesterday's luxury becomes today's necessity. In economically developed countries we need only think of clocks, radios, movies, televisions, stereos, automobiles, washers, microwaves, and telephones for prior examples of luxuries that have become necessities. Today, in the more economically-developed world, cellular telephones, foreign travel, computers, fax machines, and numerous other consumer goods appear to be shifting from luxuries to necessities. The definition of what specific goods constitute luxury is therefore specific to a particular time and place and is always socially constructed. As a generalization, however, we can identify several typical characteristics of luxury goods. Luxuries tend to be rare or expensive. Partly as a result of this, luxuries speak of privilege and those who possess luxuries are seen as privileged. We also find or imagine luxuries to be pleasurable, although what constitutes pleasure is also a social construction. Because luxuries are for the privileged few and are seen to bring pleasure, consuming luxuries may also produce feelings of desire mixed with feelings of transgression. Transgressive feelings can heighten the (forbidden) pleasure of luxury consumption, but they can also lead to guilt for consuming what others cannot have or what is seen as a highly indulgent good. An example of both guilt and indulgence may be seen with chocolates. It is not unusual to find people who hide chocolates and secretly consume them in order to avoid openly admitting a weakness or psychological dependence on these treats (Belk and Costa 1998).

Chocolates seem to violate the first characteristic of luxury in that they need not be either rare or expensive. Unlike other former luxury foods and beverages that have entered world markets, such as coffee, tea, and sugar, they have not made the move from luxury to daily necessity. We generally don't consume chocolates as a routine part of daily meals and they remain "special." They are more like alcohol and tobacco in that they are constructed as guilty pleasures or as special substances for celebration and not for ordinary use. Furthermore, there is often an additional fear that we may become dependent on these substances and no longer be in control of our own desires. While psychological dependencies can also occur for coffee, tea, and sugar, we have normalized such consumption and attach less stigma to the use of these "drug foods" (Mintz 1993). But in the contemporary West, all of these foods and beverages in their common forms might be construed as "little luxuries" rather than "big luxuries." They lie somewhat farther toward the normalizing side of a continuum that may be seen to run from big luxuries to little luxuries to comforts to decencies to necessities. The closer an item is to being regarded as a necessity, the less likelihood that any opprobrium (or prestige) will attach to its use. Furthermore, while both large and small luxuries are thought to bring pleasure, having necessities, decencies, and comforts is instead construed as avoiding the pain and deprivation of being without what many others have. It is this distributional aspect that makes the possession of luxuries seem indulgent and the possession of necessities seem more of a human right in a just society.

Again, it is important to note that something at a particular place on this continuum in one culture may be at quite a different place on the continuum in another culture. Yan (1997) provides the example of a couple in their seventies who in 1993 celebrated Chinese National Day by coming from the countryside to Beijing. In Beijing their children took them by taxi to a McDonald's restaurant for a celebration banquet. They were all dressed in their finest clothes and the couple had their picture taken in front of the Golden Arches. They sent the photo to their hometown newspaper which published it along with a 1949 photo the couple had sent in of their celebration of the first National Day of the People's Republic of China, also in Beijing. The headline in the paper read "Forty-Four years: From *Tu* to *Yang*," which means from rustic, uncouth, and backward to foreign, fashionable, and progressive. McDonald's, which is seen in the West as a convenience and as a restaurant totally devoid of prestige and fashionableness, is still seen in Beijing as an important luxury treat, even though it has become quite ordinary in Hong Kong where the first McDonald's opened in 1975 (Watson 1997). Although luxuries in transitional economies are often Western goods, as in the Beijing example, the issue of globalism in consumption patterns is distinct and will not be addressed here (Ger and Belk 1996b).

LUXURY IN CHINA

Not just McDonald's, but a wide variety of luxury and pseudo-luxury goods have begun to become popular. During the 1990s I have seen designer sunglasses proudly worn in Guangzhou (with their labels still attached), been driven in chauffeured Audis in Shanghai, and watched young men in Shen Zhen wearing "Armani" sports coats (with labels proclaiming the brand name on the outside of the sleeve). As elsewhere in Asia, counterfeit luxury brands are prevalent in China. Ronald Groves and I have recently done some observations, focus groups, tastings, and questionnaires in Hong Kong and southern China examining beverage preferences, especially for luxury beverages such as cognacs, whiskeys, and wines (Belk and Groves forthcoming). With Hong Kong as a nearby role model, XO cognacs first started to supplant *mao tai*, the traditional Chinese fermented rice beverage, as a celebratory and status beverage in southern China. More recently, however, Hong Kong cosmopolitans with educational and travel experiences abroad have begun to adopt grape wines, with the first-growth Bordeaux wines of France being the first choice and most prestigious. This pattern is again influencing southern Chinese who are starting to drink grape wine as well. In both countries, red wines outsell white wines 20 to 1, despite a near parity in other parts of the world. In addition to status considerations, this is partly because of the perceived health benefits of red wine, which like dog meat and snake wine is seen as a "hot" beverage, especially for winter consumption by men (Anderson 1988). In both countries grape wines are primarily consumed at Western-style restaurants, revealing the status associations of drinking Western wines and eating Western foods. Strongly implicated are the *mian zi* aspects of face, whereby a person would lose face if someone at a table near them in a restaurant ordered a more prestigious bottle of wine (Bond 1986).

That this adoption of wine in China is not driven by taste is affirmed by our wine tastings with college students and by the current pattern in southern China of sweetening fine wines by adding Sprite or 7-Up (Belk and Groves forthcoming). Reportedly similar practices occurred in Hong Kong not too long ago. The rush for status brands has also led to wine counterfeiting in China with Chateau names sometimes misspelled or logos from one Chateau used with the name of another Chateau in order to make the label more visually appealing. In answer to projective questions we asked in Hong Kong, if red wine were a car, it was most often reported that it would be a sports car, Rolls Royce, Volvo or BMW. In southern China it was most often reported that it would be a Mercedes or a Lincoln. Beer, by contrast, would be a small sedan, Jeep, or Ford (Hong Kong), or a Mitsubishi (mainland China). In both countries the most likely beverage for a succesful businessperson was seen to be wine (followed by cognac on the PRC mainland), whereas beer, rice wine, or tea were seen as most likely beverages for a clerk or factory worker. Red wine was also seen (along with champagne in mainland China) as the beverage of choice for a wedding banquet or in a karaoke club. These findings affirm the special luxury status of Western red wines in China and the contrasting non-luxury image of other beverages.

Recent luxury beverage preferences in China stand in marked contrast to the first 30 years of Communism in China, and especially the Cultural Revolution of 1966–1976. These were austere times when "decadent" luxuries were condemned, as illustrated by the following parable about the Cultural Revolution, "Right to The Heart of the Matter," by Wang Meng.

> A meeting to discuss cold drinks for summertime was held in a place called "M." MA put forward his proposal to raise the quality level of osmanthus-flavored sour-plum nectar, and voiced his opinions on the issue of beverage production facilities in general. MB made a recommendation regarding the opening up of additional sources of cold milk and liquid yogurt. MC advocated an energetic expansion of the production and supply of bottled beer, ale, and light beer. MD made known his ideas regarding the production of top-grade soft drinks. ME demanded the return of the traditional thirst-slaking dried fruit from North China. MX stood up, pounded the table, raised his index finger, and sounded a warning: "Gentlemen, friends, since we are discussing the issue of beverages, we mustn't forget for a single moment man's most basic, his principal, his most essential, his most important beverage, the one that can never be overlooked: not beer, not fruit juice, not yogurt, and not soft drinks, but H_2O—that's water! Talking about beverages and ignoring water is a perfect example of reversing the relationship between principal and subordinate, which can only lead to chaos. At this rate, before long the people will

> be drinking urine, lime wash, maybe even lubricating oil. Why? Because they will have forgotten that water is *the* source, that water is at the heart of all things, that they must hold on to water at all costs! If we can tolerate this sort of trend, then what's left for us *not* to tolerate?" All the other, from MA to ME, gazed at each other in blank dismay, not knowing what to do now. MF was the first to respond to the challenge. "I'm in total agreement with MX's point of view," he shouted, "and I want to go even further by stating that it's not enough just to drink water, that in order to ensure its survival, mankind must also eat! Whether it's flour or rice, vegetables or seafood, makes no difference at all, as long as we eat. Just ponder for a minute the serious consequences of drinking water and not eating! Therefore, of primary. . ." MA was clearly getting worked up. He unbuttoned his shirt to expose his chest, shouting as he did so: "I want to solemnly declare that I have never opposed the eating of food or the drinking of water, not in the past, not now, and certainly not tomorrow, or the day after, or the day after that. . ." His declaration thus completed, he took a biscuit out of his pocket, poured himself a glass of cool water, and began eating and drinking right there in front of the others. MB entered the fray at that moment, calling the others to account: "I want you all to take note that it's not nearly enough just to eat food and drink water. We must also wear clothing! Clothing is necessary to keep us warm *and* to keep our bodies concealed from view. Without clothing we would be no better than beasts!" And the debate goes on (Meng 1995).

But the post-Mao era is hardly China's first brush with luxuries. As Clunas (1991) details, the race for luxuries became so rampant in late Ming China (1550–1650) that an elaborate set of sumptuary laws specified just what occupations' wine cups must be made of gold, silver, porcelain, or lacquer, who could dress in various fabrics and colors, what types of coaches each rank was entitled to, and what house designs were allowed each profession. Even such details as sedan chairs, parasols, horse trappings, seals, and utensils were regulated by sumptuary laws. But as with sumptuary laws elsewhere, they were followed more in the breach than observance (Belk 1995). Style manuals helped aspiring status-seekers to choose tasteful and prestigious luxury goods, including clothing, furnishings, dwellings, and decorations. And as with contemporary counterfeit goods, counterfeit paintings became so common in late Ming China that only one in ten paintings were estimated to be genuine (Clunas 1991, p. 114). These historical and cultural changes suggest that in considering the role of luxuries in contemporary Russia and eastern and central Europe, it may be best to start before the rise of Communism and to attempt to trace a path to the present. This is the goal of the next section.

LUXURY AT THREE POINTS IN RUSSIAN HISTORY

Luxury Before the Bolshevik Revolution

A history of consumption in pre-communist Russia has yet to be written. But as I detail elsewhere (Belk forthcoming), there is a compelling illustration of the lure of luxury in Nikolai Gogol's (1985) tale "The Overcoat." The story focuses on Akaky Akakievich, a lowly Russian clerk, who is ignored by his office superiors and treated rudely by his fellow workers. Before the Moscow winter sets in, he takes his threadbare overcoat to the tailor to be mended once again. But the tailor tells him that the coat is beyond repair and that he will have to spend the huge sum of 150 roubles for a new one. At first Akaky is miserable about such an unaffordable expenditure, but gradually he resigns himself to it and begins to scrimp and save. He gives up eating evening meals and burning candles at night and goes to his landlady's room if he must work after dark. He even walks on his tiptoes in order that the soles of his shoes might last a bit longer. Eventually his utilitarian sacrifices give way to fantasies of luxury and a new and better existence as possessor of a new overcoat:

> . . . he carried ever in his thoughts the idea of his future overcoat. His whole existence had in a sense become fuller, as though some other person were present with him, as though he were no longer alone but an agreeable companion had consented to walk the path of life hand in hand with him, and that companion was none other than the new overcoat with its thick padding and its strong, durable lining. He became, as it were, more alive, even more strong-willed, like a man who has set before himself a definite goal. . . . the most bold and audacious ideas flashed through his mind. Why not really have marten on the collar? (Gogol 1985, 316–317).

Eventually Akaky Akakievich's sacrifices result in his new overcoat; a coat not trimmed with marten, but with cat fur. As soon as he begins to wear it, his co-workers begin to welcome him into their midst and not long after he is invited to a party. He proudly wears his new coat of course and is very attentive to the admiring glances of others at the party. But on his way home from this party he is accosted in the streets and robbed of his beloved coat. He pleads to an indifferent police chief to no avail. Without his treasured coat he quickly becomes pale, withers, and dies. His ghost begins to haunt the streets of Moscow annoying those with nice overcoats and menacing the unsympathetic bureaucrats who failed to help him recover the coat.

Gogol's "The Overcoat" has been variously interpreted as showing the rebirth of the human spirit under the influence of love (of the coat) or as a pitiful obsession with a consumer good (Belk forthcoming). It more generally raises the question of weather luxury consumption is a worthy goal in life. A decade or two after "The Overcoat," during the 1850s and 1860s, another overcoat played an indirect role in Russian history. It was the overcoat that Karl Marx wore at the time he was working on *Das Kapital.* As Stallybrass (1998) details, this coat was lost not just once, but repeatedly, as Karl Marx and his family of seven struggled to survive in London. It was only one of the many family possessions pawned, including Jenny Marx's inheritance of silver and linen from her aristocratic Scottish family, and even the children's clothing. But for Karl Marx, the coat was more than just a utilitarian garment to keep warm and to exchange for money to pay the rent and bills to the butcher and greengrocer. It was for him a symbolic garment that he needed in order to pass as a gentleman and gain entrance to the Reading Room at the British Museum where he was researching *Das*

Kapital. He wrote to Engels in February of 1852 that "A week ago I reached the pleasant point where I was unable to go out for want of the coats I have in pawn" (Stallybrass 1998, p. 187). He may have ridiculed society at large for its commodity fetishism, but for Karl Marx himself, his overcoat was much more than just a garment with which to resist the English winter. Without it he was "not fit to be seen." In order to retrieve his coat and help pay other bills, he made the sacrifice of writing journalistic accounts for newspapers, although even this was sometimes hampered by his inability to afford writing paper and daily chronicles of world events. Like her husband, Jenny Marx pawned her best clothing, and in 1866 she felt she could not go out because she had pawned all those things that might bring her some respect. When the Marx children's clothing was pawned in 1862, they were unable to go to school. Apparently to give them some hope that things would get better, their father made up episodes of a tale about Hans Röckle, a magician and toy maker who had many wonderful toys in his shop (McLellan 1981, quoted in Stallybrass 1998, p. 198). In these stories Hans could never pay his bills, and constantly had to sell his magical toys to the Devil as a result. Nevertheless, the enchanted toys inevitably marched back to Hans Röckle's shop where they took their places once again.

As both Marx's stories for his children and his own regard for the magical transforming power of his overcoat suggest, these things were valued as much for the happiness and self-esteem they were able to create as for their functional benefits. Ironically, even as Marx was writing his critique of commodity fetishism, he had made a fetish of his overcoat (Pels 1998, p. 97). While Marx's overcoat sometimes had to be pawned to allow the family to live, like Akaky Akakievich he was willing to make extraordinary sacrifices (petty journalism in Marx's case) to bring it back. The extra-utilitarian character of the two coats clearly reveal that they were luxuries more than necessities. Most likely these are not exceptional examples and luxuries have a long role in Russian history for those of even the most modest means.

CONSUMER LUXURIES IN COMMUNIST RUSSIA

The initial plans following the Bolshevik Revolution privileged efficient production and egalitarian distribution over any attention to consumption. But while the decadent consumption of capitalism may have been initially reviled, by the 1930s ideals of egalitarianism began to give way to special luxury consumption privileges for the best workers, including holiday travel, summer homes, private cars, and free standing houses. Status symbols such as Parker pens and imported cigarettes also began to become available if one had the right connections (Gronow 1997). And cultural status markers such as ballet and classical music were encouraged (Stites 1992). At this time, the state also set out to create a "worker's paradise," at least as imagined based on the perspective of pre-Revolution consumption patterns among Russian aristocrats. As a result, the state created affordable luxury goods including crystal, champagne, caviar, fur hats, perfumes, chocolates, and cakes (Gronow 1997). But like the counterfeit goods of contemporary Russia and China, these goods were often cheap imitations that bore little resemblance to the real thing. Boym (1994) called such goods "totalitarian kitsch." Nevertheless, Russian media as well as museum propaganda and official speeches continued to herald the Soviet Union as a worker's paradise where everyone was able to live a life of luxurious privilege.

By the 1950s the transparency of this fiction had increased to the point that it became clear that consumer goods in the Soviet Union were nothing like those of the West. In the mid-1950s David Riesman (1964) had only half-seriously suggested that rather than the cold war, the Soviet Union and the U.S. should engage in a "nylon war" in which the U.S. would embarrass the Soviets into shifting from military, industrial, and scientific production to catering to newly insistent consumption desires. This, he suggested, was to be accomplished by sending cosmetics and appliances to Moscow in abundance. In fact something quite like this did occur. As the first salvo in a reciprocal trade show agreement, the Soviets mounted a show in the New York Coliseum in June of 1959, featuring Sputniks and space capsules, the products of Soviet industry, heavy machinery, a model of a nuclear ice-breaker, and what were by U.S. standards dated fashions, televisions, furniture, and refrigerators (Marling 1994). The following month in Solkoniki Park in Moscow, then U.S. Vice-President Richard Nixon accompanied Soviet Premier Nikita Krushchev to the U.S. exhibit which featured an ultramodern $250,000 Whirlpool miracle kitchen, a more modest kitchen, American cars, hi-fi sets, sewing machines, furniture, TV dinners, cosmetics, and Pepsi-Cola. It was at the more modest kitchen that Nixon lured Krushchev into what has become known as the kitchen debate. What Nixon lauded as the achievements of the American lifestyle of freedom, leisure, and choice, Krushchev first criticized as mere gadgets, wretched excess, and bourgeois trivia (Marling 1994). Soviet newspapers asked whether this was the exhibit of a great nation or a branch of a department store. But the propaganda for the good life for American consumers eventually led Krushchev to declare that within seven years the Soviets would meet and pass the Americans in providing the good life through consumer luxuries for Soviet citizens.

Thus did the trivial American kitsch of rampant consumerism in the golden age of American affluence begin to sow what may have been the seeds of the demise of Soviet Communism. The Soviets did create a plan to increase production of radios, films, televisions, refrigerators, hi-fis, and affordable automobiles, high rise apartments, and fashion clothing (Gronow 1997). But the promise of equaling and surpassing American consumerism proved untenable. In the eyes of a number of analysts, it was precisely this failure that caused the collapse of the Soviet Union (e.g., Bauman 1990–91; Kohak 1992; Kozminski 1992). As Kohak (1992) put it, the collapse had "very little to do with liberty and justice for all and a great deal to do with soap operas and the Sears catalogue."

LUXURY GOODS IN CONTEMPORARY RUSSIA

One more overcoat gives us an entry point for considering the current status of luxury goods in Russia, although it comes from Romania. The coat was the recent proud purchase of 25-year-old Angela, interviewed two years after the Romanian revolution. She had shopped for the coat in the best Bucharest shops, which were now carrying stylish clothes from the West. When she tried on a particular blue coat, she was ecstatic and had to have it. Asked how she would have felt if she could not have afforded it, she said:

> I wouldn't give up. I would be very anxious. I would think about that coat night and day; that it would match with other clothes I have—which meanwhile would become without any value.

Echoes of Akaky Akakievich and Karl Marx seem to ripple through these reflections. After acquiring the coat, Angela said that she was far happier than she would have been with a boyfriend. The overcoat is a powerful luxury good in Romania and is a source of fervent contemporary consumer desires (Lascu, Manrai and Manrai 1994). Other former luxury goods such as books have meanwhile been sacrificed for new consumer temptations. As a 32-year-old woman with a 6 year-old daughter observed:

> Now that I have the opportunity to gain more money, above my current salary, I don't give up. Although I'm revolted when I realize I can't read a book, I can't take good care of my child because I want to earn more.

For her, the sacrifice is more than monetary and might even be seen as a modern variant of human sacrifice before the altar of luxury.

In contemporary Russia there is also evidence of a boom market in consumer luxuries. A five-night Moscow fashion show in massive Rossiya Concert Hall in December of 1995 had to have two showings a night, despite ticket prices ranging from $6 to $111. One account of the show proclaimed:

> Audiences, including many of Moscow's beau monde, got to see first-hand the current fall-winter collections, shown in Paris last summer, of the French couture houses Nina Ricci, Lanvin, Jean-Louis Scherrer, Torrente and Lecoanet-Hemant. Other shows included collections from Gerard Watelet of Belgium, Enrico Coveri of Italy and leading Russian designers Slava Zaitsev and Valentin Yudashkin. . . . Helmant Sagar of Lecoanet-Hemant said, . . . "You can't be as sophisticated in Moscow as you can in Paris, but then again, Russia's style evolution was broken [by 70 years of Communism]. Russians are much more enthusiastic about fashion than Parisians. No one but the press comes to the Paris shows" (Singer 1995).

Foreign fragrances also do well in Russia (Lindsay 1997), and when Calvin Klein opened a CK boutique in Moscow in 1997, it joined others by Revlon, Estee Lauder, Guy Laroche, Louis Feraud, Gucci, Max Mara, Givenchy, Fendi, and Ermenegildo Zegna. GUM shopping plaza, just off Red Square, houses other Western stores, including Benetton, Lancome, L'Oreal, Body Shop, Pierre Cardin, Galeries Lafayette, Sisley, Reebok, and Nike. As Singer (1997) observes:

> Fashion is paramount on the minds of many of Moscow's 15 million citizens. Twentysomething secretaries with moneyed boyfriends have no problem shelling out their entire $300 monthly salary on a pair of Bally pumps, while teenagers happily spend their monthly allowances on $5 copies of Russian editions of Marie Claire and Cosmopolitan. "Moscow shoppers focus on value. They'd rather save $20 and spend it on a high-quality beautifully packaged lipstick than on a cheaper, less exclusive one," ex-

> plained Elizabeth Susskind, vice president of Estee Lauder International. "To Moscow consumers, the Clinique and Estee Lauder brand names represent affordable luxury."

Such comments about fashion-consciousness remind me of a Romanian accountant I knew in 1991–92 who paid 8 to 10 times more for the pack of French or English cigarettes that she bought each day than she would have for a Romanian brand. In so-doing she smoked the equivalent of her entire salary and relied on her physicist husband's salary to live. The extent of her sacrifice for the sake of a small luxury makes palpable the strength of her desire for a symbol of a more luxurious life. Like Marx and his journalism for the sake of reacquiring his overcoat, this represents a substantial sacrifice for the sake of prestige, although it has precedents in pre-revolution Romania as well (Ger, Belk and Lascu 1993). In Russia and Romania, as in China, counterfeit brands also abound to feed this desire for a little glamour. Other avidly sought luxury goods in Russia include pets (especially pedigrees – Jenk, Michel and Margotin-Roze 1995), Coca-Cola and Pepsi Cola (Hall and Dawson 1995), and imported foods (Whitworth 1995). In men's cosmetics, domestic products have only about 20 percent of the market, with higher-priced and higher-status imported brands being strongly preferred (Cosmetics International 1997).

Of course not everyone can participate in the market for luxury goods in Russia and the gap between rich and poor has become markedly greater since the 1992 break up of the Soviet Union (Bonnell 1997; Humphrey 1995). But the drive for luxuries is widespread and goes considerably deeper than income profiles would suggest. Initially at least, after years of deprivation, when the opportunity for a little luxury suddenly emerges, it seems irresistibly seductive (Belk 1997). As one Romanian man said, "You are exactly like children. You see something different and you want it." It remains to be seen if this desire for novelty and luxury will persist, and there are some evidences that it eventually loses some of its strength. Nevertheless, in the words of another Romanian informant: "Wealth is like a disease. The more you have, the more you want." There is also the social pressure exerted as new consumption norms are constructed. One Romanian sheepherder suggested that he would be *ruşinea satului*, the shame of the village, if he could not match his neighbors' escalating consumption.

LUXURY IN TRANSITIONAL ECONOMIES: AN EVALUATION AND CONCLUSION

Why do consumers in transitional economies so improbably want extravagant luxury goods? The answer differs somewhat depending on the culture, but part of the explanation seems to be the increasing visibility of consumer lifestyles elsewhere in the world. The propaganda of the kitchen debate and the American exhibition in Moscow in the late 1950s has now been replaced by global television, films, travel, multinational corporations, foreign tourists, the Internet, and other windows on a shrinking world. Some would argue that the consumption of luxuries in transitional economies is only a factor among the fortunate few who have managed to quickly become rich. But as the examples above suggest, the demand for luxuries among consumers in transitional economies is considerably broader than this. The desire for luxuries is also exacerbated by feelings of deservingness due to prior deprivations, as was the case with the Cultural Revolution in China and the Ceauescu's decade-long consumer austerity program to repay Romanian foreign debt at the expense of Romanian consumers (Belk 1997). In small-scale Third World cultures there are barriers to status seeking through consumption, often couched in the fear of provoking the envy of others (Belk 1988). All are known in such societies, and fears such as that of the evil eye tend to keep luxury consumption in check (Gell 1986). But in formerly Communist societies where suspicions of even family members were built up over periods of "cultural purification," such barriers are more negligible. Fear of envy may persist longer in rural villages than in more *anonymous* cities, but the world is shrinking in this respect also; what comes to the city comes to the village, often sooner rather than later.

Then, too, there is the national equivalent of the nouveau riche desire to suddenly join what are perceived to be a finer class of people, even though the luxuries consumed in this pursuit may lack what these "betters" take to be taste and sophistication. That is, on the world stage, newly wealthy nations may lack the subtlety of consumption that has been gained by nations that are heirs to old wealth. And like the rags-to-riches millionaire entrepreneur, these nations may well echo a Queen song lyric that was popular in Romania in the early 1990s: "I want it all! I want it now!" But perhaps the most basic explanation for the desire for luxuries by consumers in transitional economies is the desire that Karl Marx showed with his overcoat: a desire for respectability. As Wilson (1972) notes:

> Respectability at its material level, at its level of signification, is a show of luxury. It is a grand, well-furnished home, well equipped with modern appliances, fine furniture, china and linens, good stylish clothes, an expensive education, manners and deportment. These signifiers are also the foci of ambition for the population as a whole (p. 226).

More poignantly, Drakuli (1991) asks:

> . . . what is the minimum you must have so you don't feel humiliated as a woman? It makes me understand a complaint I heard repeatedly from women in Warsaw, Budapest, Prague, Sofia, East Berlin: 'Look at us—we don't even look like women. There are no deodorants, perfumes, sometimes even no soap or toothpaste. There is no fine underwear, no pantyhose, no nice lingerie. Worst of all, there are no sanitary napkins. What can one say except that it is humiliating?' (p. 31).

Similarly, a 25-year-old Romanian woman complained that:

> You make love with a man. Your panties are broken or your underwear is old. You are ashamed to switch on the light. Afterword you would like to drink something good; not filthy water.

Seen in this way, the pursuit of luxuries is a basic and innocent human right. It also helps make some sense of the "wish lists" that my Romanian informants provided, including both large luxuries like cars, houses, and computers, and things that would be considered necessities in much of the world, like soap, deodorant, heat, and clean water.

Of course many objections might be raised about a conclusion that luxury consumption in transitional economies is good, humane, and desirable. Have we not learned that the materialistic pursuit of happiness is generally illusory? Mightn't the sacrifices made on behalf of luxury consumption be at the expense of health, nutrition, education, child care, and other "higher" and more humane goals like those suggested by Maslow? Isn't the growing prospect of a billion Chinese consumers driving cars an invitation to environmental disaster? And can't a drive for material luxury overwhelm concern for others and cultivate a passive dependency on novel trinkets (Ger 1997)? Yes. But at the same time, following a "Do as I say, not as I do" philosophy is as hypocritical as it is ineffective. Long-standing critiques of luxury as enervating, dissipating, and frivolous have never been very successful for very long (Berry 1994). And if a key role of desire for luxuries is to provide hope and the motivation for achieving a better life, it would be small, paternalistic, and wrongheaded to attempt to curb these desires. There will always be a socially constructed line between outrageous decadent luxury and morally justified decencies. But as long as this line is not crossed, marketing luxuries in the least likely of places is no more problematic, and arguably less so, than marketing them in the most likely of places. After all, by far the greatest resource depletion and environmental threat comes from the consumption of the more economically developed world. If someone is to be targeted on these grounds, those in transitional economies are far down on the list of logical candidates. It also seems apparent that there is a cycle of desire and that what is once fervently wanted loses its appeal soon after it is acquired (Belk, Ger and Askegaard 1997). This suggests that the strong desire for luxury goods among consumers in transitional economies may quickly pass. While there is some evidence of this already, the social comparison to those in more affluent countries continues to provide an engine for further consumption aspirations among transitional consumers. Furthermore, as Russia learned under Communism, democratized luxury is oxymoronic. When everyone has something it is no longer a luxury. Under these circumstances new luxuries must be created as the old ones fall from this category. This becomes part of the motor for consumer culture. And as the histories of China, Russia, and prehistoric communities all suggest, the desire luxury has long been with us and will likely persist into the indefinite future. Dignity through more luxurious consumption appears to be a strong pan-human motivation.

Finally, we should try to avoid reestablishing the same situation that led to the collapse of Communism. It might be argued that to attempt to impose Maslow's need hierarchy by giving people what we believe they need rather than what they want, harks back to Meng's (1995) parody about the purity of water during the Chinese Cultural Revolution. These days in China, people want *Perrier*, *Yibao* [a local Chinese brand], and other expensive bottled waters (Belk and Groves forthcoming; Li 1998; Wong and Ahuvia 1997). And why should they not have it? Regardless of whether the product is water or cellular phones, the proliferation of the desire for luxury is nothing new. It is only its pace and geographic place that have leaped traditional boundaries in our postmodern world.

References

Anderson, Eugene N. *The Food of China*. New Haven, CT: Yale University Press, 1988.

Bauman, Zygmont. "Communism: A Post Mortem." *Praxis International* 10, nos. 3–4, (October 1990–January 1991): 185–192.

Belk, Russell W. "Third World Consumer Culture." In *Marketing and Development: Toward Broader Dimensions*, edited by Erdoan Kumcu and A. Fuat Firat, 103–127. Greenwich, CT: JAI Press, 1988.

_____. *Collecting in a Consumer Society*. London: Routledge, 1995.

_____. "Romanian Consumer Desires and Feelings of Deservingness." In *Romania in Transition*, edited by Lavinia Stan, 191–208. Aldershot, UK: Dartmouth, 1997.

_____. "In the Arms of the Overcoat: On Luxury, Romanticism, and Consumer Desire." In *Romancing the Market*, edited by Stephen Brown. London: Routledge, forthcoming.

Belk, Russell W. and Janeen Arnold Costa. "Chocolate Delights: Gender and Consumer Indulgence." In *Gender, Marketing, and Consumption: Proceedings of the Fourth Conference*, edited by Eileen Fischer and Daniel L. Wardlow, 179–193. San Francisco: San Francisco State University, 1998.

Belk, Russell W., Güliz Ger and Søren Askegaard. "Consumer Desire in Three Cultures: Results from Projective Research." In *Advances in Consumer Research*, Vol. 24, edited by Merrie Brucks and Debbie MacInnis, 24–28. Provo, UT: Association for Consumer Research, 1997.

Belk, Russell W. and Ronald Groves. "Luxury Beverage Consumption in Hong Kong and China," (abstract). In *Asia Pacific Research in Consumer Behavior*, Vol. 3, edited by Kineta Hung and Kent B. Monroe. Provo, UT: Association for Consumer Research, forthcoming.

Belk, Russell W. and Richard W. Pollay. "Materialism and Magazine Advertising During the Twentieth Century." In *Advances in Consumer Research*, Vol. 12, edited by Elizabeth C. Hirschman and Morris B. Holbrook, 394–398. Provo, UT: Association for Consumer Research, 1985.

Berry, Christopher J. *The Idea of Luxury: A Conceptual and Historical Investigation*. Cambridge: Cambridge University Press, 1994.

Bond, Michael Harris, ed. *The Psychology of the Chinese People*. Hong Kong: Oxford University Press, 1986.

Bonnell, Victoria E. "Winners and Losers in Russia's Economic Transition." In *Identities in Transition: Eastern Europe and Russia After the Collapse of Communism*, edited by Victoria E. Bonnell, 13–28. Berkeley, CA: Center for Slavic and East European Studies, University of California, 1997.

Boym, Svetlana. "The Archaeology of Banality: The Soviet Home." *Public Culture* 6, no. 2 (Winter 1994): 263–292.

Clunas, Craig. *Superfluous Things: Material Culture and Social Status in Early Modern China*. Urbana, IL: University of Illinois Press, 1991.

Drakuli, Slavenka. *How We Survived Communism and Even Laughed*. New York: Norton, 1991.

Gell, Alfred. "Newcomers to the World of Goods: Consumption Among the Muria Gonds." In *The Social Life of Things: Commodities in Cultural Perspective*, edited by Arjun Appadurai, 110–138. Cambridge: Cambridge University Press, 1986.

Ger, Güliz. "The Positive and Negative Effects of Marketing on Socioeconomic Development: The Turkish Case." *Journal of Consumer Policy* 15, no. 3 (1992): 229–254.

_____. "Human Development and Humane Consumption: Well-Being Beyond the Good Life." *Journal of Public Policy and Marketing* 16 (Spring 1997): 110–125.

Ger, Güliz and Russell W. Belk. "Cross-Cultural Differences in Materialism." *Journal of Economic Psychology* 17, no.1 (February 1996a): 55–78.

_____. "I'd Like to Buy the World a Coke: Consumptionscapes of the 'Less Affluent World'." *Journal of Consumer Policy* 19, no. 3 (1996b): 271–304.

Ger, Güliz, Russell W. Belk and Dana-Nicoleta Lascu. "The Development of Consumer Desire in Marketizing and Developing Economies: The Cases of Romania and Turkey." In *Advances in Consumer Research*, Vol. 20, edited by Leigh McAlister and Michael L. Rothschild, 102–107. Provo, UT: Association for Consumer Research, 1993.

Gogol, Nikolai. "The Overcoat." In *The Complete Tales of Nikolai Gogol,* edited by Leonard. J. Kent, 69–111. Chicago: University of Chicago Press, 1985. Translated by C. Garnett, 1842.

Gronow, Jukka. *The Sociology of Taste*. London: Sage, 1997.

Hall, Tony P. and Havis Dawson. "Consumerism Russian-Style." *Beverage World* 114, no. 1589 (April 1995): 36–41.

Humphrey, Caroline. "Creating a Culture of Disillusionment: Consumption in Moscow, A Chronicle of Changing Times." In *Worlds Apart: Modernity Through the Prism of the Local*, edited by Daniel Miller, 48–68. London: Routledge, 1995.

Jenk, Justin, Carl H. Michel and Valerie Margotin-Roze. "The Russian Consumer Revolution." *The McKinsey Quarterly,* no. 4 (Spring 1995): 34–46.

Kohak, Erazim. "Ashes, Ashes . . . Central Europe After Forty Years." *Daedalus* 121, no. 2 (Spring 1992): 209.

Kozminski, Andrzej K. "Consumers in Transition from the Centrally Planned Economy to the Market Economy." *Journal of Consumer Policy* 14, no. 4 (1992): 351–369.

Lascu, Dana-Nicoleta, Lalita A. Manrai, and Ajay K. Manrai. "Status-Concern and Consumer Purchase Behavior in Romania: From the Legacies of Prescribed Consumption to the Fantasies of Desired Acquisition." In *Consumption in Marketizing Economies*, eidted by Clifford J. Shultz, Russell W. Belk and Güliz Ger, 80–122. Greenwich, CT: JAI Press, 1994.

Li, Conghua. *China: The Consumer Revolution*. Singapore: John Wiley & Sons, 1998.

Marling, Karal Ann. *As Seen on TV: The Visual Culture of Everyday Life in the 1950s*. Cambridge, MA: Harvard University Press, 1994.

Maslow, Abraham H. *Motivation and Personality*. New York: Harper & Row, 1954.

McLellan, David, ed. *Karl Marx: Interviews and Recollections*. London: Macmillan, 1981.

"Men's Lines Grown in Russia." *Cosmetics International* 25 (March 1997): 473–474.

Meng, Wang. "Right to the Heart of the Matter." In *The Columbia Anthology of Modern Chinese Literature*, edited by J. Lau and Howard Goldblatt, 298–300. New York: Columbia University Press, 1995. Originally written in 1982.

Mintz, Sydney. "The Changing Roles of Food in the Study of Consumption." In *Consumption and the World of Goods*, edited by John Brewer and Roy Porter, 261–273. London: Routledge, 1993.

Nevis, Edwin C. "Cultural Assumptions and Productivity: The United States and China." *Sloan Management Review* 24, no. 3 (Spring 1983): 17–29.

Pels, Peter. "The Spirit of the Matter: On Fetish, Rarity, Fact, and Fancy." In *Border Fetishisms: Material Objects in Unstable Spaces,* edited by Patricia Spyer, 91–121. New York: Routledge, 1998.

Riesman, David. *Abundance for What? And Other Essays*. Garden City, NY: Doubleday, 1964.

Singer, Natasha. "Testing the Waters in Russia: Couture's Mission to Moscow." *WWD* 170, no. 103 (December 4, 1995): 103–104.

_____. "The Russians are Buying." *WWD* 174, no. 15 (July 22, 1997): 60–64.

Stites, Richard. *Russian Popular Culture: Entertainment and Society Since 1900*. Cambridge: Cambridge University Press, 1992.

Stallybrass, Peter. "Marx's Coat." In *Border Fetishisms: Material Objects in Unstable Spaces,* edited by Patricia Spyer, 183–207. New York: Routledge, 1998.

Watson, James L. "McDonald's in Hong Kong: Consumerism, Dietary Change, and the Rise of Children's Culture." In *Golden Arches East: McDonald's in East Asia*, edited by James L. Watson, 77–109. Stanford: Stanford University Press, 1997.

Whitworth, Mick. "Feeding the Hungry Russian Bear is Challenge for the Brave." *Grocer* 217 (November 1995): 16–17.

Wilson, Peter. *Crab Antics: The Social Anthropology of English Speaking Negro Societies of the Caribbean*. New Haven, CT: Yale University Press, 1972.

Wong, Nancy and Aaron Ahuvia. "From Tofu to Caviar: Conspicuous Consumption, Materialism and Self-Concepts in East Asian and Western Cultures." Paper presented at Association for Consumer Research Conference, Denver, CO, October, 1997.

Yan, Yunxiang. "McDonald's in Beijing: The Localization of Americana." In *Golden Arches East: McDonald's in East Asia*, edited by James L. Watson, 39–76. Stanford: Stanford University Press, 1997.

3 RESOLVING CONSUMPTION DISAGREEMENTS IN MAINLAND CHINESE FAMILIES: AN INTER-GENERATIONAL COMPARISON

David K. Tse
University of Hong Kong
Leo Y. Sin
Chinese University of Hong Kong
Oliver H. Yau
City University of Hong Kong
C. Joseph Yu
National Chengchi University

Introduction

How families resolve their disagreements in consumption decisions has long been a topic of interest in marketing. Past findings have broadened our understanding on how family consumption decisions are made, which in turn provides insights to marketing managers. In particular, studies have identified six types of conflict resolution strategies in family decisions. Spouses are known to influence their partner's decision by playing the role of an expert in the decision; emphasising each party's role; bargaining the decision in question with other decisions; using reinforcements; adopting emotionally-loaded behavior; and attributing a particular course of action to external causes (Spiro 1983). These conflict resolution strategies follow an individualistic orientation that approaches family disagreement within a dyadic power struggle context. They also emphasize rationality, a dominant core value of the North American culture.

Yet, there are indications that family disagreements are resolved in totally different ways in other cultures, such as those in Mainland China, for three reasons. First, studies in comparative philosophy indicate that Chinese people assume a broad, non-fixed context in their behavior (Sun 1983). Accordingly, when couples disagree, they often involve members outside the nucleus family including relatives, friends and even leaders of their work units. Second, studies in cross-cultural psychology (Leung and Bond 1989) have found that Chinese people tend to assume a longer time horizon in their behavior, implying that spouses may assume ways to delay solving their disagreements. Third, social studies confirm that divorce is tabooed in Chinese societies (Yan 1998). As a result, spouses are motivated to deliberately reduce the extent of the disagreement so as to avoid the possibility of divorce. While the above are implications from studies that investigate how women behave in general, an interesting question is: would Mainland Chinese women assume similar indigenously Chinese ways to resolve disagreements when they disagree with their spouse in their purchase decisions?

This question is especially interesting because Chinese lifestyles are changing rapidly, in response to globalization trends. Fueled by globalization of mass media, emphasis on materialistic lifestyles, and the rising influence of women in societies, women's normative roles in Mainland China are changing dramatically (Yan 1998). As reflected in a content analysis of women's magazines, women in Mainland China are rediscovering their family roles in addition to their social and professional roles (Ng 1989). Given the trend of globalization, would Chinese families also accept the prominent conflict resolution strategy of the West?

Women in today's Mainland China grow up in distinctly three generations. Senior women (50 years and older) were born before the birth of the People's Republic of China. Compared to the younger generations, these seniors are brought up following the traditional Chinese value system. As such, traditional Chinese norms may prevail in their choices of disagreement strategies. In contrast, the middle-age group (30–49) are brought up to accept the communist women model, which emphasizes societal norms and sacrifices for the nation. The young generation (under 30) will likely be more influenced by the Western model of individualistic life and its orientation. As Mainland China continues to open up and change, would there still be substantial differences among the choice of disagreement resolution among these three generations in today's Mainland China? Would the normative models of women during the time when they were exposed affect their choice of disagreement resolution today?

One of the most important and yet least understood global markets is that of Mainland China. There have been some recent attempts to understand how Chinese behave as consumers (Lee and Tse 1994a and 1994b; Tse 1996; Tse, Belk and Zhou 1989; Yau 1994). Yet, to date, there have not been any reported attempts to study how Chinese resolve consumption disagreements within the family, a topic that can provide interesting insights.

This paper has three objectives. First, it aims to investigate how women from Beijing resolve disagreements in their family decisions. It explores whether indigenously Chinese ways on resolving disagreements exist, in contrast to those conflict resolution strategies in the (mostly Western) literature. Second, by comparing women of three distinct generations, the paper assesses whether individual differences in age matter in the choice of conflict resolution strategies. Third, the study investigates how the choice of disagreement resolution strategies relates to individuals' socio-economic characteristics. From a broader perspective, this paper aims to understand possible social changes that are fast occurring in a transitional economy like Mainland China.

To test the above propositions, we conducted surveys with a standardized questionnaire in Beijing from June to August 1996. Around 1,000 women were randomly interviewed. Their responses were used to test our propositions.

CHARACTERISTICS AND ROLE OF FAMILIES IN CHINESE SOCIETIES

Chinese people are known to place strong emphasis in their families. This emphasis has long been regarded as a core Chinese value (Sun 1983). This core value has been suggested as a success factor in the recent resurgence and future promise of Chinese economies (Boisot and Child 1996). Studies on Chinese relationship (Guanxi) have found that the presence (or absence) of family links is a fundamental determinant among Chinese when they build and maintain relations within an organization (Boisot and Child 1996) as well as in business networks labeled as clans. In the last two decades, the structures of the families in Mainland China as well as the processes of their formation and dissolution are changing. The average size of households continues to decline. In PRC, the national average reduced from 5.17 in 1911 to 3.70 persons/household in 1996 (China Statistical Yearbook 1997). In Beijing the size is even smaller at 3.08 (China Statistical Yearbook 1997). This suggests that the nuclear mode, that is, two spouses and their children have become the most dominant family mode in Chinese society. In Mainland China, 68.3 percent of all families follow this mode. The decline in family size suggests that influences from outside the nuclear family may accordingly decline while, on the other hand, the influence from within the nuclear family may increase.

Findings from social studies indicate the salience of the family in the lives of Chinese people continues to be strong as reflected by a survey on women from 5 provinces in 1989. After four decades of communist philosophy that emphasized national needs, 72.7 percent of the women survey rated "A Happy Family" as what they want from life. This was the highest among all choices, which also included good health (62.7 percent), peaceful life (54.7 percent), interpersonal relationship (27.3 percent), career success (24.0 percent), money (10.0 percent), status (9.3 percent) and power (2.6 percent). Thus, in case there is disagreement or dispute in the family, the drive to maintain a harmonious relationship will likely motivate Chinese women to try to reduce the disagreements as they emerge. Some of them may suppress their views to those of their husbands.

Chinese people value the formation of their families. Even when they are poor, they regard wedding banquets, in which extended family members and friends are generously invited, as "musts." More importantly, elders (within the extended clan, the village or the work unit) "approve" every marriage (even though this is more symbolic than realistic in contemporary China). Yet newlyweds have to pay respect to ancestors and this is part of regular rituals. Brides are accepted into the bridegroom's family. In turn, brides lose their maiden identity and simultaneously distance themselves from their original family (Yan 1998). In today's Mainland China, however, "arranged marriages" that follow a "feudal" system have dramatically been replaced. In 1953, 37.5 percent of marriages in the Mainland were arranged by parents, but from 1966 to 1982, parents arranged only 9 percent of all marriages. Interestingly, however, relatives and friends remain strong in influencing men and women in their marriages. They are obliged to introduce someone to their friends and relatives when they reach a suitable age to get married.

In short, in contemporary Chinese culture, marriage remains both an individualist as well as a family matter. Taiwan has a live TV show similar to the "dating game" in the USA, in which men and women motivated to be married are introduced. Yet in the Taiwanese version, the live TV program is eagerly attended by the participants' family members, relatives, supervisors, colleagues and friends. Almost all of them participate actively in promoting the ones they represent, describing their virtues, lifestyles and often their family culture.

Women's Normative Roles in Chinese Societies

There are three main normative roles that continue to influence most women in Mainland China. The senior group of women (age 50+) were brought up before the birth of the People's Republic of China and hence would likely be influenced by the traditional Chinese model of woman. The middle-age group (30 to 49) were brought up to accept the communist role, while the young age group (below 30) were brought up when Mainland China engaged in the modernization plan in which Western ideas are welcome. They were exposed to the Western model. While the pure form of these three norms hardly exists, one may be able to trace the influences of these three normative roles among contemporary Chinese women.

The traditional Chinese model sees a woman's role as subordinate to the family. According to strong feudal belief, an ideal woman follows her father's orders before she marries, follows her husband's orders after she has married, and follows her son's orders when she ages. It is natural for her to sacrifice everything for the goodness of the family. Women are responsible to serve their husbands and bring up the children of the bridegroom's family. An ideal woman would be a virtuous wife and a kind mother, respecting the hierarchical system within the extended family and keeping up the traditions of the extended family. Women were often deprived of education because they would be regarded as virtuous even if they didn't have education. In short, the traditional norm limits Chinese women to the family with almost no individual life.

This traditional model of women's roles lasted until the People's Republic of China was established in 1949. The communist model defines women as an equal partner in society. This is a societal or nationalistic-oriented model for women. This model implies that women are normatively treated equally, contributing as much as men and assuming as much responsibility as them. In return, a woman was expected to devote herself to her nation. Her actions and life goals were to promote the national welfare. Family matters were of lower priority than national (or communal) tasks. A communist woman maintained minimal private life; her undivided attention to the family was replaced by her duties to society. This communist model (in contemporary Mainland China, the socialistic model) of woman began in 1949 and maintained its momentum during the Cultural Revolution until the country engaged in the modernization plan in 1979.

Beginning in 1979, China opened its door to accept many ideas of the West. In so doing the Western model of woman began to influence its people. Beijing, our sample city is one of the key cities where Western influence is strong. The process is helped by the success of women in Hong Kong, where women are holding top government, management as well as professional positions. They are given equal opportunities in university education (over 51 percent of the University of Hong Kong's undergraduate enrollments are women). Hong Kong women are models to be emulated by most women in Mainland China.

Resolving Differences in Families: The North American Way

Existing Western literature on family decision making has highlighted a number of ways couples may use to resolve their differences. These ways primarily follow three orientations that are traceable to the roots of the North American culture. The first orientation can broadly be regarded as a problem solving approach. It defines family conflicts as problems both spouses would face. To solve problems, couples may gather more information relevant to the decision; follow the spouse who has more expertise in related decisions; or delegate authority to the spouse who is responsible for those decisions. In essence, this approach conceptualizes the conflict as a problem and the couples are motivated to find a solution to resolve it.

The second orientation focuses more on the external environment of the conflict. It can be labeled as an 'environmental factor dominance' approach to family conflict resolution. It conceptualizes that the limitations posted by the environment are so strong that they constrain the set of alternatives couples may take. Some examples of this approach include budgetary constraints, time pressure and other external causes, like the absence of a preferred brand.

The third orientation looks at family conflicts as dyadic interactions, that is, power plays between husbands and wives. It conceptualizes each spouse as working towards his or her own goals in the conflict situation. While those goals may either be conscious or unconscious, spouses are motivated to adopt strategies to achieve their individual goals. The alternatives a spouse may adopt range from mild influence strategies such as persuading one's spouse to adopt one's idea, to power struggles such as engaging in emotion-loaded behavior, bargaining and other power-related alternatives. Past studies have found empirical support for these strategies in each group of orientations (Spiro 1983).

Perceiving Differences: The Chinese Way

To understand how Chinese people resolve differences in family decisions, it is important to recognize how Chinese culture regards disagreements. As a culture with a long history, Chinese people have a long history in managing disagreements. They classify disagreements into roughly four categories, ranging from holding different opinions to open conflicts. One can realize such categories by their labels. The first category is usually labeled as "Bu Tun Ye Gen," a state of holding different opinions. It is a mild way to acknowledge that there is disagreement in opinion. The second stage is "Bu Hao," literally referring to "not harmonized." It acknowledges that the relationship is tense and not in harmony. The third category, labeled "Jiao Or," literally means "involve bad," that is the relationship is in a negative state. The fourth category, labeled "Zhung Du," literally refers to a more action-oriented situation of "conflict." These are categories used today; even finer categories of disagreement can be found historically.

In short, contemporary Chinese people label "disagreement" according to a set composed of two rough dimensions: (1) effect: "neutral," "non-harmonized" and "negative," and (2) "non-action" versus "action" oriented. Yet these cells are not complete. There are two additional dimensions relevant to the Chinese way of approaching disagreement. As noted in the literature, Chinese people draw a clear distinction between events that are "not-publicized" versus "publicized." A non-publicized state of disagreement refers to a situation where two spouses continue to display actions of a harmonious relationship in public; yet, consciously, the spouses know that those actions were made-up ones. "Moi Hu Zen Li" literally means "matched in appearance, separated in spirit." Once a disagreement is brought to the public, it will take much greater effort to resolve it. By then, the actors have demonstrated in public their disagreement and because of "face saving" they often opt for very extreme forms of actions. Thus, the Chinese people tend not to display any disagreement in the public eyes (flight), but once they are forced to display the disagreement in public, they are likely to engage in strong and extreme behaviors (fight) giving rise to the "flight and fight" strategies discussed by Tse, Francis and Walls (1994).

INDIGENOUS CHINESE VALUES AND DISAGREEMENT RESOLUTION

As discussed, the primary objective of this study is to substantiate that Chinese women adopt an indigenous way to resolve disagreements in their families. In the following sections we argue that there are three broad ways Chinese women follow in dealing with family consumption disagreements that differ from the current Western model. They include harmony seeking, mediator seeking and submission.

In this study, Beijing women were asked to react to a consumption decision in which they disagree with their husbands (or boyfriends, in case they are not married). They were asked to rate how likely they would be to adopt the different resolution alternatives. In total there were twenty different alternatives, including the ways of conflict resolutions reported in the literature as well as indigenous Chinese ways of dealing with family disagreements. We would like to point out that Chinese women will not necessarily limit their choice of strategies to those that are indigenously Chinese; we expect that some of the strategies adopted by North American women as reported in the literature will also be adopted by the Chinese women (H1).

Harmony Seeking. As noted by psychologists studying how Chinese people behave (Yang 1996), Chinese people are not "collectivists," rather, they are "interpersonally" driven. This means that a primary goal of the Chinese people is to maintain a harmonious relationship with all the people around them. As noted by Fi (a famous Chinese anthropologist), this harmony seeking motive can be traced to the village life where Chinese culture originates (Bei 1993). As noted in Tse, Francis and Walls (1994), Chinese managers find it easier to deal with task-related conflicts rather than interpersonal conflicts.

As discussed, the motivation to maintain a harmonious relationship and the eminence of upholding a family will likely drive the Chinese women to adopt harmony-seeking strategies. In so doing, the Chinese women may sacrifice their own preferences; at times, they may delay the decision in order to maintain harmony within the family. We hypothesise that:

> H1a: Harmony seeking is a strategy likely to be adopted by Chinese women when they face disagreement in family consumption situation.

Mediation. The Chinese philosopher Sun (1983) noted that an essential difference between traditional Chinese and contemporary Western values is the way in which people perceive the context of their decisions. While Western cultural values emphasize discrete treatment of events within a well-defined framework, the Chinese tend to define the decision context by vague and loose boundaries. When couples in today's North America disagree, it is regarded as a "personal" matter between the couple: no one has the right to step in unless invited. In most cases, parents and in-laws are bystanders of family disagreements unless they are asked to be involved. In contrast, when Chinese couples disagree, the in-laws are obliged to help. It is regarded as a matter within the family. Sometimes relatives and friends may volunteer to get involved. In Mainland China, supervisors from work units have often been invited to comment on and resolve family differences. The earlier the disagreement is resolved, the better it is. Only if it is not resolved is the next level brought in to help the dispute. This explains why mediators are so often used in Chinese culture (e.g., Tse *et al.* 1988).

Thus, the Chinese value system legitimizes parents, relatives and friends as helpers in family disagreements. Couples willingly accept counseling by others when they cannot resolve disagreements themselves. The effectiveness of mediators will likely depend on the mediator's status and expert knowledge, as well as closeness to the couple. We hypothesize:

> H1b: Use of mediators will be a frequently-used strategy chosen by Chinese women when they encounter conflicts in their consumption decisions.

Submission. The feudal system limits Chinese women's life within the family. It forges a sense of total submission of a Chinese woman to her father, then her husband and then her son. In today's Chinese societies, this norm rarely survives in younger generations, because of today's education system; it probably survives only in very remote villages where oral tradition dominates. In this study we surveyed women from Beijing, and hypothesise that:

> H1c: Submission to husbands will be perceived as a unique strategy by Chinese women, but this strategy would not likely be adopted.

INTER-GENERATIONAL DIFFERENCES

As discussed, we expected that senior Chinese women (50 or above), who were likely to be brought up before the communist regime and shortly after, would likely be affected by Chinese traditional values. When facing a family disagreement, they may opt for harmony seeking behavior. In contrast, the middle-age group (30–49) of women were brought up during the period in which the communist model of women is emphasised. Accordingly, they may opt for more rational-oriented resolution alternatives in dealing with family disagreements. Finally, the youngest age group (below 30) would be more Westernized and they would likely reject submission as a resolution strategy. Since there is no direct correspondence between resolution strategies and the normative model of women, it is difficult for us to go beyond the above general propositions. Nonetheless, we hypothesise:

> H2: There will be distinct patterns of resolution strategies among the three age groups. These distinct patterns will reflect the normative model of women these three groups of women are accustomed to.

SOCIAL CHANGES AND CORRELATES

In this study we are also interested in how specific socio-economic characteristics of the respondents correlate with their choice of disagreement resolution strategies. We have included in our survey variables such as education level, proportion of wife's income to total family income, as well as social exposure variables such as amount of local mass media exposure, amount of foreign media exposure, activities with friends and work outside the family. Our generic hypothesis is that the socio-economic characteristics we measured would be significantly related to the choice of different resolution strategies adopted by the respondents (H3). We expect the significant correlates would reflect some interesting socio-psychological processes that relate to the changing social norms that the Chinese women are experiencing.

RESEARCH DESIGN

The survey in Beijing was conducted in the summer of 1996. As in other major cities in Mainland China, Beijing is classified into different regions and within each region different units composing of varying sizes of city blocks. Each unit is managed by a team of workers who take care of the welfare and security issues with the unit. We hired two female research assistants who were studying at a renowned university in Beijing, who first contacted each of the units and sought approval to randomly choose the respondents to be interviewed within the unit. Then the research assistant visited the chosen respondents' family and conducted the interview in the family's home. This procedure is popular among marketing research companies in Beijing.

The interviewers approached the respondents, explained the nature of the survey and conducted the interview through a structured questionnaire. The entire interview lasted around 20 minutes and the respondents were given a gift worth RMB$7 (more than an hour's pay for an average worker in Beijing). With the prior approval and the gift, the response rate reached 95 percent. Table 1 displays the characteristics of the sample. Only 13.9 percent were full-time housewives; most were reasonably well educated (51 percent with post-secondary education or above); and 38.5 percent of them brought home 41 percent+ of their family income. Interestingly, their self rating as communist women was not high (3.59 on a 5-point scale: "1" strongly disagree to "5" strongly agree), and lower than their rating as women concerned about social issues.

The survey had three parts. Of particular interest to this paper was the part on consumption disagreement situations. The respondents were asked to specify how likely they would be to engage in each of the 20 items (alternatives) in case they disagree with their husband (or boyfriend, if they were not married) in their consumption decision. If the respondent's age was within the young age group, the decision scenario was whether they should have a wedding banquet; if her age was among the middle age group, the decision scenario was which school they would send their child to; if the respondent's age fell into the senior age group, the decision was whether they should buy a new set of furniture if they were to move to a new apartment/house. These three scenarios had been pre-tested before the survey, among Mainland China

Table 1. Characteristics of the Sample

	Beijing
Number of women surveyed	1000
Percentage married	74.8%
Percentage living with parents and in-laws	36.1%
Average number of children in family	1.05
Percentage of housewives	13.9%
Education:	
Below secondary school	12.0%
Secondary school	49.0
University or above	51.0
Percentage of wife's income to total family income:	
0–20%	17.4%
21–40%	35.1
41–60%	38.5
over 60%	9.1
Self rating[a] on:	
Traditional Chinese women	3.30
Modern women	3.52
Women concerned about social events	3.80
Communist women	3.59

[a]On a 5-point scale, "1" strongly disagree to "5" strongly agree.

women, and were found to have similar impact and were judged to be relevant decisions for the corresponding age group.

As seen in Table 2, the 20 items included all the alternatives from the existing literature as well as indigenous alternatives we obtained in our pretests. The items were measured by 5-point scales ranging from "1" (very unlikely to adopt) to "5" (very likely to adopt). In another part of the questionnaire, the respondent's socio-economic characteristics (education level, percentage of wife to entire family income, etc.) were measured. Another question measured social exposure variables such as the amount of local and foreign mass media (newspaper, magazine, TV, movies) exposure as well as amount of time spent with co-workers and other people outside the family.

FINDINGS AND DISCUSSION

Indigenous Chinese Disagreement Resolution Strategies

Respondents' scores on the 20 alternatives to resolve conflicts were first factor analyzed with varimax rotation. In total, six factors (called strategies hereafter to distinguish them from the 20 alternatives) with eigenvalues higher than 1 were obtained, accounting for 50.9 percent of total variance. Three items ("decide on my own without further discussion," "delay the decision" and "prepare a good meal to influence husband") had cross-factor loadings above 0.40. They were deleted from further consid-

Table 2. Factor Structure of the 17 Disagreement Resolution Alternatives

Disagreement Resolution Alternatives	Power	Submission	Persuasion	Mediator	Harmony	Information
Whoever pays, whoever decides	.681					
Bargain this decision with other decisions	.675					
Whoever has more authority, whoever decides	.668					
Engage in emotion-loaded behavior	.470					
Respect husband's view and drop my own		.748				
Give up decision		.683				
Follow the norm that husband decides		.610				
Convince husband to accept my view			.779			
Wait til husband is in a better mood			.609			.359
Get other family members on my side			.565			
Influence husband by emphasizing a "model" husband's role			.501			
Consult friends				.708		
Consult whoever has expertise				.602		
Consult parents/other senior family members				.598		
Follow the family's financial situation					.767	
Use harmony as the goal to suit each party's need		.384			.597	
Get more information for decision						.867

Note: The reported figures are the factor loadings; those loadings which were less than 0.35 are not shown.

Table 3. Mean Scores of Disagreement Resolution Strategies by Age Group and City

All Ages		Young (<30)		Middle Age (30–49)		Senior (50 or Older)	
Harmony	= 3.73	Harmony	= 3.82	Information	= 3.85	Harmony	= 3.98
Information	= 3.81	Mediator	= 3.55	Harmony	= 3.73	Information	= 3.89
Persuasion	= 3.50	Information	= 3.51	Mediator	= 3.49	Mediator	= 3.55
Mediator	= 3.48	Persuasion	= 3.50	Persuasion	= 3.47	Persuasion	= 3.49
Submission	= 2.60	Submission	= 2.49	Submission	= 2.60	Submission	= 2.74
Power	= 2.50	Power	= 2.49	Power	= 2.54	Power	= 2.45

eration. As shown in Table 2, the resultant strategies include Power (power struggle), Submission (submit to husband's view), Persuasion (persuade husband or other family members to accept one's view), Mediator (use friends, other family members to mediate difference), Harmony (emphasize harmony), and Information (get more information for the decision). Of the six strategies, Information, Power, and Persuasion have been reported in the literature. The existence of the three other strategies, namely Harmony, Mediator, and Submission suggest that Chinese women perceive other ways to approach family disagreements beyond those reported in the literature.

Table 3 displays the mean scores of each of the six strategies by age group. Turning first to the pattern for the entire sample (that is, the first column in Table 3), we find that the six strategies fall into **three** distinct groups. On a 5-point scale from 1 = very unlikely to adopt, to 5 = very likely to adopt, The Information (3.81) and Harmony (3.73) are the highly-preferred strategies. They are followed by Persuasion (3.50) and Mediator (3.48). The less preferred strategies are Submission (2.60) and Power (2.50). It is important to also note that the mean scores for both Submission and Power fall below 3.00 (the mid-point of the 5 point scale). In short, these two strategies were "rejected" by the women surveyed.

We ran multi-group comparison mean tests and found that across-group differences (for example, Information versus Persuasion) were significant at $p < .01$, while within-group differences (for example, Information and Harmony) were not significant at $p < .01$. As discussed, the generic hypothesis of our study (H1) proposes that Chinese women would use some indigenous ways to resolve family disagreements. The existence of the indigenous Chinese resolution strategies (namely Harmony, Mediator and Submission as separate factors), and the favorable mean scores of Harmony and Mediator, imply not only that these strategies exist among the Chinese women, but also that two of the three indigenous Chinese strategies have a reasonable chance of being adopted. This confirms H1.

CULTURAL ROOTS AND RANKS AMONG THE RESOLUTION STRATEGIES

Let us now examine the cultural roots of the six strategies and see how they are ranked. As discussed, the Information, Persuasion and Power strategies are rooted from Western culture, while the Harmony, Mediator and Submission are traceable to the traditional Chinese value system. As mentioned, the six strategies form three distinct groups. Within each of the three distinct groups of strategies, there is one Western value-based and one Chinese value-based strategy. This suggests that in the minds of contemporary Beijing women, strategies originated by either culture are freely grouped according to their preference rather than according to the cultural roots. Does this imply that Chinese traditional culture values no longer matter?

One way to understand the phenomenon is to apply insights derived from acculturation studies in which researchers study how individuals change their behaviors when they come into contact with other cultures. When individuals come into contact with another culture either temporarily (Stayman and Deshpande 1989) or permanently as immigrants (Lee and Tse 1994b), practices that do not generate conflicts with an individual's cultural roots will be more readily accepted than practices that generate conflicts. As a disagreement resolution strategy, Information does not work against any Chinese values and therefore women readily accepted this strategy to the extent of ranking it as highly preferred. In contrast, Power strategy originates from the conception that the family is an arena of dyadic power structure. This is in conflict with the Chinese value system that regards Harmony as a priority principle within the family. Accordingly, Power is rated the lowest (and lower than 3.0) among the Beijing women surveyed. As discussed, Persuasion is a milder form that regards family as a place where husband and wife compete for their influential roles. This strategy is likely to arouse some resistance from Chinese cultural values. Traditionally, Chinese women are taught to be led in their opinions by their father, their husband and their son. Thus women who actively engage in Persuasion may be regarded as stepping beyond their conventional role. This may explain why Persuasion is rated in between Information and Power. The absolute mean score of 3.50 also reflects its moderate level of acceptance.

Let us turn now to the three indigenous Chinese strategies. As the most important objective underlying family formation, it is not surprising that Harmony is most highly preferred. In addition, a harmonious family is the aspired hope for the Chinese women. As such, Harmony is the most ideal strategy to follow in accordance with the Chinese value system. On the other extreme, Submission (i.e., "husband is always right") is lowly rated and found to be unacceptable (mean rating below 3.00) by the women surveyed. This suggests that according to the social norms within today's cities, contemporary Beijing women find the feudal system that promotes submissive women as being unacceptable. Mediator is rated in between the two extremes, suggesting that this strategy receives moderate support (3.48) from the samples.

Taken as a whole, the ranking of the six strategies seems to be driven by two major forces, cultural resistance and modernization. Information (being culturally neutral and modern) and Harmony (culturally encouraged and modern) are highly ranked; they are followed by Persuasion (mild cultural resistance and modern) and Mediator (culturally accepted and fairly modern). In contrast, Submission (feudal and outdated) and Power (culturally opposed though modern) are rejected by the women surveyed.

AGE GROUP DIFFERENCES

As discussed, we are also interested in the age group differences because we expect different generations to exhibit some differences in their preferences for disagreement resolution strategies (H2). These differences are traceable to the differences in the normative models of the women surveyed.

Table 3 also reports the mean scores of the disagreement strategies of each age group. When we ran the ONEWAY ANOVA with each of the 6 strategies with age group as the independent variable, only the Information strategies registered significant age group differences. A closer look showed that, in the Young age group, Information was rated lower (3.51) than the mean scores of the other two age groups (3.85 and 3.89). This suggests that the Young age group does not find Information a highly-preferred strategy in resolving disagreement.

In addition, there are some indications that the senior Beijing women rated Submission highest among the three age groups, though the difference was only marginally significant ($p < .08$). Aside from that, there were no significant age group differences observed. The lack of significant difference among the three age groups raised an interesting question: why doesn't age matter? There are two possible answers. First, there may be a very strong trans-generational transfer of normative value on how women should behave. From one generation to the next, Chinese women may have passed on what is the best way to work with family differences among different generations. Second, there may be strong social changes in Mainland China that erode all age differences. Such changes may come from global or national trends (Pollay, Tse and Wang 1990). Whichever the reason, more research is needed to understand this finding.

RESOLUTION STRATEGIES AND CORRELATES

As a first study in how Chinese women resolve their family consumption conflicts, we would also like to find out the significant demographic and social-psychological variables that correlate with different conflict resolution strategies. As hypothesized in H3, we expect the significant correlates to reflect some interesting socio-psychological processes that relate to the changing social norms that Chinese women are experiencing. Let us examine four constructs: personal predispositions (demographic characteristics) and social exposure.

Personal Predispositions. Table 4 reports the sign and the level of significance of the Pearson correlation coefficients between each of the six resolution strategies and the socio-demographic variables. For the demographic characteristics, age bears a positive significant relationship with the two least-preferred strategies of Submission and Power, suggesting that women's preference for these least-liked strategies goes up as age goes up. It is important to note that these findings for Submission and Power contradict the conventional literature. The more a woman engages in Power strategies, conventional thought assumes that she would also less likely be to submit to her husband. The finding that age correlates positively with both strategies suggests that Chinese women may show a 'bimodal' inclination as they age. They will submit more, as well as engage in more power strategies, as ways to resolve their differences with their husbands.

Level of education correlates positively with Information, Persuasion and Mediation, and negatively with the two least-preferred strategies, Submission and Power. This suggests that among Chinese women, education brings in new perspectives in resolving disagreements: getting more information, actively engaging in persuading family members, as well as rejecting Submission. Yet education also serves a dual

Table 4. Disagreement Resolution Strategies and Their Correlates

Disagreement Resolution Strategies	Demographic Characteristics			Social Exposure (Amount)			
	Age	Education	Percentage of Income	Local Mass Media	Foreign Mass Media	Activities with Friends	Work Outside Family
Information		+		+ +	+ +	+	
Harmony				+ +		+	
Persuasion		+ +					
Mediation		+ +	-			+ +	- -
Submission	+ +	- -		- -	- -		- -
Power	+ +	- -	-	- -	- -		

+ + positively significant at $p < .01$ - - negatively significant at $p < .01$

\+ positively significant at $p < .05$ to .01   - negatively significant at $p < .05$ to .01

role, promoting Mediation and rejecting Power strategy. This implies that as Chinese women acquire education, they will treasure their family more and adapt Western ways to resolve it. Yet they would reject the feudal values as well as reject the concept that the family is an arena for power.

Surprisingly, the percentage of wife's income to total family income has few significant correlates with the resolution strategies, correlating only marginally (at $p < .05$) with Mediation and Power. The higher the proportion of income a woman contributes to the family, the more they prefer not to ask others to mediate family differences. In addition, the higher the proportion of income a woman brings to the family, the less likely they are to engage in a Power strategy in their family disagreement. This differs from the past literature that suggests just the opposite (more contribution leading to more power which leads to more struggle between couples).

Social Exposure. The traditional Chinese value system confines women to their family. Accordingly, the less exposure they have beyond the family, the more likely they should be to accept the traditional Chinese norms, which in turn would encourage them to assume particular disagreement resolution strategies. We use four variables to capture four different dimensions of social exposure women may have: with friends, in the workplace, local mass media (including TV, movies, newspaper and magazines) and foreign mass media (again the four types). Columns 4 to 7 in Table 4 report the correlation coefficients. The more they interact with friends the more likely are they to engage in Information (probably they have more sources of information through friends), Harmony (social circles may reinforce the Chinese norm that emphasizes Harmony) and Mediation (more chance to ask friends to mediate) strategies. The more work the women assume outside their family, the less likely they are to engage in Mediation (maybe they don't want to publicize their family matters) and Submission (because they are more independent).

Exposure to both local and foreign mass media seems to generate similar results. It seems to follow a dual process: mass media exposure seems to encourage "Westernized" ways such as Information, and discourage Submission; it also promotes less Power and more Harmony. This dual process may reflect the transition many Chinese women are embracing. The above findings confirm H3.

CONCLUSION

Taken as a whole, the significant correlations between the demographic characteristics and the resolution strategies reflect some underlying social processes that have significant implications for understanding how women in Mainland China behave. The processes reflect an indigenous rather than a Westernized social process. In particular, based on past studies that assume families have dyadic power structures, one would have predicted that as women acquire more power through education and their percentage contribution to family income, they would be more likely to engage in Power strategy. The fact that the women in the sample behaved differently from the dyadic power structure reinforce the expectation that contemporary Chinese women approach family disagreement differently from what is in the Western culture. This finding highlights the need to assume an indigenous orientation as we study how people of other cultures behave.

Another significant finding is that there is no strong difference among the three generations of Chinese women in dealing with family disagreements. The strategy pattern we found suggests that a combination of old and new, Western and Chinese forces seem to be operating at the same time. The consistency of a transgenerational behavioral pattern suggests that social change in China is a rich and complicated process. However, we did find some simple and reasonable socio-demographic correlates as well. The pattern of results suggests that the social processes that are occurring in Mainland China can indeed be partially explained. The country is certainly undergoing major social changes caused by, and also fueling, other changes.

The results suggest some promising future research directions. To tease out whether the stability of the disagreement resolution is due to Chinese traditional values or global trends, it may be useful to have results from other Chinese societies including Hong Kong and Taiwan. These additional samples may enable us to trace the source of the consistency across the senior, the middle age and the young generation. In addition, other dimensions of family consumption behavior such as consumption values would also be interesting topics to research.

Note

This study was supported by the Research Grant Council of the Hong Kong SAR government.

References

Bei, Xiao Tong. *Xiang Te Zhang Kuo Ru Xiang To Zhung Jian*. Taipei: Feng Yun Xei Dei Publishing Company, 1993.

Boisot, Max and John Child. "From Fiefs to Clans and Network Capitalism: Explaining China's Emerging Economic Order." *Administrative Science Quarterly* 41 (December 1996): 600–628.

China Statistical Bureau. *China Statistical Yearbook*. Beijing: China Statistical Bureau, 1997.

Lee, Wei-na and David K. Tse. "Becoming Canadian: Understanding How Hong Kong Immigrants Change Their Consumption." *Pacific Affairs* 67, no. 1 (Spring 1994a): 70–95.

_____. "Changing Media Consumption in a New Home: Acculturation Patterns Among Hong Kong Immigrants in Canada." *Journal of Advertising* 23, no. 1 (March 1994b): 57–70.

Leung, Kwok and Michael Bond. "On the Empirical Identification of Dimensions for Cross-Cultural Comparison." *Journal of Cross-Cultural Psychology* 20, no. 2 (June 1989): 133–151.

Ng, Miranda. "A Longitudinal Content Analysis of Women's Magazines in Mainland China." Unpublished Master's Degree Thesis, University of British Columbia, 1989.

Pollay, Richard, David K. Tse and Zheng-Yuan Wang. "Advertising, Propaganda and Value Change in Economic Development: The New Cultural Revolution in China and Attitudes Toward Advertising." *Journal of Business Research* 20, no. 2 (March 1990): 83–96.

Spiro, Rosann L. "Persuasion in Family Decision-Making." *Journal of Consumer Research* 9, no. 4 (March 1983): 393–402.

Sun, Long-ji. *The Deep Structure of Chinese Culture*. (in Chinese). Hong Kong: Yishan, 1983.

Stayman, Douglas M. and Rohit Deshpande. "Situational Ethnicity and Consumer Behavior." *Journal of Consumer Research* 16, no. 3 (December 1989): 361–371.

Tse, David K. "Understanding Chinese People as Consumers: Past Findings and Future Propositions." In *Handbook of Chinese Psychology*, edited by Michael Bond, 352–363. New York: Oxford University Press, 1996.

Tse, David K., Russell W. Belk and Nan Zhou. "Becoming a Consumer Society: A Longitudinal and Cross-Cultural Content Analysis of Print Ads from People's Republic of China, Hong Kong, and Taiwan." *Journal of Consumer Research* 15, no. 4 (March 1989): 457–472.

Tse, David K., June Francis and Jan Walls. "Cultural Differences in Conducting Intra- and Inter-Cultural Negotiations: A Sino-Canadian Comparison." *Journal of International Business Studies* 25, no. 3 (Third Quarter 1994): 537–555.

Tse, David K., Kam-hon Lee, Ilan Vertinsky and Donald A. Wehrung. "Does Culture Matter? A Cross-Cultural Study of Executive's Choice, Decisiveness and Risk Adjustment in International Marketing." *Journal of Marketing* 52, no. 4 (October 1988): 81–95.

Yan, Nan. *Prophecy of Chinese Families.* (in Chinese). Beijing: Xin Hua Publishing Limited, 1998.

Yang, K. S. *The Inter-Personality of the Chinese People*. Taiwan: Psychology Department, National Taiwan University, 1996.

Yau, Oliver. *Consumer Behavior in China*. London and New York: Routledge, 1994.

4 CONSUMER SEGMENTATION IN CHINA

Bernd H. Schmitt
Columbia Business School and
CEIBS (Shanghai)

Introduction

Before 1979, when Deng Xiao Ping declared his open-door policy, China's consumers had little choice in the marketplace. They had to consume products of dismal quality produced by state-owned enterprises in a regulated market. Today, China's consumers have vast selection in a large variety of categories from low-end/budget items to luxury goods. They have access to new media and information. They are exposed to branded goods and their logos and advertisements. Modern retail stores are rising everywhere (Schmitt forthcoming).

This consumer revolution represents a transformation of historical proportions, and offers Western companies an unprecedented opportunity to capitalize on events. In order to do so, marketers of consumer goods need to have a detailed understanding of China's complex and rapidly-changing consumer market (Li 1998).

How do consumers make purchase decisions in this new environment? How important are different product attributes (e.g., product features, price, quality, the brand image, the retail environment) to them? How do they feel about advertising? What are their attitudes toward brands? Most importantly, are there differences in attitudes and behavior among groups of consumers so that we can segment the Chinese consumer market into meaningful geographic, socio-demographic or lifestyle segments?

Until now, an understanding of the Chinese consumer market has been severely limited due to the lack of reliable data regarding consumer perceptions and consumption patterns. As a result, little is known about Chinese consumer behavior and how to segment the market. A major reason for this lack of knowledge is the lack of an infrastructure of market research. As a result, most of the research is rather impressionistic rather than based on quantitative data collections (cf., Li 1998). Although quantitative market research is increasingly being conducted to provide information and intelligence for market decisions, the quality of most research remains suspicious. Samples are frequently biased (e.g., mail and telephone surveys are biased toward those consumers that can easily receive mail and have phones). Responses can be unreliable (due to untrained interviewers who, in the worst case, fake data), and consumers have little experience with Likert scales and semantic differentials, and show strong inclinations to give socially desirable responses in group situations.

Most importantly, research data mostly consists of focus groups or surveys that concentrate on broad-scale geographic segments. The results are often presented in an intuitive and methodologically unsophisticated manner and without consideration of patterns that are useful for segmentation, i.e., data that examine differential responses (perceptions, attitudes and behaviors) and relate them to relevant descriptors. As a result, knowledge of consumer behavior and consumer segmentation is often insufficient for formulating marketing strategies and programs.

This current research was conducted to close this knowledge gap. In contrast to prior research, the data of the survey describe consumer segments on a more fine-tuned scale, focusing on geographic, demographic and lifestyle characteristics. The questions asked in the survey included a range of perceptual, attitudinal, and behavioral variables as well as geographic, socio-demographic and lifestyle background information. Data analyses were conducted using standard research techniques for segmentation such as factor analyses, cluster analyses and discriminant analyses. A subset of the data was analyzed using self-organizing maps; these analyses and visual maps have been reported in Schmitt and Deboek (1998).

In this chapter, I first review the few consumer and segmentation studies that have been published or made publicly available about the Chinese consumer market. Most of this research, using descriptive analyses of surveys and focus groups, has been conducted by commercial research firms rather than academic researchers. I then present the methodology and results of the survey that research associates Sally Lee, Ivy Fei and I conducted in Beijing and Shanghai.

REVIEW OF PRIOR RESEARCH: THE GALLUP CHINA SURVEY

Most marketing research conducted in the People's Republic of China today has focused on product ownership and identified differences between rural and urban consumers. Major differences are typically found between urban and rural households in terms of which household items consumers already own and intend to purchase within the next two years.

This type of research was pioneered by Gallup China in 1994. The survey was repeated in 1997 (The Gallup Organization 1998). Gallup is the only research firm that is licensed to conduct nationwide surveys. The survey results are based on interviews conducted as in-home interviews in every province, municipality and autonomous region of China with a roughly representative sample of the adult Chinese population.

Aside from the product ownership data, the Gallup research also identified differences among regions of the country in terms of the importance of advertising, price sensitivity, brand sensitivity and brand awareness. For example, results indicated that the urban population was significantly more likely than the rural population to study advertisements before the purchase of a "da jian"- a big ticket item or durable good. Moreover, urban respondents would pay higher prices for products of high quality. Urban consumers were also more likely to buy a leading brand regardless of price. Brand-name recognition of foreign brands was also the highest in the cities.

In terms of lifestyles, in the latest Gallup survey, urban Chinese compared to rural Chinese showed a growing interest in self-fulfillment by non-material means. Also, when asked to rate life quality, urban citizens give a higher rating than rural citizens. Moreover, urbanites tend to show more satisfaction than those in countryside with regard to home electronics and durable goods, clothing, savings, education, family life, standard of living, leisure activities, and personal income.

OTHER SEGMENTATION SCHEMES

The "urban - rural" segmentation is important but a segmentation of the Chinese consumer should not stop there. One key issue is the identification of subsegments in the overall urban segment.

For a start, there may be noteworthy differences among cities. Unfortunately, little research has been conducted on this topic but some data are suggestive. For example, Dynamics Decision, a research firm, compiles statistics about Chinese consumers from public sources. Each month, a sample of 9000 families is surveyed in cities across China on their income level and expenditures. The average per capita income as well as disposable income is roughly the same in Beijing, Tianjin and Shanghai but more than twice in Shenzhen. Moreover, there are cultural differences in language, traditions and food preferences among, for example, Beijing, Shanghai and Guangzhou. Like Dynamics Decision, advertising firms in China typically distinguish between 5 to 8 city markets.

Coopers and Lybrand regularly conducts focus groups, i.e., small-group focused discussion sessions with consumers, in Shanghai and distinguishes three segments: men aged 30–45, women aged 30–45, and a segment of both men and women aged 19–25. Coopers and Lybrand claims that these three segments are distinct in their shopping habits: women aged 30–45 appreciate "value and convenience." Men aged 30–45 are "utility shoppers"; they buy whatever they need or their wives and children ask them to buy. Shanghai consumers aged 30 and under are "highly aspirational and interested in ownership and leisure." They are more likely to spend their disposable incomes, frequent foreign-invested department stores and consume Western products. However, these results are often based on four or five focus groups conducted with 10–15 consumers each, thus questionable in terms of their reliability and generalizability.

Three other demographic variables may also be of interest: income, education and occupation. In 1995, affiliates of Louis Harris conducted a survey of 2500 consumers in Beijing, Shanghai, Guangzhou, Tianjin and Chengdu. The methodology was based on studies by Yankelovich and Skelly, who are considered pioneers in the measurement of social attitudes in the United States.

In this research, differences emerged for attitudes toward new products, trial of new products and orientations toward other people. The survey indicated that young, more-affluent and better-educated consumers were much more likely to try new products than older, less-affluent and less-educated consumers. Based on their attitudes and behavior toward new product categories or new brands within a category, they are the innovators. Turning to occupations, the survey also found that entrepreneurs and others working in the private sector are more likely to experiment with new products than government employees. Moreover, the young, affluent and educated are also more likely to try products admired by others. They have a strong desire to conform to the norms of the reference group.

The objective of the present research is to extend prior research, using more rigorous sampling techniques and data analyses. The study focused on relevant perceptions of product and brands, media, promotions, and retailing as well as on consumer behavior.

DATA COLLECTION

Methodology

The research was conducted in the spring of 1997 in Beijing and Shanghai. Beijing and Shanghai were selected as target cities for the research based on several factors:

(1) From a managerial perspective, these two cities evoke the greatest business interests in China at the present time.
(2) Since the objective of the current research is not only geographic segmentation, but also socio-demographics and lifestyles, the research required data collection in places where these types of segmentations were likely to emerge.
(3) Beijing and Shanghai are easily accessible for market research due to a fairly developed infrastructure for market research.

Sampling

A total of 925 consumers (434 in Beijing and 491 in Shanghai) participated in the research. Consumers were recruited for participation in the study on two major shopping roads in Beijing and Shanghai: Wang Fu Jing Road and Huaihai Road, respectively. The sample was stratified based on four age levels (20–29, 30–39, 40–49, 50–65) and three income levels (less than 800 RMB per month, 800-3000 RMB, more than 3000 RMB). (At the time of data collection, the exchange rate was roughly 1 USD = 8 RMB.) In addition, because of the market potential of the young generation, we also included a group of college students (without stable incomes). The final sample of respondents consisted of a minimum of 30 respondents each in the age/income cells described, though the required number of at least 30 participants could not be obtained for 50–65 year olds with an income above 3000 RMB due to the mandatory retirement from many firms at the age of 55.

Procedure

In Beijing, the study was conducted by BMS, a high-quality market research firm. In Shanghai, an equivalent study was conducted by the research team of the BAT Chair of Marketing at CEIBS (China-Europe International Business School). Respondents were approached by an interviewer and asked about their age and income. If the person was deemed to be an appropriate participant, then he or she was invited to participate in the survey on a one-by-one basis in a location nearby. The questions were read aloud to the respondent who had a copy of the questionnaire as well. The use of rating scales was explained if the respondent was unsure about how to use them. This procedure provided a safeguard against the frequent practice of faking data by either respondents or field assistants.

Each interview lasted approximately 15 minutes. Survey data were collected regarding brand perceptions, product influences, media perceptions, media behavior, customer loyalty, and perceptions of brand parity. We also collected background information including Age, Sex, Income, Education, Occupation, and Type of employer. Data on several other variables were also collected, not described here for brevity. Based on the results of a factor analysis, a "degree of engaging in a social lifestyle variable" was constructed based on responses to a number of measures regarding engagement in personal (housekeeping), personal/social (sports, shopping and traveling) and social activities (going to the movies, karaoke, dancing, restaurants and visiting friends).

DATA ANALYSIS AND RESULTS

Factor Analyses

To reduce the number of variables and determine the underlying dimensions of (1) brand perceptions and product influence, (2) media perceptions and behavior, and (3) customer loyalty and perceived brand parity, we conducted factor analyses for each of these three categories of variables. Eigenvalues greater than one, variance explained and interpretability were considered to determine the number of factors. The factor analyses explained between 54 and 57 percent of the variance. Table 1 shows the factors for each category and the factor loadings (>.4).

The factor analysis on brand perceptions and product influences revealed four factors, which were labeled: (1) brand image; (2) reference group influence; (3) promotion; and (4) product functionality. The factor analysis on media perceptions and behavior also revealed four factors: (1) positive attitudes toward advertising; (2) point of sales; (3) time spent on media; and (4) negative attitudes toward advertising. Finally, the factor analysis on customer loyalty and perceived brand parity revealed three factors: (1) loyalty to nondurables; (2) loyalty to durables; and (3) perceived brand differentiation.

Determining Consumer Segments

To identify consumer segments that differ from each other in their perceptions and behavior, we conducted a k-means cluster analysis (PROC FASTCLUS in SAS) on the factor scores, varying the number of clusters from 2 to 8. We used variance explained and cluster size to determine the number of clusters. Five clusters provided the most appropriate solution. Clusters 4 and 5 had small cluster sizes of 73 and 64 respondents, respectively, compared to the clusters 1–3 which included 353, 256 and 195 consumers, respectively. Table 2 shows the percentage of respondents in each cluster, the cluster means and an interpretative label for each clustered segment.

Segment 1 (38 percent of the sample) are the Market Rejectors. They say they are not influenced by promotions and do not have a positive attitude toward advertising. They also do not pay attention to point-of-sales marketing elements and are not influ-

Table 1. Factor Analysis

1. Brand perception and product influence

Final Communality Estimate: Total = 5.95 (54%)

Factors	Eigenvalue	Variable	Variable Loading
Brand image	2.16	Importance of brand image for purchase	0.62
		Buy brands because of high quality	0.68
		Buy brands because special	0.80
		Buy brands because fashionable	0.61
Reference group influence	1.53	Friends and relatives	0.77
		Colleagues	0.75
		Prices (not significant)	0.48
Promotion	1.20	TV ads	0.72
		Sales persons	0.71
Product functionality	1.06	Numbers of features	0.70
		Quality	0.76

2. Media perception and behavior

Final Communality Estimate: Total = 5.79 (58%)

Factors	Eigenvalue	Variable	Variable Loading
Positive attitudes toward ads	2.19	Entertaining	0.83
		Fun to watch	0.82
		Informative	0.42
Point-of-sales stimuli	1.33	Packaging	0.81
		Retail environment	0.80
		Advertising and promotion	0.60
Time spent on media	1.14	TV	0.76
		Radio	0.77
Negative attitudes toward ads	1.12	Deceptive	0.70
		Reason for high prices	0.73

Table 1. Continued

3. Customer loyalty and perceived brand differentiation

Final Communality Estimate: Total = 6.70 (56%)

Factors	Eigenvalue	Variable	Variable Loading
Loyalty to nondurables	3.43	Food	0.56
		Cosmetics	0.81
		Personal care	0.77
Loyalty to durables	2.13	Clothes	0.43
		Tools	0.82
		Electrical appliances	0.81
Perceived brand differentiation	1.15	Food	0.68
		Cosmetics	0.81
		Personal care	0.79
		Clothes	0.76
		Tools	0.68
		Electrical appliances	0.76

enced by brand image. Segment 2 (26 percent) are the Marketing Affected. Their decisions are affected by promotions but less by the functional aspects of a product. They do not hold negative attitudes toward ads. They are brand loyal to durables, and they think brands are different. Segment 3 (21 percent) represents a group that was interpreted as the Brand Explorers. They are very sensitive to brand images but not affected by reference groups. They pay attention to point-of-sales stimuli but they are brand switchers (especially for nondurables). Segment 4, a fairly small segment of 8 percent, was difficult to interpret. They are not at all affected by brand image. They are influenced by promotions. They hold both positive and negative attitudes toward ads. They are loyal to nondurables but switchers for durables. And they believe that brands are largely the same. As a result, they may be labeled the Undefined in the sense of possessing a lack of a distinct identity as consumers. Since they are in a sense outliers in our sample, we therefore removed this segment from further analyses. Segment 5 is a small segment as well of just 7 percent but they are fairly distinct in their perceptions and behaviors. They are the Traditional Functionalists who are affected by reference groups, not affected by promotions, but do pay attention to the functional aspects of the product. They ignore point-of-sales aspects, do not spend much time on media, have a negative attitude toward advertising, but are very loyal consumers for both nondurables and durables.

After we have identified the segments in terms of their essential perceptions of brands, product and media and in terms of their behavior in the marketplace,—i.e., in terms of what they think, feel and do—the question arises, "Who are they?" To answer this question, two analyses were conducted. First, we constructed profiles for each

Table 2. Cluster Analysis

Segment	Market Rejectors	Marketing Affected	Brand Explorers	Undefined	Traditional Functionalists
Percentage	38%	26%	21%	8%	7%
		Cluster Means			
Brand image	**–0.29**	0.06	**0.77**	**–1.12**	0.28
Reference group	0.06	0.13	**–0.48**	0.24	**0.42**
Promotion	**–0.66**	**0.71**	0.26	**0.59**	**–0.44**
Product functionality	–0.04	**–0.48**	0.35	0.44	**0.41**
Positive attitude toward ads	**–0.60**	0.36	0.38	**0.49**	0.28
Point of sale	**–0.30**	0.25	**0.62**	0.13	**–1.38**
Time spent on media	0.08	0.04	–0.18	0.33	**–0.50**
Negative attitude toward ads	–0.03	**–0.52**	0.32	**0.64**	**0.49**
Loyalty to nondurables	–0.12	0.14	**–0.57**	**0.89**	**1.24**
Loyalty to durables	–0.25	**0.46**	–0.25	**–0.45**	**1.06**
Perceived brand differentiation	0.01	0.31	–0.28	**–0.50**	0.30

Approximate Expected Overall $R^2 = 0.21$

segment, on the basis of the geographic, socio-demographic and lifestyle descriptors assessed in the study. Second, we conducted a stepwise discriminant analysis to determine significant descriptors and their prevalence in each segment.

In the profiles (contingency tables of descriptors by segments), all the descriptors were statistically significant at $p < .05$ except for sex and education. Table 3 shows the profiles for each segment. Examining the table in terms of being noticeably overrepresented (above the line) or underrepresented (below the line) relative to the sample as a whole, suggests the following key characteristics for each segment.

The Market Rejectors are more likely to be from Beijing than Shanghai. They are overrepresented in the group of the above 55 years old and underrepresented in the less than 20 and 20–30 year old group. In terms of lifestyle characteristics, the socially inactive are more likely to be in this segment. They are more likely to work for state-owned enterprises.

The Marketing Affected are more likely from Shanghai. In contrast to the Market Rejectors, the Marketing Sensitive are underrepresented in the age group above 55 and overrepresented in the youngest age group of less than 20 years old. They are likely to be socially active. They are overrepresented among joint ventures/foreign employees and students.

The Brand Explorers are mostly from Shanghai and in the mid-age groups of 20–55. They are likely to be socially active. Although sex was not statistically significant overall, in this one segment, women tended to be more likely to be part of this segment than men. The segment also showed an overrepresentation in the higher income categories and white collars.

The Undefined showed few distinct characteristics in perceptions and behavior. They were also difficult to identify in terms of geographic, socio-demographics or lifestyles,

Table 3. Segment Profiles

Segment	Market Rejectors	Marketing Affected	Brand Explorers	Undefined	Traditional Functionalists
City					
Shanghai		8.1%	6.0%	1.8%	
53.0%	9.1%				7.7%
Beijing	9.1%				7.7%
47.0%		8.1%	6.0%	1.8%	
Age					
15–19		8.5%			
12.7%	0.8%		7.1%	3.1%	1.8%
20–29		9.2%	4.7%		
27.6%	5.2%			5.6%	15.1%
30–39			3.2%		1.0%
20.9%	0.7%	1.8%		0.3%	
40–49	1.3%		5.2%		1.4%
17.4%		5.1%		5.1%	
50–65	5.4%			14.1%	14.4%
21.5%		9.3%	6.1%		
Segment	Market Rejectors	Marketing Affected	Brand Explorers	Undefined	Traditional Functionalists
Income					
No income		8.5%			
12.7%	0.8%		7.1%	3.1%	1.7%
Below 800					12.8%
24.7%	1.6%	0.5%	2.1%	3.4%	
800–3000	0.1%		5.4%	4.9%	
38.7%		2.7%			9.0%
Above 3000	1.8%		4.2%		
24.0%		5.4%		0.8%	2.1%
Sector					
State-Owned	2.6%		0.6%		3.8%
40.5%		4.8%		2.1%	
Collectively-			1.7%	2.0%	
owned 6.2%	0.2%	1.5%			1.3%
Government			2.3%	2.7%	
8.3%	0.2%	1.9%			1.7%

Table 3. Continued

Segment	Market Rejectors	Marketing Affected	Brand Explorers	Undefined	Traditional Functionalists
Sector (continued)					
JV/wholly foreign-		2.6%	3.4%		
owned 17.4%	1.6%			3.0%	7.4%
Education	0.4%	6.8%			0
18.0%			9.0%	7.0%	
Private			2.4%	4.8%	4.5%
10.3%	1.4%	2.6%			
Other	0.3%			2.6%	2.0%
2.9%		0.8%	1.3%		

Segment	Market Rejectors	Marketing Affected	Brand Fickle	Undefined	Traditional Functionalists
Occupation					
Blue collar			3.3%	8.2%	2.6%
16.5%	1.8%	3.0%			
White collar	3.3%		4.9%		
50.7%		3.7%		4.1%	14.2%
Student		9.5%			
14.0%	0.8%		8.1%	4.4%	1.3%
Teacher	0.5%	0.4%		0.2%	1.1%
5.3%			1.8%		
Other			1.6%	0.3%	11.6%
13.4%	1.0%	3.0%			
Social lifestyle					
High		9.5%	5.4%		
48.6%	9.6%			3.4%	4.8%
Low	9.6%				4.8%
52.4%		9.5%	5.4%	3.4%	

Note: All variables above are significant at $p < 0.01$. Variables gender and education are not significant.

except that they are more likely consumers above 55 years old and blue collar workers.

The Traditional Functionalists are mostly from Beijing, and above 55 years old. They are not socially active. They are overrepresented for state-owned enterprises and in the second lowest income category and underrepresented among white collars.

There is an another way of getting an understanding of the clusters and descriptors, using the results of the stepwise discriminant analysis. In the discriminant analysis,

Table 4. Discriminant Analysis

	Solitary City Dwellers	Socialites	Hard Workers
Lifestyle	**–0.49**	**0.46**	**–0.26**
Gender	0.07	0.42	0.11
City	**0.53**	–0.03	0.14
Income	0.11	**0.34**	**0.82**
Middle school	0.10	0.50	–0.14
College and above	0.24	0.15	0.03
Blue collar	–0.09	0.12	0.38
White collar	–0.09	–0.19	**0.79**
Student	0.21	**–0.54**	**0.48**
Age	**0.67**	**0.26**	**–0.43**

three discriminant functions were significant at the $p < .05$ level. Table 4 reports the discriminant coefficients. The three discriminant functions were interpreted as follows.

The following descriptors best describe discriminant dimension 1: a nonsocial lifestyle, Beijing and old age. Dimension 1 was interpreted as representing the Solitary City Dweller. The following descriptors best identify dimension 2: an active social lifestyle, female, nonstudent, mid-income and mid-age. Dimension 2 was interpreted as the Socialites in the sense of socially active, visible and popular. Finally, dimension 3 represents people with a nonsocial lifestyle, high income, white collar (but also some blue collar), students and young people. Dimension 3 represents the Hard Workers.

SUMMARY AND CONCLUSIONS

The current research presented a segmentation of the Chinese consumer market in terms of perceptions and behaviors and geographic, socio-demographic and lifestyle characteristics as descriptors. The results indicate the presence of five segments; four of these segments are interpretable, distinct in their perceptions and behaviors and well differentiated in terms of background descriptors. In future research it will be important to include other perceptions and behaviors that may better distinguish among the undefined segment.

The largest segment are the Nonmarket driven. This segment, as well as the Traditional Functionalists, underscore the traditional aspect of Chinese consumer behavior. However, both the Marketing Affected and Brand Explorers segments underscore the consumer revolution, albeit in a different way. The latter group may be evidence of the consumer learning process that occurs at the face of dramatic changes, whereas the former group may be more experienced consumers.

The study reported here, as well as other prior research, strongly suggests that managers should not treat the Chinese market as one market of 1.3 billion consumers. Instead China is a differentiated market, based not only on geography but also on socio-demographics and lifestyles—a market that therefore requires differentiated implementation campaigns.

References

The Gallup Organization. *1997 Survey: The People's Republic of China—Consumer Attitudes and Lifestyle Trends.* Princeton: The Gallup Organization, 1998.

Li, Conghua. *China: The Consumer Revolution.* Toronto: John Wiley and Sons, 1998.

Schmitt, Bernd. *From Politics and Production to Markets and Consumption: Capitalizing on China's Consumer Revolution.* New York: The Free Press, forthcoming.

Schmitt, Bernd and Gito DeBoek. "Differential Patterns in Consumer Purchase Preferences Using Self-Organizing Maps." In *Visual Explorations in Finance*, edited by Guido DeBoeck and Teuvo Kohonen. London: Springer, 1998.

5 VALUE PRIORITIES AND CONSUMER BEHAVIOR IN A TRANSITIONAL ECONOMY

Steven M. Burgess
University of Witwatersrand and
William Davidson Institute
Jan-Benedict E. M. Steenkamp
Catholic University of Leuven,
Wageningen University and
William Davidson Institute

Introduction

Little consumer research has been conducted in transitional economies, and even less with broadly representative groups of consumers. That is unfortunate from a *practical* point of view. Significant commercial opportunities are emerging as transitional economies increasingly move from a product(ion)-orientation to a market-orientation in which consumer desires become paramount and as economic systems that were geared toward fulfilling the needs of the state and of a privileged minority of its population embrace the needs of a wider population. Clearly, although many transitional economies have a long way to go, the economic importance of these countries is growing rapidly.

The lack of knowledge and insight concerning consumer behavior in transitional economies also is unfortunate from an *academic* point of view. Transitional economies are undergoing rapid changes that are unique in history. This allows for a "natural experiment" in which the effects of radical changes in society on consumer behavior can be studied in a real world setting. Moreover, it is not at all clear that the concepts and theories developed for western countries are equally relevant and applicable to transitional economies. Cunningham and Green (1984, p. 9) argued that there is "a need for more fundamental research in international marketing in order to adapt established marketing concepts to the realities of the international marketing place." In similar vein, Monroe (1993) stated that: "In this age of globalization, we need to move beyond the relative security of our own backyards and investigate issues relative to consumption on an international basis." Mindful of Quelch and Austin's (1993) admonition that firms ignore Africa at their own peril, we attempt to contribute to rectifying this situation by studying *value priorities* of consumers in the most important African transitional economy, viz., the *Republic of South Africa.*

South Africa entered this decade as the world's most isolated country; politically, economically, and socially. In the years since Mandela's election, the extensive web of international anti-Apartheid laws has been repealed and South Africa has become a full partner in the world economic and political system again. These external transitions hide the extent of internal change South Africa must undergo before the transition to a market-based economy can be said to be a true success. South Africa is essentially a two-tier society in that most Whites live and work in a modern economy while the majority of the Black population often interact with that economy only superficially and experience a living standard comparable to the rest of Africa (United Nations Development Program 1996). These two worlds in which South Africans live are the legacy of an Apartheid state that effectively excluded 80 percent of the population from free economic and political participation. The ambitious reforms of the new South African government share a fundamental goal of using the full potential of South Africa's human capital to build a stable, free, and market-based economy. Economic reforms are beginning to spread ownership of companies more widely in an economy where 80 percent of Johannesburg Stock Exchange shares are owned by a handful of companies. Parastatal companies in many industries are being privatized.

There are interesting parallels to the situation in Eastern Europe. In the former communist countries, there was also a clear distinction between the elite (i.e., Communist Party members) and the majority of the population. In Eastern Europe, economic and political freedom of the majority of the population was also severely restricted. Moreover, the concentration in South Africa of economic power in a few hands is in important respects similar to (pre-transition) Eastern Europe.

In this study, we will examine the *value priorities* of South African consumers, their antecedents, and their relevance for understanding key aspects of consumer behavior. Values underlie a large and important part of human cognition and behavior (Schwartz 1992). They transcend specific objects, in contrast to attitudes, which must be examined in relation to specific and carefully defined objects (Rokeach 1973). An examination of values provides both an overall picture of a central cognitive structure of the individual, as well as a means of linking central beliefs to specific attitudes. Values provide potentially powerful explanations of human behavior because they serve as standards of conduct, tend to be limited in number, universal across cultures, and temporally remarkably stable (Kamakura and Mazzon 1991; Rokeach 1973; Schwartz 1992). Consequently, it is not surprising that values have been found to be important in explaining a variety of attitudes and behaviors in the consumer context.[1]

In the following sections, we will first discuss the construct of personal values and its role in consumer behavior. Following a discussion of the research methodology, we present our empirical findings. We close with a discussion of the results, and provide suggestions for future research.

THE SCHWARTZ VALUE THEORY

Values may be defined as beliefs pertaining to desirable end states or modes of conduct that transcend specific situations (e.g., consumer-related contexts), guide selection or evaluation of behavior, and are ordered by importance vis-à-vis each other to form a system of value priorities (Rokeach 1973; Schwartz and Bilsky 1990). Building on and extending Rokeach's (1973) work, Schwartz and his colleagues (e.g., Schwartz 1992, 1994; Schwartz and Bilsky 1987; 1990, Schwartz and Sagiv 1995) have conducted the most important programmatic stream of research on personal values in the last decade.

Schwartz derived a typology of values in which ten motivationally distinct *value types* are distinguished. Table 1 outlines Schwartz's value types and the individual values typically included in the content of each type. The value types reflect a continuum of related motivations. This continuum gives rise to a circular structure (see Figure 1) that captures the notion that the pursuit of different value types can be com-

Table 1. Value Types in Schwartz's Value Theory

Value Type	Definition	Exemplary Values
Power	Social status and prestige, control or dominance over people and resources.	Social power, authority, wealth
Achievement	Personal success through demonstrating competence according to social standards.	Successful, capable, ambitious
Hedonism	Pleasure and sensuous gratification for oneself.	Pleasure, enjoying life
Stimulation	Excitement, novelty and challenge in life.	Daring, varied life, an exciting life
Self-direction	Independent thought and action-choosing, creating, exploring.	Creativity, curious, freedom
Universalism	Understanding, appreciation, tolerance, and protection for the welfare of all people and nature.	Broadminded, social justice, equality, protecting the environment
Benevolence	Preservation and enhancement of the welfare of people with whom one is in frequent personal contact.	Helpful, honest, forgiving
Tradition	Respect, commitment, and acceptance of the customs and ideas that culture or religion provide.	Humble, devout, accepting my portion in life
Conformity	Restraints of actions, inclinations, and impulses likely to upset or harm others and violate social expectations or norms.	Politeness, obedient, honoring one's parents or elders
Security	Safety, harmony, and stability of society, of relationships, and of self.	Social order, clean

Source: Excerpted from Schwartz (1994).

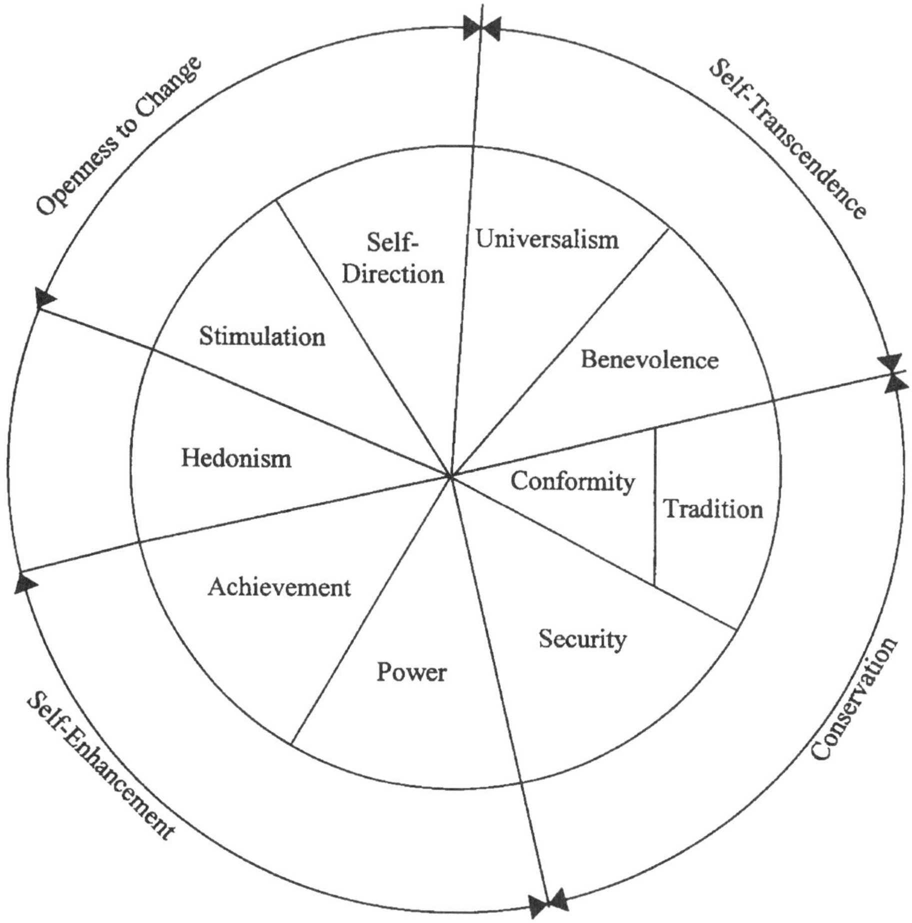

Source: Adapted from Schwartz (1994)

Figure 1. Schwartz's Model of Relations Among Motivational Types of Values and Higher-Order Value Types

patible or in conflict, depending on the proximity of the value types (Schwartz 1992). Each value type in the typology is distinguished by the motivational goal it expresses. For example, stimulation and self-direction are adjacent in the typology. The simultaneous pursuit of these value types is compatible as both involve intrinsic motivation for mastery and openness to change. On the other hand, stimulation is located opposite to conformity and tradition, as the former emphasizes challenge, risk, and change while the latter favor self-restriction and preservation of the status-quo. Simultaneous pursuit of both groups of value types would give rise to psychological and social conflict (Schwartz 1992).

The ten value types are organized in four higher order *value domains* viz., openness to change, self-transcendence, conservation, and self-enhancement. Openness to change emphasizes one's own independent thought, exploration, creativity, and action, and favors novelty, variety, and stimulation through change from established patterns. The domain of self-transcendence captures values emphasizing acceptance of others as equals and concern for their welfare. Conservation emphasizes submissive self restriction, preservation of traditional practices, and the protection of stability. Finally, self-enhancement emphasizes the pursuit of one's own relative success and dominance over others.

The structure and content of Schwartz's value system (see Figure 1) have received impressive empirical support in research in more than 200 samples from 60 countries from every continent, involving over 100,000 persons (Schwartz 1992; Schwartz and Sagiv 1995; Schwartz *et al.* 1997). Despite the impressive empirical support for Schwartz's theory and its sound conceptual basis, it has received little attention in the marketing and consumer behavior literature.[2] In this study, we will use the Schwartz value system to study value priorities of South Africans and their relations with other aspects of consumer behavior.

PERSONAL VALUES AND CONSUMER BEHAVIOR

Antecedents of Values

Values are the consequence of encounters with cultural, institutional, and personal forces that act upon, and are internalized by, the individual during life. Personal value priorities are shaped by sociodemographic and cultural factors that include, among others, gender, age, income, cultural ethnic group, marital and working status, religion, education, and urbanization (Rokeach 1973; Pitts and Woodside 1984). Several studies have examined the effects of certain antecedents on specific values. The importance of self-direction increases and the importance of conformity decreases with a person's level of education (Rokeach 1973). Individual religiosity has a positive effect on the priority given to conformity and tradition values and is related negatively to the importance attached to hedonism, self-direction, and stimulation (Schwartz and Huismans 1995). Schwartz *et al.* (1997) found that females give more importance to benevolence values than males, while males tend to give more importance to power. Inglehart (1991) theorized that higher income brings more security and more opportunities to live one's own life independently. This suggests that people with higher incomes attach more importance to openness to change values and less importance to conservation values. However, previous empirical findings often are contradictory. Not much systematic, comprehensive evidence is available on the effects of antecedents on value priorities.[3] Hence, our study will examine the effects of value antecedents in an exploratory fashion.

Values, Lifestyle and Behavior

Several authors have distinguished between central and secondary dispositions (Lastovicka 1982; Vinson, Scott and Lamont 1977). Central dispositions are dispositions that are not limited to a particular behavioral domain such as consumer behavior, but instead apply to a wide range of situations, contexts, and behaviors. On the other hand, secondary dispositions are context specific, in this case specific to the consumer context. Central dispositions are hypothesized to affect secondary dispositions (Lastovicka 1982; Vinson, Scott and Lamont 1977). Values are important central dispositions (Homer and Kahle 1988) while *lifestyle* traits are important dispositions in the consumer context (Lastovicka 1982). In line with previous theorizing, we hypothesize that a person's value priorities affect his/her lifestyle.

Moreover, because of their centrality to the individual's cognitive structure, personal values provide a powerful basis for understanding purchase and consumption *behavior* (Burgess 1992). In this study, we examined two types of consumer behavior, viz., the number of different brands the respondent had ever used across a large number of consumer product categories and the consumption of innovative financial products. Although brand switching and consumption of innovative products will be affected by a number of factors, both types of behavior share an exploratory component (Baumgartner and Steenkamp 1996; Steenkamp and Baumgartner 1992). They have the capacity to lead to exciting and novel consumption experiences, to offer a change of pace and relief from boredom, and to satisfy one's desire for knowledge and the urge of curiosity.

Openness to change emphasizes exploration and favors novelty, variety, and stimulation through change from established patterns. Thus, one may expect that the importance attached to this value domain will have a positive effect on the number of brands used and consumption of innovative products. Conservation emphasizes submissive self-restriction, preservation of traditional practices, and the protection of stability. The importance given to conservation values should have a negative effect on these two types of behavior (Steenkamp, ter Hofstede and Wedel 1999). The value domains of self-enhancement and self-transcendence appear less relevant for predicting brand switching and consumption of innovative products. They deal with the pursuit of one's own relative success and dominance over others versus emphasizing acceptance of others as equals and concern for their welfare. Thus, we hypothesize that these value domains will be less important for explaining brand switching and consumption of innovative products (cf., Steenkamp, ter Hofstede and Wedel 1999).

METHOD

Data

Data were collected by a leading professional marketing research firm among a representative national sample of 3,493 South Africans. The questionnaire was developed in English and translated into Afrikaans, North Sotho, South Sotho, Tswana, Venda, Xhosa and Zulu using back-translation techniques (Brislin, Lonner and Thorndike 1973). People were interviewed personally in their homes. All interviewers were from the ethnic group of the respondents and were chosen and trained to fit into the respondent's social class. Data were collected on the respondents' value priorities and sociodemographic characteristics. Respondents further indicated their interest in 37 lifestyle activities and products, covering a broad range of topics and interests.

Questions were also asked about brand purchase behavior for seven categories (alcoholic beverages, cigarettes, soft drinks, major food chains, major clothing retailers, gas stations, and food products). For each category, a comprehensive list of up to 12 brands was shown, and respondents were asked to indicate which of these brands they had ever used. Other brands not listed could be added. Consumption of innovative products was measured within the context of financial services products. South Africa has a large segment of the population that has no existing commercial relationship with a bank or insurance company and informal sector savings schemes are prevalent. (Interestingly, this even applies to more advanced transitional economies such as the Czech Republic, Hungary and Poland; Woodruff *et al.* 1998.) As people enter the formal employment sector, they increasingly turn to the formal sector products. Products included were whole-life policy, endowment policy, retirement annuity, medical insurance, short-term casualty insurance, checking account, savings account, transmission account, investment account, credit card, gas/garage card, ATM card and a loan from a bank. For each product, respondents indicated whether they had ever used it. The study also included other questions that are not the focus of this study.

Operationalizing Values in Transitional Economies

Transitional economies vary greatly in their human development characteristics; especially education levels (United Nations Development Program 1996). Whereas some countries are relatively close to the level of Western countries (e.g., Czech Republic, Hungary, Poland), other transitional economies are in a less favorable position (e.g., China, India, South Africa, Uzbekistan). Limited literacy and numeric skills are among the special threats to reliability and validity researchers encounter in less developed economies (Lonner and Berry 1986). Brief scales reduce cognitive demands on respondents, shorten interview completion time and open less-advanced transitional economies to values research that would previously have been precluded. These can be important benefits in any environment when the demands of longer scales might threaten the broader reliability and validity of a research project (such as in syndicated marketing research projects or in research with adolescent or elderly target populations), when respondents have limited human development (especially limited literacy and numeric skills), or when budgetary constraints preclude the use of longer scales (McDaniel, Verille and Madden 1985).

Measuring Value Priorities

Research using the Schwartz value system typically has used the Schwartz Value Survey (SVS; Schwartz 1992), an instrument that remains the first choice in values research in more developed research settings because of its demonstrated validity across more than 60 countries and its usefulness for studying relations to a wide range of individual differences and environmental influences on consumers (Schwartz *et al.* 1997). The SVS presents 57 values selected *a priori* to represent the ten motivationally distinct value types. Respondents rate the importance of all 57 values as "a guiding principle in my life," on a 9-point scale labeled ranging from –1 = opposed to my values, 0 = not important, 3 = important, 6 = very important, and 7 = of supreme importance; the other categories are unlabeled. This judgment task requires thinking about and evaluating abstract concepts. It provides no specific life contexts within which to weigh one's application of values. Because people rarely spend time thinking about the guiding principles in their life, this task is novel and intellectually demanding for most respondents. Completion of the SVS requires an average of about 15 minutes in student and 25 minutes in adult samples, with a range from 10-60 minutes (Schwartz *et al.* 1997). Problems with completing the SVS are most serious among the less educated, the elderly, and in samples from sub-Saharan Africa, India, and rural areas of less-developed nations (Schwartz *et al.* 1997).

In response to these limitations of SVS, Schwartz, Lehmann, and Roccas (1997) recently developed the new Portraits Questionnaire (PQ) instrument to assess the value priorities of populations for which the SVS is less suitable, such as are found in many transitional economies. This permits extension of values research to important groups not studied effectively in the past. The PQ includes short, textual portraits of 29 different people (see Appendix). In the PQ, value importances are measured indirectly as they are inferred from the self-reported similarity to people holding a particular value to be important (Schwartz *et al.* 1997). Each portrait describes a person to whom certain goals, aspirations and wishes—all expressive of the same single value type—are important. For example (the PQ has a male and a female form): "He likes surprises and is always looking for new things to do. He thinks it is important to do lots of different things in his life." describes a person for whom stimulation values are important. "Being very successful is important to him. He likes to stand out and to impress other people" describes a person who considers achievement values important. By emphasizing what is important to each person—the goals and wishes he or she pursues—the portraits describe the person's values rather than his or her behavior or other traits. For each portrait, respondents answer: "How much like you is this person?" They check one of six boxes labeled: very much like me, like me, somewhat like me, a little like me, not like me, and not like me at all. In the current research, we added a 7th box labeled "do not know" in order to lessen the incidence of "I-can-answer-any-question" bias and courtesy bias (cf., Brislin, Lonner, and Thorndike 1973) and to encourage respondents who found a particular scale item too challenging to respond accurately. Prior to analyses, scores were reversed so that high ratings indicated high value importance.

Schwartz *et al.* (1997) extensively tested the validity of the PQ. They found good convergent validity between ratings on the SVS and the PQ. Moreover, SVS and PQ exhibited a similar pattern of correlations with other constructs. Further, the correlation between the mean importance scores for the ten value types as measured by the two instruments was .95. Thus, there is substantial evidence that the PQ and the SVS measure the same motivational value types. However, the PQ takes much less time to complete (usually less than ten minutes) and is cognitively less demanding.

Three hundred and seventy (10.6 percent) respondents were dropped due to nonresponse to items or carelessness.[4] When compared to the overall sample, the dropped respondents were somewhat more likely to be Black (68.4 percent of the dropped respondents were Black while 57.3 percent of the total sample were Black) and to have not completed high school (71.9 percent vs. 64.3 percent) but the association between being dropped and race or education was not strong in either instance (Cramer's V $\leq$ .080).

RESULTS

Measurement Validation of PQ Form

The current research provides a particularly rigorous and realistic test for the PQ scale in a less advanced research environment. The PQ scale was administered within a large, syndicated survey questionnaire and respondents had already been responding to the survey about twenty minutes on average when they encountered the scale. Nevertheless, with one exception, the theoretical structure of the instrument was supported.

Smallest Space Analysis (Guttman 1968) revealed the theoretical value structure as shown in Figure 1 emerged, with the exception that security values emerged with benevolence and universalism. Thus, security seems to be serving self-transcendence goals rather than conservation goals. This finding appears to be unique to sub-Saharan populations (Schwartz *et al.* 1997). Importance ratings were mean-centered within respondents across all 29 values to control for differences in scale use in rating values (Bass and Wilkie 1973). An index of the importance of a value type was obtained by averaging the ratings for the values within the value type in question. Similarly, the importance of a value domain was obtained by averaging the importances attributed to the value types within each domain.[5] This procedure ensures equal weighting of all values (value types) in the construction of a particular value type (value domain) (Schwartz 1992). Table 2 provides the mean importances of the value types and value domains. Self-transcendence values are on average the most important, self-enhancement and openness to change values are the least important.

Antecedents of Values

The importance attached to a value domain was regressed on the following antecedents (categories in parentheses): gender (female, male), age (in years), monthly house-

Table 2. Mean Value Importances in South Africa

	Mean Importance
Value types	
Stimulation	–.747
Self-direction	.113
Universalism	.368
Benevolence	.514
Security	.651
Conformity	–.073
Tradition	.061
Power	–.257
Achievement	–.222
Hedonism	–.341
Value domains	
Openness to change	–.317
Self-transcendence	.511
Conservation	–.006
Self-enhancement	–.239

hold income (in Rands), education (lower, higher), urbanization (major metropolitan areas, urban areas [i.e., cities and larger towns], rural), marital status (single, married/cohabiting, ex-married [i.e., divorced, widowed, separated]), working status (not working, working), religion (Westernized Christian, Afro-Christian, Hindu, Muslim, other, adherence to no particular religion) and cultural ethnic group (English White, Afrikaner White, Coloreds, Zulu, Xhosa, North Sotho, South Sotho, Tswana, other).[6] The results are reported in Table 3.[7]

People that gave more importance to openness to change tended to be male, younger, single, and had higher incomes. This value domain was relatively less important for people living in rural areas, and for the Xhosa. Females, older people, and Coloureds attached more importance to self-transcendence, while various Black cultural ethnic groups and Muslims gave less importance to this value domain. Conservation was relatively more important for females, older people, people with lower incomes and less education, and people living in rural areas. It was relatively less important for people who do not identify themselves with any religious group and for English Whites.[8] Self-enhancement was more important among younger people, males, people with no religious adherence, and for the various Black cultural ethnic groups, while it was less important among Coloreds and Afrikaner Whites.

The negative effect of age on openness to change is in line with research on optimum stimulation level in which it consistently has been found that a person's desired level of stimulation in life declines with age (e.g., Zuckerman 1979). The positive effect of income on openness to change and the negative effect on conservation are in line with Inglehart's (1990) theorizing. The finding that females attach more importance to self-transcendence and males to self-enhancement is consistent with Schwartz *et al.* (1997). The weak effects of education observed in this study contrast with Rokeach's (1973) finding of strong differences between subjects on 25 of his 36 values. The low level of education in the current research—17.3 percent have not completed primary school and 63.4 percent have not graduated from high school—and the uneven quality and content of education for different racial groups in the Apartheid era, even when formally it was the same level (e.g., high school) may be important factors influencing this result. The finding that people who do not identify themselves with any religious group attach less importance to conservation has strong validity. Respect and acceptance of religion is an important element of the conservation domain. On the other hand, most religions do not promote values related to self-enhancement, and we indeed find that people who adhere to a particular religion give less importance to self-enhancement than people who do not adhere to a religion. The finding that people living in rural areas attach less importance to openness to change and more importance to tradition and conformity is consistent with the literature on diffusion of innovations (Rogers 1983). When we take the total picture of antecedent effects into account, it is found that gender, age and cultural ethnic group have the largest and most consistent influence on people's value priorities.

Schwartz's specific structure of the value domains allows for an even more fine-grained examination of the associations of values with their antecedents. Associations with a particular antecedent should decrease monotonically as one goes around the

Table 3. Antecedents of Values[a]

	Criterion variables			
Predictor Variables[b]	Openness to Change	Self-Transcendence	Conservation	Self-Enhancement
Gender				
Male	.098[d]	–.089[d]	–.135[d]	.081[d]
Age				
Age	–.147[d]	.149[d]	.214[d]	–.171[d]
Household Income				
Income (SA Rand)	.104[d]	–.010	–.121[d]	.036
Education				
High school grad	.037	.047	–.085[d]	–.015
Urbanization				
Urban	.004	–.005	.022	–.003
Rural	–.102[d]	.034	.095[d]	–.028
Marital status				
Married or Cohabiting	–.067[c]	.042	.001	.019
Ex-married	–.072[c]	.051	.002	.001
Working status				
Working	.033	–.026	–.033	.027
Religion				
Afro-Christians	.013	–.036	.011	.014
Hindu	–.011	.015	–.009	.001
Muslims	.041	–.052[c]	–.014	.018
Other religions	.021	–.019	–.029	.037
No religion	.026	.005	–.097[d]	.053[c]
Ethnic cultural group				
Afrikaner Whites	–.025	.000	.164[d]	–.129[d]
Coloreds	–.049	.073[c]	.080[c]	–.102[d]
Zulu	–.033	–.234[d]	.096[c]	.182[d]
Xhosa	–.087[c]	–.241[d]	.074[c]	.176[d]
N Sotho	.024	–.239[d]	.030	.136[d]
S Sotho	–.006	–.124[d]	.021	.087[d]
Tswana	.020	–.230[d]	.070[c]	.090[d]
Other	–.019	–.111[d]	.032	.089[d]
R^2	.111[d]	.211[d]	.159[d]	.160[d]

[a]Reported are standardized regression coefficients.

[b]Except for age and income, all antecedents are coded as dummies. Baseline is for gender: female; education: lower; urbanization: major metropolitan areas; marital status: single; working status: not working; religion: Westernized Christian; cultural ethnic group: English White.

[c]$p < .01$

[d]$p < .001$

circular structure of value domains in both directions from the most positively associated value domain to the most negatively associated value domain (Schwartz 1992). This creates a sinusoid curve of associations from most positive to most negative, and back. Thus, a further validation of the role of values and of the validity of Schwartz's value structure in South Africa is obtained by examining the total pattern of regression coefficients for any antecedent.[9]

Taking the most positive effect of an antecedent on a value domain as point of departure, we see that the expected sinusoid pattern is strongly supported. For example, the largest positive effect for gender was observed for openness to change. The effect decreases if we move around the circle via self-transcendence to conservation for which the largest negative effect was found. It increases again if we move from conservation via self-enhancement to openness to change. A similar pattern can be observed for income, rural areas, and the various Black ethnic cultural groups.

The monotonic relation predicted by the Schwartz framework can also be observed for age, education, ex-married people, Muslims, people with no particular religious affiliation, Coloreds and Afrikaner Whites. For example, for age, the largest positive effect was observed for conservation, and this effect decreases if we move around the circle in both directions to self-enhancement for which the largest negative effect is found. However, the structure is somewhat different, in that for all these antecedents the most positive and most negative effect were found for adjacent value domains. Thus, the pattern of effects across value domains provides strong support for the validity of the Schwartz value system in Sub-Saharan countries.

Values and Lifestyle Interests

For 37 lifestyle activities and products, respondents indicated whether or not they were interested in each item. These 0-1 ratings were factor analyzed. Based on the scree test, two factors explaining 27.4 percent of the variance were extracted. The factors could be interpreted as "masculine" lifestyle interests and "feminine" lifestyle interests. Examples of items loading high on the first factor include car purchasing, investment opportunities, sport and outdoor activities, insurance, and car maintenance, accessories, and information. Women's clothing, children's clothing, furniture and home furnishing, cosmetics and toiletries, and interior decorating were some of the items loading high on the feminine lifestyle interests dimension. Summated scores were computed for each lifestyle factor based on all items loading at least .4 on that factor. There were no items with salient loadings on both factors. These summated lifestyle scores were regressed on the four value domains. Given the nature of the two lifestyle dimensions identified, gender of the respondent was added as covariate in the regression analyses. The results are reported in Table 4.

Masculine lifestyle interests were positively affected by the importance attached to openness to change, and negatively affected by conservation and self-enhancement. Further, self-transcendence and conservation had a moderately negative effect ($p < .025$) on feminine lifestyle interests. The covariate gender exhibited the expected effects. As expected, males rated higher on masculine lifestyle interests while females exhibited more interest in feminine lifestyle products and activities. It is interesting

Table 4. Effect of Value Priorities on Lifestyle Interests[a]

Predictor Variables	Criterion Variables	
	"Masculine" Lifestyle Interests	"Feminine" Lifestyle Interests
Value domains		
Openness to change	.129[c]	.056
Self-transcendence	−.004	−.053
Conservation	−.152[c]	−.061
Self-enhancement	−.068[b]	−.019
Covariate		
Gender (male)	.196[c]	−.481[c]
R^2	.110[c]	.227[c]

[a]Reported are standardized regression coefficients.
[b]$p < .01$
[c]$p < .001$

to note that while the effect of gender clearly dominated the effects of the value dimensions for feminine lifestyle interests, this was much less the case for masculine lifestyle interests. This was caused by asymmetry in lifestyle interests by gender. Of the male respondents, 39.2 percent had the lowest possible score on the feminine lifestyle interest factor versus only 4.7 percent of the females; a ratio of 8.3:1. On the other hand, only 23.1 percent of the females and 9.3 percent of the males had the lowest possible score on the masculine lifestyle interest factor; a ratio of 2.5:1. Thus, males expressed much less interest in "feminine" items than females expressed in "masculine" items. Two reasons for this asymmetry in interests are: (a) South African women enjoy a degree of economic and political empowerment that surpasses many industrialized nations and ranks in the top 20 nations (gender empowerment measure; United Nations Development Program 1996) and (b) many females are single heads of households, and hence have full responsibility for both masculine and feminine lifestyle activities and products.

Values and Behavior

Although the link between value priorities and most forms of consumer behavior is well-established (Burgess 1992; Pitts and Woodside 1984), few studies have explored the link between values and innovativeness or brand-switching behavior. However, there is support in the literature for such links (McQuarrie and Langmeyer 1985; Steenkamp, ter Hofstede and Wedel 1999). We hypothesize that values will be related to brand-switching behavior and to the consumption of innovative financial products.

The number of different brands the respondent had ever used was measured for seven categories (see above). The responses were summed into a multiple-category behavioral index (Epstein 1979) of brand-switching behavior. It is a measure of the generalized tendency to use different brands across a wide range of categories. A behavioral index of consumption of innovative financial services products was constructed by summing the number of innovative financial services products a household used, based on the list of such products included in this survey (see above).

These measures were regressed on the value domains. Household income, age, and cultural ethnic group of the respondent were added as covariates to provide for a more precise test of the value effects. It was expected that a higher income increases the possibilities of a person to buy different brands and financial services products. Age captures experience effects, as older people have had more time to use multiple brands and to consume innovative products. Given the legacy of separate development under the Apartheid system, a person's cultural ethnic group is likely to have a great impact on actual consumer behavior. The results are reported in Table 5.

Income and cultural ethnic group had the greatest effect, and these effects were consistent across the two behavioral measures. People with higher incomes and Afrikaner Whites have used more brands and consumed more innovative financial products. On the other hand, all Black cultural ethnic groups scored significantly lower on both measures. Further, age had a positive effect on the consumption of financial products while Coloreds had consumed fewer financial products. Compared to these sociodemographic effects, the effects of the value domains were modest. As expected, conservation had a negative effect on both behavioral measures. Further, in line with our hypothesis, openness to change had a positive effect on the number of brands ever used, but contrary to expectations, no effect was found on consumption of innovative financial products. As hypothesized, the effects of self-transcendence and self-enhancement tended to be of minor importance, with only one out of four effects reaching statistical significance. Thus, the findings suggest support for our basic hypothesis that openness to change and conservation

Table 5. Effect of Value Priorities on Consumer Behavior[a]

	Criterion Variables	
Predictor Variables	Number of Brands Ever Used	Consumption of Innovative Financial Services Products
Value domains		
Openness to change	.068[b]	–.002
Self-transcendence	.070[b]	.029
Conservation	–.109[c]	–.086[c]
Self-enhancement	.007	–.008
Covariates		
Age	–.028	.148[c]
Income	.176[c]	.436[c]
Africaner White	.138[c]	.118[c]
Coloreds	.002	–.146[c]
Zulu	–.276[c]	–.259[c]
Xhosa	–.257[c]	–.219[c]
North Sotho	–.166[c]	–.149[c]
South Sotho	–.119[c]	–.131[c]
Tswana	–.159[c]	–.123[c]
Other	–.093[c]	–.095[c]
R^2	.352[c]	.569[c]

[a]Reported are standardized regression coefficients.
[b]$p < .01$
[c]$p < .001$

are more relevant for explaining these behaviors than self-transcendence and self-enhancement.

The relatively weak effects for the value domains compared to the covariates indicates that in South Africa, "external" constraints limit the possibility of consumers to express one's value priorities in behavior. The classic "budget constraint" of economics is more important in markets where incomes are on average much lower. Moreover, the legacy of the Apartheid system can still be felt in contemporary South Africa. Even when we control for income, we can note that all Black ethnic groups rate lower on both behavioral measures. This is a direct consequence of their impoverished living and consumption environment. However, it is important to note that even in environments imposing such significant constraints on behaviorial expressions, significant effects of values priorities were found.

CONCLUSIONS

In this paper, we examined value priorities in South Africa—Africa's most important transitional economy. To the best of our knowledge, this is the first extensive study of value priorities with a representative sample in a transitional economy. We examined the structure of the value priorities, their antecedents, and their effects on lifestyle interests, brand purchase behavior, and consumption of innovative products.

We found strong evidence on the validity of the structure of value priorities in South Africa and on the relation of the value priorities with other constructs. The role of a large number of sociodemographic/cultural antecedents of value priorities was examined. The results emphasize the generalized importance of gender, age, and the ethnic cultural group or subculture to which the person belongs. Other relevant antecedents include household income, degree of urbanization, and choice of religious membership or not. The observed sinusoid pattern of effects for most antecedents across the four value dimensions was consistent with the predictions made by Schwartz's theory and further validates this theory and its conceptual usefulness and applicability in South Africa.

Systematic and predictable relations could be observed with brand purchase behavior and consumption of innovative financial products. The effects found were mostly consistent with our hypotheses: openness to change (positive) and conservation (negative) taken together were more important than self-enhancement and self-transcendence.

Income and ethnic cultural group were found to be more important than value priorities in explaining actual behavior, at least for the behaviors examined in this study. It appears they act as powerful constraints on the potential of consumers to express their value priorities in actual behavior. We expect that the relatively weaker link between values and behavior also occurs in other countries where there are significant constraints on full participation of consumers in the marketplace. We conjecture that this may apply, for example, to other less affluent transitional economies (e.g., Central Asian Republics of the former Soviet Union, China, India and Vietnam). However, it is important to note that even in environments imposing such significant constraints on consumer behavior expressions, significant effects of values were found. This attests to the robustness and power of value priorities in understanding consumer behavior, also in transitional economies. Their conceptual power for understanding consumer behavior in transitional economies will further increase the less severe the external constraints will become due to increased wealth and general liberalization of the economy.

People often adapt their value priorities to be compatible with the reinforcement contingencies that their life circumstances allow (Schwartz and Bardi 1997). Kohak (1992) argued that people adjust in a manner analogous to the adaptation of long-term prisoners to jail: they develop a set of skills and attitudes that enable them to live reasonably under the circumstances. The results of our study suggest that on average, South Africans have shown remarkable resistance to adapt their value priorities to the life circumstances created by the Apartheid system. For example, it was found that South Africans on average attach relatively high importance to universalism and benevolence. These values capture the notion of acceptance of others as equals and concern for their welfare. These values are in contradiction to the Apartheid system with a legacy of stimulating divisions in society. If anything, Apartheid should have been detrimental to fostering such values. As another example, people in jobs that afford little freedom of choice increase the importance of conformity values and decrease the importance of self-direction values (Kohn and Schooler 1983). Seriously limited job options were typical for the large majority of South Africans. Nevertheless, the mean importance of self-direction values (.182) was greater than the mean importance of conformity values (.003) when the sample is limited to those who are working. Moreover, the analysis of the value antecedents does not indicate that conformity or conservation values (to which conformity belongs) are systematically more important to those people who had systematically fewer economic options (e.g., for non-Whites).

The apparent lack of adaptation of the value priorities of South Africans to their prevailing life circumstances stands in stark and encouraging contrast to the findings of Schwartz and Bardi (1997) for Eastern Europe. In their research among students and teachers, they found strong evidence of adaptation of people's value priorities to the Communist system.[10] Numerous factors may contribute to this difference between the transitional economies of Eastern Europe and South Africa. To our opinion, one factor that plays an important role is the perceived acceptance of the system. In the case of South Africa, it was not accepted by the non-Whites (as well as by many Whites), and by the international community. However, the Communist system was accepted by at least part of the population (without sharp division along racial lines), and was regarded as legitimate by the international community, as exemplified by the Helsinki Accords of 1975, among others (Kissinger 1994).

On the negative side, the aggregate value structure of South Africa indicates that values that are the basis for the system of free enterprise are not well-established. On average, achievement values are not considered to be important and self-direction is only marginally more important than tradition. This suggests a reluctance to develop own thoughts and take own action, be independent and ambitious, and to apply one's own talents and achieve one's own goals. This may present a serious barrier to the spread of the market-based free-enterprise system among the entire population of South Africa. On the positive side, a large proportion of the South African population is under 25 years old. For young people, value priorities are less crystallized and less anchored in a large number of past experiences (Inglehart 1991; Schwartz and Bardi 1997). Younger people may hence adapt more quickly to the changed reinforcement contingencies of post-Apartheid South Africa. Moreover, openness to change and self-enhancement (conservation) values are already more (less) important to young South Africans than to older South Africans (see Table 3). Thus, we may expect that in the future, the value structure of South Africans may become more favorable to the growth of free enterprises.

In sum, this research has contributed to the emerging body of knowledge on consumer behavior in transitional economies. Future research should extend this work to other transitional economies, including countries like China and Vietnam. In terms of human development, numeric skills, literacy, etc., these markets are more similar to South Africa than to the transitional economies of Eastern Europe. Instruments like the PQ may also be of great value in these markets. Another issue for future research is to study the change in value importance over time. As an economy moves along the path of transition to a free, market economy, the value structure of its population may gradually change as well. Value structures that were instrumental in the old days will be less "suitable" in the new economic and social environment. By monitoring value changes over time, we deepen our understanding of the role of values in shaping consumer behavior. That will allow companies to increase their marketing effectiveness in transitional economies.

Notes

This research was supported by a grant from Markinor (Pty) Ltd. to Steven M. Burgess and by a grant from the William Davidson Institute to Jan-Benedict E. M. Steenkamp. We gratefully thank Sue Grant and Mari Harris of Markinor for their support, Shalom Schwartz for assistance with, and use of, his Portraits Questionnaire, and the participants of the William Davidson Institute conference, *Marketing in Transitional Economies*, for their useful suggestions. Order of authorship is alphabetical.

1. See Burgess 1992; Homer and Kahle 1988; and Kamakura and Mazzon 1991 for overviews.

2. See Burgess and Blackwell 1994; and Steenkamp, ter Hofstede and Wedel 1999 for exceptions.

3. See Schwartz *et al.* 1997.

4. See Burgess and Steenkamp 1998 for details.

5. Schwartz (1992) theory posits that hedonism may be related to openness to change or to self-enhancement in different groups. Hence, we excluded hedonism from the computation of the importance attached to the higher order value domains. Further, consistent with the results of the Smallest Space Analysis, security was included in the self-transcendence domain.

6. Zulu, Xhosa, North Sotho, South Sotho and Tswana are the main Black cultural ethnic groups in South Africa.

7. Note unless indicated otherwise, we will use $p = .01$ as cutoff for statistical significance throughout the paper because of the large sample size.

8. Note that the coefficients for all cultural ethnic groups were positive and mostly significant.

9. We will only consider antecedents that showed a significant effect on at least one value domain.

10. Note that both in Schwartz and Bardi (1997) and in our study, data were collected after the collapse of Communist and Apartheid regime, respectively. However, value priorities are highly stable and only change gradually over time, even when the reinforcement contingencies have changed dramatically. Thus, the past will have a large influence on value priorities long after the environment has changed (Rokeach 1973). This was shown in detail by Schwartz and Bardi (1997).

References

Bass, Frank M. and William L. Wilkie. "A Comparative Analysis of Attitudinal Predictions of Brand Preference." *Journal of Marketing Research* 10, no. 3 (August 1973): 262–269.

Baumgartner, Hans and Jan-Benedict E. M. Steenkamp. "Exploratory Consumer Buying Behavior: Conceptualization and Measurement." *International Journal of Research in Marketing* 13, no. 2 (May 1996): 121–137.

Brislin, Richard W., Walter J. Lonner and Robert M. Thorndike. *Cross-Cultural Research Methods.* New York: Wiley, 1973.

Burgess, Steven M. "Personal Values and Consumer Research: An Historical Perspective." In *Research in Marketing*, Vol. 11, edited by Jagdish N. Sheth, 35–79. Greenwich, CT: JAI Press, 1992.

Burgess, Steven M. and Roger D. Blackwell. "Personal Values and South African Financial Services Brand Preference." *South African Journal of Business Management* 25, no. 1 (1994): 22–29.

Burgess, Steven M. and Jan-Benedict E. M. Steenkamp. *Value Priorities and Consumer Behavior in a Transitional Economy: The Case of South Africa.* The William Davidson Institute Working Paper No. 166. Ann Arbor: University of Michigan Business School, 1998.

Cunningham, William H. and Robert T. Green. "From the Editor." *Journal of Marketing* 48, no. 1 (Winter 1984): 9–10.

Epstein, Seymour. "The Stability of Behavior." *Journal of Personality and Social Psychology* 37, no. 7 (July 1979): 1097–1126.

Guttman, Louis. "A General Nonmetric Technique for Finding the Smallest Coordinate Space for a Configuration of Points." *Psychometrika* 33, no. 4 (December 1968): 469–506.

Homer, Pamela M. and Lynn R. Kahle. "A Structural Equation Test of the Value-Attitude-Behavior Hierarchy." *Journal of Personality and Social Psychology* 54, no. 4 (April 1988): 638–646.

Inglehart, Ronald. *Cultural Shift in Advanced Industrial Society.* Princeton: Princeton University Press, 1991.

Kamakura, Wagner A. and José Alfonso Mazzon. "Value Segmentation: A Model for the Measurement of Values and Value Systems." *Journal of Consumer Research* 18, no. 2 (September 1991): 208–218.

Kissinger, Henry. *Diplomacy.* New York: Simon & Schuster, 1994.

Kohak, Erazim. "Ashes, Ashes . . . Central Europe After Forty Years." *Daedalus* 121, no. 2 (Spring 1992): 197–216.

Kohn, Melvin L. and Carmi Schooler. *Work and Personality: An Inquiry into the Impact of Social Stratification.* Norwood, NJ: Ablex, 1983.

Lastovicka, John L. "On the Validation of Lifestyle Traits: A Review and Illustration." *Journal of Marketing Research* 19, no. 1 (February 1982): 126–138.

Lonner, Walter J. and John W. Berry, eds. *Field Methods in Cross-Cultural Research.* Beverly Hills, CA: Sage, 1986.

McDaniel, Stephen W., Perry Verille and Charles S. Madden. "The Threats to Marketing Research: An Empirical Reappraisal." *Journal of Marketing Research* 22, no. 1 (February 1985): 74–80.

McQuarrie, Edward F. and Daniel Langmeyer. "Using Values to Measure Attitudes Toward Discontinuous Innovation." *Psychology and Marketing* 2, no. 4 (Winter 1985): 239–252.

Monroe, Kent B. "Editorial." *Journal of Consumer Research* 19, no. 4 (March 1993): 487.

Pitts, Robert E. and Arch G. Woodside, eds. *Personal Values and Consumer Psychology.* Lexington, MA: Lexington Books, 1984.

Quelch, John A. and James E. Austin. "Should Multinationals Invest in Africa?" *Sloan Management Review* 34, no. 3 (Spring 1993): 107–119.

Rogers, Everett M. *Diffusion of Innovations.* 3d ed. New York: The Free Press, 1983.

Rokeach, Milton J. *The Nature of Human Values.* New York: The Free Press, 1973.

Schwartz, Shalom H. "Universals in the Content and Structure of Values: Theoretical Advances and Empirical Tests in 20 Countries." In *Advances in Experimental Social Psychology,* Vol. 25, edited by Mark Zanna, 1–65. Orlando, FL: Academic Press, 1992.

_____. "Are There Universal Aspects in the Structure and Contents of Human Values?" *Journal of Social Issues* 50, no. 4 (Winter 1994): 19–45.

Schwartz, Shalom H. and Anat Bardi. "Influences of Adaptation to Communist Rule on Value Priorities in Eastern Europe." *Political Psychology* 18, no. 2 (June 1997): 385–410.

Schwartz, Shalom H. and Wolfgang Bilsky. "Toward a Universal Psychological Structure of Human Values" *Journal of Personality and Social Psychology* 53, no. 3 (September 1987): 550–562.

_____. "Toward a Theory of the Universal Content and Structure of Values: Extensions and Cross-Cultural Replications." *Journal of Personality and Social Psychology* 58, no. 5 (May 1990): 878–891.

Schwartz, Shalom H. and Sipke Huismans. "Value Priorities and Religiosity in Four Western Religions." *Social Psychology Quarterly* 58, no. 2 (June 1995): 88–107.

Schwartz, Shalom H., Arielle Lehmann, Gila Melech, Steven M. Burgess, Mari Harris and Vicki Owens. "Validation of a Theory of Basic Human Values with a New Instrument in New Populations." Hebrew University Working Paper. Jerusalem: Hebrew University (submitted, 1997).

Schwartz, Shalom H., Arielle Lehmann and S. Roccas. "Multimethod Probes of Basic Human Values." In *Social Psychology and Cultural Context: Essays in Honor of Harry C. Triandis*, edited by J. Adamopoulos and Y. Kashima. Newbury Park, CA: Sage, 1997.

Schwartz, Shalom H. and Lilach Sagiv. "Identifying Culture-Specifics in the Content and Structure of Values." *Journal of Cross-Cultural Psychology* 26, no. 1 (January 1995): 92–116.

Steenkamp, Jan-Benedict E. M. and Hans Baumgartner. "The Role of Optimum Stimulation Level in Exploratory Consumer Behavior." *Journal of Consumer Research* 19, no. 2 (December 1992): 434–448.

Steenkamp, Jan-Benedict E. M., Frenkel ter Hofstede, and Michel Wedel. "A Cross-National Investigation into the Individual and National-Cultural Antecedents of Consumer Innovativeness." *Journal of Marketing* 63 (forthcoming, 1999).

United Nations Development Program. *Human Development Report 1996.* New York: Oxford University Press, 1996.

Vinson, David E., Jerome E. Scott and Lawrence M. Lamont. "The Role of Personal Values in Marketing and Consumer Behavior." *Journal of Marketing* 41, no. 2 (April 1977): 44–50.

Woodruff, David, James Drake, Christopher Condon and Peggy Simpson. "The New Consumers: How Business Is Chasing the Rising Middle Class of Central Europe." *Business Week* (May 25, 1998): 40–44.

Zuckerman, Marvin D. *Sensation Seeking: Beyond the Optimal Level of Arousal.* Hillsdale, NJ: Lawrence Erlbaum, 1979.

APPENDIX

Portraits Questionnaire Instructions and Items (Male Form)

Here we briefly describe some people. Please read each description and think about how much each person is or is not like you. Put an X in the box to the right that shows how much the person in the description is like you.[A1]

---

1. It is important to him to be polite to other people all the time. He believes he should always show respect to his parents and to older people. (Conformity)
2. Thinking up new ideas and being creative is important to him. He likes to do things in his own original way. (Self-Direction)
3. Being very successful is important to him. He likes to stand out and to impress other people. (Achievement).
4. He thinks it is important to do things the way he learned from his family. He wants to follow their customs and traditions. (Tradition)
5. He thinks it is important that every person in the world should be treated equally. He wants justice for everybody, even for people he doesn't know. (Universalism)
6. He likes surprises and is always looking for new things to do. He thinks it is important to do lots of different things in his life. (Stimulation)
7. The safety of his country is very important to him. He wants his country to be safe from its enemies. (Security)
8. He always wants to help the people who are close to him. It's very important to him to care for the people he knows and likes. (Benevolence)
9. He likes to be in charge and tell others what to do. He wants people to do what he says. (Power)
10. He really wants to enjoy life. Having a good time is very important to him. (Hedonism)
11. He likes to make his own decisions about what he does. It is important to him to be free to plan and to choose his activities for himself. (Self-Direction)
12. He thinks it's important not to ask for more than what you have. He believes that people should be satisfied with what they have. (Tradition)
13. It is important to him to be rich. He wants to have a lot of money and expensive things. (Power)
14. He looks for adventures and likes to take risks. He wants to have an exciting life. (Stimulation)
15. Honesty is very important to him. He believes he must be honest in any situation and always tell the truth. (Benevolence)
16. It's important to him that everything is clean and in order. He really doesn't want things to be a mess. (Security)
17. He looks for every chance he can to have fun. It is important to him to do things that give him pleasure. (Hedonism)
18. He strongly believes that people should care for nature. Looking after the environment is important to him. (Universalism)
19. He believes that people should do what they're told. He thinks people should follow rules at all times, even when no-one is watching. (Conformity)
20. He likes people to know that he can do well. He is ambitious and ready to work hard to get ahead. (Achievement)
21. His family's safety is extremely important to him. He would do anything to make sure his family is always safe. (Security)
22. It is important to him to listen to people who are different from him. Even when he disagrees with them, he still wants to understand them and to get along with them. (Universalism)
23. He doesn't like to boast or draw attention to the things he does. He wants to be modest. (Tradition)
24. He thinks it's important to be interested in things. He is curious and tries to understand everything. (Self-Direction)
25. It is important to him to fit in and do things the way other people do. He thinks he should do what others expect of him. (Conformity)
26. He thinks everyone should work to get people in the world to live together peacefully. Peace everywhere in the world is important to him. (Universalism)

27. It's very important to him to show his abilities. He wants people to admire what he does. (Achievement)
28. It is important to him that his friends can always trust him. He wants to be loyal to them and always to look out for their interests. (Benevolence)
29. Being religious is important to him. He tries hard to follow his religious beliefs. (Tradition)

[A1] Shown in parentheses is the value type to which the portrait refers. This is not shown in the questionnaire.

Market Orientation in Firms

6 AN EXAMINATION OF THE DIMENSIONS OF MARKET ORIENTATION IN THE POLISH RETAIL SECTOR

Patricia Huddleston
Michigan State University
Linda Good
Michigan State University

Introduction

Today, the retail sector in Poland is a combination of privatized state-owned firms, start-up private firms and foreign investment/joint-venture firms. Prior to "shock therapy" in 1989, 95 percent of retail sales in Poland were generated by state and cooperative organizations (Wojciech and Jeffrey 1997). Of all of the Polish state industries to be privatized, retailing was the first. By 1998, the Polish Ministry of the Treasury estimated that close to 100 percent of retail firms in Poland were privately owned.

In successive trips to Poland (1992–1997), we have gathered anecdotal evidence that retailers are attuned to marketing mix variables and that they apply marketing strategies in varying degrees depending on their competitive situations and form of ownership. Are the firms we visited aberrations or has a wider spectrum of Polish retail managers grasped fundamental marketing strategies? Do they perceive a need to gather and respond to customer data? These questions have not yet been addressed in the empirical literature.

THE POLISH RETAIL SECTOR

We see Polish entrepreneurial spirit in the plethora of small "mom and pop" operations, most of which have evolved since 1994. Growth of these small outlets can be attributed to both the elimination of state distribution system, and low barriers to entry (Murphy 1997). Currently, Poland's retail sector can be characterized as very fragmented and extremely competitive, having 3 times more shops per capita than any other country in Europe (McQuaid 1994). The estimated number of retail sales points is 414,000 and represents 10 shops for every 1000 residents (Smorgorzewska and

Markiewicz 1997). Of this number, an estimated 20 percent are food and grocery retailers, 5 percent cosmetics and pharmaceuticals, and 25 percent general outlets. Kiosks comprise the remaining 50 percent (Keller 1995). The vast majority of shops are less than 400 square feet and employ 5 or less (Wojciech and Jeffrey 1997).

Large scale retailing is just beginning in Poland (U.S. Embassy 1998). The leaders are foreign firms, perhaps because supermarkets were not well developed in Poland; the supermarket and hypermarket formats represent less than .02 percent of the total number of retailers (*Eurofood* 1997). Since 1995, fourteen European retail firms have seized opportunities to capitalize on the 38 million Polish consumer market. These entrants include hypermarkets, supermarkets and discounters such as Billa (Austria), Globi (Belgium), Auchan, LeClerc, Robert, Géant, Casino (France), and Hit and Real (Germany). The presence of these foreign retailers is causing a great deal of consternation among the "mom and pop" firms who view foreign entrants as unfair competition because of their access to capital and vast business experience. Approximately 20 percent of the food trade in Poland has been absorbed by these chains and domestic trade associations estimate that they will control 80 percent of the market by 1999 (Smorgorzewska and Markiewicz 1997). "Polish retailers feel increasingly threatened by foreign shopping chains and want the state to protect them"... (*The Warsaw Voice* 1996, p. 10). They want the government to limit where supermarkets can locate their operating hours. They also want subsidies to support domestic retail trade (*The Warsaw Voice* 1996). In 1997, a bill was put forward by the Ministry of the Economy to introduce supermarket licenses and require special permission to build stores over 400 square meters or trading complexes over 1000 square meters (Smorgorzewska and Markiewicz 1997).

Given its fragmented nature, consolidation of the Polish retail sector is expected (McQuaid 1994). Between 1995 and 1996, 20,000 retail shops disappeared (*Polish News Bulletin* 1998). Polish retail firms are scrambling to compete. Their current approach of seeking government intervention has not yet succeeded. A recent survey revealed that over half the Poles questioned opposed the licensing measure (*Eurofood* 1997) and President Kwasniewski assured French entrepreneurs that he would block such a measure (*PAP News Wire* 1998). Further, Polish consumers have proven to be more demanding and price sensitive as competition enters and their price sensitivity has not engendered store loyalty. Firm survival will be dependent on an ability to understand and respond to their customers, as well as to their foreign competitors. Under previous conditions, a retail firm did not need to understand its customers, nor was it necessary to gather information about them. An entire generation of managers in Poland was socialized in a system in which consumer needs were minimized and there was little need for firms to manipulate the marketing mix of their products. Customers simply bought what was available. Retail firms operated in seller's market conditions where the supplier, not the buyer was king. Competition was non-existent, so it is no wonder that small retail firms are feeling very threatened by the new business landscape. This raises a question: rather than employing reactive competitive strategies such as government intervention, would it be more effective to employ pro-active competitive strategies?

To survive, retail firms must focus on those activities which increase revenues, decrease costs, and result in bottom-line profits. As competitive forces increase and consumers become more informed, retail organizations in Poland have been forced to shift organizational activities to recognize and understand customer needs and predict their buying behavior. This requires a mechanism for generating, disseminating and responding to information about target markets. This mechanism is referred to in the empirical literature as a market orientation.

MARKET ORIENTATION

Market orientation is defined as the "organization wide generation of market intelligence across departments and organization wide responsiveness to it." (Jaworski and Kohli 1993, p. 53). Three activities characterize market orientation: 1) generating market intelligence about customer needs, 2) disseminating this information throughout the organization and 3) organizational response to this information (Day 1994; Jaworski and Kohli 1993; Ruekert 1992). Market orientation is viewed alternatively as a company philosophy or company behavior (Avlonitis and Gounaris 1997). Dimensions of a market orientation commonly cited in the literature are: gathering market intelligence (Ruekert 1992; Trout and Ries 1985; Kohli and Jaworski 1990; Jaworski and Kohli 1993), prioritization of customer needs (Elliot 1987); strategies, plans and information (Piercy 1992).

Empirical and managerial interest in market orientation in firms is tied to its positive relationship with economic performance. Jaworski and Kohli (1993) found mixed support for a significant, positive relationship between market orientation and business performance. The relationship was significant when using judgmental measures but not with objective measures. Using self-report measures, market orientation was tied to performance improvements and performance against the competition (Avlonitis and Gounaris 1997). Narver and Slater (1990) found market orientation to be a determinant of profitability for commodity and non-commodity businesses. Degree of market orientation was the highest discriminating factor between high and low performing business units (Ruekert 1992).

The scant literature regarding marketing strategies in transition economies has focused primarily on Russia. Many former state-owned businesses are described as "rust" in the new market economy (McCarthy and Puffer 1995) and tend to be less competitive than new, start-up ventures. Lowry (1995) concluded that many U.S./Russian joint-venture failures can be attributed to lack of understanding of the management culture and a misperception of the exposure Russian businesses and consumers have to marketing strategies. However, even prior to the collapse of the command economy, there was evidence of some understanding of marketing strategies. Data collected in 1991 on 200 Russian manufacturing, construction, retailing and service firms revealed a stronger market orientation in an uncertain business environment (Golden *et al.* 1995). Russian firms used the traditional marketing mix to implement their market orientation and there was a positive relationship between high-service levels, product quality and firm performance (Golden *et al.* 1995).

More recently, we found differences in customer profiles between privatized state-owned retail firms and new start-up ventures (Good and Huddleston 1995). Newly privatized (former state-owned) firms tended to attract less affluent, more ethnocentric customers, while the start-up private and joint-venture firms enjoyed patronage of younger, more affluent, less price-sensitive customers. We identified no studies which examined the market orientation of Polish firms.

CONCEPTUAL FRAMEWORK

The Kohli and Jaworski (1990)/Jaworski and Kohli (1993) model served as the conceptual framework for the study (see Figure 1). **Antecedents to market orientation** refer to organizational characteristics and relationships (e.g., top management emphasis, interdepartmental conflict and connectedness, centralization and departmentalization) which facilitate or deter market orientation development. **Components of market orientation** (market intelligence, intelligence dissemination and responsiveness) are the activities which comprise market orientation. The end result of the interaction of these factors are posited to either enhance or retard business performance.

Assessing the cross-cultural applicability (e.g., measurement equivalence, construct reliability and validity) for measures developed in the United States is the first step prior to making statistical inferences and drawing conclusions from international samples (Parameswaran and Yaprak 1987). Our earlier exploratory study (Huddleston and Good 1997), using open-ended questions as well as personal interviews, found Polish retail managers to demonstrate a surprisingly sophisticated level of understanding of marketing, contrary to some of the previous literature about Eastern European managers. The dimensions of market orientation cited by Western researchers were elicited in the definitions of marketing provided by our respondents. However, even though they provided "textbook" definitions, we don't know whether this translated to understanding or practice.

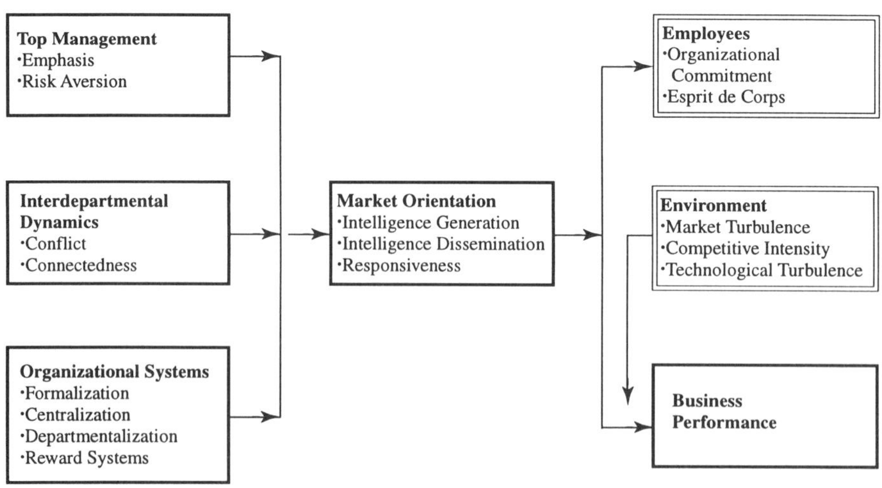

Figure 1. Antecedents and Consequences of Market Orientation

The preceding review of literature raises the following questions. Are antecedents to market orientation present in Polish retail firms? Are activities comprising market orientation in Polish retail firms similar to those found by Jaworski and Kohli (1993)? Are dimensions of market orientation as proposed by Jaworski and Kohli (1993) valid and reliable for a sample of Polish retail managers?

OBJECTIVE AND PURPOSE OF THE STUDY

The following objectives contribute to the overall purpose of our study which is to assess cross-cultural applicability of the measures used.

1. To test the cross-cultural equivalence of the Jaworski and Kohli (1993) market orientation instrument and its applicability to a retail setting.
2. To assess the reliability and validity of the Jaworski and Kohli (1993) market orientation instrument among Polish retail executives.
3. To assess the construct validity of antecedents to market orientation (top management interdepartmental dynamics, organizational systems) and market orientation.

METHOD

Measures

Jaworski and Kohli (1993) used the approach proposed by Churchill (1979) to develop and purify an instrument measuring antecedents to the dimensions of and consequences of a market orientation. To the extent possible, we tried to replicate their measurement procedures. It was necessary to modify the wording of questions to reflect our focus on the retail sector. See Appendix 1 for a complete list of the scale items.

Antecedents to market orientation were measured similarly to Jaworski and Kohli (1993). *Top management emphasis* on marketing and *risk aversion* were measured by two separate scales of four and six items respectively. Sample items were: "Top managers often tell employees to be sensitive to the activities of our competitors" and "Top managers in our firm like to take big financial risks." The interdepartmental dynamics constructs (*conflict* and *connectedness*) were measured by six and seven items. Sample items for departmental conflict were: "Most departments in this store get along well with each other"; for departmental connectedness, a sample item was "People around here are quite accessible to those in other departments."

Formalization and *centralization* employed the Aiken and Hage (1966, 1968) scales as utilized by Jaworski and Kohli (1993). Sample items for these scales were: "I feel that I am my own boss in most matters" (formalization) and "I have to ask my boss before I do almost anything" (centralization). *Reward system orientation* was measured by a 6-item scale with items such as: "Customer satisfaction assessments influence senior managers' pay in this store."

Dimensions of market orientation measured by the instrument included *intelligence generation*, which used nine items. A sample item was: "In this store we do a lot of in-house market research." The *intelligence dissemination* scale consisted of eight items such as: "A lot of informal 'hall talk' in this store concerns our competitors tactics or strategies." *Response design* used seven items, a sample item being: "It takes us forever to decide how to respond to our competitors price changes." *Response implementation* was captured by seven items such as: "Customer complaints fall on deaf ears in this store."

Due to the unavailability and unreliability of financial data from firms in transition economies, financial performance was captured by a 2-item self-assessed comparison to competitors regarding overall performance and scored on a 5-point scale (1 = poor) (Golden *et al.* 1995). A third measure of the performance construct asked the respondents whether the firm made a profit, broke even or lost money. All items except performance were scored on a 5-point Likert scale (1 = strongly disagree).

Reliability of the original instrument dimensions ranged from .66 (top management emphasis) to .88 (centralization) (Jaworksi and Kohli 1993).

Measurement Equivalence

Using measures developed in one country to collect data in another can cause problems with measurement equivalence; measurement equivalence addresses the question of whether the same models hold across different populations (Mullen 1995). To insure that the instrument means the same thing before and after translation (translation equivalence) the questionnaire was translated into Polish by native speakers and then back translated by another bilingual person who was unfamiliar with the study (Mullen 1995; Nasif *et al.* 1991). We evaluated the back translations to identify ambiguous or confusing questions and those were revised by the forward translator.

DATA COLLECTION

To cross validate the dimensions of market orientation within retail firms, our sample consisted of three levels of retail management. In order to insure that a firm would employ three levels of management, only retail firms with 20 or more employees were included in the population. Trade directories by business sector for Polish firms are, as yet, unavailable. Lists of retail firms with more than 20 employees were purchased from the Warsaw and Katowice Region Statistical Offices and were gleaned from the Warsaw and Katowice telephone directories. The lack of published business directories made a random sample not feasible and can be considered a limitation of the study. A sample size of 250 firms was targeted.

Data were collected by native-speaking academic colleagues in Warsaw (Warsaw Agricultural University) and Katowice (University of Silesia), Poland during spring and summer 1997. Prior to data collection, we conducted a training session to review the purpose of the study, research protocols and provide the opportunity for the data collectors to ask questions. The multiple informant approach employed by Jaworski and Kohli (1993) was replicated in our study. Three levels of retail managers in each firm were contacted for participation in the study. Top management included either the owner/director, president or marketing director. Middle management included buyer/expert in goods and the third level of management included store or department manager. Data collectors contacted each firm personally, dropped off the questionnaires and returned at a later time to pick them up. Retrieving questionnaires from some firms required multiple visits from the data collectors in order to get responses from all 3 levels of management.

SAMPLE

One hundred and one firms participated in the study, yielding a total of 305 respondents. 7.8 percent were state owned, 12.9 percent were cooperatives, 65.2 percent were private and 13.7 percent were joint ventures (Table 1). Number of sales employees averaged 51 per store, with an average of 10 managers per store. However, most firms in our sample were small (60 percent), had 1–5 managers and 25 employees or less (64.5 percent). Food accounted for the majority of sales volume for 44.9 percent of the sample, followed by "Other" such as home chemical products, shoes and books (34.8 percent).

Table 1. Sample Characteristics

Descriptor	N	Percentage
Ownership		
State	20	7.8
Cooperative	33	12.9
Private	167	65.2
Joint venture	35	13.7
Stores in firm		
1–5	45	48.5
6–10	9	12.9
11–25	13	20
>25	7[a]	10
Managers per firm		
1–2	51	24.7
3–5	73	35.3
6–10	36	17.4
11–25	23	10.9
>25	24	11.5
Salespeople per firm		
1–10	36	16.8
11–25	10	47.7
26–50	30	14.0
51–100	13	6.1
>100	33	15.4
Highest sales category		
Food	129	44.9
Clothing	10	3.5
Appliances	31	10.8
Furniture	17	5.9
Other	100	34.8

[a]Frequency total may vary due to missing data.

ANALYSIS AND RESULTS

While we were careful to establish translation equivalence, this process does not imply reliability or validity of the constructs (Mullen 1995). If the scales used in this study can be used cross nationally, then they should exhibit high reliabilities, and similar factor loadings to the original scale. Therefore, we conducted reliability analyses on the 12 sub-scales as suggested by Churchill (1979).

The scale reliability scores as well as reliabilities for the original scale are reported in Table 2. Intelligence generation, intelligence dissemination, top management emphasis, interdepartmental connectedness, centralization and reward system orientation all meet or exceed the threshold proposed by Nunnally (1978) for exploratory research. Two dimensions, response design and response implementation, have α scores of .69. Top management risk aversion, interdepartmental conflict and formalization fall below the threshold.

Several constructs (intelligence generation, top management emphasis and reward system orientation) had reliability scores which exceeded those of the original instrument. These finding support Parameswaran and Yaprak's (1987) findings that the same scales may exhibit different reliabilities in different cultures. All were within or quite close to the acceptable cutoff. Because of the exploratory nature of the study, all constructs were used in subsequent analyses.

Each of the 12 sub-scales was subjected to a confirmatory factor analysis (CFA) using LISREL VIII (Jöreskog and Sörbom 1996). In testing for the factorial validity of an instrument, CFA assists in determining the extent to which items designed to assess a particular factor actually do so and measures the strength of relationships among those items (Byrne 1989; Maruyama 1998). Items with low factor loadings (<.40) or large standardized residuals were removed. Thirty-four items were retained for analysis with three to five items per construct. Bolded items in Appendix 1 were used for further analysis. Reliabilities for the purified constructs were recalculated and are reported in Table 2. Two constructs *(response design and top management risk aversion) remained* slightly below the .70 threshold.

Table 2. Comparison of Reliability Scores

Dimension	Reliability (Jaworski and Kohli 1993)	Reliability (Huddleston and Good 1997)	Reliability after CFA (Huddleston and Good 1997)
Intelligence generation	.71	.72	.78
Intelligence dissemination	.82	.80	.71
Response design	.78	.67	.60
Response implementation	.82	.72	.71
Top management emphasis	.66	.83	.78
Top management risk aversion	.85	.68	.68
Interdepartmental conflict	.87	.66	.71
Interdepartmental connectedness	.80	.75	.77
Formalization	.76	.59	.72
Centralization	.88	.83	.90
Reward system orientation	.73	.74	.72
Overall performance	.83	.76	NA

Discriminant validity among the four scales for *market orientation* was assessed by comparing the fit of correlated four-factor models with that of single factor models for each possible pair of scales (Anderson and Gerbing 1988). A four-factor model produced a better fit than a single or two-factor model. Model one hypothesized that the 13 items related to market orientation formed one unidimensional construct. The value of chi-square for this model was 497.04 ($df = 65$, $p < .001$). The GFI, AGFI and RMS were .71, .60 and .15 respectively. Model two hypothesized that the items for intelligence generation and dissemination would form one construct and the items for response design and response implementation would form a second construct. For this model the GFI, AGFI and RMS were .92, .89 and .084 respectively, thus indicating a better fit to the data. Model three hypothesized that market orientation items would form four separate constructs. Results revealed GFI = .93, AGFI = .90 and RMS = .074.

Generally models with good fit are characterized by GFI > .95, AGFI > .90 and RMS < .05. (Jöreskog and Sörbom 1989). A comparison of the fit statistics for models two and three show that the two models were almost identical. The difference in the chi-square values between the two models was significantly large [$\Delta\chi^2(5) = 24.91$, $p < .05$], thus indicating that the four-factor model was the better fit.

We used the same approach for *organizational systems* as for market orientation. The three-factor model produced a better fit than the one-factor model. Model one proposed the nine items would form a unidimensional construct. The first model fit the data poorly with the following results: GFI, AGFI and RMS were .79, .65 and .25 respectively. The second model proposed a three-factor model with the GFI, AGFI and RMS being .96, .92 and .071 respectively, indicating a better fit to the data.

For *top management*, the two-factor model provided a superior fit to the data. GFI, AGFI and RMS for model one .80, .64 and .20 respectively versus .96, .92 and .07 for model two. The two scales for *interdepartmental dynamics* were analyzed similarly and again, the two-factor model produced a better fit. GFI, AGFI and RMS for model one were .96, .90 and .04 respectively versus .97, .91 and .004 for model two. While the results were very similar for these two models, the difference in the chi-square values between the two models was significantly large [$\Delta\chi^2(1) = 6.05$, $p < .05$], thus indicating that the four-factor model was the best fit.

CONCLUSION

Using a sample of retail managers for a transition economy, we have confirmed reliability for eight of the twelve constructs proposed by Jaworski and Kohli (1993). Reliabilities for the original scales met or exceeded the threshold proposed by Nunnally (1978) for the following dimensions: (antecedents) *top management emphasis*, *interdepartmental connectedness*, *centralization* and *reward system orientation* and (market orientation) *intelligence generation*, *intelligence dissemination* and *response implementation* as well as *overall performance*. Three others: *response design, top management risk aversion and interdepartmental conflict* yielded reliabilities very close to this threshold. Only one construct, *formalization*, did not approach the cutoff when considering all items in the original scale. After CFA, the reliability exceeded the threshold. However, *response design* and *top management risk aversion* fell below the .7 cutoff.

A closer examination of these constructs is useful. That formalization proved to be the least reliable dimension is less than astounding. Formalization deals with autonomy on the job—not a common characteristic under the command economy. Becoming "one's own boss" is more prevalent, but vestiges of the old system may still be present in management and employee attitudes. Risk taking was not encouraged (and sometimes not tolerated) under the old system, so that top management risk aversion is a less reliable construct is also understandable. As managers become more comfortable with autonomy and risk-taking behaviors, we expect future results to more closely parallel those from western firms. As for the response design dimension, formal feedback from customers was not required in the former command economy. In seller's market conditions, an understanding of customer preferences was not considered.

The results of our study established support for the reliability and discriminant validity of market orientation constructs established in previous research (Day 1994; Jaworski and Kohli 1993; Ruekert 1992). These constructs appear to be valid for the Polish retail sector. The four-factor model for market orientation (*intelligence generation, intelligence dissemination, response design* and *response implementation*) proposed by Jaworski and Kolhi (1993) provided the best fit to our data and lends further empirical support to their work. We found similar support for the antecedents to market orientation constructs. Confirmatory factor analysis revealed *top management, interdepartmental dynamics* and *organizational systems* relationships were similar to those proposed by Jaworski and Kohli (1993). Our earlier findings (Huddleston and Good 1998) regarding knowledge of marketing strategies are confirmed as well. Polish retail managers do appear to implement market-oriented strategies.

Based on our results it appears that the Jaworksi and Kohli (1993) instrument can be used cross-culturally in a transition economy. However, researchers who study transition economies should exercise caution when using the *formalization, response design* and *top management risk aversion* constructs because of their relatively low reliability scores. Future research should make other cross-country comparisons to further confirm the reliability and validity of the antecedents to market orientation and market orientation constructs. Use of a random sample whenever feasible would lend further credibility to future results.

References

Aiken, Michael and Gerald Hage. "Organizational Alienation." *American Sociological Review* 31 (1966): 497–507.

______. "Organizational Independence and Intra-Organizational Structure." *American Sociological Review* 33, no. 6 (December 1968): 912–930.

Anderson, James C. and David W. Gerbing. "Structural Equation Modeling in Practice: A Review and Recommended Two-Step Approach." *Psychological Bulletin* 103, no. 3 (May 1988): 411–423.

Avlonitis, George J. and Spiros P. Gounaris. "Marketing Orientation and Company Performance: Industrial vs. Consumer Goods Companies." *Industrial Marketing Management* 26, no. 5 (September 1997): 385–402.

Byrne, B.M. *A Primer of LISREL: Basic Applications and Programming for Confirmatory Factor Analysis.* New York: Springer-Verlag, 1989.

Churchill, Gilbert A. "A Paradigm for Developing Better Measures of Marketing Constructs." *Journal of Marketing Research* 16 (February 1979): 64–73.

Day, George S. "The Capabilities of Market-Driven Organizations." *Journal of Marketing* 58, no. 4 (October 1994): 37–52.

Golden, Peggy A., Patricia M. Doney, Denise M. Johnson and Jerald R. Smith. "The Dynamics of a Marketing Orientation in Transition Economies: A Study of Russian Firms." *Journal of International Marketing* 3, no. 2 (Summer 1995): 29–49.

Good, Linda K. and Patricia Huddleston. "Ethnocentrism and the Eastern European Consumer: Are Feelings and Intentions Related?" *International Marketing Review* 12, no. 5 (1995): 35–48.

Huddleston, Patricia and Linda K. Good. Personal interviews with retail executives in department, specialty and food stores in Russia and Poland, 1992–1995.

_____. "An Exploration of Marketing Orientation in the Russian and Polish Retail Sectors." Paper presented at the 5th International Conference on Recent Advances in Retailing and Services Science, Baveno, Lago Maggiore, Italy, August 25–28, 1998.

Jaworski, Bernard J. and Ajay K. Kohli. "Market Orientation: Antecedents and Consequences." *Journal of Marketing* 57, no. 3 (July 1993): 53–70.

Jöreskog, Karl G. and Dag Sörbom. *LISREL 8*. 3d ed. Chicago: SPSS Inc., 1996.

Keller, T. "Establishing Effective Retail Distribution in Poland." *Encyclopaedia of Polish Industry* (1995): 59–60.

Kohli, Ajay K. and Bernard J. Jaworski. "Market Orientation: The Construct, Research Propositions and Managerial Implications." *Journal of Marketing* 54 (April 1990): 1–18.

Lowry, James R. "A Partnering Approach to Mass Merchandising in Russia." *Business Horizons* 38, no. 4 (July–August 1995): 28–31.

"Major Retailers Have Long Way to Go in Poland." *Eurofood* 4 (May 8, 1997).

Maruyama, Geoffrey M. *Basics of Structural Equation Modeling*. Thousand Oaks, CA: Sage Publications, 1998.

McCarthy, Daniel J. and Sheila M. Puffer. "'Diamonds and Rust' on Russia's Road to Privatization: The Profits and Pitfalls for Western Managers." *The Columbia Journal of World Business* 30, no. 3 (Fall 1995): 57–69.

McQuaid, David. "Retailing: When Will the Shakeout Come?" *Business Eastern Europe* 23, no. 36 (September 5, 1994): 7.

Mullen, Michael R. "Diagnosing Measurement Equivalence in Cross-National Research." *Journal of International Business Studies* 26, no. 3 (Third Quarter 1995): 573–596.

Murphy, K. "European Retail Environment: Market Turbulence in Eastern Europe." *European Retail Digest*, no. 16 (Autumn, 1997): 4–10.

Nasif, Ercan C., Hamad Al-Daeaj, Bahman Ebrahimi and Mary S. Thibodeaux. "Methodological Problems in Cross-Cultural Research: An Updated Review." *Management International Review* 31, no. 1 (First Quarter 1991): 79–91.

Narver, John C. and Stanley F. Slater. "The Effect of Marketing Orientation on Business Profitability." *Journal of Marketing* 54, no. 4 (October 1990): 20–35.

Nunnally, Jum C. *Psychometric Theory*. 2d ed. New York: McGraw-Hill Book Company, 1978.

Parameswaran, Ravi and Attila Yaprak. "A Cross-National Comparison of Consumer Research Measures." *Journal of International Business Studies* 18, no. 1 (Spring 1987): 35–50.

Piercy, Nigel. *Market Led Strategic Change*. Oxford: Butterworth-Heinemann, 1992.

"President Against Limiting Foreign Investments." *PAP News Wire* (March 31, 1998).

"Retailers Should Get Together to Survive." *Polish News Bulletin* (January 13, 1998).

Ruekert, Robert W. "Developing a Market Orientation: An Organizational Strategy Perspective." *International Journal of Research in Marketing* 9, no. 3 (August 1992): 225–245.

Smorgorzewska, Lidia S. and Tadeusz Markiewicz. "Inching Toward Licenses." *The Warsaw Voice* 16, no. 443 (April 20, 1997).

"Supermarkets: Super Targets." *The Warsaw Voice* 47, no. 422 (November 24, 1996): 10.

Trout, J. and A. Ries. "Colas' Thirst for Battle." *Marketing* 23, no. 8 (November 21, 1985): 36–38.

U.S. Embassy. *Poland: Large Scale Retailing*. [Homepage of TradePort]. [Online]. Available: http://www.tradeport.org/ts/countries/poland/mrr/mark0279.shtml. [Access Dates July 1998]

Wojciech, Roman and John Jeffrey. "Poland: Underdeveloped But Promising." *Chain Store Age: Global Retailing: Assignment Eastern Europe,* Section 3 (January 1997): 14–15.

APPENDIX

Scale	Scale Items	Coefficient Alpha of Original Constructs
Market Orientation (Intelligence Generation)	**1. In this store, we meet with customers at least once a year to find out what products or services they will need in the future.**	.71
	2. Individuals from our buying department interact directly with customers to learn how to serve them better.	
	3. In this store, we do a lot of in-house market research.	
	4. We are slow to detect changes in our customers' product preferences. (R)	
	5. We poll end users at least once a year to assess the quality of our products and services.	
	6. We collect industry information through informal means (e.g., lunch with industry friends, talks with trade partners).	
	7. In our store, intelligence on our competitors is generated independently by several departments.	
	8. We are slow to detect fundamental shifts in our industry (e.g., competition, technology, regulation). (R)	
	9. We periodically review the likely effect of changes in our business environment (e.g., regulation) on customers.	
Market Orientation (Intelligence Dissemination)	10. A lot of informal "hall talk" in this store concerns our competitors' tactics or strategies.	.82
	11. We have interdepartmental meetings at least once a quarter to discuss market trends and developments.	

APPENDIX (continued)

Scale	Scale Items	Coefficient Alpha of Original Constructs
	12. Marketing personnel in our store spend time discussing customers' future needs with other functional departments.	
	13. Our store periodically circulates documents (e.g., reports, newsletters) that provide information on our customers.	
	14. When something important happens to a major customer or market, the whole store knows about it in a short period.	
	15. Data on customer satisfaction are disseminated at all levels in this store on a regular basis.	
	16. There is minimal communication between marketing and manufacturing departments concerning market developments. (R)	
	17. When one department finds out something important about competitors, it is slow to alert other departments. (R)	
Market Orientation (Response Design)	**18. It takes us forever to decide how to respond to our competitors' price changes. (R)**	.78
	19. Principles of market segmentation drive new product development efforts in this store.	
	20. For one reason or another we tend to ignore changes in our customers' product or service needs. (R)	
	21. We periodically review our product development efforts to ensure that they are in line with what customers want.	
	22. Our business plans are driven more by technological advances than by market research. (R)	
	23. Several departments get together periodically to plan a response to changes taking place in our business environment.	

APPENDIX (continued)

Scale		Scale Items	Coefficient Alpha of Original Constructs
	24.	The product lines we sell depend more on internal politics than real market needs. (R)	
Market Orientation (Response Implementation)	25.	If a major competitor were to launch an intensive campaign targeted at our customers, we would implement a response immediately.	.82
	26.	The activities of the different departments in this store are well coordinated.	
	27.	**Customer complaints fall on deaf ears in this store. (R)**	
	28.	Even if we came up with a great marketing plan, we probably would not be able to implement it in a timely fashion. (R)	
	29.	**We are quick to respond to significant changes in our competitors' pricing structures.**	
	30.	**When we find out that customers are unhappy with the quality of our service, we take corrective action immediately.**	
	31.	**When we find that customers would like us to modify a product or service, the departments involved make concerted efforts to do so.**	
Top Management Emphasis	**32.**	**Top managers repeatedly tell employees that this store's survival depends on its adapting to market trends.**	.66
	33.	**Top managers often tell employees to be sensitive to the activities of our competitors.**	
	34.	**Top managers keep telling people around here that they must gear up now to meet customers' future needs.**	
	35.	**According to top managers here, servicing customers is the most important thing our store does.**	

APPENDIX (continued)

Scale	Scale Items	Coefficient Alpha of Original Constructs
Top Management Risk Aversion	**36. Top managers in this store believe that higher financial risks are worth taking for higher rewards.**	.85
	37. Top managers here accept occasional new product failures as being normal.	
	38. Top managers in this store like to take big financial risks.	
	39. Top managers here encourage the development of innovative marketing strategies, knowing well that some will fail.	
	40. Top managers in this store like to "play it safe." (R)	
	41. Top managers around here like to implement plans only if they are very certain that they will work. (R)	
Interdepartmental Conflict	**42. Most departments in this store get along well with each other.**	.87
	43. When members of several departments get together, tensions frequently run high. (R)	
	44. People in one department generally dislike interacting with those from other departments. (R)	
	45. Employees from different departments feel that the goals of their respective departments are in harmony with each other.	
	46. Protecting one's departmental turf is considered to be a way of life in this store. (R)	
	47. There is little or no interdepartmental conflict in this store.	
Interdepartmental Connectedness	48. In this store, it is easy to talk with virtually anyone you need to, regardless of rank or position.	.80
	49. There is ample opportunity for informal "hall talk" among individuals from different departments in this store.	

APPENDIX (continued)

Scale	Scale Items	Coefficient Alpha of Original Constructs
	50. In this store, employees from different departments feel comfortable calling each other when the need arises.	
	51. Managers here discourage employees from discussing work-related matters with those who are not their immediate superiors or subordinates. (R)	
	52. People around here are quite accessible to those in other departments.	
	53. Communications from one department to another are expected to be routed through "proper channels." (R)	
	54. Junior managers in my department can easily schedule meetings with junior managers in other departments.	
Formalization	**55. I feel that I am my own boss in most matters.**	.76
	56. A person can make his own decisions without checking with anybody else.	
	57. How things are done around here is left up to the person doing the work.	
	58. People here are allowed to do almost as they please.	
	59. Most people here make their own rules on the job.	
	60. The employees are constantly being checked on for rule violations. (R)	
	61. People here feel as though they are constantly being watched to see that they obey all the rules. (R)	
Centralization	62. There can be little action taken here until a supervisor approves a decision.	.88
	63. A person who wants to make his own decision would be quickly discouraged here.	
	64. Even small matters have to be referred to someone higher up for a final answer.	

APPENDIX (continued)

Scale	Scale Items	Coefficient Alpha of Original Constructs
	65. I have to ask my boss before I do almost anything.	
	66. Any decision I make has to have my boss' approval.	
Reward System Orientation	67. No matter which department they are in, people in this store get recognized for being sensitive to competitive moves.	.73
	68. Customer satisfaction assessments influence senior managers' pay in this store.	
	69. Formal rewards (i.e., pay raise, promotion) are forthcoming to anyone who consistently provides good market intelligence.	
	70. Salespeople's performance in this store is measured by the strength of relationships they build with customers.	
	71. Salespeople's monetary compensation is almost entirely based on their sales volume.	
	72. We use customer polls for evaluating our salespeople.	
Overall Performance	73. Overall performance of the store last year.	.83
	74. Overall performance relative to major competitors last year.	

(R) Indicates item is reverse scored.

7 RELIABILITY IN MEASURING MARKET ORIENTATION AND FINANCIAL PERFORMANCE IN TRANSITION ECONOMIES

Rohit Deshpandé
Harvard Business School
John U. Farley
China-Europe International Business School and
Amos Tuck School

Introduction

The successful transition of command economies to market economies clearly implies a need to develop effective marketing. As we have pointed out elsewhere (Deshpandé and Farley 1998a),

> "Market Orientation is the central component of the more general notion of the Marketing Concept, the pillar upon which the modern study of marketing is based. Because of its significant managerial relevance, measuring Market Orientation has for the past five years been assigned top priority status in terms of research needs by the Marketing Science Institute."

The purpose of this paper is the following:

1. To compare how existing scales for measurement of Market Orientation function in applications in emerging economies and in the industrial world. We put particular emphasis on command economies transitioning to market economies.
2. To extend our work to consider reliability of a measure of Firm Performance which might prove useful in the study of transition economies where more standard performance measures may be difficult or lacking.
3. To consider some preliminary results on relationships between measured Performance and Market Orientation in industrial and emerging economies.

EMPIRICAL MEASUREMENT OF MARKET ORIENTATION

We first briefly review the history of three scales developed to measure Market Orientation, and also discuss a scale which synthesizes the three scales. We then review published data on reliability of the scales.

The Three Market Orientation Scales

About a decade ago, working more or less without knowledge of each others' results, three groups of researchers developed scales to measure Market Orientation. Deshpandé and Farley (1998a) showed that the three scales produced almost identical substantive conclusions when tested on a common sample.

- The Narver and Slater 15-item factor-weighted scale used as one of nine measures to explain return on investment (ROI). In the *Journal of Marketing* (1990), they report positive and significant differential effects of Market Orientation on Performance for commodity and non-commodity businesses in a multi-divisional firm.
- Kohli, Jaworski and Kumar developed MARKOR, using non-linear factor analysis of matched samples of senior marketing and non-marketing executives (*Journal of Marketing Research* 1993). Their approach was later used in Scandinavia.
- Deshpandé, Farley and Webster (1993, 1998) used a Customer Orientation scale as part of a study of Organizational Culture and Organizational Innovativeness on Performance in several countries, the first of which was Japan. Their nine-item scale was developed by factor analysis from a list of thirty items, also using measures of item salience to determine choices. Personal in-office interviews with questionnaires in the local language were conducted with double dyads of suppliers and customers. These produced significant inter-rater reliabilities at the firm level.

Synthesizing a Market Orientation Scale

Deshpandé and Farley (1998a) show that the three scales appear interchangeable in the sense that substantive conclusions reached with each apply generally to the others. The synthesis is based on results from a sample composed of 82 marketing executives from 27 participating companies, which represented 45 percent of the Marketing Science Institute (MSI) 1995 membership. Individual companies were asked to submit three or four independently-completed questionnaires which contained all 43 items from the three Market Orientation scales discussed above, two Performance scales and some demographics.

The 43 items in the three scales combined can be used together, but (unsurprisingly) they are not only numerous but rather redundant, and the task of using all items is somewhat tedious to the respondent. In work with managers on Market Orientation, we were strongly advised to seek a set of perhaps ten to a dozen item with face validity and with technical rigor as a parsimonious measurement device based on the three existing scales.

Such a synthesis was developed based on a factor analysis of the 43 individual items from the three original scales, which produced a first factor significantly separated from two others on a scree test. The ten items (which included items from all three of the component scales) with the highest loading on the first factor were used in the summary Market Orientation Scale, which is also called "MORTN."

Reliability Measures

Published reliabilities for Market Orientation scales are generally encouraging for all four scales as shown in Table 1. The geographically wide-spread set of tests for the Deshpandé-Farley-Webster scale is a result of the fact that Market Orientation is an element of a broader cross-national research program for the study of how marketing-related organizational factors relate to Performance.

There is a clear pattern of reliability for all four scales in all settings. The published studies provide a sort of "natural experiment" which indicates robustness in a wide variety of settings. Further, reliability is not dependent on industry or data collection method, nor does it vary systematically over the four scales. Data on India, China and Vietnam indicate reliability in Transition Economies.

Table 1. Reliability of First Applications of Market Orientation Scales as Measured by the Cronbach α

First Application of Narver-Slater Scale		
U.S.[f]		.81
First Reported Reliabilities of Kohli-Jaworski-Kumar Scale		
Scandinavia[g]		.89
U.S.[g]		.89
First Applications of Deshpandé-Farley-Webster Scale		
Industrial countries		
Japan[b]		.72
U.S.[c]		.73
France[c]		.60
England[c]		.70
Germany[c]		.61
Industrializing countries		
India[c]		.72
Vietnam[e]		.64
China[d]		.72
First Application of All Four Scales in International MSI Member Sample[a]		
	U.S. Sample	European Sample
Narver-Slater Scale	.90	.83
Deshpandé-Farley-Webster Scale	.81	.75
Kohli-Jaworski-Kumar Scale	.67	.61
MSI Synthesising Scale (MORTN)	.88	.89

[a]Adapted from Deshpandé and Farley (1998)
[b]Deshpandé, Farley and Webster (1993)
[c]Deshpandé, Farley and Webster (1996)
[d]Desphandé and Farley (1997)
[e]Desphandé and Farley (1996)
[f]Narver and Slater (1992)
[g]Selnes *et al.* (1997)

EMPIRICAL MEASUREMENT OF PERFORMANCE

Empirical measurement of Performance does not have the immediate currency of empirical measurement of Market Orientation, but it involves more abiding problems which probably make it more difficult. For example, all three teams working on Market Orientation chose to develop batteries of scales to be used either for self-evaluation of an internal sample or for evaluation by outsiders such as customers. While the particular items varied, the syntax did not.

Measuring Peformance in these studies, on the other hand, was done in a number of ways. In fact, measuring Performance offers a number of quite different alternatives. For example, measurement using financial records is often suggested and is probably the preferred approach. In several countries in our samples, however, financial records are not at all as transparent as they are in some Western countries. In the extreme, for example, a substantial portion of the Indian samples reported in Table 1 are made up of large privately-owned (usually family-owned) companies.

Others suggest measuring Performance in terms of stock market returns, but this is not feasible in either privately-owned firms or in those Emerging Economies where few of the members of our sample are listed on an exchange. (Only 14 of the 100 Chinese firms reported in Table 1 are listed, for example.) Of course, complicating all of the above is the fact that marketing is seldom carried out at the highest level of the firms where the financial accounts are actually aggregated and financial markets operate, but rather further down in the organizations where the publicly-available financial accounts or market data may shed little or no light on causes of micro perfomance.

Deshpandé, Farley and Webster (1993) chose to use a four-item scale based on the work of PIMS (Buzzell and Gale 1987) for their work in Japan, and this choice was continued in work in the industrializing and emerging economies. The use of a measure like self-reported ROI used by Narver and Slater (1990) was considered, but collaborating research firms in four countries suggested that the questions would cause interviewing difficulties and would have a large number of refusers. Literature-based searches in 1998 on measurement of Performance by Chinese state-owned enterprises had the goal of examining the four items in the scale and seeking alternatives or additional items in the Chinese context. A number of specific financial items were found, but these were not different in spirit from the four items in the scale. No new dimensions were found in consistent use. (An example is a debt-covering ratio of revenue to debt.) Nonetheless, consistent cross-national measurement of Performance at the business or product level is a relatively undeveloped area and should be the focus of considerably more research.

MARKET ORIENTATION AND PEFORMANCE

In-depth discussion of the relationship between Market Orientation and Performance is beyond the scope of this paper, largely because such relationships have generally been developed as the partial effect of Market Orientation as one element of a broader model of Performance. Of course, the basic hypothesis, sometimes implicit and sometimes explicit, is that Market Orientation has a significant positive (partial) effect on Performance. Further, it is usually assumed that improving measured Market Orientation can improve Performance. The weight of the empirical literature is in the direction of supporting this hypothesis (Narver and Slater 1998), but there are important exceptions (Deshpandé, Farley and Webster 1993; Deshpandé and Farley 1998a, b).

RESULTS

Our discussion of results focuses on the emerging economies and includes some new results and some unpublished details about scale reliability. We discuss:

1. The general pattern of reliability of the Market Orientation and Performance scales in emerging economies;
2. Detailed item-by-item analysis of one scale for emerging economies; and
3. Some bivariate analysis of Market Orientation and Performance.

Scale Reliabilities

This discussion focuses on work using the Deshpandé-Farley-Webster measures, primarily because a multi-country research program using these measures has involved several emerging economies including China, Vietnam, Russia and India. Further, item-by-item data are available for in-depth evaluation of both the Market Orientation and Performance measures in applications in the emerging economies. Methodologically, all work outside the industrial world except in India was done using single respondents from supplier firms for samples of about 100 firms in a major city or cities. In-office interviews were conducted in the local language by international market research firms from representative samples drawn from sample frames maintained by the research firms for industrial markets. Industry has been shown not to affect conclusions in any significant way.[1]

The pattern of published reliabilities in Market Orientation in Table 1 carry over both to new samples and to the measure of Performance using the Deshpandé-Farley-Webster measures (Table 2).

The synthesizing MSI scale has only been used in Russia, and its performance in terms of reliability is about the same as for the more established scales.

Item-by-Item Analysis in the Emerging Economies

Item-by-item analysis involves assessing whether the reliability of the scale would be improved by removal of one or more items in the scale. The pattern of results in aggregate indicates that the scales are quite robust in application to four emerging economies—China, Russia, India and Vietnam. In no case does removal of an item materially improve the reliability of a scale. This is true of the Deshpandé-Farley-Webster Orientation Scale (Table 3), for the Farley-Webster Performance Scale (Table 4) and for the 10-item synthesizing scale (Table 5) in Russia.

Table 2. Reliability for Market Orientation and Performance Scales in Seven Market Economies and Eight Samples in Four Emerging Economies

	Deshpandé-Farley-Webster Market Orientation Scale	Deshpandé-Farley-Webster Performance Scale
In five industrial countries		
(Japan, U.S., France England and Germany)[a]	71[a]	.71
In other market economies		
Hong Kong	.67	.70
Thailand	.77	.86
Emerging economies (all)	.70	.78
All Chinese samples	.66	.75
Shanghai	.72	.81
Shenzhen, Guangzhou and Wuxi	.64	.74
Vietnam	.64	.70
India	.72	.68
Russia	.73	.76
(MSI Synthesizing Scale)	.74	.76

[a]As measured at supplier.

Market Orientation and Performance

As discussed earlier, the analysis of partial effects of Market Orientation and Performance involves considerable complexity. Table 6 shows indications of a pattern of positive relationships.

Section A of the table shows average Market Orientation scores in Vietnam, in the Shanghai sample in China and Japan. The analysis of significance of differences, which is done in the context of multivariate F analysis, shows a generally positive effect in both Industrial and Emerging Economies. Section B of the table shows a set of consistently significant positive correlations on a U.S.-Europe sample of all four Market Orientation scales with two Performance measures, including the Narver-Slater self-reports of Return on Investment.

CONCLUSION

We have taken the rather narrow perspective of scale reliability in our discussion of the analysis of Market Orientation and Performance in emerging economies. The question of the reliability of measures developed in one setting (in our case the Industrial World) for use in others (in our case the emerging economies) is an important first hurdle for the measures to clear in a search for ways to make relevant comparisons of such important concepts as Market Orientation.

Our approach is essentially etic, with the goal of setting benchmarks for comparisons of countries using similar research technologies. The approach is consistent with the view that the conceptual underpinnings of Market Orientation, like the Marketing

Table 3. Item-By-Item Reliability Analysis of Deshpandé-Farley-Webster Market Orientation Scale—Four Emerging Economies (Cronbach α for all items = .70)

	Strongly Disagree	Disagree	Neither Agree Nor Disagree	Agree	Strongly Agree	Alpha if Item is Deleted
1. We have routine or regular measures of customer service.	1	2	3	4	5	.68
2. Our product and service development is based on good market and customer information.	1	2	3	4	5	.67
3. We know our competitors well.	1	2	3	4	5	.67
4. We have a good sense of how our customers value our products and services.	1	2	3	4	5	.66
5. We are more customer focused than our competitors.	1	2	3	4	5	.68
6. We compete primarily based on product or service differentiation.	1	2	3	4	5	.67
7. The customer's interest should always come first, ahead of the owners.	1	2	3	4	5	.68
8. Our products/services are the best in the business.	1	2	3	4	5	.68
9. I believe this business exists primarily to serve customers.	1	2	3	4	5	.66

Concept itself, have not developed with a strong cultural component incorporated into it. This does not mean that an emic approach of building measures of Market Orientation in each culture with entirely new building blocks would be useless or undesirable, and we urge that work be developed along these lines as well. However, we also believe that our results should be considered in the design of the building blocks for such a venture:

1. We find that levels of reliability of measures of Market Orientation on samples of managers from relatively large business firms (which include both public sector and private firms) are comparable in Industrial and Emerging Economies. These levels are well above the bare minimum of .6 for reliability as measured by the Cronbach α. We further find that the levels of reliability in four individual Emerging Economies (which include Vietnam, China, Russia, and India) are similarly

Table 4. Item-by-Item Reliability Analysis of the D-F-W Performance Scale in Four Emerging Countries (Cronbach α for all items = .78)

	(1)	(2)	(3)	(4)	(5)	Alpha if Item is Deleted
(a)	Are much less profitable	Are less profitable	Are about equally profitable	Are more profitable	Are significantly more profitable	.75
(b)	Are much larger	Are larger	Are about the same size	Are smaller	Are much smaller	.70
(c) (R)	Have a much larger market share	Have a larger market share	About the same market share	Have a smaller market share	Have a much smaller market share	.67
(d)	Are growing much more slowly	Are growing more slowly	Are growing at about the same rate	Are growing faster	Are growing much faster	.76

(R) = Reverse-scored

homogeneous. Tests in Russia of two Market Orientation scales (one of three pre-existing scales and the other a scale synthesized from elements of these three scales) produced similar results. In no case does the analysis suggest that removal of any item from an existing Market Orientation scale would improve scale reliability.

2. We have tested a scale for measuring Firm Performance and found it to have similarly high levels of reliability in both industrial and emerging economies. We acknowledge that the use of a scale to measure Performance stands on a weaker basis than does the use of measures drawn directly from financial reports. However, the latter face issues related to unwillingness in many countries to report performance measures, as well as differences over countries in transparency in financial accounting systems.
3. We have reported results from industrial and emerging economies that indicate a positive relationship between Market Orientation and Firm Performance. Market Orientation is probably the central element of marketing management as governed by the marketing concept. As a result, measuring a firm's Market Orientation (and hence a firm's marketing health) is of considerable interest in the shift of economies from central plans to markets as governing mechanisms.

To conclude: we have examined three different scales measuring Market Orientation which were developed more or less independently at about the same time. In a

Table 5. Item-by-Item Reliability Analysis for the MSI Market Orientation (MORTN) Scale in Russia (Cronbach α for all items = .74)

	Strongly Disagree	Disagree	Neither Agree Nor Disagree	Agree	Strongly Agree	Alpha if Item is Deleted
1. Our business objectives are driven primarily by customer satisfaction.[a]	1	2	3	4	5	.74
2. We constantly monitor our level of commitment and orientation to serving customer needs.[a]	1	2	3	4	5	.73
3. We freely communicate information about our successful and unsuccessful customer experience across all business functions.[a]	1	2	3	4	5	.73
4. Our strategy for competitive advantage is based on our understanding of customers' needs.[a]	1	2	3	4	5	.73
5. We measure customer satisfaction systematically and frequently.[a]	1	2	3	4	5	.73
6. We have routine or regular measures of customer service.[b]	1	2	3	4	5	.74
7. We are more customer focused than our competitors.[b]	1	2	3	4	5	.71
8. I believe this business exists primarily to serve customers.[b]	1	2	3	4	5	.72
9. We poll end users at least once a year to assess the quality of our products and services.[c]	1	2	3	4	5	.73
10. Data on customer satisfaction are disseminated at all levels in this business unit on a regular basis.[c]	1	2	3	4	5	.73

[a]Item from Narver and Slater (1990).
[b]Item from Kohli and Jaworski (1990).
[c]Item from Deshpandé, Farley and Webster (1993).

Table 6. Relationships of Market Orientation and Performance

A. Average Market Orientation for

	Top Performers	Others	Significant Difference at $\alpha = .05$?
Vietnam[a]	36.2	34.8	Yes
Shanghai, China[b]	39.4	36.8	Yes
Japan[c]	32.7	31.0	Yes

B. Correlations of Market Orientation and Performance Measures on U.S. and European MSI Members[d]

	Performance Measure	
Market Orientation Scale	Deshpandé, Farley and Webster	Narver and Slater
Kohli-Jowarski	.30[e]	.44[e]
Narver-Slater	.67[e]	.35[e]
Deshpandé, Farley and Webster	.54[e]	.39[e]

[a]Deshpandé and Farley 1996.
[b]Deshpandé and Farley 1997.
[c]Deshpandé, Farley and Webster 1993. Market Orientation measured at customer in Japan.
[d]Deshpandé and Farley 1998a.
[e]Significant at $\alpha = .01$

dozen international applications we find that the measurement procedures are reliable in different cultural settings—both industrialized and industrializing, in North America, Asia and Europe, and in emerging economies in particular. A more parsimonious and managerially-oriented scale constructed from the three existing scales is now available for use in future applications—especially when Market Orientation is part of a broader study in which interviewing time is short.

Admittedly, we use a narrow definition of Market Orientation. As Webster (1988) has suggested, focusing on competitors as part of a corporate strategic planning agenda might have taken many firms' eyes off their customers. Nonetheless, "the set of cross functional processes and activities directed at creating and satisfying customers through continuous needs-assessment" is a definition which seems conceptually and in practice equally applicable in economies emerging from command structures as in economies already governed by market forces.

Notes

1. For example, Deshpandé and Farley 1996, 1997.

References

Buzzell, Robert D. and Bradley J. Gale. *The PIMS Principle: Linking Strategy to Performance.* New York: The Free Press, 1987.

Deshpandé, Rohit and John U. Farley. "Managing Markets Under Doi Moi: Marketing in Vietnam." Amos Tuck School Working Paper. Hanover, NH: Amos Tuck School, 1996.

_____. "Chinese Corporate Culture, Market Orientation, Innovation and Firm Performance." China Europe International Business School, Shanghai, China, 1997.

_____. "Measuring Market Orientation: Generalisation and Synthesis." *Journal of Market-Focused Management* 2, no. 3 (1998a): 213–232.

_____. "The Marketing Orientation Construct: Correlations, Culture and Comprehensiveness." *Journal of Market-Focused Management* 2, no. 3 (1998b): 237–239.

Deshpandé, Rohit, John U. Farley and Frederick E. Webster, Jr. "Corporate Culture, Customer Orientation, and Innovativeness in Japanese Firms: A Quadrad Analysis." *Journal of Marketing* 57, no. 1 (January 1993): 22–27.

_____. "Factors Affecting Organisational Performance: A Five Country Comparison." Marketing Science Institute Working Paper, Report No. 97-108. Cambridge, MA: Marketing Science Institute, May, 1997.

Grover, Rajiv. "Editorial: Market-Focused: Some Fundamental Issues." *Journal of Market-Focused Management* 1, no. 2 (1996): 115–117.

Kohli, Ajay and Bernard J. Jaworski. "Market Orientation: The Construct, Research Propositions, and Managerial Implications." *Journal of Marketing* 54, no. 2 (April 1990): 1–18.

Kohli, Ajay, Bernard J. Jaworski and Ajith Kumar. "MARKOR: A Measure of Market Orientation." *Journal of Marketing Research* 30, no. 4 (November 1993): 467–477.

Narver, John and Stanley F. Slater. "The Effect of a Market Orientation on Business Profitability." *Journal of Marketing* 54, no. 4 (October 1990): 20–35.

_____. "Additional Thoughts on the Measurement of Market Orientation: A Comment on Deshpandé and Farley." *Journal of Market-Focused Management* 2, no. 3 (1998): 233–236.

Selnes, Fred, Bernard J. Jaworski and Ajay Kohli. "Market Orientation in U.S. and Scandinavian Countries: A Cross-Cultural Study." Marketing Science Institute Working Paper, Report No. 97-107. Cambridge, MA: Marketing Science Institute, May, 1997.

Slater, Stanley F. and John C. Narver. "Does Competitive Environment Moderate the Market Orientation-Performance Relationship?" *Journal of Marketing* 58, no. 1 (January 1994): 46–55.

Webster, Frederick E., Jr. "Rediscovering the Marketing Concept." Marketing Science Institute Working Paper, Report No. 88-100. Cambridge, MA: Marketing Science Institute, 1998.

8 THE PROSPECTS OF BECOMING MARKET ORIENTED: EVIDENCE FROM THE CZECH REPUBLIC

Ronald Savitt
The University of Vermont

Introduction

Dramatic changes have taken place in the industrial structure of the Czech Republic as a result of the economic transformation of the last seven years. However, while macro economic studies and business reports have discussed changes in companies such as reductions in labor and changes to product lines (e.g., Myant 1997), what marketing programs they have implemented and how far they have gone in becoming market oriented has not been established. All we have is scattered evidence about what Czech firms are doing in adapting to the market.

This chapter explores the hypothesis that neither marketing nor market orientation programs are really well understood by managers in the recently restructured "old state enterprises." We argue that, in spite of the major restructuring activities, these firms are moving at a relatively slow pace in changing their previous structures and behaviors toward anything that is similar to the practice of marketing in firms in developed market economies.[1] While there have been major changes in the structure and operations of these firms, most of it has focused on financial and ownership issues with less emphasis on what in Czech transformation activities is referred to as "commercial planning."

Such a situation is not hard to understand. One of the greatest challenges in the area of organizational restructuring that Czech firms are going through is recognizing the importance of the market and buyers. In the past, what was produced had little relevance to what buyers wanted. Enterprises were driven by production goals set by central plans that showed little concern for market demand. Central planning provided production quotas and hence managers did not have to understand the needs of the intermediate and final user. These enterprises were shaped to take advantage of economies of scale and as a result were very large and "the small number of enterprises and the high degree of vertical integration have implied rather strong ties between suppliers and customers" (Elster, Offe and Preuss 1998). For example, the average number of workers in each firm in Czechoslovakia in 1989 was 3,000 compared to approximately 300 in the West (Estrin and Takla 1993). Creating new relationships was going to be difficult in so far as it meant that most of the past relationship had to be abandoned. This often meant breaking social and political ties as well as economic ones. It is a process that requires new thinking and the willingness to change and it results in replacing the comfortable and familiar previous social and institutional bases of authority (Clark and Soulsby 1996). Most confounding about the process is that there are no instructions or maps.[2]

The absence of market coordination led to what became known as "the shortage economy" in which there was forced consumption (Kornai 1992). Ultimate consumers and intermediate buyers learned how "to make do" within the system. They were exceedingly skilled negotiators around the gathering, hoarding, and allocation of materials (Newman and Nollen 1996). Enterprises had no need to deal with marketing activities because responding to demand was not a critical element for managers in the individual organization. Even in those cases in which state enterprises exported to non-socialist markets, they were able to use the service of state-operated export agencies. Customer satisfaction was not an issue.

Marketing in the Restructuring Process

An important element of organizational restructuring is marketing. The challenges for accomplishing this objective were significant because of the widely-held attitudes about marketing, limited resources and a lack of understanding about what marketing should be in the organization and how it operates. Basically, two approaches were taken. The first has been to establish a separate marketing department to undertake and direct marketing activities for the entire organization or for specific units. This often took the form of integrating what managers thought were marketing functions in a single department structure. Packaging, distribution and sales were often merged to become the marketing department. In other cases, old functions such as data collection were brought into marketing. In still other cases, activities including market research, new product development and promotion were also combined (Hitchens *et al.* 1995). Not only were there the internal difficulties of how to organize a marketing department, there were other issues. Most important of these was how the new marketing department should relate to the traditional departments in the enterprise. In theory all should have equal footing, however, that was not to be achieved. Production remained and remains fairly dominant. There has been only limited movement toward the integration of marketing with other management functions.

The second approach has been to combine what management views as marketing within the traditional organizational divisions. In this case, something like "marketing" or more correctly, selling, became part of the historical production divisions. People who were once "technical representatives" now became the marketing representatives for individual lines of insulation, resins and steel products. In such cases, the goal was to build better relationships with consumers (Edwards and Lawrence 1994). In an extensive study of the transformation of an East German pharmaceutical company, researches concluded: "There appeared to be a problem within the company with understanding the role of marketing (rather than sales). This was compounded by the cost of marketing activities and the internal lack of experience" (Edwards and Lawrence 1994). What often prevailed in this process was an attempt to be seen as moving toward marketing. Adapting Western concepts and words, printing business cards in English and producing slick promotional materials represent some of the artifacts that are easily found. More than once this has been described as moving from "the Marxian dialectic to the marketing dialectic."[3]

What is missing is some overall strategic view of what the organization should look like and how it should behave. Whether the Western model is the most appropriate or not, what the transforming enterprises did not have was a clear idea of what they should become. The past was clear; however, the future was not and the broadly defined elements of market orientation were understandably beyond their grasp. "In short, it has proven impossible to erase forty years of state socialism, ideology, institutions, and behavioral patterns, and simply inscribe the new values, structures and appropriate conduct of market capitalism" (Clark and Soulsby 1995).

Some Czech firms have indeed been moving toward some market-oriented practices, but they do not have a clear idea of what they are and more importantly how to implement and manage them. "Quality, customer orientation, and competitiveness became the mantras of top management in 1992," for example; however, they were not a part of a comprehensive strategy for managing the enterprise (Newman and Nollen 1996). As a result of the socialist culture and highly vertical organizational structure, managers had great difficulties in understanding a concept that transcends the organization. Managers were "well-qualified to make short-run adjustments to the production process, for example by closing particular product lines, changing the product mix toward more saleable goods . . . and reorganizing production toward cheaper or higher quality inputs" (Estrin, Gelb and Singh 1995). However, they have had difficulty with developing "the strategic direction for a business that plays a critical role in achieving a business's long-run objectives with respect to growth, financial performance, and market position" (Best 1997).

There are only a few examples of old state enterprises that have been able to make significant changes without extensive foreign investment. The most interesting case is from Poland where a shipyard, not yet privatized though fully restructured, carried out a sophisticated market-oriented program. It came as the result of the ingenuity of a single individual who had both the insights and the authority to make major changes in the enterprise. He was able to move it quickly from a traditional state-owned shipyard building ships for local use or building ships for hard currency without regard for efficiency or profits to one that successfully competed in world markets. The strategy concentrated on understanding market conditions and then adapting production to demand. "The creation of a focused marketing and product strategy was driven by a careful assessment of the fit between the market conditions and the shipyard's relative advantage vis-à-vis world wide competition" (Johnson, Kotchen and Loveman 1995).

In summary, given the challenges in getting marketing established and operating, it is little wonder that the more complex concept of market orientation has been difficult to develop.

THE RESEARCH AGENDA

The Environment for Undertaking Research

The great challenge in this research was to recognize and then adapt to the dramatic turbulence that continues to go on in the Czech Republic. Beyond the fact that that there is no clear direction, there is a lack of understanding of widely-used concepts. At the same time, language is in flux. Managers are keen to adopt Western managerial terminology; some of the words exist in Czech; others are directly drawn from English. Many create problems because they do not share commonly agreed meanings. Even though words can be translated, there is no guarantee that underlying differences will be clearly established. As managers almost everywhere, Czech managers use American jargon freely even in Czech. What market segmentation may mean to Johnson & Johnson management in the United States or the United Kingdom may not be the same to a Czech manager.

Because of these factors, great effort was given to the development of the questionnaire. There were three phases of back translation as a means of insuring accuracy in the meaning of various concepts for the respondents as well as the researchers. In each phase great attention was placed in making certain that the Western jargon provided meaning and that responses to various questions and statements would best represent what respondents thought the ideas meant. Such concepts as business strategy and planning have different meanings in Czech and English. For example, 'planning' takes on a negative connotation. Central planning with its negative aspects has not yet been replaced by firm-level planning.

Purposes

The primary purpose of the research is to add to our understanding of how well the "old state enterprises" in the Czech Republic are doing in changing their business and marketing practices to bring them in line with demands of the market economy. A secondary purpose is to determine how far these firms have traveled in the development of market-oriented programs. The importance of this task to our understanding stems from the fact that it is cast in terms of Czech perceptions rather than the Western constructs in the Czech context. The final purpose of the research is to develop an understanding of the complex factors that affect the adoption, implementation and effectiveness of marketing and market-oriented programs.

Methodology

The methodology was composed of three highly-integrated phases. The first was an extensive review of several academic literatures including marketing and market orientation, economic transformation and Czech economy and society. The results of this phase provided an overall framework that structured the second and third phases. The second phase was a series of in-depth interviews with a number of Czech firms and managers (Savitt 1998a). The purpose of this part of the methodology was to understand what a cross section of Czech managers believe marketing is all about as well as determining what they understood market orientation to mean. In addition, these interviews provided a means for putting in perspective the important events in the economy and their impact on developing marketing activities in their enterprises. This phase of the research took place in March 1997. Four firms that represented various types of Czech enterprises were included. Two were old state enterprises, similar to those that were included in the large field study; one was a wholly owned subsidiary of an American firm that had just implemented a market-oriented program. The last firm was a new enterprise that was formulated around the concept of market orientation as found in the Western literature. These interviews clarified concepts, refocused research objectives and formed the basis for developing the research instrument.

The final phase of the research was a formal survey of "top managers" in 82 old state enterprises that took place in November 1997. The data were collected by a market research agency familiar with administering questionnaires to managers in these enterprises. The purpose of the questionnaire was to capture as much information about the basic issues of marketing and market orientation as possible for each of the firms for the previous three years. Also, demographic information was collected about each of the respondents.

The Sample

The sample is a convenience sample based on approximately 1,200 old state enterprises contained on the sampling frame of STEM/MARK, a major Prague marketing research firm with whom they have conducted previous studies. All of the firms met the following criteria:

1. All had been restructured, that is, they had been a state enterprise prior to 1991; now they were in either a joint stock company or a limited liability company;
2. There was little or no foreign ownership or participation in their operations;
3. They all produce goods and services that compete on a limited basis with both domestic and foreign firms in the Czech market. Most have export operations where they compete with foreign firms;
4. All employ more than 250 people;
5. The sample was divided approximately between industrial and consumer goods as defined by the Czech Statistical Office, 54 and 46 percent, respectively. There are no retailers or distributors among them; and,
6. They represent approximately the geographic distribution of such enterprises among Bohemia, Moravia and Prague, the major economic regions.

The final number of firms used in the analysis was 76. Six firms were eliminated from the analysis. Although they were private, they had spun off from other enterprises that now were their sole client and as such did not participate in the market.

Respondents

The selection of respondents was important to obtaining reliable information in each of the firms. One person from each was selected with very specific conditions. The person had to come from what is known in Czech management circles as "top management." This represents a group of senior managers that have appeared in almost all of the restructured firms. While there are some differences among them, they share a common organizational pattern that includes a "managing director" at the top of the organization supported by an executive management group. This usually includes an executive director, a chief financial officer, a chief personnel director and a chief commercial director. The latter often represents marketing activities. Underneath this level is "top management" that normally includes a variety of titles representing divisional, functional and product responsibility.

The use of "top managers" as respondents provided an important opportunity to see how well organizational values if not practices were set. That is, for the most part, these were the very same people who were responsible for the introduction of marketing in the restructuring plans. If they understood marketing and marketing orientation, we would expect that the organizations they represented would in some way be implementing such programs. If they did not understand market orientation and marketing, then there should be little evidence of these practices in their organizations. Of the 76 respondents, 91 percent reported directly to the managing director; the remaining reported to either the commercial or financial directorates.

MARKETING AND MARKET ORIENTATION

The Czech Context

With rare exception, managers in Czech enterprises up to 1991 had very little to do with marketing and as a result they had very little idea about what it meant and what they would have to do if given the chance. In the study sample, only 14.3 percent of the firms had marketing departments prior to 1991; 45.8 percent of them added marketing departments since 1994. The most significant position for marketing had been in the state-operated export agencies and even there, while marketing concepts were used, they were at a very primitive level.

Studying Market Orientation

Originally, the research set out to measure the incidence of market orientation among transforming firms in the Czech Republic. The framework for the analysis began with the traditional Western definition of market orientation though it was clear that it would not adequately fit Czech circumstances. Market orientation is acknowledged to have a common set of characteristics: "three behavioral components—customer orientation, competitor orientation, and interfunctional coordination—and two decision criteria—long term focus and profitability" (Narver and Slater 1990). Further, the level of market orientation in any business is "the degree to which the business unit: (1) obtains and uses information from customers; (2) develops a strategy which will meet customer needs; and (3) implements that strategy being responsive to customers needs and wants" (Ruekert 1992).

Early in the fieldwork it became very clear that the Western construct was not going to be helpful in understanding what was happening in the Czech economy. Interviews with a number of managers at various levels in several Czech firms clearly indicated that there were numbers of different views about both market orientation and marketing and while many contained elements similar to those in Western definition, there was no universal agreement about the concepts. These respondents often had great difficulty in separating becoming private, becoming business oriented, and becoming market oriented. These findings required that the Western constructs be abandoned. While some of the responses discussed later appear to be similar to those presented in the previous paragraph, they should be interpreted as the views that Czech managers hold.

In order to develop the survey instrument, a series of in-depth interviews were undertaken; this resulted in the development of four case studies. These served to establish how well a cross-section of Czech managers, similar to ones to be included in the survey, understood market orientation and marketing practices. These interviews focused on developing a clear understanding of what managers believed was necessary for their enterprises to achieve success in the market economy. It was hoped that they would be able to describe something like "market orientation." They were given no direction nor definitional structure of the basic concepts; rather, they were encouraged to fully develop their ideas, as they knew them. Their responses were linked to the basic characteristics of market orientation.

They identified three elements.

1. They identified customer orientation which was defined as the shift from the past production orientation to a recognition of the importance of the customer in establishing a direction for the firm.
2. They recognized the importance of having a competitor orientation that was deemed to represent a process in which they searched for understanding of what their competitors were and how they operated and, most importantly, how they should treat them.
3. These respondents recognized the need to integrate several business functions in order to carry out plans.

While this did not approach the idea of inter-functional coordination as seen in the literature, it did represent awareness that further organizational changes were required. There was no general agreement as to which of the functions should be brought together though most saw the need for marketing to be more closely related to production.

Although there are some interesting findings as a result of this approach, especially with regard to those firms that have been exposed to Western management and marketing ideas, the lasting impression was that substantial changes would have to be made in the methodology if anything were to be learned about what really was taking place. This precipitated the shift from trying to fully integrate the Western concepts and methodology and to determine what respondents viewed as the issues about how to perform in the market. Once again this limits the ability to make comparisons across economies; however, it provides better insights into how Czech managers are dealing with their search for market strategies.

Four Case Studies

Some evidence of market orientation does exist within the four cases though what was found can be related to specific circumstances.[4] Summary findings are presented in Table 1.

Table 1. Evaluation of Market Orientation Components

Company:	JORAN	HP[a]	KAUCUK	SPOLCHEMIE
Component				
Customer orientation	I	I	N	N
Competitor orientation	P	P	A	P
Inter-functional coordination	I	I	N	N
Implementation				
Customer information	I	I	N	N
Develop strategy	I	I	P	P
Implement strategy	I	I	A	A

Where:
A is absent from market planning activities.
P is present but not implemented.
I indicates component is at least partially implemented.
N indicates that the component is not clearly understood.

[a]HP is Hewlett-Packard.

There is no surprise that the Hewlett-Packard (H-P) wholly-owned subsidiary has a strong market-oriented program. The Czech operation was based on the corporate philosophy and practices. JORAN CS spol s. r. o., as it was known in early 1997, was a "green field development" begun in 1991. With the luxury of having no managerial and structural legacies and the enthusiasm of young entrepreneurs actively pursuing management education, the firm defined itself around the principles of market orientation.[5] The company is a full-line merchant wholesaler with wholly-owned retail stores supplying construction tools, electric power tools, construction adhesives and fixings for concrete, steel and wood. Although management has not fully implemented all of the components of market orientation, that is part of their goals. What they have done is to clearly establish the fundamentals for reaching them. For example, they have a mission statement, which in English and Czech, states that their interests are to ". . . satisfy the needs of customers at high quality through selling tools, instruments and fixation technologies with maximum effectiveness and efficiency both in the short term and in the long term." It goes on: "JORAN regards itself as a full-service wholesaler serving both merchant and industrial segments with a full product line in which the greatest attention is paid to customer training, technical assistance and advice and rapid shipment (24 hour) of merchandise." Marketing information including that of aggregate demand, competitors, consumer wants and needs and internal costs drive the operations. Finally, purchasing, financial management and marketing are integrated. The company is truly a textbook example of what a market-oriented firm should look like. Implementing the practices in the Czech economy have been difficult and management has had great challenges in convincing customers and suppliers about what they are doing and why. Early in 1998, however, economic conditions forced JORAN to seek an outside investor and to selectively cut back on market-oriented practices as a means of cutting costs and dealing with a number of foreign firms that compete solely on a price basis. The results were devastating and in June 1998, the person who implemented and managed the market orientation program was fired.

Kaucuk is a major Czech petrochemical firm that has not developed market orientation principles. Restructuring lead to the establishment of a marketing department with a variety of ill-defined responsibilities including everything from strategic planning to gathering market information. It is both a strategic function and an operating division with an emphasis on developing "direct contact with clients," although that has not been defined. At the center of the department is the collection of market information, though there is very little evidence to suggest that the information that is collected is used. The firm purchases data from every source related to the petrochemical industry without regard to whether it is relevant to its current markets. In spite of sophisticated computing systems, little is done with the data except to develop aggregate demand forecasts by sector. Within the data are significant findings about competitors, new product development and pricing. Little of this is used in the formulation of programs. At the core of the matter is the fact that they don't understand what marketing is all about and therefore have no idea of how to use this information. The department has become a catchall for all those activities that top management does not know what to do with. It has had to compete for resources with other departments and has had great difficulty in establishing the value of its services to management.

The major success in their restructuring has been the expansion of sales force responsibility to the collection of information from customers. The sales force is now responsible for gathering information from current clients about future demand. They use this information to support forecasting models; however, the data are neither shared across various divisions serving the same customers nor moved back up into the planning process. Unfortunately, they have not gotten to the point where they inquire about specific product characteristics and ways that they can better serve the market. Each salesman holds on to the information that is collected; there is great suspicion among them, that their colleagues might exploit the situation if the information is shared across the various divisions. They show an intense fear of internal competition. Also, they are afraid that if the information was incorrect or if the clients did not purchase what they had indicated, the salesman would be held responsible. At best, Kaucuk has brought in some marketing activities but certainly does not have a full understanding of what marketing is all about, let alone what it means to be market oriented.

Spolchemie is also a petrochemical firm founded in 1856; it has experienced all the economic machinations of the twentieth century.[6] It was restructured in 1994 as a holding company with three separate chemical divisions. Senior management is responsible for developing marketing programs throughout the company and has clearly stated its direction. "We will increasingly depend on marketing and on the potential of our employees for development." The mission statement is perfectly clear about how it should operate: "Our business is not producing or selling products, but solving the problems and meeting the needs of our customers." As important as this statement is, there have not been the dramatic series of events to clearly establish the role of marketing or to implement a market-oriented strategy. While there is inter-functional coordination at the top of the organization, little of that has seeped down into the three divisions, let alone the various product-line organizations within the three. The marketing manager of one division said that he was thinking of purchasing products from one his competitors to sell to his customers rather than sell products from one of the other divisions within his own firm!

As in Kaucuk, a great deal of market information is collected though very little of it is used beyond aggregate-demand forecasting. They do no research about individual needs and wants or about ways of better serving customers. While there is much discussion about marketing, there is little agreement as to what it should do within the company. Some view it as the rightful replacement for the "central planning" unit of the past, though now to be described as strategic planning. But what marketing can contribute is not well established. The customer base has not changed since restructuring and with a great concentration on meeting or beating competitors' prices, marketing has only a limited value. Marketing was defined as "product knowledge, product applications, and technical problem solving." It might include such activities as advertising, marketing research and selling. Finally, there was no clear perspective of what programs would move the company toward becoming market oriented. All agreed that it had something to do with "focusing on consumer needs," though that was left undefined.

What Was Learned?

The case studies clearly indicated the paucity of understanding among state enterprises about marketing and market orientation. While there are glimpses of awareness that there are important changes to be made, little action has been taken in the direction that is needed. The two cases where market orientation was found provided important insights about what questions needed to be in the larger field study. It became apparent that it would be necessary to approach the topic of market orientation in a dramatically different manner than had been used in Western research. While the concepts had currency for some Czech managers, what they were saying really was something different. While the words might be shared, there were differences in meaning between theory and these managers. It was necessary, therefore, to develop a research instrument that would more accurately allow Czech managers to tell what they thought the various concepts were all about than to enforce one on them.

MARKET ORIENTATION AND MARKETING

The Concepts

From the twenty individuals involved in phase two of the research, ten from the organizations discussed in the previous section, a list of concepts related to market orientation based on a Czech perspective was developed. As a means of eliminating the confusion about what market orientation might mean, the question was framed in terms of "what it takes to have the most appropriate business strategy for the market economy."[7] This, as will be seen later, was used as the major question for determining what respondents thought market orientation was. The six items are as follows:

1. Collection and use of market information;
2. Short-run planning;
3. Prompt response to consumer needs and wants;
4. Cooperation of all departments in your firm in the process of new product development;
5. Product development management by research and development; and
6. Full cost pricing.

The first three approximate market-oriented characteristics. How those factors relate to what Czech managers view as market orientation is shown in Table 2.

Understanding the Elements that Approximate Market Orientation

The items presented in Table 2 offer insights into how these respondents define something approximating marketing and perhaps market orientation. Each reflects the efforts that their enterprise has taken in developing some kind of marketing program, their understanding of what they are supposed to understand, and what they incorporate in their thinking as a result of seeing the actions of firms in the market. The composite is primitive in one sense; however, it may represent the starting point of the development of a particularly Czech approach for defining marketing.

Prompt response to consumer needs and wants are similar to consumer orientation. There is an understanding that the consumer is now an important element in what they do; however, the level of understanding focuses on reaction to the consumer. This has been noted earlier as a common part of current management policies. *What was clear is that Czechs do not see the importance of anticipation of consumer wants and needs; what they stress is the importance of responding to consumer complaints or dissatisfaction.* While the questionnaire did not collect information about what these responses were, earlier interviews suggested that most of the actions here were with regard to logistical issues such as on-time delivery, damaged merchandise and completeness of orders. Further, there is little indication that these firms have developed their information systems to the point that they can systematically collect information about activities affecting consumer satisfaction.

Table 2. Definition and Application of Market Orientation Factors

Western Definitional Elements	Conversion to Firms in Economic Transformation
Behavioral components:	
1. Customer orientation	1. Prompt response to consumer needs and wants
2. Competitor orientation	2. Collection and use of market information
3. Inter-functional coordination	3. Cooperation of all departments in product adaptation and development decisions
Decision criteria:	
1. Long-term perspective	1. Measurement of organizational goals
2. Profitability	2. Several market performance measures

The collection and use of market information can be thought of as part of elements relating to competitor orientation. Throughout the study, there was a clear recognition of the importance of collection market or marketing information. What is interesting is the disparity in the type of information that is collected. Case evidence showed that a great deal of secondary information was collected about consumers and buyers, but the only primary information that was collected was about competitors. It is important to note that there is little evidence, however, to suggest that this information is used in any significant way to develop a competitive strategy. At best what we see is an awakening of the importance of understanding competitors and competition. The act of gathering information is a first step in the integration of marketing to the organization, though it is still not clear how of much of the information, primary or secondary, is actually used in making decisions. This makes sense in the context that "many East European companies are more or less noncompetitive when facing a western style, market-oriented environment" (Villinger 1996).

The idea that disparate departments would work together is still underdeveloped. This is especially true with regard to the integration of financial functions with others and especially marketing. The idea that there is a need to have closer relationships between production and sales appears to have become more widely accepted, though once again it is difficult to determine the degree of actual performance. Based on the analysis of open-ended questions, it would appear that this is more rhetoric than reality. Inter-functional coordination was amended to include "all departments" related to product adaptation and product development. The former represents what they think will improve their current problems. Adaptation really represents what these firms are doing in light of the limited resources to develop new products. It is difficult to document how much of either are taking place. It is reasonable to conclude that these firms are undertaking very little new product development. Moreover, there is great variation in the meaning of adaptation. It seems to run the gamut from packaging to product improvement changes.

Other Elements Related to Market Orientation

Besides these three elements, case research turned up another three elements that some Czechs saw as part of being market oriented. These three were incorporated in the study. The results are presented in a following section. The inclusion of short-run planning, product development by research and development and full-cost pricing need explanation. At first glance, they seem inconsistent or irrelevant to market orientation. What they do represent is a refinement of what such managers see as part of their need to become more business oriented. They are part of the managerial instruments needed to be successful for operating in the market economy. They go beyond marketing and reflect the larger set of managerial skills. Short-run planning represents an interesting movement away from central planning in that it now places the planning responsibility within the firm. This is a new function in so far as the firm must create the type of information to direct its operations on its own, rather than having it passed down from central planning authorities. Unlike market orientation that explicitly has a long-run dimension, short run becomes the focus for these firms. This reflects the turbulent environment in which they operate. It also represents their understanding of the need to move from the external central planning mode of the past to the internal planning mode that is found in private firms. It is once again a significant indication of the movement toward Western business practices.

Although product development managed by research and development may appear to be a variant to product adaptation and development elements discussed previously, it is not. What we have here is a major step in the integration of the organization's departments. The production orientation system of the past gave great latitude to the production function to undertake product development. Much of this came as a result of shortages and the need to adapt, change and refocus production as a result of shortages. While research and development departments existed in these enterprises, much of their responsibility was in the development of "grand ideas," many of which had little chance of ever being produced. It is fair to suggest that these departments engaged in pure rather than applied research. Their responsibility was to create new ideas; they were not evaluated on whether they came to fruition, nothing similar to commercialization criterion.

Full-cost pricing is a pressing issue in organizational transformation because managers have for the first time the responsibility of setting pricing. It reflects the shift from the "soft budget" regime of the past in which costs were never fully recognized and accounted. Pricing is a difficult issue for Czech managers in spite of the fact that "cost based pricing is deeply rooted" (Matesova 1994). What is left out, of course, is demand's role in pricing; something that might be considered part of market orientation. It is not that demand is irrelevant but that costs are seen to be most relevant. This stems in great part from the industrial rather than consumer nature of Czech management and the general view that Czech competitiveness can be based on high quality at low prices (costs). Even though this is some distance from those that make up market orientation, the fact that pricing is viewed as part of the orientation required to make these firms effective is an important factor.

If Not Market Orientation, Then What?

Question 1 of the survey asked "Which of the following three items, when combined, represent your understanding of what it takes to have the most appropriate business strategy in terms of the market economy?" As noted earlier the question stayed away from directly asking about market orientation. The choice of three items was also a deliberate decision to see if respondents would structure the choices into those that are more and less important. The responses to this question are found in Table 3.

The percentage responses are ranked in order and they offer interesting insights about what these managers understand about what represent strategic elements. Two items, collection and use of market information and response to consumer wants and needs, were indicated more than 80 percent of the time as key elements.

An open-ended "How do you define market orientation?" was used to obtain another perspective. An extensive content analysis of the written answers developed seven categories. Customer satisfaction received more than half of the responses with 33 out of the 63 who answered the question. The remaining items are "adjusting products to markets" (7), "better selling practices" (6), "selling directly to consumers" (5), "competitive pricing" and "maximizing profitability" (each with 3), and don't know

Table 3. Do Czech Managers Understand What It Is to Be Market Oriented?

QUESTION: Which of the following three (3) items, when combined, represents your understanding of a market-oriented strategy?

Items	Percent
Collection and use of market information	86.8
Prompt response to consumer needs and wants	80.3
Cooperation of all departments in product adaptation and development	39.5
Full-cost pricing	38.2
Product development decisions managed by Research and Development	30.3
Short-run planning	21.1

(2). It was hoped that respondents would take the advantage to provide greater depth to the question with the structured responses. They did not and in spite of significant time (about four minutes) and significant space on the questionnaire, provided only one or two sentences. While similar elements are found in both, the lack of detail in the second leads to the conclusion that these respondents are uncertain about these concepts.

Marketing Is Not Well Understood

There was great confusion and lack of certainty by these respondents as to what marketing is all about. While over 75 percent of the firms in the sample had a marketing department (see Table 4), having such a unit is not the same as being market oriented (Lamb, Harr and McDaniel 1994). Other parts of the survey provided insights about what the respondents understood about marketing. Two separate questions were used. The first asked them to indicate what functions their marketing departments were responsible for, and in the second question they were asked about marketing's function.

The responses for the first question are found in Table 4 for those enterprises with marketing departments. Of the eight functions that are indicated only two were mentioned more than 90 percent of the time; these are advertising and marketing research. Advertising was defined narrowly in the European context—"reklam." That basically

Table 4. What Is the Role of Marketing in Your Organization?

QUESTION: Does your company have a Marketing Department? 75%

QUESTION: For which of the following functions is the Marketing Department responsible?

Function	Percent
Advertising (reklam)	95.4
Marketing research	92.3
Customer service (delivery confirmation)	72.3
Pricing	59.4
Strategic planning	54.7
Sales	38.5
New product development	35.4
Physical distribution	13.8

is related to the use of mass media. Note that sales were included only 38.5 percent of the time as being part of marketing. Customer service is not seen as a critical part of marketing and once again is defined in the narrow context of "delivery confirmation." Respondents were asked to define marketing through the question "What do you understand 'marketing' does?" Here the findings are inconsistent with those in the previous question. Once again, given the opportunity to write extensively, the respondents chose to focus in on single concepts. Content analysis lead to the creation of four mutually exclusive categories. These are market surveys (39), customer satisfaction and sales promotion (13 each) and management of the firm (4).

The prominence of marketing research in these responses is important even though the case studies indicate that what takes place is not particularly sophisticated. Based on follow-up interviews with several firms it is apparent that managers view marketing research as the first step in developing marketing activities and in the longer run as a key component of market-oriented business policies. Those enterprises that have not been directly influenced by foreign partners do believe that this is an important first step in making better decisions. For example, when Nestlé entered into a joint venture with Cokloladovny in the confectionery market, its first step was to establish a marketing department to "provide market research into new products, changes and improvements in packaging" (Hitchens *et al.* 1995). Both Kaucuk and Spolchemie may be bogged down in the collection and use of their market information; however, they represent old state enterprises who are taking the first step toward marketing (Matesova 1994). The formalization of the process and placing it within an organizational structure should be regarded as an important step forward regardless of the extent of its activities. This in itself is an important sign of change (Soulsby and Clark 1996).

RESTRUCTURING AND MARKETING

Basic Finding

The basic finding suggests that "shallow restructuring," restructuring that does not contain significant programs and processes for operating in the market economy, has curtailed the development of market orientation. Restructuring that primarily focuses on changes in ownership and financial structure leads to passive and reactive actions by managers in charge of the production and marketing of goods. Given uncertainty, lack of direction, and the risk of losing their jobs, they are not going to engage in the development of dramatic activities such as marketing (Carlin and Aghion 1996). Marketing may be part of the rhetoric of restructuring but creating marketing programs has not been part of the process.

Privatization as a Source of Problems

Mass privatization programs in the Czech Republic have resulted in highly dispersed ownership patterns in which the state-owned banks remain the dominant owners. Privatization has created very complicated ownership patterns and many private or privatized enterprises are owned by state-owned enterprises. The most prominent examples are of the Czech investment funds: seven of the nine largest funds, which now own the bulk of shares in privatized enterprises, were established by the larger state controlled banks (Elster, Offe and Preuss 1998).

Continuity of Senior Managers

Only in rare cases (and basically in the case of foreign investment) have there been the removal of significant numbers of Czech managers. In many cases there have not been opportunities to replace the old managers simply because there are very few new managers with the skills to implement marketing programs. To the extent that market orientation represents a strategic direction, it must come from the top and "unless an organization gets clear signals from top managers about the importance of being responsive to customer needs, the organization is not likely to become market oriented" (Jaworski and Kohli 1993). Given that top management does not understand these principles, there is little reason to suspect that much more than limited understanding will be passed down through the organization in the short run. What we have is a continuation of the post-communist senior management structure (Clark and Soulsby 1996). In the survey, 56 percent of the respondents were above 45 years of age and had, on average, 12 years before retirement. A relevant question is whether there is a propensity to change. Although no such data were collected as part of this study, an on-going survey of general Czech propensities finds that the average managerial propensity toward change is low (Pribova 1998).

What Will It Take to Develop Market Orientation?

Market orientation may take a long time to develop in the Czech Republic. Its development is a complex process that probably requires a greater amount of time than anyone expects. In spite of extensive research in Western firms, there is no idea of how much time it takes to move a firm to a market orientation program, let alone what resources are required. When one factors in the need for the extensive change of attitudes, the replacement of the current managerial group and the resources, the process is probably going to be lengthy. What we might see in the short run is a series of changes in programs that provide some breathing room but clearly are not market oriented in nature. Many of the passive and reactive behaviors of Czech managers are visible. "Instead of undertaking substantial organizational and behavioral changes, they have confined themselves to labor shedding and real wage cuts" (Elster, Offe and Preuss 1998). It is going to be difficult to see the end of the legacies of the past.

One way to bring market orientation to Czech firms is through foreign control and/or ownership (such as Volkswagen's purchase of Skoda automobiles). The challenge is to find foreign firms that would be interested in investing in these old state enterprises given their relatively weak positions. Current management practices can otherwise only be affected at a slow rate, in several ways. For instance, management education programs provide an exposure to a small number of managers to Western, market-oriented programs. However, even such exposure to new ideas does not guarantee change. Nearly 40 percent of the respondents in this study had attended such programs, yet their understanding of the most basic concepts was not good.

A great deal about the need for marketing and market orientation will be learned by these firms in the marketplace as they begin to compete with others, especially foreign companies. Whether managers are able to go beyond reactive behaviors is not clear. They have a long history of being excellent at reaction, but market orientation requires more. The market will be a cruel teacher; it may be the only one that works.

Notes

I want to offer my most sincere appreciation to those who have helped me through this work. Professor Marie Pribova, of the Marketing Faculty of the Czech Management Center in Celakovice and a Research Director of STEM/MARK in Prague, provided enormous direction, support and advice during the entire project. Also, I would like to thank all of the Czech managers who took time from their schedules to help me try to understand what has been taking place, who completed questionnaires, and who shared their views about the larger issues in Czech life.

I greatly appreciate the significant efforts of the William Davidson Institute at the University of Michigan Business School for helping bring order to a first proposal and then supporting the project. I also want to acknowledge the School of Business Administration and The University of Vermont that provided me with a research leave in the fall of 1997 and a sabbatical in the spring of 1998. The Czech Management Center also provided important resources. Professor John Dawson, Head of the Department of Business Studies at the University of Edinburgh, provided a quiet place to work, access to the Library and computing facilities, and interesting colleagues who are involved in similar work in Central Europe. Jim Sinkula, a colleague at Vermont, was exceedingly helpful in the early stages of the data analysis.

At the end I am fully responsible for the errors of commission and omission.

1. It is not clear whether marketing is a prerequisite for the development of market orientation. In transforming economies, the presence of marketing, regardless how loosely defined, is most likely an important first step in the process because it forces managers to pay attention to consumers. Jaworski and Kohli (1993) provide a discussion of antecedents, however, the scope of the issue is greater; see Nevett (1991).

2. This is an important issue that we in the West often ignore. Living in a market economy provides experiences that shape our behavior. We know what prices mean, how to write checks, and how to behave. The issue here is the ultimate cultural transformation, probably best thought of in terms of what aliens from outer space might face landing in America.

3. Ivan Dudek, Sales Manager, JCS s. r. o., a "green field operation" near Prague uses this to describe both his suppliers and customers.

4. This section is drawn from R. Savitt (1998a).

5. The materials about JORAN are drawn from the case study by R. Savitt (1998b).

6. The materials about Spolchemie are drawn from the case study by R. Savitt (1998c).

7. We learned from the second phase of the research that whether in Czech or English "market orientation" had several distinct meanings. Some respondents obviously used the Western context; others defined it in terms of the overall transformation process, but did not see it as an issue for individual firms. Finally, others saw it as the market economy. This confusion forced us away from using the concept directly in the survey.

References

Best, Roger. *Market-Based Management: Strategies for Growing Customer Value and Profitability.* Saddle River, NJ: Prentice-Hall, 1997.

Carlin, Wendy and Philippe Aghion. "Restructuring Outcomes and Evolution of Ownership Patterns in Central and Eastern Europe." *Economics of Transition* 4, no. 2 (October 1996): 371–388.

Clark, Ed and Anna Soulsby. "Transforming Former State Enterprises in The Czech Republic." *Organization Studies* 16, no. 2 (1995): 215–242.

_____. "The Re-Formation of the Managerial Elite in The Czech Republic." *Europe-Asia Studies* 48, no. 2 (March 1996): 285–303.

Dudek, Ivan. Interview by author. Prague, Czech Republic, May 3, 1998.

Edwards, Vincent and Peter Lawrence. *Management Change in East Germany*. London: Routledge, 1994.

Elster, Jon, Claus Offe and Ulrich K. Preuss. *Institutional Design in Post-Communist Societies: Rebuilding the Ship at Sea*. Cambridge: Cambridge University Press, 1998.

Estrin, Saul, Alan Gelb and Inderjit Singh. "Shocks and Adjustments by Firms in Transition: A Comparative Study." *Journal of Comparative Economics* 21, no. 2 (October 1995): 131–153.

Estrin, Saul and Lina Takla. "Competition and Competition Policy in the Czech and Slovak Republics." In *Competition and Competition Policy: A Comparative Analysis of Central and Eastern Europe,* edited by S. Estrin and M. Cave, 44–61. London and New York: Pinter, 1993.

Hitchens, David M. W. N., J. E. Birne, J. Hamaar, K. Wagner and Z. Zeinplinerova. *Competitiveness of Industry in the Czech Republic and Hungary.* Aldershot: Avey, 1995.

Jaworski, Bernard J. and Ajay Kohli. "Market Orientation: Antecedents and Consequences." *Journal of Marketing* 57, no. 3 (July 1993): 53–70.

Johnson, Simon, David T. Kotchen and Gary Loveman. "Complementarities and Managerial Challenges of State Restructuring from Two Shipyards." *Journal of Transition* 4, no. 1 (1995): 31–42.

Kornai, Janos. *The Social System: The Political Economy of Communism.* Oxford: Clarendon Press, 1992.

Lamb, C. W., Jr., J. F. Harr and C. McDaniel. *Principles of Marketing*. 2d ed. Cincinnati, OH: Southwestern Publishing Co., 1994.

Matesova, Jana. "Will the Manufacturing Heart Beat Again?" *East European Economics* 31, no. 6 (Winter 1994): 3–35.

_____. Interview by author. Prague, Czech Republic, March 19, 1997.

Myant, Martin. "An Incomplete Transformation?" In *Successful Transformations? The Creation of Market Economies in Eastern Germany and the Czech Republic*, edited by P. Hill, 128–162. Cheltenham: Edwar Elgar, 1996.

Narver, J. C. and S. F. Slater. "The Effect of Market Organization on Business Profitability." *Journal of Marketing* 54, no. 4 (October 1990): 20–35.

Nevett, Terence. "Historical Investigation and the Practice of Marketing." *Journal of Marketing* 55, no. 3 (July 1991): 12–23.

Newman, Karen L. and Stanley Nollen. "Managerial Challenges During Organizational Recreation: Industrial Firms in the Czech Republic." In *Privatization and Entrepreneurship: The Managerial Challenges in Central and Eastern Europe*, edited by Arich Ullman and Alfred Lewis, 115–140. Binghamton: International Business Press, 1996.

Pribova, Marie. (Dr. and Senior Market Analyst, STEM/MARK). "Comments on the Draft." E-mail to author. June 29, 1998.

Ruekert, Robert W. "Developing a Market Orientation: An Organizational Strategy Perspective." *International Journal of Research in Marketing* 9, no. 3 (August 1992): 225–245.

Savitt, Ronald. "Evolving Management Practices in the Czech Republic." *Journal of East European Management Studies* (forthcoming 1998a).

_____. JSC s. r. o. Case Study. Department of Business Studies Working Paper. Edinburgh: University of Edinburgh, January 15, 1998b.

_____. Spolek Pro Chemickou A Hutni Vyrobu Case Study. Mimeo, the William Davidson Institute, University of Michigan Business School, Ann Arbor, MI, 1998c.

Sedlar, L. "Bankruptcy in the Balance: Unjustice for All?" *The Prague Tribune* (January 1998): 14–21.

Soulsby, Anna and Ed Clark. "Post-Communist Management in the Czech Republic." *Organization Studies* 17, no. 2 (Spring 1996): 227–247.

Villinger, Roland. "Post-Acquisition Management Learning in Central Eastern Europe." *Organization Studies* 17, no. 2 (Spring 1996): 181–206.

Distribution

9 TOWARDS A NEW DISTRIBUTION PATTERN: THE CASE OF ROMANIA

Carmen Balan
Academy of Economic Studies, Romania

Introduction

Distribution is one of the most dynamic and rapidly-changing sectors of the Romanian economy. These changes have affected the range and the quality of the products traded, the manner in which transactions are conducted, the types of operators involved in the distribution process, the forms of ownership and the relations among distribution entities.

These changes have occurred in the context of the other changes taking place in the Romanian economy: the privatization of enterprises; the opening up of imports to private operators; the reduction of tariffs; the removal of price controls; the elimination of state subsidies for consumer goods; the setting up of legal frameworks concerning franchising and trademarks; and the growth in demand for all goods, especially imported goods. They have been slowed, however, by the many problems that still remain, including the lack of financial liquidity among many enterprises, high inflation, the reduction of domestic production of consumer goods and continuing low levels of purchasing power.

Such an environment is typical of many economies in transition. We now describe how the Romanian distribution system is changing in such an environment.

MAJOR SHIFTS IN ROMANIAN DISTRIBUTION

Between 1990 and 1998, numerous changes have taken place in the distribution of consumer goods. The most outstanding of them refer to the dimensions of the marketing channels, the emergence of new distribution formulae, the development of the retail network, the logistical activities, the relationships with the other market operators and the role of business information. Later, the main aspects relative to these major shifts will be presented.

Dimensions of the Marketing Channels

Before 1989, the average length of the distribution channels was 1.5 levels.[1] The decentralization and deregulation process that took place in industry, agriculture and trade has resulted in the emergence of a multitude of channels in terms of length, beginning with 1990. *The increase in the diversity of marketing channels* was due to the following causes:

- The freedom of each operator to choose its business partners;
- The growth in the number of market operators, due to the privatization of public companies and to the setting up of new private companies;
- The mushrooming of small operators (for example, retail trade transactions are conducted mostly by private small/medium enterprises (SMEs), which have accounted for 49 percent out of the total number of SMEs in 1997);
- The diversification in the types of the services offered by middlemen in the distribution channels, leading to the emergence of operators with full or partial functions.

The new types of operators appeared within the distribution channels mainly under the direct influence and requirements of the foreign companies interested in the Romanian market. A specific type was the distributor, who allowed for the simplification of the selling activities and the penetration of the Romanian market—an advantageous alternative for the foreign exporters. The distributor bore the responsibility for the market coverage and territorial dissemination of the merchandise, for sales promotion, customer service and inventory management.

The distributors acted in their own name and on their own account, whether or not they were granted exclusivity. In addition, the distributor might have the obligation to develop and maintain a sales network. Usually, the distributor has the right to set the reselling prices and terms.

The large suppliers (like Procter & Gamble) selected their distributors on the basis of a well-defined set of criteria. The usual criteria were: market coverage, capacity to ensure distribution to the store, financial status, ability to communicate and desire to learn.[2] Market coverage was a primary aspect considered when choosing distributors, in order to expand the reach of the marketing channels beyond the major metropolitan areas. In Romania, Procter & Gamble, for example, has invested in establishing subdistributors for counties where the company did not have an appropriate system for intensive distribution.[3] The company has also applied operating methods, like cash-and-carry and van-distribution, adapted to the needs of small and remote retail outlets.

Another type of operator was the sales agent who dealt in the name of and on account of a company (domestic or foreign). The sales agent received a commission for the activities carried out.

Despite the diversity of the marketing channels, many operators expressed their *preferences for direct channels* at the beginning of the 90s. This trend started because of the sharp increase in the retail prices generated by the interference of numerous intermediaries adding their mark-ups. Although desirable, the direct channel has not become the unique channel used. This is because the small operators are not able to integrate themselves backward or forward nor are they able to perform the functions of firms acting upstream or downstream in the channel.

The preference for direct channels led to severe difficulties for the public companies specialized in wholesale activities. By 1994, these companies still owned 630 warehouses with approximately 974 thousand sq.m. of warehouse surface, 46.6 percent for food products, 34.9 percent for metallic and chemical products and 18.5 percent for textiles and footwear.[4] At the beginning of the 90s, these wholesale companies were considered unnecessary operators by the other members of the marketing channels. Consequently, they faced a decapitalization process and unsatisfactory financial results. In 1993, for example, the gross profit rate (based on the total revenues obtained) was 0.78 percent and the net profit rate 0.48 percent.[5]

The width of the marketing channels has also modified. The number of retailers downstream has gone up. Manufacturers and wholesalers have larger opportunities to sell their products. Nonetheless, not all the retailers who emerged on the Romanian market have been able to provide the same range and quality of services for their customers.

The increase in the number of companies specialized in distribution activities was intrinsically associated with a job creation process. Between 1992 and 1996, the Romanian economy had a net loss of 545,000 jobs (or 11 percent of employment) and created a net 182,000 enterprises. In stark contrast with the non-service sector, trade had a positive contribution to this change.

In retail trade (except for motor vehicles and motorcycles and repair of personal and household goods), the total change in the number of enterprises was +105,947 and in the number of employees was +25,193. The total growth rate for the number of retail trade employees was 6.2 percent for the period 1992–1996. The wholesale distribution was characterized as well by a net job creation. However, due to the specific activities entailed by this sector of distribution, the change in the number of companies was 3.3 times smaller than for the retail trade, while the net change in the number of employees was higher, +32,221 persons.[6]

From the viewpoint of *channel depth*, there is a trend towards getting closer to the ultimate consumer. This is evident from:

- The emergence of convenience shops;
- The direct selling at the customer's residence and the "party selling" used by companies like Oriflame, Amway and Zepter;
- The teleshopping method gaining ground due to the ever wider access of the population to satellite TV channels;
- The mail-order selling of various products such as books;
- The selling based on orders for merchandise delivered by the company's personnel "at the door," in the case of several foodstuffs.

Channels of various lengths will continue to emerge on the Romanian market for each type of consumer good. In the future, new distribution opportunities wait for daring entrepreneurs. One of them is in the area of electronic commerce on the Internet, which provides almost equal chances of success for small and large firms.

Emergence of New Distribution Formulae

In order to increase the profitability of distribution, the market operators themselves and the Ministry of Commerce have promoted new formulae. These include cash-and-carry wholesaling, wholesale markets for fruits and vegetables and franchising.

The cash-and-carry system achieved a great success as early as 1990. At present, there are many wholesale centers for food and non-food products, such as Prisma, Europa, IDM, etc. Their setting up was welcomed by the small retailers who wanted to rapidly purchase the products required by customers, to choose from a large range of products and to buy extremely small quantities of goods at affordable transportation costs.

One of the examples that attracted the interest of the market was "Metro," the cash-and-carry center opened in autumn 1996 at Otopeni, near Bucharest; the first of ten centers the company, MetroRom Invest, intends to build up in Romania. This center reduces the number of middlemen between producer and consumer to a maximum of two, as the goods offered are bought either directly from producers or from authorized distributors. On a surface of 10,000 sq.m., 20,000 food and non-food items are displayed.[7] The selling method is self-service and payment is made on the spot, in cash.

The wholesale markets for agricultural products appeared in Romania after 1990, as in other countries from Central and Eastern Europe. Two distinct projects were initiated. One of them started with the support of the PHARE Program of the European Union and aimed to refurbish and outfit several warehouses of the former State wholesalers of agricultural products in more than ten localities all over the country. The other project was initiated by the Ministry of Commerce and financed by the European Bank for Reconstruction and Development. It benefited from the technical assistance of the Federal Government of Germany. The objective was to set up a wholesale market near to the Capital, which is an important consumption area (about 10 percent of Romania's population). The Bucharest Wholesale Market (BWM) was designed after an in-depth analysis of the Western examples of France (Rungis and the M.I.N.), Spain (Mercassa), Great Britain (Covent Garden) and Germany. The BWM, inaugurated in 1997, was based on eight centers for the collection of agricultural products from the individual farmers and their associations.

BWM was the largest market of this type in Romania. It had an area of 16 hectares and four commercial buildings. The market capacity allowed for 160 stalls. Any wholesaler could rent at least 192 sq.m., out of which 60 sq.m. represented the stall, 12 sq.m. the display area and 120 sq.m. the parking area.[8]

The market will accomplish its functions with the direct support of six collecting centers located close to the Capital: Mihaesti (Arges county), Movilita (Ialomita), Brezoaiele (Dambovita), Giurgiu (Giurgiu), Cuza Voda (Calarasi) and Vidra (Ilfov). The centers from Mihaesti and Movilita were inaugurated in the first half of 1998. Each center has a central hall of 1,500 sq.m. (for the reception, sorting, storage and dispatch of products), as well as appropriate equipment. The centers are used by associations of farmers who combine their efforts to ensure the distribution of agricultural produce.

The aim of these wholesale markets is the improvement of the supply of fruits and vegetables for the population. This new level in the marketing channels will improve relations between farmers and traders. The role of the wholesale markets consists of reducing the losses of agricultural products—losses due to the inability of farmers to transfer the produce to the important consumption centers, as well as to the lack of information on prices and on demand—in the regulation of prices and in reducing the number of intermediaries.

Another form of distribution is the contractual vertical marketing system type of franchising. The main type of franchising arrangement existent at the present moment on the Romanian market is the *service-sponsored retail franchise system*. Since 1993, McDonald's has been present in Romania. By the end of 1996, its network was composed of 16 restaurants. In 1997, another 15 units were planned for the Bucharest area, and for the cities of Pitesti, Ploiesti, Timisoara, Arad, Oradea and Cluj. By the year 2000, the total investment of the "golden arches" in Romania will exceed US$150 million.[9] The number of employees in the 30 units will reach 6,000 persons; 3.75 times more than in 1996.

By the end of 1998, the company intends to open the first outlet managed by a Romanian entrepreneur. There are two alternative contracts which McDonald's agrees to include with a franchisee. According to the first type, the entrepreneur participates with an initial investment of US$75,000 and pays a monthly rate of 28 percent of the gross sales (without VAT). The second type stipulates the obligation of the franchisee to pay about US$300,000 at the beginning and a monthly rate of 23 percent of the gross sales.[10] The franchisee may develop the business by concluding franchising contracts for other McDonald's outlets.

Besides McDonald's, there are several other examples. MBL Computers ("Computerland") is able to conclude subfranchising contracts. Companies that have obtained the right to subfranchise prefer to develop only their own network for the moment. Examples are U.S. Foods Network ("KFC") and American Restaurant System ("Pizza Hut").

Among the new approaches to distribution is a trend consisting of *setting-up sales forces*. This trend is visible both at manufacturers' and distributors' level. The sales force is a real promotional tool also is an improved selling method, compared to the classic ones. Still in its infancy, this process shows a change in the mentality of the companies regarding marketing and sales departments. More operators feel an ever greater need for being proactive, for influencing the market and identifying their sales leads and prospects.

Development of the Retail Network

During the period 1990–1995, the retail sales of consumer goods have been severely affected by inflation: retail sales have grown from ROL 306 billion to ROL 20,850 billion in current prices. In fact, the physical volume of sales decreased gradually in the interval 1990–1993, after a rise of 17.2 percent in 1990 compared to 1989 (rise due to the imported goods, the reserves of products and the temporary augmentation of the individual income). In 1993, the physical volume of sales represented 66.7 percent of the volume registered in 1989; while in 1995, it was 87.2 percent.[11]

The retail sales of US$6.6 billion, achieved in 1995, mirror the development gap still existent between Romania and other countries of Central and Eastern Europe. The retail sales per capita did not exceed US$289.9 in 1995. In 1996, the level registered in the Czech Republic was US$2,005.3, in Slovakia US$1,651.4 and in Poland US$1,234.9.[12]

In accordance with the provisional data provided by the National Commission for Statistics, for eleven months of 1997, compared to the similar period of 1996, retail sales have registered a 28.8 percent decline. For food products, beverages and tobacco, the drop was sharper (32 percent). The private sector accounted for 70.4 percent of the total value of the retail sales achieved in the specified period of 1997, 77.5 percent in the case of food, beverages and tobacco.[13]

The evolution of the retail network was diametrically opposed to that of sales. Beginning with 1990, the number of retail outlets has continuously risen. In 1994, there were 179,502 outlets, 2.2 times more than in 1991.[14] From the viewpoint of the ownership form, the private retail units have gained a significant share in the total network, 76.8 percent in 1994 as opposed to 27.6 percent in 1991 (the rest being public, mixed, cooperative and community units). Retail sales grew from 0.8 percent in 1990 to 21.7 percent in 1991 and the share of the private sector expanded to 71.1 percent in 1994.

The retail network is dominated by stores. However, the number of kiosks increased from 10,192 in 1991 to 40,595 in 1994. Thus, the share of the kiosks in the total number of units increased from 12.9 percent to 22.61 percent.[15] This evolution was the result of the initiative of small entrepreneurs with limited financial resources.

Besides the aspects mentioned, several trends are worth noticing:

- *Emergence of chain stores.* Relevant examples are as follows: "Mega Image" supermarkets, "Panasonic" and "Mega Vision"—chains of stores specialized in selling electronic products; "Optinova"—for optical products; "Angst" and "Plus"—for food products; "Panipat"—for confectionery and pastry products, and "Steillman" —for ready-made clothes. However, with several exceptions, these chains do not contain many stores. In the case of "Steillman," the expansion strategy is not focused only on separate stores. The products with the brand "Steillman" are also sold in specially created departments inside stores having a diversified offer (department stores).
- *Renting of commercial space in the large stores.* The private retailers have had the opportunity to rent small areas inside the large stores in Bucharest and in the larger cities. Some of these spaces have been separated from the rest of the store becoming "boutiques." In Bucharest, there are numerous examples of large stores with spaces rented to private retailers including Unirea, Cocor, Bucur-Obor and Victoria. This situation has caused an acute crisis for the large stores, due to fierce competition and the decline in the purchasing power of the ultimate consumers.
- *Development of small street trade.* The enhancement of the private initiative of the entrepreneurs with limited material and financial resources led to the mushrooming of stalls and kiosks in the affluent areas. They have provided consumers with advantages such as accessible location, prices lower than those existent in various stores and products of current or periodic use. Their main disadvantages are the negative impact on urban aesthetics, the agglomerating in high traffic areas and the inappropriate selling and display conditions. Due to these less desirable effects, in the Capital area, strict regulations have been enacted by the Bucharest and sector Municipalities. The regulations limit the presence of street

stalls in the central areas and stipulate more severe conditions relative to the characteristics of the kiosks. At present, a large number of kiosks are located in the proximity of the public transportation stops and in the subway stations.
- *Cooperation of public companies with foreign partners.* Relevant examples are some Bucharest-based companies. The company "Bucharest" S.A. associated with partners from Israel and Great Britain, creating the companies "Optinova Romanian AME," "Rican," "MBM" and "Olympic." The company "Cocor" S.A. set-up three joint ventures: "Teamcor," "Maco," and "Neoset Cocor" with investors from Italy, Great Britain and Greece. The company "Meteor" S.A. established the joint venture "Mega-Vision" S.A. with German partners and the company "Universal" S.A. laid the bases of the chain "Stefanel" with an Italian counterpart.

With these market pressures, retailers will look for new ways of increasing profitability. Their marketing mix will be adjusted according to the needs of specific market segments. Thus, new formulae will come to life in the field of distribution.

Logistics Activities

In the 90s, significant changes took place in the area of purchasing and physical distribution. Besides the structure of the marketing channels, the logistics activities have represented another area of distribution change during the first decade of transition.

The most visible changes relative to logistics have been the following:

- *Higher involvement of producers* in the distribution of their products and in the physical distribution to the ultimate consumer;
- *Emergence of new operators* specialized in providing transportation services, under the pressure of a larger number of companies involved in the distribution sector and of the greater transportation needs;
- *Renting out of warehouse space* by the wholesale public companies, especially at the beginning of this decade when most of them had storage space in excess, compared to their merchandise turnover;
- *Setting up logistical alliances* by non-competing companies, one partner putting at the disposal of another operator its logistical capabilities, for example the warehouse network at national scale;
- *Assessment of suppliers* for the quality of their products: the large manufacturing companies, created with foreign partners, selecting their suppliers after a preliminary analysis of the quality level and its consistency;
- *Participation of Romania* in the intermodal multinational transportation network. A significant example of this was made on October 31, 1996 when a new international train of transcontainers ("Danubia Express") circulated between the terminal "16 Februarie 1933" Bucharest and the terminal "Sopron Hatar" in Hungary, with the merchandise further sent to Hamburg and Rotterdam.[16]

As for transportation, some changes in the quality of the network may be expected in the near future. A vast rehabilitation program of 4,500 km of motorway network was scheduled to begin in 1998. The importance attached to this program evolved from the fact that Romania's road network accounts for 80 percent of the total volume of merchandise and passenger transportation. Up to 60 percent of the financial backing will be provided by the World Bank, EBRD, EIB, BIRD and PHARE; the remainder being the direct contribution of the Romanian Government.[17] The rehabilitation process will be achieved in three stages: first - 1,000 km, US$250–280 million, deadline September 1998; second - 1,000 km, US$520 million, deadline year 2001; and third - 2,500 km, US$1,500 million, deadline year 2006.

In addition, the Romanian section of the European railway corridor will be modernized. In January 1998, Law No. 10 passed through the Parliament. It approved further participation of the Government of Romania to the agreement between UN-ECE and the governments participating in the "Trans-European Railway" Project, during the period 1998–2000.

An important shift, with direct impact on the logistics activities of the companies, is the introduction of bar coding. In 1993, EAN Romania, an association for the international coding of articles, was set up for the coordination of the EAN system in Romania and of the electronic communication based on the EANCOM standard. The expansion of bar coding will improve the communication and the correlation of the logistics activities within the supply chain, between producers, wholesalers and retailers.

Relationships Between Distribution Operators

The transition towards the market economy generated many changes in the commercial infrastructure, in the volume and quality of the supply, and in the number and types of market operators. At the same time, major shifts have taken place in the relations established among these operators.

The most relevant changes having a direct impact upon the relationships between the operators engaged in distribution activities are presented below:

- *Setting up employers' organizations*. They aim to better represent the interests of the public and private companies as well as to improve the coherence of the sector. In the field of distribution, there are distinct organizations for food products, for metallic and chemical products and for textiles and footwear. They periodically organize specialized fairs in order to facilitate the conclusion of selling contracts.
- *Direct unrestricted relations*. Each market operator may establish relations with any other partner. There are no regulations limiting the territorial area. Each distributor will purchase from the supplier he considers appropriate and will sell to various downstream operators.
- *Creation of the Romanian Committee of Distribution*. In 1996, the RCD was created in Romania in order to develop this sector and to lay the basis for an exchange of expertise among the operators. At the same time, the relationships between Romanian distributors and foreign ones have expanded. For example, Romania became a member of the International Association of the Distribution of Food Products and a member of its Administration Council. The 24th Congress of A.I.D.A. was organized in Bucharest, in May 1998.

- *Suppliers' support to retailers.* The development of the sales forces led to a new type of specialist - the merchandiser. He helps the retailers in displaying the merchandise, in order to set the products off to advantage, to attract customers and to yield higher profits.

As for the contractual relations among companies, there is no single law governing all types of economic contracts (as once existed, before 1989). The utility of such law has been the core subject of a lively debate at the beginning of the 90s.

In the relationships area, exclusivity is one of the issues whose importance has emerged. The Romanian regulatory environment has precise provisions in this respect. Relevant examples are the exclusivity clauses allowed in the franchising agreements, such as:

- Obligation of the parties to refrain from concluding franchising agreements with third parties—the franchisor within the territory covered by the contract and the franchisee outside this area;
- Obligation of the franchisee to operate directly on the territory specified in the contract;
- Obligation of the franchisee to refrain from looking for customers outside the area subject to the contract;
- Obligation of the franchisee to sell only the products or to provide only the services of the franchisor and no competing products or services.

According to Law No. 21/1996, relative to competition, the clauses included in the franchising contracts should not restrict competition. Clauses such as the following are forbidden:

- Interdiction of the franchisee to supply products of quality similar to that provided by the franchisor;
- Obligation of the franchisee to sell only the products and use only the services offered by the franchisor or by the third parties appointed by the franchisor;
- Interdiction of the franchisee to use, after the termination of the franchising agreement, licensed know-how, in the case that it has become easily accessible and widely known;
- Limitation of the franchisee's right to set the selling price for the products and services traded within the framework of the franchising agreement.

The competition law regulates many aspects of the relationships between companies acting on the Romanian market. However, the law does not discriminate between the "horizontal" and the "vertical" agreements (article 5), while their implications for competition are extremely different.

At present, many companies are considering only the rivalry they have with other market players. Nevertheless, in the future, the concept of partnership and long-term relationships may gain ground in the field of the Romanian distribution.

Role of Business Information in Distribution

One of the major changes in distribution is related to information. As merchandise of the twentieth century, information is more diversified and available.

Some of the most significant examples consist in the setting up of the following:

- *National Office of The Trade Register.* The Office puts at the disposal of all physical and legal persons, on commercial basis, information on the operators listed in the Central Register regardless of their activity: production, foreign trade, wholesaling, retailing and services. At the outset of 1998, the former Law relative to the Trade Register (Law No. 26/1990) has been modified and completed by Law No. 12.
- *Business Information Center.* This is a specialized department of the Chamber of Commerce and Industry of Romania and of the Bucharest Municipality. The Center is affiliated with international networks of business information such as BRE (of the European Union), which covers more than 70 countries, and IBCC-Net (administered by the International Chamber of Commerce from Paris).[18] Presently, the testing of networks such as ABC Infos and BSNet (targeting the Balkans and the Black Sea region) is under way. Robix, a new product of this Center, provides information on firm profiles, Romanian and foreign business opportunities, trade fairs etc.
- *Euro-Info Center.* This center was created in 1995 in Bucharest by the Romanian Chamber of Trade and Industry, through a cooperation with the European Union and the Chamber of Industry and Trade from Brussels.[19] It has established seven subcenters countrywide and exchanges information with 249 centers existing in Europe. The main data provided refer to the EU programs, economic and statistical issues, as well as SMEs. The Center provides information especially for the small and medium-sized operators who want to find partners in Europe, for export and import transactions.
- *Trade Point Romania.* Within the Romanian Foreign Trade Center, a Trade Point was set up with the support of UNCTAD and the financial backing of the Swiss Government. This point will be an important part of the Global Trade Point Network. The information provided ranges from data on business opportunities and company profiles to market data. A virtual presentation of the Romanian handicrafts is already available on-line on the UNCTAD web site and could be accessed within the GTPN.
- *World Trade Center Association.* Business information is also made available by the Trade Information Department of WTCA.[20] The range of services consists of the following: trade opportunities, Dun & Bradstreet's Exporters' Encyclopaedia (on 22 countries), World Business Directory (Gale) and Trade Pricing System (for USA export/import products). WTCA on-line has organized a Virtual Trade Fair where the companies may introduce themselves and their products/services to the potential partners on a multimedia platform.

All the changes that have been presented intertwine and create the multi-colored and contrasting "puzzle" of the Romanian distribution of consumer goods.

CONCLUSION

The changes which took place in Romania during the present decade until 1998 have fundamentally reshaped the micro and macro environment of consumer goods distribution. With a structure dominated by the private initiative and characterized by an increasing openness to competition and consumers' needs, Romanian distribution is much more oriented now towards the rules of the "free market" than before. Other changes are expected in the years to come, including the greater usage of market information, further specialization, the greater importance of merchandising and electronic commerce, more vertical integration and the greater development of skills.

Notes

1. See Florescu (1985).

2. See Uriasii vand Intensiv (1998, p. 25).

3. Batra (1997, p. 107).

4. See *Definirea si Elaborarea Strategiei de Restructurare a Comertului de Gros* (1994).

5. See *Definirea si Elaborarea Strategiei de Restructurare a Comertului de Gros* (1994).

6. See *OECD Economic Surveys 1997–1998* (1998, p. 109).

7. See "Angrosistii Trec de la Modelul Arab la cel German" (1996, p. 29).

8. Gioga (1998, p. 27).

9. Pavel (1996, p. 9).

10. See *Capital* 19 (1998, p. 39).

11. Based on *Evolutia Principalilor Indicatori Economico-Sociali* (1996, p. 2).

12. *European Marketing Data and Statistics* 1998 (p. 281).

13. See "Produsul Intern Brut in Cadere Libera" (1998).

14. See *Anuarul Statistic al Romaniei 1995* (1996, p. 661).

15. See *Anuarul Statistic al Romaniei 1995* (1996, p. 661).

16. Varvici (1996, p. 5).

17. Enache (1998).

18. Juganaru (1998).

19. Carlan (1996, p. 11).

20. See *Capital* 21 (1998, p. 13).

References

"Angrosistii Trec de la Modelul Arab la cel German." *Capital* 43 (October 31, 1996): 29.

Anuarul Statistic al Romaniei 1995. Bucharest: National Commission for Statistics (1996).

Batra, Rajeev. "Executive Insights: Marketing Issues and Challenges in Transitional Economies." *Journal of International Marketing* 5, no. 4 (1997): 107.

Capital 19 (May 14, 1998): 39.

Capital 21 (May 28, 1998): 13.

Carlan, Corneliu. "De la Informatia Europeana la Parterneriat." *Adevarul Economic* 31, no. 229 (August 2–8, 1996): 11.

Definirea si Elaborarea Strategiei de Restructurare a Comertului de Gros. Bucharest: The Institute of Research for Domestic Trade (1994).

Enache, Viorica. "Drumul Reformei sau Reforma Drumurilor." *Piata Financiara* 4 (April 1998).

European Marketing Data and Statistics 1998, 33rd ed. Euromonitor, 281.

Evolutia Principalilor Indicatori Economico-Sociali. Documentar. National Commission for Statistics (September 1996): 2.

Florescu, C. *Strategii in Conducerea Activitatii Intreprinderii*. Bucharest: Editura Stiintifica si Enciclopedica (1985).

Gioga, Stere. "Proiectul Piata de Gros." *Tribuna Economica* 14 (April 18, 1998): 27.

Juganaru, Elena. "Produse Moderne de Comunicare a Informatiilor." *Mesagerul Economic* 6-7 (1998).

OECD Economic Surveys 1997–1998. Romania. OECD, 1998, 109.

Pavel, Cristian. "Paul Booth: Nu Exista Nici o Tara Fara Birocratie." *Capital* 44 (November 7, 1996): 9.

"Produsul Intern Brut in Cadere Libera." *Adevarul Economic* 309 (February 13–19, 1998).

"Uriasii van Intensiv." *Capital* 19 (May 14, 1998): 25.

Varvici, Reghina. "Danubia Express Conecteaza Romania la Pulsul Economiei Vest-Europene." *Curierul National* (November 6, 1996): 5.

10 FACTORS RELATING TO SUPPLY STABILITY AND THE REDUCTION OF OPPORTUNISM IN HUNGARIAN MARKETING CHANNELS

Debra J. Dahab
Data Transmission Network
James W. Gentry
University of Nebraska-Lincoln

Introduction

In most market systems, institutions govern trade relationships, providing for performance stability and dispute resolution and reducing opportunism. These institutions can be legal and administrative, such as contract law and the court system or social, as for example, professional, ethnic, political, and interpersonal relationships. Governance is provided either through sanctions or interdependence, depending on the institution. In transition economies some of these institutions are often missing or underdeveloped and can result in either the unbridled commerce described in the popular press or the continuation of longstanding, but often unprofitable, interfirm relationships.

Our previous work in Hungary has looked at both interpersonal and institutional factors and how they together affect trade in the current environment. In the world of business, "connections" are a global phenomenon. We have *keiretsus* in Japan and *guanxi* in China. In the United States and in European business circles, connections are sometimes associated with corruption, as being "connected" means having access to resources and opportunities that are not offered to everyone in a free market. In Russia, what we saw as "markets" in the early 1990s were really the vestiges of the web of interpersonal connections that dominated the underground economy of the socialist system. In Hungary, "connections" were reported to be very important to Hungarian entrepreneurs in attaining resources and influence (Rona-Tás 1994) following the political and economic changes of the late 1980s. Under the former system, entrepreneurs were adept at building relationships that gave them access to supplies, capital, and influence (Dahab, Gentry and Sohi 1996; Rona-Tás 1991; Stark 1992).

Yet, the pace of change in post-1990 Hungary and the drive to cast off old ways of doing business raises the question of the role of relationships in the new environment. Further, as the firm interdependencies of the former system are disrupted by competition, what will be the role of personal interdependencies in providing transaction stability? Finally, as Hungarian entrepreneurs learn more about doing business in a market economy and interact with foreign partners and suppliers, will the nature and role of Hungarian business relationships change?

This research extends our work on the nature and role of the interpersonal relationship between Hungarian retailers and suppliers (Dahab *et al.* 1996; Dahab, Gentry and Sohi 1997; Dahab, Sohi and Gentry 1998). Data collected in 1995 revealed that strong dyadic ties brought direct returns to retailers by providing access to scarce resources and enhanced stability of supplies. Finally, though unanticipated, we found that interpersonal relationships are stronger when multinational companies are perceived as being more important in the product industry. Retailers also associate branded products with better performance by the supplier, measured as on-time deliveries, correct product type and quantity, consistent quality of product, and correct price. This last finding suggests that branded products might be used as a cue for a suppliers' reputation in the absence of industry norms, enforceable contract laws, and other institutional factors that encourage and enforce performance. This may suggest that brand equity exists in supplier-retailer transactions beyond the value of the brand to the end consumer manifested in terms of retail demand. Relatively little conceptual or empirical work has been done on the value of a branded product in a channel context beyond the value of the consumer market (Kim *et al.* 1995).

The objectives of this study are as follows:

1. To determine whether the role of interpersonal relationships between retailers and suppliers has changed over time. We expect that as channel institutions develop and trade expands over a larger geographic area, more formal institutions will replace interpersonal relationships in facilitating trade (Zucker 1986). One of these institutions may be the product brand.
2. To expand on the finding that branded products are related positively to supplier performance. We suggest that the brand may play an institutional role in the channel by serving as a governance structure in developing channel relationships.

This report presents the results of an empirical study of the Hungarian supply chain from the perspective of the retailer. The study was conducted in two phases. An initial or baseline measure of key variables was taken in 1995 using a mail survey methodology. In 1997, we repeated the study with additional variables using a similar written survey with a drop-off methodology. A comparison of the results over time is presented in this report.

The report is organized by first presenting the theory underlying the original model and hypotheses. Then, a discussion of unanticipated findings from the 1995 study is presented. These findings provide a basis, in part, for the revisions made in the second study. The results of the 1997 study are presented and discussed. Finally, we address managerial issues.

Nature of Embeddedness

Economic action is embedded within dyadic relationships of varying degrees of interpersonal care and concern, reciprocity, and emotional security (Granovetter 1985). The conceptual basis and operationalization of embeddedness is described in detail in Dahab, Sohi and Gentry (1998). We suggest that embeddedness is an integrated construct with several dimensions, since each dimension of the social context acts in concert with the others to influence exchange behaviors (Granovetter 1985). Our dimensions are based on Granovetter's work and are supported by empirical work as well (Uzzi 1997). They are 1) voluntary confiding associated with strong interpersonal ties; 2) expectations of fairness and reciprocity which reflect the interdependent nature of the relationship; and 3) the extent of broader connections or communication patterns that constitute links to social others.

Voluntary confiding is associated with *tie strength*, which is the degree of personal closeness, intimacy, support, and association between two parties (Marsden and Campbell 1984). Tie strength is closely related to but distinct from trust, as the emotional bonds associated with tie strength may form the basis for trust based on strong affect or liking (McAllister 1995).

Fairness is associated with the interdependent utility function that underlies an embedded relationship. The purchaser's utility function includes both the acquisition value of the product or service and the transaction value that represents the perceived fairness of the deal (Thaler 1985). The embedded context would not have exchange value if it were perceived as unfair, as this would indicate a relationship based on coercion and dependence rather than the mutuality or reciprocity that is embeddedness (Frenzen and Davis 1990; Uzzi 1997). Reciprocity is a part of expectations of fairness (Granovetter 1985; Uzzi 1997). Reciprocity can change from an obligation that is clearly incurred and requires a like response to a reciprocity that has been internalized and is of a more generalized nature. Tie strength and fairness-reciprocity are strongly linked. In a strong tie relationship, the parties are assured that their actions will be reciprocated; it makes no difference at any given point who owes whom as part of the value is in the knowledge of the assurance of reciprocity.

The third dimension of embeddedness is *communication density* that connects the dyad to the broader community of relationships. Tight networks, where communication is frequent and ties are strong, affect the breadth of resources available to the dyad and can make or break reputations (Granovetter 1973, 1985). These communication patterns determine the level of information impactedness or whether and with whom information about resource availability and reputations is shared. For example, in Weigand's (1994) ethnographic study of high-risk trading activities, where interpersonal relationships were important in establishing trust, the rapid spread of information throughout an industry regarding violations of trust by individuals ultimately affected an individual's desirability as a trading partner. In Hungary, we found in our preliminary interviews with retailers that these connections were instrumental to retailers' independent financing for a project when capital was scarce.

The Role of Embeddedness

The literature in sociology, organizational theory and marketing suggests that the quality of interpersonal ties shapes opportunities and expectations. An embedded relationship represents an investment in social capital that creates obligations that may affect performance and provide specific returns through access to scarce or special information and influence (Frenzen and Nakamoto 1993; Granovetter 1985, 1992; Uzzi 1997). We use outcome variables of *supply stability* to reflect expectations, and *access to resources* to represent opportunities. Each is discussed in the following paragraphs.

Supply Stability

Ties have been suggested to create switching costs that discourage seeking other sources of supply (Seabright, Levinthal and Fichman 1992) are associated positively with compliance and cooperation (Murry and Heide 1997), and may be used to pre-qualify potential suppliers (Doney and Cannon 1997). These findings are all examples of interpersonal ties creating expectations of performance. Providing a consistent and reliable assortment of products to consumers is important to Hungarian retailers trying to differentiate themselves in the new market environment. While shortages from the command system may have been alleviated over time, retailers we spoke with in 1994 still complained that suppliers did not deliver products on time, substituted or diverted merchandise to another retailer or provided poorer quality goods than anticipated. Many reported that a considerable amount of time was spent qualifying and monitoring suppliers. Embedded relationships represent a mechanism for ensuring performance and reducing the need to monitor supply partners. In earlier work we found strong positive relationships between embeddedness and supply stability (Dahab *et al.* 1996; Dahab, Gentry and Sohi 1997). *Supply stability* represents the extent to which the retailer perceives the performance by the supplier to be stable and predictable. We generated items for this measure based on interviews with Hungarian retailers and wholesalers in which we asked them to specify the activities that affect the evaluation of the supplier's performance.

H1: Embeddedness is related positively to supply stability.

Access to Resources

Part of the importance of social capital is in creating the ties and obligations that increase the returns to yourself from favors that others owe you. Interpersonal ties are related to patterns and types of information exchange (Larson 1992). During the transitional period from 1989 to 1992, personal relationships reportedly continued to provide access to information about prices, demand and the availability of goods (Rona-Tás 1994). Our interviews with Hungarian retailers in 1994 suggested that suppliers who could provide access to financial capital and had political "clout" within local governments that controlled retail locations were highly prized. This leads to the hypothesis:

H2: Embeddedness is related positively to access to resources.

Moderating Effects

Uzzi (1997) observed that the same firm used embeddedness selectively in certain relationships—that is, certain relationships were more embedded than others. This suggests that embeddedness is a strategy that firms use to "match" certain conditions in the environment and to achieve certain goals.

Institutional Trust

In Hungary, both the history of relationships between people and the state and the current political conflict surrounding the nature of the developing legal infrastructure may have affected the level of trust that people have in formal institutions that guide business relationships. An institutional approach to trust production holds that interpersonal trust development need not precede economic transactions if other cues such as institutional guarantees serve as signals for trust (Zucker 1986). A Western bank, for example, is trusted in certain financial circles because of the legal status and protection afforded by the institution. The situation in post-1989 Central and Eastern Europe may parallel Zucker's (1986) description of changes that took place in the United States from 1840–1920 when massive social disruption and internal migration broke long-standing relational and social ties resulting in the development of a market for institutional trust. As trading distances and the number of players increase, a market for institutional trust will develop and we would eventually expect a lower reliance upon relational embeddedness as a governance structure.

This discussion suggests that the use of embeddedness as a governance structure may be related to the extent of trust in formal institutions such as the system for arranging and enforcing business contracts. As *institutional trust* increases, we would expect the embedded relationship to become less important as a mechanism for encouraging supply stability. Finally, at higher levels of institutional trust, government institutions such as contract law and courts might provide assurances of more equal access to resources or redress when access is denied to one party by another. Thus, we would expect embeddedness to have lower instrumental value because of the availability of these trusted alternative mechanisms. To our knowledge, *institutional trust* has not been measured empirically. The measure used in this study is intended to capture the degree to which institutions such as government, contract law, the legal system and banks are perceived as providing a trusted, reliable framework for transactions (Borner, Brunetti and Weder 1995).

H3: An increase in institutional trust offsets the strength of the positive relationship between embeddedness and supply stability.

H4: An increase in institutional trust offsets the strength of the positive relationship between embeddedness and access to resources.

Opportunism

Opportunism represents a state of self-interest (Williamson 1975). Opportunistic behavior may exist within an industry in the absence of industry norms that provide a standard of conduct for doing business. Further, in Hungary, trading interdependencies under the old system may have constrained opportunism; with increased trading opportunities, retailers will be less certain that their supply partners will not behave opportunistically. Personal relationships can provide a foundation for trust and have been used to pre-qualify business partners (Doney and Cannon 1997) and to reduce subsequent monitoring (Stump and Heide 1996). We suggest that the role of embeddedness as a governance structure is enhanced in an environment where industry opportunism is perceived as high. When many other actors are behaving opportunistically, strong social ties are cultivated to protect oneself from opportunistic others as well as provide resources and stability.

The business climate in Hungary seems appropriate to test the role of embeddedness as a governance structure in an opportunistic environment as we heard many complaints from retailers about the general "lack of trading morals" in the supply sector. One reason given for this was that the government does not license traders (wholesalers); thus, the presence or absence of industry norms may reflect, in part, the level of development of the legal system (Axelrod 1984; Macauley 1963). Further, an influx of foreign traders may have disrupted prior trading relationships and contributed to the overall confusion and disagreement on industry rules of conduct (Dahab, Gentry and Sohi 1996).

We would expect opportunism to moderate the relationship between embeddedness and access to resources and supply stability as follows:

> H5: An increase in industry opportunism enhances the strength of the positive relationship between embeddedness and supply stability.
>
> H6: An increase in industry opportunism enhances the strength of the positive relationship between embeddedness and access to resources.

Environmental Uncertainty

Uncertainty in the channel environment reduces the ability to predict the behaviors of channel partners (Williamson 1975) and makes it difficult to use markets or contracts to govern all possible occurrences (Noordewier, John and Nevin 1990). Empirically, more flexible, bilateral decision-making processes led to higher performance in a study of industrial markets (Noordewier, John and Nevin 1990). Further, the normative kinds of contracting behaviors one associates with embeddedness may be more important in an uncertain environment (Lusch and Brown 1997). Uzzi's (1997) work also suggests that managers use embeddedness to reduce uncertainty such as when mechanisms that provide market price information are weak, when product development risk is high and when the market is highly competitive or turbulent. The measure of *environmental uncertainty* was adapted from Achrol and Stern (1988) and Noordewier, John and Nevin (1990).

> H7: An increase in the degree of environmental uncertainty enhances the strength of the positive relationship between relational embeddedness and supply stability.

H8: An increase in the degree of environmental uncertainty enhances the strength of the positive relationship between relational embeddedness and access to resources.

Expected Changes Over Time

Given the rationale provided earlier and the current stage in Hungary's transition, we would expect that the relative strength of its economy (compared to its Central European counterparts) would result in movement towards Western channel practices and norms. These would include greater institutional trust, reduced industry opportunism, reduced environmental uncertainty, lower levels of embeddedness, improved supplier stability and improved access to resources. As will be discussed below, the 1997 sample involved a different mix of retailers (far more urban, far fewer rural stores), presenting a second explanation for expected changes in the constructs. Given the more collective nature of the rural environments, we expect that the different sample composition would yield much lower levels of embeddedness in the 1997 data given the weaker ties to be found in more individualistic, urban environments.

Importance of the Brand

An unanticipated finding in the 1995 study was that the importance of the brand to the retailer was associated with superior supplier performance. Further, the importance of the brand was not related to access to resources, suggesting that the value of the brand is not in the additional resources that might be provided by suppliers of strong manufacturers' brands. We suggest that brands in Hungary, particularly European and global brands, play an institutional role within the channel. Suppliers of well-known, major brands are attractive to retailers in two ways. First, the brand signals that the supplier is trustworthy and serves as a guarantee of performance. This is particularly useful in an environment where the choice of trading partners is expanding rapidly, where the supply sector has a history of opportunistic behavior and new entrants may be suspect and where business associations are struggling to deal with the lack of regulation of "traders." Further, retailers do not have the time nor the resources to verify the identity and integrity of individual supply partners.

Second, the brand provides a source of retail differentiation. Initially in Hungary, companies such as Levi Strauss invested heavily in developing their own stores and building distribution channels that delivered goods promptly to company-owned stores where their retail image associated with the brand name could be protected. This was a resource decision that represented a trade-off with developing consumer demand. Now, carrying manufacturers' brands gives retailers a distinct image that differentiates them from the competition in a highly competitive environment. This suggests a strategy that is in contrast to the decreased investment in manufacturers' brands in the United States. We expect brands to still be related to supplier stability in 1997 and not to access to resources as it is the brand itself and not the resources behind the brand that has value. Similarly we expect to find low levels of supplier support for promotion, in-store displays, credit and other supplier assistances for the same reason. We also expect global brands to be perceived as more important to retail sales than Hungarian brands.

METHODOLOGY

Measure Development

Wherever possible, we incorporated existing multi-item measures from prior channel research making minor modifications for the Hungarian context. For some constructs, new multi-item scales were developed. For example, *Access to resources* was developed by first identifying through personal interviews the kinds of resources that are valued by Hungarian retailers. Items were developed first in English, then translated into Hungarian by a professional translator in Budapest. The items were then back-translated into English by another Hungarian national.

Sample and Data Collection

Data were collected from retailers in 1995 and 1997. Our methodology in 1995 is described in Dahab, Gentry and Sohi (1996). In 1997, a drop-off, self-administered survey methodology was used to reach retailers across product industries. We drew 25 percent of the sample from a list of members of the Hungarian Retailers' Association provided by the Association President. We had hoped for a larger sample from this source; however, the Association President controlled the selection method and the number of names provided. (We have heard from other industry sources that Hungarian managers are often reluctant to provide or use names of members or customers for any purpose, including direct mail, even when it will benefit the Association or company. One of the underlying issues in these examples may be the deliberate accumulation of social capital by controlling access to resources.) Seventy-five percent of the sample came from a purchased database of companies registered to do business in Hungary. We selected from the database only those firms engaged in retailing.

The interviewers were students trained by faculty at Budapest University of Economic Sciences. They were instructed to make a personal visit to the store, ask for the person who is responsible for purchasing supplies and obtain that person's commitment to complete a survey. They left a survey with verbal and written instructions for completion and returned at a prescribed time to pick up the completed questionnaire. If the store on the list was no longer at the indicated address, the interviewer substituted the store occupying the location. If the location was not a retailer, the interviewer selected the retailer geographically closest to the original address. Interviewers contacted 345 stores; 65 refused to participate and 162 completed surveys were collected. The response rate was 64 percent.

Table 1 provides characteristics of the 1997 sample compared to the sample from the 1995 study. Rural retailers dominated the 1995 sample (142 rural versus 17 urban), while the 1997 sample was predominantly urban (127 urban versus 35 rural ones). In 1997, respondents from outside Budapest came from Veszprem, Varpalota, Szombathely, Szekesfehervar and Ajka. The respondents represent a variety of retail product lines, which was our intent; many reported merchandise mixes from several product areas, which precluded subsequent analysis by industry. The mail survey in the 1995 study yielded a response rate under 10 percent limiting its representativeness. The 1997 survey used more costly procedures to contact retailers, yielding a

Table 1. Comparison of 1997 and 1995 Samples by Product Line, Size, Geographic Location and Length of Relationship

Types of Products	Percent of Retailers Who Reported Carrying the Product in Their Store (a)	
	1995 N = 141	1997 N = 163
Food	33	26
Housewares	17	11
Clothing	24	32
Health and beauty	20	14
Electronics	14	6
Books, stationery	14	23
Furniture	10	4
Large home appliances	16	4
Hardware	15	7
Pharmaceuticals	3	NA
Other	21	33
Number of employees	Percent of Total Respondents (b)	
Ten or fewer	76	
More than ten	24	78
		22
Geographic location	Respondent Percentage	
Budapest	11	
Other city, village	89	78
		21
Length of relationship	Mean/Standard Deviation	
Business	5.7 (6.5)	5.0 (4.8)
Personal	6.1 (6.5)	3.8 (5.6)

much higher response rate while at the same time limiting the geographical scope due to cost concerns.

Respondents were asked to identify either a major or a non-major supplier as the subject for the queries in the survey (we used a split sample to control for this characteristic). Table 2 shows that of the suppliers identified by respondents, 55 percent were wholesalers, 37 percent were manufacturers, 3 percent were cash-and-carry warehouses and 5 percent represented other types of supplier organizations.

Analysis Section

The first stage of the analysis was to investigate the reliability and unidimensionality of the constructs. The reliabilities for all measures meet Nunnally's standards.

The factor structures of the measures were very consistent between the two data sets, with much similarity in the patterns of loadings observed (the factor structures are not reported here due to space constraints, but they are available from the authors). One change in the structure of the constructs was observed in Access to Resources, where access to credit loaded with the supplier providing information and other sup-

Table 2. Suppliers by Type—1997

Type of Supplier	Percentage of Respondents	
Cash-and-carry warehouse	3	
Manufacturer	37	
Wholesaler	55	
Other	5	
	Manufacturers (Number)	Wholesalers (Number)
Foreign ownership	11	8

port in 1995 but loaded on a separate factor in 1997. It may be that the nature of valued resources has changed over time, or that access to credit is a different phenomenon in Budapest than it is in the outlying areas of the country. (Mean values in 1995 were: urban 2.5, rural 2.7; in 1997: urban 3.1, rural 2.8.). In 1997, we also added two items to the access to resources scale relating to access to exclusive information for decision-making and to information about special offers before other retailers. These behaviors emerged from our preliminary interviews as being important in the 1997 retail environment. Further, we had expected the nature of valued resources to change over time with changes in the external environment.

The means and standard deviations of the measures are reported in Table 3. The small urban sample size in 1995 and small rural sample size in 1997 make tests of mean differences problematic. However, the overriding result is the consistency between the 1995 and 1997 results, despite the varying geographical sources of the data and the changing economic conditions. The key construct, Embeddedness, showed very similar levels over time and across geographical areas. Rather than diminishing over time as expected, the mean values increased (though not significantly).

Surprisingly, environmental uncertainty increased over time periods, while opportunism decreased and institutional trust increased. The latter two findings are consistent with our observation that Hungary is adjusting well to the market economy. At the same time, there appears to be growing apprehension about the levels of risk required on the part of retailers, possibly due to the acknowledgement that the government was playing less of a role in retail transactions. Alternatively, the high levels of environmental uncertainty may be related to decreasing perceptions of supplier stability from 1995 to 1997.

Overall, the key finding in the comparison of the two samples is the amount of consistency over time in terms of the emic meanings of the constructs (as noted by the factor structures) and in the means of the constructs themselves. The exception is in Access to Resources where apparent urban/rural differences have disappeared in the last two years.

Tests of the Role of Embeddedness and Moderating Effects

We used regression analysis to test the hypotheses. Table 4 reports the results. We include the results of the 1995 study for comparison purposes. A detailed discussion of those results appears in Dahab, Sohi and Gentry (1998). Hypothesis 1 was supported as there was a positive relationship between embeddedness and supply stability

Table 3. Comparison of Embeddedness-Related Constructs in Hungary Over Time

	1995				1997			
	Urban n = 17		Rural n = 142		Urban n = 127		Rural n = 35	
Construct	Mean	SD	Mean	SD	Mean	SD	Mean	SD
Embeddedness	3.3	.54	3.4	.52	3.4	.56	3.4	.49
Tie Strength	2.7	.68	3.1	.81	3.0	.88	3.1	.74
Fairness	3.8	.61	3.8	.56	3.0	.63	3.8	.62
Communications Density	3.2	.58	3.4	.65	3.4	.87	3.3	.72
Environmental Uncertainty	2.6	.86	2.7	.74	3.3	.67	3.2	.66
Opportunism	3.1	.52	2.8	.84	2.5	.87	2.4	.90
Institutional Trust	1.8	.67	2.1	.81	2.5	.87	2.4	.93
Access to Resources	2.3	.89	3.8	.56	2.7	1.03	2.7	.79
Supplier Stability	4.5	.47	4.3	.71	4.2	.60	3.9	.76

Table 4. Regression Results
Standardized Estimates with t-Values in Parentheses

	Supply Stability		Access to Resources	
	1995	1997	1995	1997
Main Effects				
Embeddedness	.15 (2.04)[b]	.20 (2.36)[c]	.42 (5.12)[c]	.38 (4.49)[c]
Institutional Trust	.10 (1.58)[b]	.01 (.16)	.02 (.29)	.18 (2.20)[b]
Opportunism	–.29 (–4.04)[c]	–.20 (–2.59)[c]	.15 (1.88)[b]	.08 (.98)
Environmental Uncertainty	–.16 (–2.28)[b]	.06 (.75)	.00 (.02)	–.08 (–1.05)
Brand	.22 (2.94)[c]	.23 (2.88)[c]	–.02 (–.21)	.08 (.96)
Interaction Effects				
Embeddedness × Institutional Trust	–.08 (–1.14)	.03 (.35)	.03 (.42)	–.00 (–.08)
Embeddedness × Opportunism	.20 (2.82)[c]	.02 (.31)	–.10 (–1.33)[a]	–.06 (–.72)
Embeddedness × Environmental Uncertainty	–.11 (1.63)[b]	.15 (1.90)[b]	–.10 (–1.43)[a]	–.13 (–1.60)[a]
Full model R^2	.33	.23	.20	.19
F – Ratio	8.76	5.02	4.62	3.97

[a]$p < .10$
[b]$p < 0.05$
[c]$p < 0.01$
(One-tailed tests)

($\beta = .20$, $t = 2.3$, $p < .01$). Hypothesis 2 was also supported; the more "embedded" the relationship with the supplier, the greater access to resources ($\beta = .38$, $t = 4.5$, $p < .01$). These results were consistent over the two studies.

Hypotheses 3 and 4 address the moderating role of institutional trust on the outcome variables. The results show a lack of support for both hypotheses, showing no changes from the 1995 study (For stability: $\beta = .03$, $t = .35$, $p = .36$; For access: $\beta = -.01$, $t = -.08$, $p = .46$). Hypotheses 5 and 6 suggest that at high levels of industry opportunism the relationship between embeddedness and the outcomes will be enhanced. Neither hypothesis was supported (For stability: $\beta = .02$, $t = .31$, $p = .38$; For access: $\beta = -.07$, $t = -.08$, $p = .46$). This is in contrast to the finding in 1995 that when the industry is perceived as opportunistic, embeddedness *enhances* supplier stability and *reduces* access to resources. Hypotheses 7 and 8 suggest that when environmental uncertainty is high, embeddedness will enhance supplier stability and access to resources. Both of these moderating effects were significant, however for access to resources the effect was in the opposite direction (For stability: $\beta = .15$, $t = 1.90$, $p < .03$; For access: $\beta = -.13$, $t = -1.60$, $p < .06$).

Several unhypothesized direct effects were also significant. Greater institutional trust provided enhanced access to resources ($\beta = .18$, $t = 2.20$, $p < .01$). Importance of the brand to the retailer was again associated with greater stability ($\beta = .23$, $t = 2.89$, $p < .01$) but not access to resources ($\beta = .08$, $t = .96$, $p = .17$).

FINDINGS AND CONCLUSIONS

We tested a model of factors hypothesized to provide stability in supplier performance and access to resources, and compared our results to a similar study conducted in 1995. We found that embeddedness, our key construct, has remained important over time in Hungarian retailer-supplier relationships. Being embedded with a supplier provides stability and access to resources, although the types of resources have changed. In 1997, we found that access to exclusive information was important; access to credit in Hungary is still difficult to arrange. Only 6 percent of all respondents said that they get credit from their supplier.

We also found that the uncertain environment moderates the role of embeddedness although the direction of the effects is different for each outcome variable. Uncertainty enhances the effects of embeddedness on supplier stability but offsets the effects of embeddedness on access to resources. While social capital encourages suppliers to perform and may discourage opportunism, as the environment becomes more uncertain because of the number of players and uncertainties in demand, it becomes more difficult to provide access to information and other resources even when one has social capital. Opportunism is decreasing and institutional trust is increasing even at a time when the market is seen as increasingly uncertain.

For multinational corporations (MNCs) that have been disappointed with prior distribution decisions in Hungary, this may mean that investing time in cultivating relationships within supply channels, including relationships with suppliers who are themselves "well-connected," might bring long as well as short-term benefits. This may be at odds with an environment that appears to be increasingly transaction oriented as supply choices multiply. For example, we found that retailers were very reluctant to form exclusive distribution arrangements with suppliers given the high level of uncertainty in the marketplace. This reluctance to form long-term relationships is supported in part by the price sensitivity of the retailers in our sample. However, given the importance of relationships in providing tangible returns, arms-length trading may not be the best approach.

In addition to highlighting the managerial importance of developing interpersonal relationships, our research suggests that manufacturers' brands not only differentiate the retail outlet, but provide brand equity within the channel. Further, regional or global brands have better reputations with retailers based on the performance of the channel. This gives MNCs a clear advantage over local brands in establishing reliable channels of distribution.

Acknowledgements

We would like to thank our colleagues at the Budapest University of Economic Sciences for their assistance and support on this project. Dr. András Bauer and Zsófia Kenesei were instrumental in the project conceptualization and design, conducting preliminary interviews, reviewing the translation, and in training the interviewers. Erzsebet Malota translated the survey instrument and managed all phases of the data collection. We also thank Dr. Ravipreet Sohi for his insights and participation during phases of this project and the William Davidson Institute for their funding.

References

Achrol, Ravi and Louis Stern. "Environmental Determinants of Decision Making Uncertainty in Marketing Channels." *Journal of Marketing Research* 25, no. 1 (February 1988): 36–50.

Axelrod, Robert. *The Evolution of Cooperation.* New York: Basic Books, 1984.

Borner, Silvio, Aymo Brunetti and Beatrice Weder. *Political Credibility and Economic Development.* London: St. Martin's Press, 1995.

Dahab, Debra J., András Bauer, Zsófia Kenesei and James W. Gentry. "Relational Embeddedness in Retailer-Supplier Transactions in Hungary." In *Proceedings of the European Marketing Academy*, 1585–1594. Budapest: European Marketing Academy, 1996.

Dahab, Debra J., James W. Gentry and Ravipreet Sohi. "Interest Domination as a Framework for Exploring Channel Changes in Transforming Economies." *Journal of Macromarketing* 16, no. 2 (Fall 1996): 8–23.

_____. "Measuring the Nature of Retailer-Supplier Embeddedness: Differences in Meaning Across Cultures." In *Proceedings of the American Marketing Association Summer Educator's Conference*, 83–89. Chicago: American Marketing Association, 1997.

Dahab, Debra J., Ravipreet Sohi and James W. Gentry. " Embeddedness in Retailer-Supplier Transactions: An Empirical Test in the United States and Hungary." Department of Marketing Working Paper. Lincoln: University of Nebraska, 1998.

Doney, Patricia M. and Joseph P. Cannon. "An Examination of the Nature of Trust in Buyer-Seller Relationships." *Journal of Marketing* 61, no. 2 (April 1997): 35–51.

Frenzen, Jonathan K. and Harry L. Davis. "Purchasing Behavior in Embedded Markets." *Journal of Consumer Research* 17, no. 1 (June 1990): 1–12.

Frenzen, Jonathan K. and Kent Nakamoto. "Structure, Cooperation, and Flow of Market Information." *Journal of Consumer Research* 20, no. 3 (December 1993): 360–375.

Granovetter, Mark. "The Strength of Weak Ties." *American Journal of Sociology* 78, no. 6 (May 1973): 1360–1380.

_____. "Economic Action and Social Structure: The Problem of Embeddedness." *American Journal of Sociology* 91, no. 3 (November 1985): 481–510.

_____. "Problems of Explanation in Economic Sociology." In *Networks and Organizations: Structure, Form, and Action*, edited by Nitin Nohria and Robert G. Eccles, 25–56. Boston: Harvard Business School Press, 1992.

Kim, John, David Reid, Richard E. Plank and Robert Dahlstrom. "The Role of Brand Equity in Business Markets: A Model, Research Propositions, and Managerial Implications." In *Proceedings of the American Marketing Association Educators Conference*. Washington, DC: American Marketing Association, 1995.

Larson, Andrea. "Network Dyads in Entrepreneurial Settings: A Study of the Governance of Exchange Networks." *Administrative Science Quarterly* 37, no. 1 (March 1992): 76–104.

Lusch, Robert and James Brown. " Interdependency, Contracting, and Relational Behavior in Marketing Channels." *Journal of Marketing* 60, no. 4 (October 1997): 19–38.

Macaulay, Stewart. "Non-Contractual Relations in Business." *American Sociological Review* 28, no. 1 (February 1963): 55–70.

Marsden, Peter V. and Karen Campbell. "Measuring Tie Strength." *Social Forces* 63, no. 2 (1984): 483–501.

McAllister, Daniel J. "Affect- and Cognition-Based Trust as Foundations for Interpersonal Cooperation in Organizations." *Academy of Management Journal* 38, no. 1 (February 1995): 24–59.

Murry, John P. and Jan B. Heide. "Managing Promotion Program Participation Within Manufacturer-Retailer Relationships." *Journal of Marketing* 62, no. 1 (January 1998): 58–68.

Noordewier, Thomas G., George John and John R. Nevin. "Performance Outcomes of Purchasing Arrangement in Industrial Buyer-Vendor Relationships." *Journal of Marketing* 54, no. 4 (October 1990): 80–94.

Nunnally, Jum C. *Psychometric Theory*. 2d ed. New York: McGraw-Hill, 1978.

Rona-Tás, Ákos. "The Selected and the Elected: The Making of the New Parliamentary Elite in Hungary." *East European Politics and Societies* 5 (Fall 1991): 357–393.

_____. "The First Shall Be Last? Entrepreneurship and Communist Cadres in the Transition from Socialism." *American Journal of Sociology* 100, no. 1 (July 1994): 40–69.

Seabright, Mark A., Daniel A. Levinthal and Mark Fichman. "Role of Individual Attachments in the Dissolution of Interorganizational Relationships." *Academy of Management Journal* 35, no. 1 (March 1992): 122–160.

Stark, David. "The Great Transformation? Social Changes in Eastern Europe." *Contemporary Sociology* 21, no. 3 (May 1992): 299–304.

Stump, Rodney L. and Jan B. Heide. "Controlling Supplier Opportunism in Industrial Relationships." *Journal of Marketing Research* 33, no. 4 (November 1996): 431–441.

Thaler, Richard. "Mental Accounting and Consumer Choice." *Marketing Science* 4, no. 3 (Summer 1985): 199–214.

Uzzi, Brian. "Social Structure and Competition in Interfirm Networks: The Paradox of Embeddedness." *Administrative Science Quarterly* 42, no. 1 (March 1997): 35–67.

Weigand, Bruce. "Black Money in Belize—The Ethnicity and Social Structure of Black Market Crime." *Social Forces* 73 (September 1994): 135–154.

Williamson, Oliver E. *Markets and Hierarchies: Analysis and Antitrust Implications*. New York: The Free Press, 1975.

_____. *The Economic Institutions of Capitalism*. New York: The Free Press, 1985.

Zucker, Lynne G. "Production of Trust: Institutional Sources of Economic Structure 1840–1920." *Research in Organizational Behavior* 8 (1986): 53–11.

11 PRODUCT DISTRIBUTION CHOICES IN CHINA: A TRANSACTION COST PERSPECTIVE

Louisa Ha
The Gallup Organization
Mrinal Ghosh
University of Michigan
Rajeev Batra
University of Michigan
Jie Hai Zhang
Shanghai Academy of Social Sciences

Introduction

The emergence of transitional economies (TEs) poses a great challenge to marketing scholars and practitioners alike. China provides a good illustration of the unique problems encountered in TEs. From 1991 to 1994 it boasted an average annual economic growth rate of 11.7 percent (Luk, Xu and Ye 1998) and an annual income growth rate of about 10 percent (Batra 1997). Reforms have dramatically altered the structure of its distribution system from a centralized, state-owned system where prices were fixed and retailers had to purchase their "quota" only from particular wholesalers, to a partially decentralized state and privately-owned system where parties are free to choose their own vendors and retailers. This rapid growth and enormous potential accompanied by reforms have made China an attractive market for foreign investors. For example, in 1993, foreign direct investments in Mainland China amounted to US$26 billion (Tseng, Kwan and Cheung 1995).

Yet, such ventures have been fraught with immense difficulties. Manufacturers routinely complain that *the* major impediment to effective marketing in China is its complex, inefficient and poor infrastructure in distribution. Critical problematic areas include lack of adequate and timely (a) logistics and transportation facilities; (b) market research information; (c) proper financial institutions and; (d) legal infrastructure, to support exchanges. Marketing managers hence experience difficulty in choosing and organizing effective channel structures for their products.

In spite of the vital role played by the channels of distribution in the long-term success of a company's venture into China, research in the area has been scant. Existing studies (e.g., Tseng, Kwan and Cheung 1995; Luk, Xu and Ye 1998) document the development of post-reform distribution systems in China but do not provide a generalized conceptual framework to address the issues faced by managers. Other studies (e.g., Pan 1996) focus exclusively on market entry-level decisions made by foreign companies in the manufacturing sector (e.g., the level of equity participation in joint ventures) but not in the distribution sector. Furthermore, no study has focused on the different set of problems faced by domestic companies as compared to foreign manufacturers.

The purpose of this study is to provide a framework that would enable us to explain some of the strategies used by domestic and foreign manufacturers in their attempt to overcome the barriers encountered in distribution. We draw not only on existing research on transitional economies (e.g., Batra 1997) but also on transaction cost analysis (e.g., Klein 1991) to gain some preliminary understanding of the issues involved *and* actions undertaken by domestic and foreign manufacturers in China. We then present our analysis based on in-depth interviews of marketing managers from 18 companies in China.

LITERATURE REVIEW

The choice and implementation of an appropriate distribution structure is critical for the long-term success of a company, especially so because distribution decisions happen to be "sticky." Such decisions are relatively easy to make when the economic, social and legal environments are stable. Unfortunately, this is not the case in TEs like China, where presently both domestic and foreign marketers are confronted with a near-absence of distribution channels (Batra 1997). The pre-reform, predominantly state-owned distribution network, where decisions like wholesale price and "quota" were made centrally, has been replaced in the post-reform era by a partially decentralized network, where channel members are free to choose their own suppliers, set their own prices within a certain range and generate their own operating funds. Yet, this abandonment of the state-owned network has not been completely compensated by the rise in private-sector enterprises. One probable reason could be that the implications of converting to a market economy have not been well understood by policy makers, manufacturers and distribution channel members alike.

For instance, it is imperative that the move towards a decentralized economy be supported by a concurrent change in the institutional environment of contract law and legal enforceability (North 1990; Williamson 1996). In the absence of appropriate informal social norms of exchange, legal uncertainty leads to a lower level of trust and commitment between manufacturers and their channel partners because of the lack of a robust judicial system in case of disputes. On a similar note, a distribution system will not become effective just because of the transfer of appropriate technology from multinational corporations (MNCs). To be successful, channel members will not only have to adopt Western business practices (Mueller and Baron 1994) but also have to understand the mechanics of working proactively and cooperatively with each other in terms of gathering and disseminating information and implementing marketing actions based on the information. Yet, it is hard to change the customs and value system instilled under the communist regime (Savitt 1994). Batra (1997) rightly points out that, given the state of transition in China, companies should be very cautious while making channel structure decisions because these structures are difficult to change and a wrong decision may lead to adverse consequences (Klein 1991).

The dominant paradigm for analyzing channel structure issues has been the transaction cost analysis (TCA) framework as developed by Williamson (1985) and elaborated on by subsequent scholars (e.g., Anderson and Coughlan 1987). The framework argues that governance structures are designed to minimize the sum of production and transaction costs. Transaction costs are the costs of organizing and managing transactions, and include not only the direct costs of negotiating and monitoring contracts but also the opportunity costs of foregone transactions. These costs become critical determinants of channel design under conditions of bounded rationality and contractual incompleteness, where parties are vulnerable to opportunistic expropriation by their exchange partners. Hence, TCA would suggest that if the monitoring and enforcement costs of distribution are high, then even if the out-of-pocket costs of using independent distributors are low, manufacturers should opt to internalize the distribution operation (Anderson and Coughlan 1987). This framework has also been applied to many important channel issues like incentive design for channel participation and use of qualification systems for selecting an appropriate channel partner.

It should be noted here that different features of the same transaction or transactional environment might have contrasting influences on the choice of appropriate governance structures. Consider the following illustration. It has been well documented that TEs not only have very uncertain legal environments to support transaction-specific investments but companies operating in TEs also possess scarce information about their customer needs and lack accurate market forecasts (Batra 1997). The former problem dictates internalizing the distribution function to protect oneself from contractual hazards but the latter problem dictates use of cooperative arrangements with independent channel partners to seek valuable information. Understandably, mitigating one important problem exacerbates another. Under such circumstances, parties might opt for a basic structure that alleviates the most important problem, as per their perception, and then look for additional mechanisms to overcome the disadvantage generated in other problems. This form of "tiered" decision making is, in principle, analogous to Williamson's idea of first-order and second-order economizing.

As we subsequently show, many manufacturers in China, both domestic and foreign, seem to be making such "tiered" decisions to overcome certain problems. The four-channel structure decisions we document are: use of "internal" versus "external" sources, use of incentives, use of appropriate contractual structures and use of qualification criteria by the manufacturers. For each decision we will try to hypothesize the conditions in China that influence these decisions and then look at evidence for the proposed directional effects from our data.

PERTINENT ISSUES AND TENTATIVE PROPOSITIONS

Issue 1: Should the Distribution Function be Internalized?

This is arguably the most important decision facing marketing managers in China. In TCA jargon, this is the classic "make" versus "buy" problem where use of the company's own agents constitutes the 'make' option and use of independent channel intermediaries constitutes the 'buy' option. This decision can be looked at from both the production costs as well as transacticn costs' perspectives.

Volume of sales should be a key determinant of the channel integration decision. The greater the volume of sales, the greater the potential to exploit the advantages derived from economies of scale and internal specialization (Klein 1991). This influence of channel volume has received empirical support in international markets (e.g., Klein, Frazier and Roth 1990) and we can expect it to hold in China. Hence:

> P1: *The higher the volume of sales, the more likely a manufacturer is to use its own salesforce.*

Another important determinant of the channel integration decision would be the level of expertise and knowledge a particular company has in operating in China. Companies having little prior experience will not possess adequate local market information to make appropriate marketing decisions. These companies are more likely to lack relevant information about the legal restrictions imposed by the central government and the regional provinces. They are also less likely to possess knowledge about specific relationship building, or "guanxi" features. Hence, we can expect that companies with less operating experience in China might try to overcome these disadvantages not by setting up their own in-house distribution but by allying themselves with independent channel intermediaries. Hence:

> P2: *The lower the operational experience in China, the less likely a manufacturer is to use its own salesforce.*

Issue 2: Should the market research function be internalized?

Securing information about customer needs and preferences and obtaining accurate sales forecasts is important for undertaking appropriate marketing actions. Many MNCs have traditionally made decisions using market research data and realize the critical importance of such data. Furthermore, as they might not have an adequate understanding of the Chinese market, they are more likely to consider such information crucial to their success than domestic companies. In contrast, domestic Chinese companies, having operated under a 'command' regime, would have been less likely to find market information of much importance for their success. MNCs should therefore seek market research information more than domestic companies. In acquiring such information, however, they are likely to want to collect it themselves, partly because domestic market research companies do not have the relevant expertise and skills, and partly because the MNCs already have in-house market research departments to service these needs. Hence MNCs are likely to seek more control over their market research activities. Therefore we propose that:

P3: *MNCs are more likely to conduct their own market research than domestic manufacturers in China.*

For which activities should incentives be provided to the intermediaries?

Even though we claim that MNCs might value market research information more than domestic companies, it does not mean that domestic companies in China consider market research to be of no value. Rather, we would expect that domestic companies would organize this activity commensurate with the lower level of importance they place on market research. Hence, instead of incurring additional transaction costs by internalizing the activity, domestic companies would provide incentives to (or penalize) their distributors for providing (not providing) information about customer needs and sales forecasts. Therefore:

P4: *Domestic manufacturers in China are more likely than MNCs to provide incentives to, or impose penalties on, their distributors for (a) providing customer information and (b) providing accurate sales forecasts.*

Issue 3: What Are the Appropriate Contractual Structures?

Many scholars contend that the essential premise of TCA can also be used to look at intermediate forms of governance like the structure of implicit norms (e.g., Bradach and Eccles 1989) and explicit contracts (e.g., Joskow 1987) that exist between contracting parties. Structuring of contracts becomes vitally important in TEs like China where legal and financial uncertainty faced by manufacturers is immense. The legal uncertainty arises because the judicial system is not independent of the political system and hence is susceptible to be manipulated by opportunistic parties (Williamson 1996). The inability of the system to credibly commit "fair enforcement" leads to lower levels of trust and commitment between the manufacturers and their distributors. Long-term contracts, with their accompanying incompleteness and complexity, become relatively inefficient. Similarly, financial uncertainty is quite high because of high levels of inflation. Under such circumstances, manufacturers are vulnerable to being "locked-in" into providing long-term credit to their channel partners. Hence we would expect that:

P5: *Contracts between manufacturers and distributors in China would be of short duration.*

P6: *Manufacturers are more likely to use cash-in-advance payment terms than extending long-term credit to their channel partners in China.*

Issue 4: What Qualification Criteria to Use for Selecting Channel Partners?

As distribution decisions are "sticky," qualifying appropriate channel partners is crucial for manufacturers. Such qualification efforts serve the purpose of eliminating parties lacking in requisite skills and motivations for conducting the business, and hence the criteria for selecting distributors should be commensurate with the key benefits sought by manufacturers from their distributors. In our discussions, managers indicated that availability of financing, availability of technical information about the product and after-sales service were the most important features desired by their end-customers. Manufacturers therefore will have to undertake channel actions to provide these valuable services. Hence we would expect that while qualifying their distributors, manufacturers would be more likely to use the aforementioned attributes as criteria. Therefore:

> P7: *Manufacturers in China are more likely to use financial strength, product knowledge and ability to provide after-sales service as the key criteria for selecting distributors.*

RESEARCH SETTING

To gain some preliminary understanding of the strategies adopted by manufacturers, we conducted in-depth interviews with marketing managers of 18 manufacturing companies in Shanghai and Beijing in 1996. Of these 18 companies, nine were domestic companies, five were joint ventures between MNCs and Chinese domestic companies, and four were wholly-owned subsidiaries of MNCs. The MNC partners' country of origin for the five joint ventures were Japan (Koyo), Belgium (Eternit), The Netherlands (Philips), Finland (Nokia) and Hong Kong (Zhejiang NIC Daily Use Chemical Co). The country of origin for the four wholly-owned subsidiaries were the United States (Johnson and Johnson), South Korea (Samsung), The United Kingdom (Taikoo Sugar) and Hong Kong (Winifred International). We obtained information on the distribution practices for a total of 37 products (32 percent industrial, 49 percent consumer and 19 percent mixed). We selected companies with different countries of origin and product types to obtain a general picture of product distribution practices followed in China. The annual sales volumes of the companies ranged from US$35,000 to over US$125 million. Their time of operation in China ranged from 2 to 47 years. Almost 75 percent of the managers interviewed saw the market for their product categories to be highly competitive, with more than five competing brands.

RESULTS

Our propositions cannot be tested using rigorous statistical techniques because of the lack of a large and representative sample. Nonetheless, in the spirit of exploratory analysis, we attempt to discern some patterns in the data using techniques like percentages and cross-tabulations.

Our observations support Proposition 1. We find that companies having higher sales volume in China generally use their own salesforce and companies having lower sales volumes generally used independent channel intermediaries. Consistent with government regulation, we also found that companies integrated only the first level of distribution. The wholesale and retail sectors were completely independent. Incidentally, all the companies using their own salesforce marketed consumer products. We also find support for Proposition 2 and observe a polarized trend between companies with greater and lesser experience in China. Companies with more experience seemed to use their own salesforce. In contrast, newer companies seemed to use a more diversi-

Table 1. Distributor Selection Criteria

Criterion	Percentage of Responses
Financial background	65%
Reputation	50%
Product knowledge	47%
Size of salesforce	30%
Support systems	24%
Aggressiveness	24%
Trade connections	18%
Delivery service	12%
Location of distributor	12%

fied portfolio of distributors. Many of them supplemented their own salesforce with independent distributors and still others completely outsourced the distribution function.

Our observations provide support for Proposition 3. MNCs are more likely to conduct their own market research. They did not seem to value the skills of their distributors in providing information about both customer needs and sales forecasts. MNCs also claimed to be more knowledgeable about their end-customers than the Chinese domestic companies. Proposition 4 finds partial support in the data. There seems to be no difference between MNCs and domestic companies in their proclivity towards offering incentives for securing customer information. About 25 percent of both MNCs and domestic companies provided incentives to distributors for providing customer market information. On the other hand, we find that domestic companies are more likely to provide incentives to (or levy penalties on) their distributors for providing accurate (inaccurate) sales forecasts. About 43 percent of domestic companies offered such incentives compared to none of the MNCs.

The data provides general support for Proposition 5. All manufacturers had short-term contracts with their distributors. None of the 37 products in our sample had contract renewal terms longer than one year. Proposition 6 is also supported. Manufacturers seemed to avoid providing financial credit to their distributors. Forty-four percent of the manufacturers accepted only cash-in-advance of delivery. Only 25 percent of the companies provided credit to their distributors and these credit terms were provided only to state-owned distributors. Manufacturers were concerned about the ability of private distributors to pay back outstanding credit and hence offered them only cash-in-advance financial terms.

Table 1 shows that financial background was the most commonly mentioned criteria in selecting a distributor, followed by distributor reputation and product knowledge. In general, therefore, Proposition 7 is supported.

OTHER ANALYSIS

Apart from the core propositions, our interviews provided additional insights. One problem that managers consistently seemed to cite was the poor transportation infrastructure in China. Problems encountered included an inability to distribute goods according to schedule (33 percent), theft during transit (19 percent) and poor inventory management (12 percent). Managers have tried to tackle these problems by using

Table 2. Distributor Status by Type of Manufacturer

Distributor Status	Domestic Co.	Joint Venture	MNC Subsidiary
State-owned	45%	40%	0%
Mixed	27%	10%	43%
Private	27%	50%	57%

more diversified forms of transportation as well as using more diversified forms of communication with their distributors. Another problem that was brought to our notice was the residual effect of government control in the distribution sector. State-owned distributors still dominated the system and such distributors were not aggressive in pushing the sales of the manufacturers. To overcome these problems, newer companies (basically joint ventures and MNCs) diversified their portfolio by increasing the use of private distributors. Table 2 shows the pattern of distributor status by type of company.

Consistent with other market economies, the number of channel intermediaries used for consumer products (mean = 3.9 levels) was higher than for industrial products (mean = 2.5 levels). The profit margins for distributors of industrial products ranged from 7 percent to 35 percent compared to the range of 2 percent to 20 percent for distributors of consumer products. We also noticed that companies with less experience in China (JVs and MNCs) were more interested in the trade connections of the distributor than its financial background.

CONCLUSIONS AND FUTURE RESEARCH

This paper explored the perceived problems faced and prospective solutions designed by domestic and foreign manufacturers while distributing their products in China. Our preliminary analysis shows that managers demonstrate a discriminating ability to align various aspects of their distribution activities and that the governance structures put in place are consistent with the broad predictions of the transaction cost analysis framework. Our analysis suggests that companies with higher sales volume and more experience in China use their own salesforce instead of independent distributors. We also find that MNCs are more likely to internalize their market research activity whereas domestic companies are more likely to provide incentives to their distributors to provide relevant information. The duration of contracts is quite short and cash-in-advance is the most widely used payment term.

Our paper has numerous limitations. First, the lack of a sufficiently large sample size has prevented us from systematically looking at the joint influences of the core factors. Lack of adequate control over some of the variables could possibly confound our findings. Second, our data is at the firm level, which is not consistent with the TCA focus on a particular transaction. Third, we have ignored the influence that informal social norms and implicit contracts (Stinchcombe 1985), informal information exchanges (Johnson, Sakano and Onzo 1990) and power considerations (Lederhaus 1984; Lusch and Ross 1985) might have on the design of governance structures. We hope that future studies expressly look at some of these issues to provide an even better understanding of the issues involved while distributing products in China in particular and TEs in general.

References

Anderson, Erin and Anne T. Coughlan. "International Market Entry and Expansion via Independent or Integrated Channels of Distribution." *Journal of Marketing* 51, no. 1 (January 1987): 71–82.

Batra, Rajeev. "Marketing Issues and Challenges in Transitional Economies." *Journal of International Marketing* 5, no. 4 (1997): 95–114.

Bradach, Jeffrey L. and Robert G. Eccles. "Price, Authority, and Trust: From Ideal Types to Plural Forms." *Annual Review of Sociology* 15, no. 1 (1989): 97–118.

Johnson, Jean L., Tamoaki Sakano and Naoto Onzo. "Behavioral Relations in Across Culture Distribution Systems: Influence, Control and Conflict in U.S.-Japanese Marketing Channels." *Journal of International Business Studies* 21, no. 4 (Fourth Quarter 1990): 639–655.

Joskow, Paul L. "Contract Duration and Relationship-Specific Investments: Empirical Evidence from the Coal Market." *American Economic Review* 77, no. 1 (March 1987): 168–185.

Klein, Saul. "Selection of International Marketing Channels." *Journal of Global Marketing* 4, no. 4 (1991): 21–37.

Klein, Saul, Gary L. Frazier and Victor J. Roth. "A Transaction Cost Analysis Model of Channel Integration in International Markets." *Journal of Marketing Research* 27, no. 2 (May 1990): 196–208.

Lederhaus, Mary Ann. "Improving Marketing Channel Control Through Power and Exchange." *Journal of the Academy of Marketing Science* 12, no. 3 (Summer 1984): 18–34.

Luk, Sheriff T. K., Yin Zhou Xu and Wan Chun Ye. "Distribution: The Chinese Puzzle." *Long Range Planning* 31, no. 2 (April 1998): 295–307.

Lusch, Robert F. and Robert H. Ross. "The Nature of Power in a Marketing Channel." *Journal of the Academy of Marketing Science* 13, no. 3 (Summer 1985): 39–56.

Mueller, R. D. and P. J. Baron. "The Evolution of Distribution Systems: A Framework for Analyzing Market Changes in Eastern Europe: The Case of Hungary." *International Marketing Review* 10, no. 4 (1994): 52–56.

North, Douglass. *Institutions, Institutional Change, and Economic Performance*. Cambridge: Cambridge University Press, 1990.

Pan, Yigang. "Influences on Foreign Equity Ownership Level in Joint Ventures in China." *Journal of International Business Studies* 27, no. 1 (First Quarter 1996): 1–26.

Savitt, Ronald. "Comment: The Evolution of Distribution Systems." *International Marketing Review* 11, no. 2 (1994): 47–51.

Stinchcombe, Arthur L. "Contracts as Hierarchical Documents." In *Organization Theory and Project Management*, edited by Arthur L. Stinchcombe and Carol Heimer, 121–71. Oslo: Norwegian University Press, 1985.

Tseng, Choo-sin, Paula Kwan and Fanny Cheung. "Distribution in China: A Guide Through the Maze." *Long Range Planning* 28, no. 1 (February 1995): 81–91.

Williamson, Oliver E. *The Economic Institutions of Capitalism: Firms, Markets, and Relational Contracts*. New York: The Free Press, 1985.

_____. *The Mechanisms of Governance*. Oxford: Oxford University Press, 1996.

Strategy and Tactics

12 A COMPARATIVE STUDY OF DISTRIBUTION AND PROMOTION STRATEGIES USED BY MULTINATIONAL VERSUS LOCAL COMPANIES IN ROMANIA

Lalita A. Manrai
University of Delaware
Ajay K. Manrai
University of Delaware
Dana-Nicoleta Lascu
University of Richmond

Introduction

The fall of communism in Central and Eastern Europe in the late 1980s has opened a market of more than 200 million people who were deprived of most consumer goods and services for nearly half a century. Consequently, companies from around the world have rushed to these markets, making a presence in a variety of ways from mere exports to setting up large-scale manufacturing operations. Today the availability of goods and services in many of these former communist countries such as Poland, Hungary, Czech Republic and Romania has increased to such an extent that their marketplaces resemble that of Western European countries. Fashionable boutiques carrying internationally-known brands, such as Benetton, Gucci, Pierre Cardin, etc., are quite a familiar sight in downtown streets of Warsaw, Budapest, Prague and Bucharest (Brucan 1992). Many U.S.-based fast-food restaurants have set franchises in these countries that are doing flourishing business catering to the foreign tourists as well as the locals, who are eager to experience a piece of Western style living.

Parallel to this invasion of the Central and Eastern European marketplace by Western companies, local entrepreneurship has also developed tremendously in the last decade. However, most of these new enterprises are small in scale. For instance, in the retailing sector, many small "mom and pop" kinds of shops and kiosks have been set up in virtually every street corner and residential neighborhood (Lascu, Manrai and Manrai 1993). Shortly after the opening of the Romanian marketplace, as many as 20,000 street vendors appeared in the capital city of Bucharest alone.

For the Western marketer, therefore, the Eastern and Central European marketplace presents a multitude of challenges. First of all they have to deal with the challenges of the foreign environment as an outsider. Second, competition is ever evolving and there is very little, if any, understanding of the competitive dynamics in these transition economies. Further, each of these Central and Eastern European countries has its own path of evolution, depending upon its environment consisting of political, legal, cultural, economic, as well as geographical, and historical considerations. Past research (Lascu, Manrai and Manrai 1996; Manrai, Manrai and Lascu 1996) has clearly suggested that a regiocentric approach should not be used and international marketers need to look at each country in its own right in terms of the unique challenges of its marketplace.

Towards this end, the research reported in this chapter investigates the nature of competitive dynamics in the country of Romania. We present some preliminary findings from a field study of multinational (MNC) versus local companies in Romania. (Most of the multinationals studied were based in the United States.) The competitive strategy investigated in this research deals with certain distribution and promotion-related issues.

This chapter is divided into five sections. In the next section we briefly overview the market economy of Romania and identify distribution and promotion as the two areas (out of the four Ps of marketing) that have been relatively less understood. Section 3 of this chapter presents the research design, methodology and research questions related to the selected distribution and promotion related issues. Section 4 reports some findings on distribution and promotion strategies used by multinational versus local companies in Romania based on the responses to the questions. Finally, section 5 discusses the findings of the field study and future research directions are identified.

MARKETING CHALLENGES IN ROMANIA

Today products and services are available in abundance in Romania. Consumers are getting increasingly status-conscious (Lascu, Manrai and Manrai 1994) and are using products as a form of status and self-expression. Many of the local entrepreneurs are basically engaged in importing merchandise and reselling it and the proportion of products made in Romania is relatively limited (*The Economist* 1991). However, recent changes in policies, such as deregulation and liberalization of foreign trade, privatization of state enterprises and shift in the focus of production from industrial and agricultural goods to consumer goods (Hooley 1993; Wood and Darling 1993), have led to a substantial boost in the development of local enterprise. Many foreign companies have set up joint ventures in Romania with a substantial percentage of investment coming from foreign capital. These include Colgate Palmolive (USA), Shell (England), Alcatel (France), Siemens (Germany) and many others. Automobile manufacturers from around the world have also set up dealership and service operations in Romania.

While there is no dearth of goods and services in the Romanian marketplace, inflation has been exceptionally high. In the year 1990, prices increased by 220 percent, whereas wages increased by 160 percent. In the year 1992, unemployment increased at the rate of 13 percent and the GDP declined by 16 percent (Shafer and Ionescu 1993). Unable to adjust to these challenges of transition, many consumers wished for communist times to come back (Ger, Belk and Lascu 1993). In a recent study, Manrai, Manrai and Lascu (1998) report that this substantial decline in the affordability of goods has led to a perception of deterioration of their quality of life for Romanian consumers.

In such dynamic, yet unpredictable transition economies, the task of the marketer is indeed very demanding. A careful balancing of marketing mix elements is needed to articulate marketing strategies that effectively deliver value to customers. While there seems to be some understanding of the product and price components of the marketing mix strategy, the other two areas, i.e., place (distribution) and promotion, are relatively much less understood. It is with this objective that the research reported in this chapter focuses on investigating certain distribution and promotion-related issues in Romania.

Multinational and local companies are likely to differ in terms of their promotion and distribution strategies. This is expected because of the differences in company structure and objectives, size and resources of the company, etc. Specifically, because the scale of the multinationals is bigger, they are expected to be more aggressive than their local counterparts. Next we present an overview of the field study investigating selected distribution and promotion-related strategies used by multinational versus local companies in Romania.

FIELD STUDY

Design

The preliminary findings presented in this chapter are part of a large-scale, comprehensive field study currently in progress in Poland and Romania on the topic of competitive marketing strategies used by multinationals versus local (Polish and Romanian) companies. The comprehensive field study will investigate several different aspects of competitive marketing strategy in Poland and Romania. However, the findings presented in this chapter provide a comparison of multinationals versus local Romanian companies in terms of various strategic issues related to two out of the four Ps of marketing, i.e., distribution and promotion of products in Romania. Further, our research design for the comprehensive study includes six different categories of products, i.e., consumer nondurables, consumer durables, industrial products—capital equipment, industrial products—supplies/intermediaries, consumer services and industrial/business services. We intend to examine the differences across these six product categories. However, considering the limited data collected so far, the six categories are regrouped into two and comparisons are drawn for consumer products (durables and nondurables) and consumer services versus industrial products (capital equipment and supplies/intermediaries) and industrial/business services.

Methodology and Research Questions

The data was collected using a field survey methodology. Company representatives in all six product categories were contacted and the surveys were completed mostly using a drop-pick methodology. This implied that the field surveyors first contacted the company representatives, explained the research study to them, sought their agreement for participation and left the questionnaires with the company representatives. The field surveyors then went back and picked up the completed surveys either after a couple of hours the same day, or within a day or two, as was agreed. In some cases, a third or fourth visit was necessary because either the respondents were not able to complete the surveys or they had additional questions.

A list of selected questions relating to a variety of distribution and promotion-related issues are given in Table 1 and Table 2, respectively. These questions were developed based on a review of past literature.

FINDINGS

Results For Distribution-Related Questions

Four categories of company-product combinations were compared using F statistics and corresponding p-values. These four combinations included multinationals—consumer goods and services, multinationals—industrial goods and services, Romanian

Table 1. Distribution-Related Questions

D1. Does your company employ its own sales force?

1 _____ Yes 2 _____ No

If YES, what activities does the sales force undertake? (Circle AS MANY AS APPLY)

1 Negotiate terms of sales with customers
2 Developing new customers
3 Trouble shooting and helping customers with complaints and difficulties
4 Information gathering and dissemination
5 Helping distributors' sales force
6 Taking orders
7 Other, pl specify_______________________

D2. Approximately what proportion of your company sales are made through each of the following intermediaries?

1 Independent wholesalers	1 ___ (<25%), 2 ___ (25–50%), 3 ___ (>50%)
2 Independent retailers	1 ___ (<25%), 2 ___ (25–50%), 3 ___ (>50%)
3 Your own wholesale outlets	1 ___ (<25%), 2 ___ (25–50%), 3 ___ (>50%)
4 Your own retail outlets	1 ___ (<25%), 2 ___ (25–50%), 3 ___ (>50%)
5 Direct sales to the end consumer	1 ___ (<25%), 2 ___ (25–50%), 3 ___ (>50%)
6 Other, pl specify__________	1 ___ (<25%), 2 ___ (25–50%), 3 ___ (>50%)

D3. How does the distribution coverage of your company compare to competitors?

1 ____ Higher than Competitors 2 ____ About the Same 3 ____ Lower than Competitors

Table 2. Promotion-Related Questions

P1. Which of the following methods of advertising and sales promotion does your company use? (Circle AS MANY AS APPLY)

1	Print advertising	8	Direct mail
2	Radio advertising	9	Telemarketing
3	Television advertising	10	Internet marketing
4	Poster advertising	11	Leaflets and brochures
5	Billboards	12	Company catalogs
6	Trade exhibitions and shows	13	Telephone directories, e.g., yellow pages, etc.
7	Public relations	14	Other, pl specify________________

P2. How does your company design & implement its advertising and sales promotion effort?

1 Mostly, it subcontracts the work to an outside agency
2 Mostly, it handles the work internally
3 About equal use of in-house effort and agency work
4 Other, pl specify________________

P3. How do the advertising and sales promotion expenditures of your company compare to competitors?

1 ____ Higher than Competitors 2 ____ About the Same 3 ____ Lower than Competitors

companies—consumer goods and services, and Romanian companies—industrial goods and services. The results for the four distribution-related questions are presented in Table 3. For the results reported next for each question, the following four abbreviations will be used for these four types of companies respectively: MNC-CON, MNC-IND, ROM-CON and ROM-IND.

Use of Sales Force (Q. D1A)

The percentage of companies employing their own sales force was compared and the differences were marginally significant ($F = 2.29$ ($DF = 3,56$), $p = .09$). All (100 percent) multinational companies (both MNC-CON and MNC-IND) employed their own sales force compared to 69.6 percent of Romanian consumer goods and services companies (ROM-CON) and 70 percent of Romanian industrial goods and services companies (ROM-IND).

Roles of Sales Force (Q. D1B)

The four category of companies differed significantly ($F = 5.89$ ($DF = 3,56$), $p = .01$) in terms of the negotiation function with highest percentage being for MNC-IND (100 percent) followed by ROM-IND (65 percent), MNC-CON (57.1 percent) and ROM-CON (26.1 percent).

The other functions on which the four types of companies differed marginally ($p \leq .10$) were trouble shooting ($F = 2.48$, ($DF = 3,56$), $p = .07$), information gathering ($F = 2.21$ ($DF = 3,56$), $p = .10$) and helping distributors ($F = 2.26$ ($DF = 3,56$), $p = .09$). The differences on the new customer-development function and order-taking function were not significant.

Table 3. Results for Distribution-Related Questions

Question/Variable	Multnatls. Cons. Goods and Services	Multinatls. Ind. Goods and Services	Romanian Cos. Cons. Goods and Services	Romanian Cos. Ind. Goods and Services	F-Value	p-value
D1A. Percent employing own salesforce	100	100	69.6	70.0	2.29 (DF = 3,56)	.09
D1B. *Role of Salesforce*					(DF = 3,56)	
Negotiation	57.1	100	26.1	65.0	5.89	.01
Develop new customers	64.3	100	39.1	45.0	1.80	.15
Trouble shooting	64.3	33.3	34.8	20.0	2.48	.07
Information gathering	35.7	0.0	8.7	10.0	2.21	.10
Helping distributors	21.4	66.7	13.0	10.0	2.26	.09
Taking orders	57.1	66.7	43.5	60.0	0.50	.69
D2. *Type of Intermediaries*[a]						
Independent wholesaler	2.7	1.5	3.0	2.6	2.74 (3,32)	.05
Independent retailer	1.5	1.0	2.0	1.3	0.95 (3,4)	.50
Own wholesalers	2.0	1.5	2.5	—	1.40 (2,7)	.31
Own retailers	2.3	1.5	2.2	1.3	4.88 (3,33)	.00
Direct sales	2.2	1.0	2.4	2.8	2.03 (3,16)	.15
D3. *Coverage Compared to Competition (%)*					(DF = 3,56)	
Higher	57.1	33.3	26.1	10.0	3.35	.03
Same	28.6	66.7	13.0	45.0	2.56	.06
Lower	7.1	0.0	43.5	45.0	2.92	.04

[a](1: < 25%, 2: 25–50%, 3: > 50%)

Note: The results reported in this chapter (Tables 3 & 4) are for combined consumer (durables, nondurables and services) versus industrial (capital equipment, supplies/intermediaries and services) products.

As regards the trouble shooting function, the percentages were 33.3 percent for MNC-IND, 64.3 percent for MNC-CON, 20 percent for ROM-IND and 34.8 percent for ROM-CON. On the information gathering function, MNC-CON companies were the highest (35.7 percent), followed by ROM-IND companies (10 percent), ROM-CON companies (8.7 percent) and none (0 percent) for MNC-IND companies. MNC-IND companies scored the highest (66.7 percent) on the function of helping distributors, followed by MNC-CON companies (21.4 percent), ROM-CON companies (13 percent) and ROM-IND companies (10 percent).

Type of Intermediaries (Q. D2)

Significant differences were found between the four types of companies in terms of their use of independent wholesalers (F = 2.74 (DF = 3,32), p = .05) and their use of own retailers (F = 4.88 (DF = 3,33), p = .00). The four types of companies did not differ significantly in terms of their use of independent retailers, own wholesalers and direct sales.

As regards the use of independent wholesalers, greater than 50 percent of the ROM-CON companies used this type of intermediary compared to about 40 percent of ROM-IND and MNC-CON companies and about 30 percent of MNC-IND companies. As regards the use of own retailers, about 35 percent of MNC-CON and ROM-CON companies and about 20 percent of MNC-IND and ROM-IND used this type of intermediary.

Coverage Compared to Competitors (Q. D3)

MNC companies, in general, responded that their coverage was the same or higher compared to competitors, whereas the Romanian companies, in general, responded that their coverage was the same or lower. On the response indicating higher distribution coverage, the differences between the four types of companies were significant (F = 3.35 (DF = 3,56), p = .03) with 57.1 percent of MNC-CON companies indicating higher coverage. On the response indicating lower distribution coverage, the differences between the four types of companies were significant (F = 2.92 (DF = 3,56), p = .04) with 45 percent of the ROM-IND companies indicating lower coverage.

Results for Promotion-Related Questions

Once again the results for the three promotion-related questions are presented using the abbreviations MNC-CON, MNC-IND, ROM-COM and ROM-IND for the four categories of companies. These results are presented in Table 4.

Media Used (Q. P1)

The four types of companies differed in terms of the use of the following media: posters (F = 3.76 (DF = 3,56), p = .02), trade promotions (F = 2.95 (DF = 3,56), p = .04), leaflets (F = 2.20 (DF = 3,56), p = .10 (marginal)), catalogs (F = 4.41 (DF = 3,56), p = .01) and telephone books (F = 4.44 (DF = 3,56), p = .01). There were no differences between the four types of companies in use of media such as print, radio, TV, billboards, public relations, direct mail, telemarketing and internet.

As regards the media, where the differences were significant, a higher percentage of MNC companies used posters (MNC-CON: 78.6 percent; MNC-IND: 66.7 percent)

Table 4. Results for Promotion-Related Questions

Question/Variable	Multnatls. Cons. Goods and Services	Multinatls. Ind. Goods and Services	Romanian Cos. Cons. Goods and Services	Romanian Cos. Ind. Goods and Services	F-Value	p-value
P1. *Media Used*					(DF = 3,56)	
Print	85.7	66.7	65.2	50.0	1.56	.21
Radio	85.7	100.0	69.6	60.0	1.31	.28
TV	78.6	66.7	52.2	40.0	1.77	.16
Posters	78.6	66.7	43.5	25.0	3.76	.02
Billboards	28.6	0.0	13.0	5.0	1.51	.22
Trade promotion	57.1	100.0	56.5	90.0	2.95	.04
Public relations	57.1	66.7	39.1	40.0	0.62	.61
Direct mail	7.1	0.0	13.0	10.0	0.22	.88
Telemarketing	7.1	0.0	17.4	10.0	0.47	.71
Internet	0.0	33.3	8.7	15.0	1.32	.28
Leaflets	71.4	100.0	39.1	55.0	2.20	.10
Catalogs	57.1	33.3	52.2	95.0	4.41	.01
Telephone books	0.0	33.3	30.4	55.0	4.44	.01
P2. *Advertising Method*					(DF = 3,56)	
Outside agency	50.0	66.7	17.4	20.0	2.65	.05
In-house	14.3	0.0	69.6	75.0	8.16	.00
Both equally	35.7	33.3	8.7	5.0	2.78	.05
P3. *Advtg. Exp. Compared to Competition* (%)					(DF = 3,56)	
Higher	50.0	33.3	13.0	0.0	6.08	.00
Same	35.7	66.7	34.8	50.0	0.64	.59
Lower	7.1	0.0	43.5	50.0	3.33	.03

compared to Romanian companies (ROM-CON: 43.5 percent; ROM-IND: 25 percent). Similarly, a higher percentage of MNC companies used trade promotions (MNC-CON: 57.1 percent; MNC-IND: 100 percent) compared to Romanian companies (ROM-CON: 56.5 percent; ROM-IND: 90 percent). On the other hand, a higher percentage of ROM-IND companies used catalogs (95 percent) as compared to MNC-IND companies (33 percent). Similarly, a higher percentage of Romanian companies (ROM-CON: 30 percent; ROM-IND: 55 percent) used telephone books as compared to MNC companies (MNC-CON: 0 percent; MNC-IND: 33.3 percent). The use of catalogs for consumer goods and services was, however, higher for MNC companies (57.1 percent) as compared to Romanian companies (52.2 percent).

Advertising Method (Q. P2)

A large percentage of MNC companies (both MNC-CON and MNC-IND) used outside agencies for advertising (50 percent and 66.7 percent respectively) compared to 17.4 percent and 20 percent respectively for ROM-CON and ROM-IND companies. These differences were significant at $F = 2.65$ ($DF = 3,56$), $p = .05$. A larger percentage of Romanian companies on the other hand (ROM-CON: 69.6 percent; ROM-IND: 75 percent) handled advertising in-house and these differences were significant at $F = 8.16$ ($DF = 3,56$), $p = .00$.

Advertising Expenditure Compared to Competition (Q. P3)

A larger percentage of MNC companies indicated higher advertising expenditures as compared to the competition. The percentages were MNC-CON: 50 percent; MNC-IND: 33.3 percent; ROM-CON: 13 percent; and ROM-IND: 0 percent. These differences were significant at $F = 6.08$ ($DF = 3,56$), $p = .00$. On the other hand, a larger percentage of Romanian companies indicated lower advertising expenditures as compared to the competition. The percentages were ROM-CON: 43.5 percent; ROM-IND: 50 percent; MNC-CON: 7.1 percent; and MNC-IND: 0 percent. These differences were significant at $F = 3.33$ ($DF = 3,56$), $p = .03$.

DISCUSSION AND FUTURE RESEARCH

As regards the findings related to distribution-related issues, the results on Q. D1A and Q. D1B indicate that 100 percent of the multinational companies employ their own sales force and their sales people play a more active role in terms of negotiation, trouble shooting, information gathering and helping the distributors. The differences between the multinational and Romanian companies on the function of developing new customers also approached marginal significance with MNC companies scoring higher. On the function of order taking, however, the MNC and Romanian companies did not differ. This suggests that the MNC companies are, in general, using their sales forces more aggressively.

The findings on Q. D2 (i.e., type of intermediaries) indicate that independent wholesalers are a popular method of distribution for MNC-CON, ROM-CON and ROM-IND companies. While this is expected for consumer products, the finding that Romanian industrial companies also heavily use this method of distribution is interesting and suggests that perhaps the wholesaling function is primarily comprised of independent organizations. This corroborates the finding relating to the use of own wholesalers where none of the ROM-IND companies reported using own wholesalers method of distribution.

The findings on Q. D3 (i.e., coverage compared to competition) indicate that MNC companies have greater market coverage compared to Romanian companies. This is surprising, and suggests that the MNC companies perhaps are more cognizant of the importance of building up distribution coverage (and may know better how to do so).

As regards the findings related to promotion-related issues, the results on Q. P1 (i.e., media used) indicate that on use of basic media like print, radio, TV, billboards, public relations, direct mail, telemarketing and internet, the multinationals and the local Romanian companies are quite comparable. This is an interesting finding that suggests that the promotion function of marketing seems to have developed and evolved at a fairly high rate in Romania. Some differences were found on the use of certain other media with most MNC companies using posters, trade promotions and leaflets and more of Romanian companies using catalogs and telephone books.

The findings on Q. P2 (i.e., the advertising method) indicate that the MNC companies made more use of outside advertising agencies, whereas the Romanian companies seem to be handling the advertising more in-house. This possibly is due to the prohibitive costs of outside advertising, which Romanian companies are not able to afford. It may also suggest that the MNCs are more conscious of the need to obtain "external" counsel and talent for their advertising efforts, because of their obviously greater need to understand the Romanian market.

Finally, Q. P3 (i.e., the advertising expenses compared to competition) indicates that MNC companies spend higher amounts and the responses of Romanian companies seem to corroborate this finding (i.e., they indicated lower spending compared to competition).

Overall, the findings of the field study reported in this chapter indicate that the distribution and promotion functions are still evolving in Romania. In some areas, such as the use of basic media vehicles, the Romanian companies seem to be fairly comparable to MNC companies but they seem to be quite behind in most other areas relating to promotion and distribution. However, the critical issue worth examining would be the extent to which the differences in competitive marketing strategies followed by multinational versus local Romanian companies are justified considering the factors such as respective company objectives, the structure of the market and demand and how eventually these strategic differences affect profitability and other performance measures. The distribution and promotion strategies need to be examined within a greater context, looking at the antecedents and consequences of these strategies. Such an analysis will provide comparative insights into operations of multinationals versus local Romanian companies. It is possible that very different strategic approaches may be equally successful for multinational versus local companies, thereby enhancing our understanding of the development of marketing theory and practice in the evolving economies of Romania. Future research should, therefore, take this antecedents and consequences approach. Also, the findings presented in this chapter dealt with Romania. It might be worthwhile to examine how the Romanian marketplace may be evolving differently than other Eastern and Central European countries.

References

Brucan, Silvia. "Freedom is Great but Expensive." *Worldpaper* (September 1992): 1–8.

Ger, Güliz, Russell Belk and Dana-Nicoleta Lascu. "The Development of Consumer Desire in Marketizing and Developing Economies: The Cases of Romania and Turkey." In *Advances in Consumer Research*, edited by Leigh McAlister and Michael Rothchild. Provo, UT: Association for Consumer Research, 1993.

Hooley, Graham J. "Raising the Iron Curtain: Marketing in a Period of Transition." *European Journal of Marketing* 27, no. 11-12 (1993): 6–20.

Lascu, Dana-Nicoleta, Lalita A. Manrai and Ajay K. Manrai. "Marketing in Romania: Challenges of Transition from Centrally Planned Economy to Consumer Oriented Economy." *European Journal of Marketing* 27, no. 11-12 (1993): 102–120.

_____. "Status Concern and Consumer Purchase Behavior in the Marketizing Economy of Romania: From the Legacies of Prescribed Consumption to the Fantasies of Desired Acquisitions." *Research in Consumer Behavior* 7 (1994): 89–121.

_____. "Value Differences Between Polish and Romanian Consumers: A Caution Against Using Regiocentric Marketing Orientation in Eastern Europe." *Journal of International Consumer Marketing* 8, no. 3-4 (1996): 145–167.

Manrai, Lalita A., Ajay K. Manrai and Dana-Nicoleta Lascu. "Eastern Europe's Transition to Market Economy: An Analysis of Economic and Political Risks." *Journal of Euromarketing* 5, no. 1 (1996): 7–35.

_____. "How the Fall of the Iron Curtain Has Affected Consumers' Perceptions of Urban and Rural Quality of Life in Romania." *Journal of East-West Business* (submitted, 1998).

"Setting up Shop." *The Economist* (January 1991): 44.

Shafer, M. and D. Ionescu. "Romania: Political Change and Economic Malaise." *RFE/RL Research Report* 2, no. 1 (January 1993): 108–112.

Wood, Van R. and John R. Darling. "The Marketing Challenge of the Newly Independent Republics: Product Competitiveness in the Global Markets." *Journal of International Marketing* 1, no. 1 (1993): 77–102.

13 DO TIMING AND MODES OF ENTRY IN CHINA MATTER TO MARKET SHARE POSITION AND PROFITABILITY?

Yigang Pan
University of Oregon
Xiaolian Li
University of Hong Kong

Introduction

There is little doubt that China has become a hot investment location in the world today. Foreign investments in China have expanded dramatically to reach an annual total of US$34 billion in 1994 and 1995, and US$42.6 billion in 1996. China was the second largest recipient of foreign direct investment in the world, after the United States, for two years in a row in 1993 and 1994. By the end of 1996, 284,000 foreign enterprises have been approved by the Chinese authorities, of which 140,000 have been in operation. According to the Industrial Census of China for 1995, foreign enterprises accounted for 17 percent of overall GDP of China. The role of foreign enterprises in China's export was phenomenal. They accounted for 47.3 percent of China's total foreign trade volume, i.e., US$137.1 billion in China's total trade volume of US$289.9 billion in 1996.

In the first quarter of 1998, foreign investment rose about 10 percent due to an increase in Taiwanese and Western investment. China took in US$8.6 billion in foreign investment from January to March, which is a 9.7 percent increase over the same period last year. Reasons for the rise are cited to be the improvement in political and investment climates. The smooth return of Hong Kong and more stable relations with Taiwan have lured back investors.

One burning question that keeps popping up again and again, especially among the business executives, is how to be successful in China. Are there any lessons that can be learned or mistakes that can be avoided? What are the opportunities in the years ahead? However, apart from a few case studies and some personal encounters, there have not been any rigorous studies that investigate the performance of foreign enterprises in China.

In this study, I will examine two strategic decisions facing foreign firms that are considering investing in China. One is the timing of entry into China. The other is the mode of entry into China. Based on the existing literature, I will argue that there are overwhelming advantages in favor of the early movers in China both in terms of market share position and profitability. I will also argue that equity joint ventures have not lost their appeal in China, when compared to wholly foreign-owned operations or non-equity arrangements.

After the conceptual discussion, I will present the empirical evidence that supports my arguments. I will draw upon several empirical studies that have been published in this area, including on-going large-scale empirical studies that I have been involved in.

At the end of the chapter, I will point out the implications of this study for business executives and policy makers.

WHY DOES TIMING OF ENTRY MATTER IN CHINA?

The timing of market entry is an important strategic issue (Caves and Porter 1977; Lambkin 1988; Mitchell 1991; Robinson, Fornell and Sullivan 1992). There are many advantages of being an early mover in a given product sector, because the early movers benefit from economic, preemptive, technological and behavioral factors (DeCastro and Chrisman 1995). Economic factors include cost advantages from the economy of scale, the experience curve effect and asymmetries in marketing costs. Preemptive factors are those that limit or prevent late entrants from gaining access to suppliers, markets and customers (Bain 1954). Technological factors include the ability of early movers to set industry standards, keep innovations proprietary and the advantage to lead continually future research and development. With respect to behavioral factors, studies have shown that early movers often enjoy a higher degree of customer preference and loyalty than late entrants (Carpenter and Nakamoto 1989). Early movers benefit from asymmetries in terms of switching costs, reputation, information and consumption experience (DeCastro and Chrisman 1995).

While early mover advantages have been shown to be empirically robust, there are circumstances under which late entrants may overcome these disadvantages (Lilien and Yoon 1990). These conditions include free-rider effects, low costs of imitation, shifts in technology and consumer preferences leading to new product and market opportunities or simply the complacency of early movers (Carpenter and Nakamoto 1989; Lieberman and Montgomery 1988). Many studies have been able to relate first-mover advantages to market performance. Early movers often command larger market shares than late entrants (Mitchell 1991; Robinson, Fornell and Sullivan 1992).

Does market entry timing matter for foreign firms in China? The answer is yes. Apart from the above reasons, there are the following reasons that are unique to China and other emerging markets:

1. The Chinese government has opened up its market to foreign firms on a gradual basis. Early movers in China seized strategic opportunities that came once in a long while. Those foreign firms that could not get in at an earlier time had a lot to lose.

The Chinese government carefully planned the time a given product sector was opened to foreign investors, the ceiling on the number and amount of foreign direct investment (FDI) in the sector and a set of state enterprises designated as potential local partners. By doing so, it hoped to protect and nurture its domestic industry in the face of foreign competition. Foreign firms that could get into the door enjoyed the monopolistic opportunity to develop the market, promote the product and tap into a variety of strategies to preempt the future entry of competitors. Those foreign firms that were shut out had to wait for a future entry opportunity. The loss of Chrysler to Mercedes in a bid to manufacture minivans in South China in 1995 was regarded as significant because the Chinese had made the decision not to take on any new major foreign operations in that sector in the near future.

The amount of lead time that the early mover has is of great importance. Early movers have a free hand establishing their products, markets, customers, business partners, suppliers and even industry standards (Lambkin 1988; Lilien and Yoon 1990). This ability to make preemptive moves against later entrants is a powerful weapon. The early movers take the first cut at the investment location, access to key natural resources, market exclusivity and even local human resources (Child 1994; Peng and Heath 1996).

For instance, the Chinese government approved only three joint ventures in automobile sectors in the 1980s, namely Volkswagen in Shanghai, AMC/Chrysler in Beijing and Peugeot in Guangzhou. In 1993, these three ventures were ranked the first, second and fourth largest foreign-invested ventures in China in terms of total sales in 1993, and reached a combined sales of US$2.84 billion (Luo 1997). The top 30 foreign-invested manufacturing firms were all established before 1984 (Luo 1997).

2. Foreign firms that entered China at an earlier time received better incentives than later entrants.

China re-opened its door to foreign investors in the late 1970s. In the first years, there was a high degree of skepticism about investing in China. Only 2,531 foreign enterprises were approved in the first five years of 1979–83 (Johnstone 1997). Those foreign investors that entered China then had shown a great deal of trust in the open-door policy of the Chinese government. In return, they were rewarded with incentives and concessions in terms of taxes, land use, supplies of energy and materials and market access that were not readily available to late entrants (Beamish 1993). The early movers were granted more flexible standards in terms of size of investment, requirements for environment protection and so forth (Osland and Cavusgil 1996; Vanhonacker 1997). These differences enhance the early-mover advantages and contribute to a higher degree of performance success in China.

The Chinese government has gradually faded out policies of incentives towards foreign investors. For instance, the State Council announced that tariff and import taxes will be levied on imported equipment and raw and semi-finished materials in accordance with the legal tax rates for newly approved foreign-funded enterprises. Foreign enterprises set up before December 31, 1997, will, within the specified grace period, continue to enjoy the preferential terms on the reduction and exemption of tariff and import taxes. The policy has not been fully implemented due to the negative response from foreign investors. Nonetheless, the State Council in February 1998 decided that all office, communication and transportation equipment used by foreign enterprises would not be subjected to an import tariff. After General Motors got the approval to produce the "Regal" sedan in Shanghai, it spent a lot of time negotiating with Chinese authorities to waive import duties on imported equipment.

3. Foreign firms that entered China at an earlier time competed against a weaker domestic industry, and had a higher chance of success.

Take China's auto sector as an example (Table 1). The whole domestic industry remained at the level of the 1950s when three auto joint ventures were approved in mid-1980s. The Chinese manufacturers lacked capital and technology. The production equipment was basically what was left over by the Russians. Research and development abilities were weak. Product innovation was non-existent. The "Liberation" brand truck produced by the First Automotive Plant in Changcun did not change its appearance in thirty years. The automotive sector has now become a pillar sector in China. From the mid-1980s, the auto sector increased at a double-digit rate to a total of 1.55 million vehicles by 1997. Only 48,000 vehicles were imported.

Foreign firms that entered this sector early met with weak local competition. They came with capital, technology, manufacturing process and equipment, product and management know-how. The most noticeable case was Volkswagen Shanghai, which sold about 200,000 Santanas in 1995, and had taken a lion's share of the sedan market. The profitability of Volkswagen Shanghai was also among the highest in the sector.

In contrast, there was only one foreign enterprise in the top ten manufacturers in the refrigerator sector in China in 1995. That foreign enterprise was started in 1994. Since then, the Chinese manufacturers have dominated the refrigerator market. The top ten brands had 91.6 percent of total sales in China by 1997, indicating a high level of competitive intensity and brand consolidation.

Table 1. Sedan Sector in China in 1995

Top 10 Firms by Revenues	Start Year	Ownership	Revenues in Million RMB	Profit in Million RMB	Number of Employees
Volkswagen Shanghai	1985	foreign	18,431	2,480	9,437
Tianjin Auto	1984	state-own	10,400	0	1,515
Beijing Jeep	1984	foreign	5,746	353	8,067
Tianjin Mini Auto	1988	state-own	3,929	572	3,479
FAW-Volkswagen	1991	foreign	2,417	8	3,046
Quangzhou Peugeot	1985	foreign	1,098	–321	3,134
Yi Qi Shunde	1992	collective	548	8	222
Quangdong Wemry	1989	state-own	289	11	501
Chongqing Suzuki	1993	foreign	269	–65	594
Pu Dong Yi Qi Assembly	1993	domestic JV	154	–1	40

Note: See *China's Industrial Markets Yearbook 1997* (1997).

4. Foreign firms that entered China at an earlier time had a longer time to learn and adjust to the Chinese market.

Direct investment in China can be seen as buying an option through which foreign firms gain the rights to future choices and flexibilities in China (Bowman and Hurry 1993). In other words, initial FDI can be a platform for obtaining rights to future opportunities. Most large multinational corporations now have dozens of investment projects in China. The earlier they jumped into the Chinese market, the more experienced they are today. Foreign firms learn about the political system, market system, distribution, logistics and so on. Also, foreign firms acquire and accumulate knowledge about how to function as an organization in China.

Early movers have a longer period of time to carry out the learning and adjustment. As pointed out in point 3, they could do it at a time when the local Chinese competition was rather weak, thus enhancing their likelihood of success (Chang 1995).

5. Foreign firms that entered China at an earlier time had less stringent requirements on environment protection, product safety, labor management and so on.

The first Santana produced by Volkswagen Shanghai was a vehicle brought from Volkswagen Brazil. It was a car of the 1980s. It did not have the latest design and comfort. But it met with the needs of China before 1995. Importantly, it met with the environment and safety requirements of that time. Now, there is an increasing public awareness that has prompted auto manufacturers to upgrade the quality of their vehicles. Major cities in China are now enforcing the use of unleaded gas, as well as plans to require air bags and anti-lock braking systems in the near future. Volkswagen introduced Santana 2000 around 1995 and was prepared for the tougher environmental and safety expectations.

6. Foreign firms that entered China at an earlier time had a longer time to develop their corporate and brand position.

The bulk of sedans were purchased by government institutions. In 1996, the government sector bought 64 percent of all domestically-produced sedans, and 50 percent in 1997. Companies, especially taxi firms, bought 21 percent in 1996, and 29 percent in 1997. Individuals bought 15 percent in 1996 and 21 percent in 1997.

It is important for firms to have a strong corporate and brand position to sell successfully to the government and institutions. A strong consumer perception, acceptance and a strong distribution network are important. The ability to work with local governments to overcome local protectionism is vital. All this takes time. An early mover has the time advantage over the late comer. Volkswagen had the time to establish a nation-wide brand recognition and distribution system.

Evidently, there are also risks and uncertainties associated with an early entry. It is imperative that the early movers be prepared to deal with them effectively. There are many early movers that did not survive. Recently, Peugeot decided to sell its joint venture in Guangzhou to Honda, thus giving up on its early-mover advantage in China.

While it is not the focus of this article, it is nonetheless worth listing the kinds of risks and uncertainties that an early mover in China might encounter. First, political uncertainty. The 1989 Tiananmen Square student movement was a case in point. Second, the cyclical nature of Chinese economy. The economy of China has gone through growth, inflation, tightening up, stagnation and growth at a cycle of around 4–6 years. Third, industry and sector policy changes. Fourth, various operational difficulties (Vanhonacker and Pan 1997).

EMPIRICAL EVIDENCE ON ENTRY TIMING

In a study of foreign firms in Jiangshu Province, Luo (1997) found that early entrants (7 firms started in 1980–81) had an average sales growth of 26.8 percent while late entrants (24 firms started in 1989–90) had 15.3 percent. Early entrants had a higher asset turnover than late entrants. However, the late entrants had a higher return on investment than early entrants. His study suffered from the problem of a small sample, among others.

A recent study by Pan and Chi (1998) offers more evidence. Their study was based on a sample of 962 foreign enterprises. Of the 962 foreign enterprises in this sample, 588 were from Hong Kong, 188 from Taiwan, 57 from the United States, 52 from Japan, 19 from EU, 42 from other Asian countries and 16 from other countries. In the sample, 123 were wholly foreign-owned operations, 746 equity joint ventures and 93 cooperative operations. The earliest time that an enterprise started production was December 1980, and the latest time was June 1993.

Pan and Chi (1998) found that foreign enterprises that entered China at an earlier time were more profitable than those that entered at a later time. Specifically, 59.6 percent of foreign enterprises that entered China prior to 1984, and 58.8 percent of those that entered during the 1984–89 period were profitable. However, only 44.3 percent of those that entered after 1989 were profitable. Furthermore, those that entered China the earliest were most profitable, because 48.1 percent of the first wave earned at least 3 percent or higher profit, while only 43.6 percent of the second wave and 32.4 percent of the third wave fell in the same category. See Table 2.

Table 2. Timing of Market Entry into China (I)

	Firm's Timing of Entry in China			
Profit Level	1978–1984	1985–1989	1990–1993	Overall
>15%	9.62	12.06	6.61	9.36
8–15%	13.46	12.94	10.13	11.64
3–8%	25.00	18.64	15.64	17.57
<3%	11.54	15.13	11.89	13.41
No profit	7.69	6.80	12.33	9.46
Minor loss	9.62	9.21	18.72	13.72
Heavy loss	7.69	7.24	8.59	7.9
Out of business	15.38	17.98	16.08	16.94
Column total	100%	100%	100%	100%
N	52	456	454	962

Note: Based on the paper written by Pan and Chi (1999).

Table 3. Timing of Market Entry into China (II)

Independent Variables		Market Share (%)	ROA (%)	N
Overall average		0.385 (2.07)	0.65 (0.133)	23518
Order of entry				
Early entrants		2.024 (7.66)	3.10 (0.120)	688
Followers:	1st 3 years	1.285 (4.91)	3.17 (0.130)	810
	2nd 3 years	0.781 (2.60)	1.89 (0.126)	2446
	3rd 3 years	0.439 (1.59)	0.54 (0.135)	5416
	4th 3 years	0.226 (0.75)	0.42 (0.131)	6606
	5th 2 years	0.111 (0.69)	0.03 (0.135)	7552

Note: The data are based on the 1995 Chinese Industrial Census (Pan, Li, and Tse 1999).

A comprehensive study was based on the 1995 Chinese industrial census done by Pan, Li and Tse (1999). The total number of enterprises (both foreign and local) in the data set was 450,233, and they accounted for 91 percent of the total industrial output by all enterprises in that year. There were 41,958 foreign enterprises, accounting for 17 percent of total industrial sales revenue in 1995. Their final sample had a total of 23,518 foreign enterprises in China.

The average market shares of foreign enterprises were 0.385 percent. As expected, early entrants had an average of 2.024 percent of the market share, which is much higher than the average for all foreign enterprises. The followers had smaller market shares. The average market shares were 1.285 percent for the followers in the first three years, 0.781 percent for those in the second three years, 0.439 percent for those in the third three years, 0.226 percent for those in the fourth three years and 0.111 percent for those in the last two years. The descriptive results (see Table 3) supported the hypothesis that early entry foreign enterprises had larger market shares than the early followers, and early followers had larger market shares than late followers.

Early entry foreign enterprises had a return on assets (ROA) of 3.10 percent, which was much higher than the overall average of 0.65 percent. Interestingly, the average ROA for the followers in the first three years was quite similar, at 3.17 percent. However, the average ROA for later followers was much smaller at 1.89 percent for those in the second three years, 0.55 percent for those in the third three years, 0.42 percent for those in the fourth three years and 0.03 percent for those in the last two years. The descriptive results showed that early entry foreign enterprises had higher profitability than late followers.

In their multivariate analysis, the results of early mover on market share and profitability came out quite strongly (Pan, Li and Tse 1999).

In short, there is significant evidence supporting the first mover advantages for foreign firms in China based on the three existing empirical studies.

WHY DOES MODE OF ENTRY MATTER IN CHINA?

In China, the number of equity joint ventures in the first fifteen years after 1979 far exceeded that of wholly foreign-owned subsidiaries (Pan 1997). However, wholly foreign-owned enterprises made up 46.6 percent of the total foreign-invested contracts approved in 1995 (Johnstone 1997). It is commonly believed that if foreign investors had had a choice of their own, many would have preferred setting up wholly foreign-owned subsidiaries in China (Vanhonacker 1997). However, there has not been a consistent empirical pattern on the impact of entry modes on performance. There has not been a satisfactory literature framework to examine this issue either.

To understand the impact of entry modes on performance, the existing literature has looked at the role of resource commitment, costs and managerial control (Anderson and Gatignon 1986; Madhok 1997; Woodcock, Beamish and Makino 1994). The basic premise of the cost argument is that the higher the resource requirements of one particular mode of entry, the harder it is for an enterprise to recoup its investment and to make a profit.

It is commonly believed that firms often simply duplicate what they have done successfully in an overseas market in the case of wholly foreign-owned operations. Firms thus incur minimal resource-based costs (Woodcock, Beamish and Makino 1994). On the other hand, in the case of joint ventures, firms incur costs in searching for appropriate local partner(s) and integrating the assets pooled together by venture partners (Madhok 1997). Additional resources are needed in coordinating the interests, goals and management of venture partners. The total combined costs are often higher for joint ventures than for wholly-owned operations, holding other things constant (Caves and Mehra 1986). Therefore, it has been argued that wholly-owned operations tend to outperform equity joint ventures in overseas markets (Li and Guisinger 1991).

From the perspective of managerial control, it is easy to see that the wholly-owned mode gives foreign firms complete responsibility and control from inception to demise (Kim and Hwang 1992; Madhok 1997). Foreign firms have few reservations about extending their competitive and proprietary assets to wholly-owned operations in an overseas country. Most importantly, foreign firms avoid conflicts of interests and objectives that occur in the case of joint ventures (Vanhonacker 1997). They can pursue wholeheartedly their own goals and objectives in the absence of local partners. Such efficient management control contributes to better performance. As a result, wholly foreign-owned operations often perform better than joint ventures (Woodcock, Beamish and Makino 1994).

In the case of emerging markets, such expectations may not hold. The importance of local partners there often is more salient than in the Western markets. Foreign firms may greatly enhance their potential by involving local enterprises (Osland and Cavusgil 1996; Yan and Gray 1994). Through joint ventures, foreign firms can do a better job in gaining acceptance by the local customers, support from the host country government, penetrate local distribution and overcome various operational difficulties (Beamish and Banks 1987). On the other hand, the burdens of a shared ownership and joint management can also break down the venture.

Therefore, many foreign firms in China have found many reasons to pursue a wholly-owned operation (Vanhonacker 1997). They believe that they can make fast decisions and act forcefully, especially in penetrating local market and to promote their products according to their positioning strategy. They do not have to worry about proprietary know-how and products in the local market (Madhok 1997). They can also avoid pressure from local joint venture partners to export more (Child 1994). Of course, the success of this strategy depends on many factors, including the degree of market openness and the adequacy of the financial resources of the foreign firm.

Given that there seems to be no consensus in the literature regarding which mode of entry should perform better, we have to turn to the empirical results.

EMPIRICAL EVIDENCE ON MODE OF ENTRY

Two studies offer relevant empirical findings. The study by Pan and Chi (1999) investigates the profitability performance question.

They found that equity joint ventures were more profitable than wholly foreign-owned operations. Specifically, 53.66 percent equity joint ventures with state-owned local firms and 52.24 percent equity joint ventures with non-state-owned local firms were profitable. (See Table 4.) Only 47.16 percent wholly foreign-owned operations were profitable. Interestingly, only 2.44 percent wholly foreign-owned subsidiaries suffered a heavy loss but 21.95 percent of them have gone out of business. This suggests that foreign firms would rather close their wholly-owned operations than keep losing money. In contrast, equity joint ventures have a low percentage of close-down, but a high percentage of heavy loss. This means that in the case of equity joint ventures, it is less easy to dissolve the operation even in the case of a heavy loss.

Cooperative operations had a high percent of close-down (29.17 percent for those with state-owned local firms and 22.22 percent for those with non-state-owned local firms). They also made a small profit. Specifically, 24.44 percent and 14.58 percent of cooperative operations made a profit of less than three percent of revenues in 1993.

The study by Pan, Li and Tse (1998) covers both market share and profitability performance. With respect to market share performance, wholly foreign-owned enterprises have the highest market shares, followed by equity joint ventures and coopera-

Table 4. Mode of Market Entry into China (I)

	Firm's Mode of Operation					
Profit Level	Wholly-Owned	JV-State	JV-Nonstate	Coop-State	Coop-Nonstate	Overall
>15%	4.88	10.00	10.76	4.17	8.89	9.36
8–15%	8.94	11.33	12.56	10.42	13.44	11.64
3–8%	17.89	18.33	17.71	12.50	15.56	17.57
<3%	15.45	14.00	11.21	14.58	24.44	13.41
No profit	11.38	8.67	10.54	4.17	4.44	9.46
Minor loss	17.07	14.67	13.68	6.25	6.67	13.72
Heavy loss	2.44	6.33	9.64	18.75	4.44	7.90
Out of business	21.95	16.67	13.90	29.17	22.22	16.94
Column total	100%	100%	100%	100%	100%	100%
N	123	300	446	48	45	962

Note: The five modes of operations are wholly-owned foreign enterprises, JV with state-owned Chinese enterprises, JV with non-state-owned Chinese enterprises, Cooperative operations with state-owned Chinese enterprises, and Cooperative operations with non-state-owned Chinese enterprises.
Based on the paper written by Pan and Chi (1999).

tive joint ventures. Wholly foreign-owned enterprises have an average market share of 0.414 percent, followed by 0.394 percent for equity joint ventures and 0.288 percent for cooperative joint ventures. See Table 5.

With respect to profitability, they found that wholly foreign-owned enterprises have significantly lower profitability and equity joint ventures have higher profitability. Wholly foreign-owned enterprises have an average ROA of –0.41 percent, while equity joint ventures have 1.03 percent and cooperative joint ventures have 0.08 percent.

If we take these two studies together, it is apparent that equity joint ventures are more profitable. Wholly foreign-owned operations are least profitable. However, wholly foreign-owned operations have slightly higher market share positions than equity joint ventures.

One possible explanation of this last result is that the primary goal of foreign firms is to penetrate the local market when they adopt wholly-owned operations. They plow their earnings back into the operations and thus report little profitability. Another possible explanation is that the costs of running a wholly-owned operation are much higher than those of equity joint ventures, thus driving down the profitability.

One thing that is clear is that the relationship between entry mode strategy and performance is much more complicated than previously thought.

To study this in detail, one has to define performance first. As we see, performance can be gauged by sales and market share position, level of profitability, acceptance of a technology as industry standard of the local market, a self-sustaining outpost in a foreign market and so on. Therefore, the right question to ask is what mode of entry maximizes what kind of firm performance.

Based on the empirical results, we would argue that foreign firms should consider wholly-owned operations when their primary goal is to maximize their local market share position. Foreign firms can avoid the disagreements and complications from the local partners as in the case of joint ventures over where to sell the products. They can also pinpoint all of their resources with such a goal. The downside of so doing is that foreign firms often underestimate or simply ignore the types and severity of difficulties in an emerging market. In other words, the costs of so doing are often higher than with the help of local partners. Therefore, it is imperative that foreign firms realize that they are trading short-term profit for long-term market share position. They should not pull out of the local market if their wholly-owned operation is not profitable on a quarterly basis.

Table 5. Mode of Market Entry into China (II)

Independent Variables	Market Share (%)	ROA (%)	N
Overall average	0.385 (2.07)	0.65 (0.133)	23518
Mode of entry			
Cooperative joint ventures	0.288 (1.07)	0.08 (0.126)	2758
Equity joint ventures	0.394 (2.17)	1.03 (0.125)	16305
Wholly foreign-owned subsidiaries	0.414 (2.16)	–0.41 (0.161)	4455

Note: The data are based on the 1995 Chinese Industrial Census (Pan, Li and Tse 1999).

I would argue that there are many situations under which equity joint ventures remain a viable entry mode choice. With local partners, foreign firms have to balance their interests with the local ones. They cannot rush to implement their own strategies. However, on the whole, it appears that profitability would be higher and business less volatile. It is not easy to make a quick and big buck with joint ventures, but there is a safety net below. Beijing Jeep joint venture is a case in point.

IMPLICATIONS

Timing of market entry affects market share and profitability performance. The empirical results show that foreign firms that entered early are now more profitable than those that entered late. This has two practical implications. If a foreign enterprise has entered China quite early, but has not been more profitable than its later competitors, it needs to identify why it has not been able to achieve the pioneer advantages it is supposed to have. It has not taken full advantage of its potential. On the other hand, if a foreign enterprise is a later entrant, it has to find out what advantages the early movers have in China. How long will their privileges last? What are the niche opportunities not captured by the early movers? Are there any changes in the market environment that will erode early movers' market positions? It should pay close attention to the host country policies.

Choice of entry mode also matters. The results show that so far equity joint ventures have a higher level of profitability than either wholly foreign-owned subsidiaries or cooperative operations. More interestingly, wholly foreign-owned operations and cooperative operations have a higher rate of close-down. A word of caution seems necessary in light of the findings and the current trend among foreign investors of favoring wholly foreign-owned operations in China. Foreign investors need, at least, to be fully aware of the potential downside of operating alone in the new market environment in China. They need to be prepared for every possibility on their own before they embark on a wholly foreign-owned operation.

In comparison, equity joint ventures can count on the support from local partners and government in terms of favorable policy, supplies, concessions, market access and so on. Chrysler's Beijing Jeep joint venture would have long been terminated had it been a wholly foreign-owned operation. We should also caution readers that it is still too early to draw a definitive conclusion on the relationship between modes of operation and performance.

From the policy maker's perspective, it is important to let foreign investors choose which mode of operation they prefer. The fear of dominance by foreign firms in sensitive sectors will gradually be reduced as China becomes more integrated into the world economy. At the same time, as the government allows an increasing number of state-owned enterprises to be separated from the state system, more and more local firms will have a truly independent status. They will be able to run their own business. When that happens, the true value of these local firms as partners to Western firms will come to light. Joint ventures in the near future may no longer be "nightmare" stories as reported sometimes in the 1980s. They will be attractive enough themselves that there is no need for the local government to "pressure" foreign investors into one of them.

CONCLUDING REMARK

What should we expect as China continues its economic and social reform? China will undoubtedly push forward such reform. The government will rely more and more on market mechanisms instead of on administrative means. This will produce a substantial positive impact on how foreign firms operate in China. They will eventually be able to compete on a level playing field with other domestic and foreign firms.

Ironically, there might also be a bit of "undesirable" change. When the local government is authoritarian and uses its power, things get done fast. In the past, the government wanted foreign investment, and they delivered quickly on what foreign firms wanted. Roads were expanded, power plants were built and so on, while the opposition was pushed aside. As market forces and rule of law take the center stage, however, this power of local government will be reduced. It is possible that things will take longer to get done, as "due process" is followed. It is our hope that policy makers in China will strive to maintain the "will do" attitude and create an even more attractive environment for foreign investors in China in the years to come.

References

Anderson, Erin M. and Hubert Gatignon. "Modes of Foreign Entry: A Transaction Cost Analysis and Propositions." *Journal of International Business Studies* 17, no. 3 (Fall 1986): 1–26.

Bain, Joe S. "Conditions of Entry and the Emergence of Monopoly." In *Monopoly and Competition and Their Regulation,* edited by Edward H. Chamberlin, 215–241. London: Macmillan & Co, Ltd., 1954.

Beamish, Paul W. "The Characteristics of Joint Ventures in the People's Republic of China." *Journal of International Marketing* 1, no. 2 (1993): 29–48.

Beamish, Paul W. and John C. Banks. "Equity Joint Ventures and the Theory of the Multinational Enterprise." *Journal of International Business Studies* 18, no. 2 (Summer 1987): 1–16.

Bowman, Edward H. and Dileep Hurry. "Strategy Through the Option Lens: An Integrated View of Resource Investments and the Incremental-Choice Process." *Academy of Management Review* 18, no. 4 (October 1993): 760–782.

Carpenter, Gregory S. and Kent Nakamoto. "Consumer Preference Formation and Pioneering Advantage." *Journal of Marketing Research* 26, no. 3 (August 1989): 285–298.

Caves, Richard E. and Sanjeev K. Mehra. "Entry of Foreign Multinationals into U.S. Manufacturing Industries." In *Competition in Global Industries*, edited by Michael E. Porter. Boston: Harvard Press, 1986.

Caves, Richard E. and Michael E. Porter. "From Entry Barriers to Mobility Barriers: Conjectural Decisions and Contrived Deterrence to New Competition. *Quarterly Journal of Economics* 91, no. 2 (May 1977): 241–262.

Chang, Sea Jin. "International Expansion Strategy of Japanese Firms: Capability Building through Sequential Entry." *Academy of Management Journal* 38, no. 2 (April 1995): 383–407.

Child, John. *Management in China During the Age of Reform.* Cambridge: Cambridge University Press, 1994.

China's Industrial Markets Yearbook 1997. Hong Kong: City University of Hong Kong Press, 1997.

DeCastro, Julio O. and James J. Chrisman. "Order of Market Entry, Competitive Strategy, and Financial Performance." *Journal of Business Research* 33, no. 2 (June 1995): 165–177.

Kim, W. Chan and Peter Hwang. "Global Strategy and Multinationals' Entry Mode Choice." *Journal of International Business Studies* 23 (First Quarter 1992): 29–53.

Johnstone, Helen. "Foreign Firms Go it Alone on the Mainland." *South China Morning Post* (July 13, 1997): Money Section, 3.

Lambkin, Mary. "Order of Entry and Performance in New Market." *Strategic Management Journal* 9, Special Issue (1988): 127–140.

Li, Jiatao and Stephen Guisinger. "Comparative Business Failures of Foreign-Controlled Firms in the United States." *Journal of International Business Studies* 22, no. 2 (Second Quarter 1991): 209–224.

Lieberman, Marvin B. and David B. Montgomery. "First Mover Advantages." *Strategic Management Journal* 9, Special Issue (1988): 41–58.

Lillien, Gary L. and Eusang Yoon. "The Timing of New Entry: An Exploratory Study of New Industrial Products." *Management Science* 36, no. 5 (May 1990): 568–585.

Luo, Yadong. "Pioneering in China: Risks and Benefits." *Long Range Planning* 30, no. 5 (October 1997): 768–776.

Madhok, Anoop. "Cost, Value and Foreign Market Entry Mode: The Transaction and the Firm." *Strategic Management Journal* 18 (1997): 39–61.

Mitchell, Will. "Dual Clocks: Entry Order Influences on Incumbent and Newcomer Market Share and Survival When Specialized Assets Retain Their Value." *Strategic Management Journal* 12, no. 2 (February 1991): 85–100.

Osland, Gregory E. and S. Tamer Cavusgil. "Performance Issues in U.S.-China Joint Ventures." *California Management Review* 38, no. 2 (Winter 1996): 106–130.

Pan, Yigang. "The Formation of Japanese and U.S. Equity Joint Ventures in China." *Strategic Management Journal* 18, no. 3 (March 1997): 247–254.

Pan, Yigang and Peter S. K. Chi. "The Promises and Challenges of Direct Foreign Investments in China." *Business & the Contemporary World* 10, no. 1 (1998): 87–105.

_____. "Financial Performance and Survival of Multinational Corporations in China." *Strategic Management Journal* 20, no. 4 (forthcoming 1999).

Pan, Yigang, Shaomin Li and David K. Tse. "The Impact of Order and Mode of Market Entry on Profitability and Market Share." *Journal of International Business Studies* 30, no. 1 (forthcoming 1999).

Peng, Mike W. and Peggy S. Heath. "The Growth of the Firm in Planned Economies in Transition: Institutions, Organizations, and Strategic Choice." *Academy of Management Review* 21, no. 2 (April 1996): 492–528.

Robinson, William T., Claes Fornell and Mary Sullivan. "Are Market Pioneers Intrinsically Stronger than Later Entrants?" *Strategic Management Journal* 13, no. 8 (November 1992): 609–624.

Vanhonacker, Wilfried R. "Entering China: An Unconventional Approach." *Harvard Business Review* 75, no. 2 (March–April 1997): 130–140.

Vanhonacker, Wilfried R. and Yigang Pan. "Impact of National Culture, Business Scope, and Geographic Location on Joint Venture Operations in China." *Journal of International Marketing* 5, no. 3 (1997): 11–30.

Woodcock, C. Patrick, Paul W. Beamish and Shige Makino. "Ownership-Based Entry Mode Strategies and International Performance." *Journal of International Business Studies* 25, no. 2 (Second Quarter 1994): 253–273.

Yan, Aimin and Barbara Gray. "Bargaining Power, Management Control, and Performance in United States-China Joint Ventures: A Comparative Case Study." *Academy of Management Journal* 37, no. 6 (December 1994): 1478–1517.

14 DEFENDING TURF: MARKETING STRATEGIES FOR EMERGING MARKET COMPANIES

Niraj Dawar
University of Western Ontario
J. Ramachandran
Indian Institute of Management, Bangalore

Introduction

In the marketplace of the global village, multinational-owned megabrands have rapidly become ubiquitous. The crumbling of the iron curtain, the institution of economic reforms in China and the liberalization of economies from India to Brazil have opened up large markets to multinational corporations (MNCs). As trade barriers have disintegrated, MNCs have rushed in, seeking sales growth and respite from their intensely competitive and saturated home markets. As a result, erstwhile protected markets have experienced an abrupt deluge of international brands. For the choice-starved consumers in these emerging markets, this a welcome change from the meager choice and low quality products to which they had grown accustomed. However, for local brands in these newly liberalized markets, the influx of foreign players spells a different reality. For many emerging market companies (EMCs), the experience is a first taste of international competition. To them, the large-scale entry of international firms is a major threat. At best, it results in erosion of local firms' market shares, and at worst it could spell their demise. Even if local firms do survive, the transition may allow powerful and well-endowed multinationals to wrest control of the rules of the market.

At first sight, the outlook for EMCs is bleak. Governments of liberalized economies are unlikely to be able to turn back the clock. Therefore, lobbying for the reinstatement of protectionism is scarcely an option. Furthermore, for EMCs, the option of selling out to MNCs or diluting control with partial foreign ownership is often only considered as a painful last resort. EMCs tend to be family or government controlled, and do not easily take to the idea of foreign ownership. Consequently, EMCs need to find a means of survival in the face of global competition while ensuring that they retain their autonomy. This often means adapting to the new market environment and competing with the new entrants. However, EMCs are rarely equipped to effectively deal with the competitive onslaught from multinationals. Long accustomed to privileged positions in protected markets, most EMCs lack the products, the technology, the financial resources and, most importantly, the skills necessary to compete. There is little advice available to such firms in the traditional management literature.

Little has been written about survival and defense strategies available to emerging market firms abruptly exposed to harsh competition.[1] Much of the strategy and marketing literature related to emerging markets adopts the perspective of developed-market companies doing business in emerging markets. An extensive literature exists, for example, on market entry strategies of MNCs. Yet the other side of the story, the effects of multinational entry on local competitors, remains a neglected topic. Given the urgency and magnitude of the competitive threat to local firms, we believe it is necessary to examine their strategic options and to draw lessons from the approaches adopted by successful local defenders. The purpose of this article is to examine the marketing strategies, and specifically, brand-level strategies available to EMCs as they attempt to survive the entry of international competitors.

ASSESSING SURVIVAL LIKELIHOOD AND OPTIONS

As it becomes evident that formidable multinational players armed with a powerful arsenal of global brands, internationally-honed marketing skills, huge financial resources and state-of-the-art production and product technology will enter the market, EMCs understandably question their ability to survive.

Multinational competitors not only have access to superior technology and knowledge garnered from operating in a number and a variety of markets worldwide, they also have the advantage of being able to treat any one market as a long-term venture, justifying short-term losses as investments in market building, while satisfying shareholders with profitable positions in other markets. The chief of Swiss transnational Nestlé in India has stated that their company is not looking for massive returns or fast money. A large profit is not going to be made in India. Helmut Maucher, Nestlé's CEO in Switzerland, strategizes that the profit in India will come from future generations.

EMCs are usually not so fortuitously placed. They generally derive all of their revenues and profits from their home market and need to demonstrate returns for the short-term, while combating their competitors.

Nevertheless, EMCs do have assets and opportunities which, if appropriately used, can provide a means of stemming the MNC advance. Among these assets are the "localness" of their brands, superior customer knowledge, low costs of production, the ability to make rapid decisions and make pre-emptive moves, selective partnering with international players and in some cases, the potential to counterattack. EMCs such as China's Shanghai Jahwa, the Philippine's Jollibee and Russia's Vist Computers have managed to defend their home turf in the face of competitive inroads made by major multinationals such as Unilever, McDonald's and Compaq. In other cases, EMCs such as India's Arvind Mills and Titan Watches, and Mexico's Cemex and Bimbo have built on their success at home and launched international expansion strategies of their own. In the following sections we examine these defensive strategies, and illustrate their use by EMCs.

EXPLOIT LOCAL-NESS

One of the clearest advantages that EMC brands have over multinational brands is that they are local. Being local involves having an established local presence, a locally-appealing proposition and positioning, a local level of service and delivery and superior local knowledge of consumer tastes and regional differences. Leveraging this local superiority is key to the survival of local brands. Unfortunately, many local firms tend to assume the opposite—that emulating successful international brands is the best means of survival. This can be a serious mistake, as it leaves EMCs playing by the international firms' rules, without the resources to do so.

Getting Close to the Customer

Local service and delivery are key to the success of VIST, a Russian personal computer manufacturer. VIST has grown from a small operation to being the largest brand of computers sold in Russia, despite stiff competition from international players such as Compaq and Hewlett-Packard. Most of the international majors have concentrated on getting a share of the large but fickle government market in Moscow. In contrast, VIST's strategy is to establish a local presence and serve small office and home-office customers through an extensive dealer network covering over 60 small cities and towns. The firm offers warranty terms and personal sales which are appreciated by consumers buying their first computer. In 1997, VIST attained a 20 percent share of the Russian PC market. VIST attributes its success to a superior understanding of the Russian consumer, and relies on its proximity to the market to provide it with knowledge about changing trends and expectations. By meeting these ahead of the competition, VIST has consolidated its position as the market leader in Russia.

Another way of looking at VIST's success is that it has focused on downstream activities in which its local nature is an advantage. The personal computer industry is characteristically global, in that the fixed costs of product development and brand building need to be amortized over large sales, leading international players to seek global markets. However, by focusing on local service and delivery, VIST is concentrating on making the downstream aspects of the industry more important in consumers' choice. These downstream aspects are inherently local.

Local Products for Local Consumers

Jollibee, a family-owned fast food company in the Philippines, has successfully staved off competition from one of the world's most global companies—McDonald's. In its home market, the company has captured 75 percent of the burger market and 56 percent of the fast-food business by developing a home-grown menu, customized for local tastes, while skilfully matching the service and delivery standards of its international competitors. Jollibee's menus, which include burgers seasoned with garlic and soy sauce, alongside spaghetti, noodle and rice meals made with fish and shrimp, have enabled it to defend its home market in the Philippines over its closest rival, McDonald's, which has a 19 percent share.

Another company which successfully uses its superior knowledge of local consumer behavior in its competitive battle with multinationals is Shanghai Jahwa, China's oldest personal hygiene and cosmetics company. Its strategy is to develop low-cost, mass-marketed brands whose positioning revolves around consumers' belief about traditional Chinese ingredients. An example is the Liushen (meaning "six spirits") brand of *eau de toilette*. Chinese consumers believe that human organs such as the heart and liver are all internal "spirits" that determine the health of the body. Liushen is the name of a traditional prescription made of pearl powder, musk and several other ingredients, usually packaged in the form of a tiny tablet, and used as a remedy for a variety of summer ailments such as prickly heat. Building on this knowledge of local consumer preferences, Shanghai Jahwa launched the Liushen *eau de toilette* positioned for summer use. The brand rapidly gained 60 percent share of the market, and has since been extended to a mainstream shower cream targeted at the traditional Liushen user. The shower cream is doing well in a competitive market dominated by Lux (Unilever), Safeguard (P&G) and Johnson Baby (Johnson & Johnson) brands, which appeal to young fashion conscious urban consumers. Today, Jahwa is the biggest of the country's 2,000 domestic skin-care and cosmetic companies, and has about 7 percent of the Chinese market. Jahwa's chairman, Mr. Ge Wenyao, believes that Jahwa is one of the few companies well poised to realize the true potential of the Chinese market by developing products which appeal to its billion-plus consumers. In contrast, foreign manufacturers tend to seek consumers which best match their existing product portfolios. As a result, they lock themselves to restricted, if lucrative, segments of the market. For example, Revlon estimates its entire market in China to consist of about 39 million consumers—less than 3 percent of the population.

Use Local Knowledge to Fragment the Market

A key element of the local-ness strategy is to segment the local market so as to serve local needs better. While international players tend to see an emerging market nation as a single market, or even simply as an extension of a global region (e.g. Vietnam is considered by many multinationals to be just another market in Asia, with characteristics similar to other Asian markets), local firms are often able to understand and profit from the subtleties of regional and other differences within the country. Local players who understand the strategic importance of these differences can fragment the market and develop offerings tailored to smaller segments within the market. Shanghai Jahwa, for example, has introduced a variety of product lines to cater to different segments, including its Chinf de Chinf line of cosmetics which competes with multinationals' products at the top end of the market, and its Maxam line of products which has a primarily rural appeal.

Regional differentiation also allows local firms to out-maneuver international competitors. Consider the fabric-whitener market in India. For decades, the Anglo-French giant, Reckitt and Colman's Robin brand, has been the market leader. It still remains the only national brand. Today however, Robin's dominance is confined only to the powder segment of the market. In the rapidly growing market for liquid fabric whiteners, Ujala, a local Indian brand is the market leader, despite only a regional presence. In urban markets, it outsells Robin's liquid fabric whitener by a factor of three to one. Ujala exploited regional differences in consumer preference. While the consumers in north and east India prefer their fabric whitener in powder form, urban consumers and those in the south and west tend to prefer it in liquid form. Through its strong presence in south India, Ujala has emerged as the overall market leader. Robin is not the market leader in the second largest zone (west) either. Another local Indian brand, Captain, is the market leader there. These local brands understand local consumer and trade preferences and develop products to fit them.

While the expenses and risks of fragmenting a market may be high, there is a definite strategic rationale for considering such investment. Naturally, fragmenting the market involves understanding differences in consumer tastes and the preferences. But in the long term, a fragmented market is also one which is more difficult and less attractive for competitors to enter—any new entrant has to provide the entire line of products, or conversely, to be satisfied with only a fragment of the overall market.

Multinationals will, in time, be driven by their growth imperatives to develop products for the large untapped mass markets in emerging economies. As a result, over time the EMC advantage of superior local knowledge may wane. Some well-entrenched multinationals have already demonstrated a keen ability to develop products and offerings adapted to local markets. Unilever, for example, has developed products such as the "Fair & Lovely" beauty cream specifically for the Indian market (and subsequently launched it in other countries in Asia). Colgate Palmolive's toothpastes are formulated for the local market, sometimes in order to meet cost criteria to make the product acceptable to the mass market. In China, Procter and Gamble's Safeguard brand was effectively able to leverage a government campaign to encourage hygiene practices to reinforce its antibacterial positioning. It also obtained an endorsement from the China Medical Association, which further boosted its local credibility.

The initial focus of multinationals on select segments of the market does not provide EMCs with a permanent defense. Instead, it is best viewed as an opportunity for EMCs to consolidate their positions in the local market. Consolidation strategies include catering to the mass market, and fragmenting this market to deliver distinct offerings to each segment.

APPROPRIATE CRITICAL RESOURCES

In anticipation of the entry of multinationals, EMCs can appropriate key market resources such as brand positions and distribution channels. By locking up these key resources, the EMC ensures that penetration of the market by new entrants is more difficult, more time consuming and more expensive.

Brand Positions

In the South African and Jamaican markets, McDonald's name was registered by local fast-food operators long before the burger giant entered the market. In South Africa, the firm was forced to litigate to obtain the right to use the name. This is a particularly stark, if unsophisticated, example of the appropriation of key resources. More sophisticated EMC competitors tend to pre-emptively appropriate key brand positions before multinationals enter the market. For example, Shanghai Jahwa launched a two-in-one shampoo and conditioner in China just as Procter & Gamble was preparing to introduce its hugely successful Rejoice shampoo, whose key proposition was the convenience of a two-in-one shampoo. Multinationals which emphasize global brands and positions are particularly vulnerable to this form of pre-emption. Their brands are developed on the premise of a single global positioning that is an open book to local competitors.

Distribution Channels

Another key market resource, which can be pre-emptively appropriated, is distribution channels. Local brands often have the advantage of an extensive and established distribution presence in channels that may be the best or least expensive means of getting the product to consumers. Asian Paints, an Indian company, sells paint through over 14,000 retail outlets, reaching some of the remotest rural areas in India. In contrast, its nearest multinational rival has fewer than half that number of outlets. The existing distribution network and the relationships Asian Paints has nurtured with its channels are a formidable barrier to entry for new arrivals. Similarly, Titan watches of India, faced with the threat of market liberalization and entry by giants such as Seiko and Citizen, quickly established 101 exclusive (owned and franchised) Titan stores in key cities in India, along with a strong presence in 85 multibrand showrooms, and a total distribution through 5,000 outlets in 1,250 towns across India. Says Mr. Vasant Nangia, Managing Director of Titan watches, "This represents a stranglehold on the domestic market." As Seiko and Citizen contemplate entry into India, they must contend with replicating these enormous distribution investments. Titan's local presence, its reach and its extensive agreements with the channels place it in a strong defensive position.

LEVERAGE COST ADVANTAGE

Local manufacturers in Brazil, Russia, Indonesia, China, India and other liberalizing markets sometimes take comfort in their cost advantage over MNCs. Their products are likely to be designed and produced locally, with local raw materials and inexpensive labor. This cost advantage is typically used by EMCs to adopt a low-price strategy in the market. Competing on price may work in the short-term, if it is not matched by the foreign competitors. However, the price advantage is illusory for two reasons. First, local manufacturers often cannot match the quality of international brands. When they do, the cost advantage generally evaporates. Secondly, international brands often adopt a long-term market-entry strategy that allows them to take advantage of both the inexpensive local inputs and their superior international technology. Unilever, for example, produces locally in most countries with local raw material and labor. Yet its marketing is clearly world class in every market. The strategy of leveraging lower costs of production can easily be replicated by MNCs, much to the discomfort of local players. Hindustan Lever, Unilever's Indian subsidiary, for example, introduced a price-brand, Wheel detergent powder, which has reclaimed market share from the remarkably successful local market leader Nirma. Local firms need to demonstrate that they can produce products of a quality similar to that of products from MNCs, and still retain their price advantage.

When they do actually have a cost advantage at equivalent quality levels, EMCs need to carefully consider their options in terms of deploying it. A cost advantage should not automatically translate into a lower price. A low-price positioning is vulnerable not just to price-wars with multinationals, but also to predatory local competitors. Instead, EMCs might consider not cutting price and spending the better margins on measures such as generating brand loyalty, investments in brand equity and positioning, buying distribution space, new product development, packaging innovation, etc. Asian Paints, for example, has consistently developed new paint products and packaging designed specifically for the Indian market. Many of its products are targeted at the low-end of the market. Yet, in each segment, Asian Paints is able to command a premium over its competitors. Returns generated form the premium pricing are ploughed back into market-building measures. These measures strengthen the firm's position in the marketplace and create the potential for additional future revenue. Asian Paints remains the dominant brand in the consumer paints market in India, despite huge efforts by multinationals to displace it. By directly translating a cost advantage into price, EMCs may be squandering an opportunity to create market positions not based on price. They may be locking themselves into a uni-dimensional price-based positioning.

COMPETE ON PACE: LEVERAGE ORGANIZATIONAL FLEXIBILITY

Relative to their MNC competitors, EMCs tend to be administratively less complex organizations. The distance between managers and owners, and that between key decision makers and key stakeholders is not as large as for multinationals. As a result, procedures and control mechanisms tend to not be as rigid. For example, local EMCs generally do not have to grapple with typical MNC tensions—such as that between forces in the organization that advocate global integration (with an eye on scale economies) and those that argue for greater local responsiveness (with a view to being customer friendly), or the tension between the product organization and the regional/ country organization.

One consequence of this is that EMCs have the option of competing on pace. Rapid product launches, entry into new segments and use of localized and customized promotions to alter the competitive nature of the market are options available to local players. MNCs may be strapped by cumbersome control procedures that make it necessary for decisions such as product launches, and even promotional campaigns, to be authorized at higher levels in the organization, which are often located outside the local market.

Another factor which magnifies the complexity of local operations for the MNC, but not for the local firm, is the nature of entry for MNCs. If the MNC's entry into the emerging market is through a joint venture or a strategic alliance (either because of regulatory requirements or due to the desire of the MNC management to diversify risk), they are additionally burdened with managing the well-documented tensions that arise from such partnering. Critically, for an MNC, the challenge of managing an operation in an emerging market with its own dynamic, and often more chaotic and less well-ordered rules of the game, is added to this potent mix of managing a multi-business multinational with multiple ownership structures. MNC managements are often unprepared for these challenges. In such cases, their superior resource positions come to naught, and the firms under-perform. The limits of the flexibility of their organizational arrangements—structure, systems and cultures—are tested in an effort to accommodate rapid responses to EMC initiatives. EMCs are well positioned to exploit this lack of MNC flexibility. Indeed the outstanding success achieved by Bajaj Auto in the Indian market place is a case in point.

In the mid-1980s, at the time of the entry of the global majors—Honda, Yamaha and Suzuki from Japan and Piaggio from Italy—into the Indian market for two-wheel motorized vehicles (scooters, motorcycles and mopeds), the local producer, Bajaj Auto, was considered heavily disadvantaged. It had dated technology, and its scooters were poorly designed. Bajaj had a huge share of the scooter market, but no presence in the fast growing motorcycle and moped segments. While it was not cash strapped, its financial resources were no match to those of the international players. Most analysts had expected Bajaj to cede the market to the powerful MNCs.

More than a decade later, Bajaj Auto remains the market leader. It has a 37 percent share of the entire two-wheeler market. Besides maintaining its leadership of the scooter segment, Bajaj has also carved out a 28 percent share of the motorcycle market, and a healthy 9 percent share of the moped segment. A significant factor contributing to the company's success has been its ability to make quick decisions, unencumbered by the complexities of a multi-business multinational with multiple ownership structures. Rahul Bajaj, the chairman, could choose to enter new segments, seek new and multiple technology partners, expand the distribution network, make investments in information technology, increase R&D and advertising expenditures and cope with initial product failures, without having to justify these decisions to a higher level hierarchy located elsewhere in the world. In sharp contrast, the country managers of Honda, Suzuki, Yamaha and Piaggio would all have had to deal with significantly less responsive organizational arrangements.

LEVEL PLAYING FIELD THROUGH SELECTIVE PARTNERING

MNC competitors often have the advantage of superior technology and strong brand equity. Both of these advantages, however, can be neutralized by EMCs through selective partnering. Shanghai Jahwa, for example, competes head-on with some powerful MNCs through its top of the line Chinf de Chinf cosmetics products. Much of the technology in this line of products is bought from a French manufacturer. Similarly, Bajaj has been effective at competing in the fast-growing motorcycle business because it brought in technology from Kawasaki through a technical collaboration agreement. Computer manufacturers, Vist in Russia, Legend in China and HCL in India, are all competing effectively with multinational giants such as Compaq and Hewlett-Packard by signing on to the "Intel inside" campaign or its local variants. The use of the Intel name provides the consumer with the assurance they need and places the local brands in the same consideration set as well-known multinational brands. A key feature of selective partnerships is that they allow the local firm to match their international rivals while maintaining their autonomy. Unlike joint ventures and sell-outs, selective partnership deals are driven by the EMC as it seeks to upgrade its capabilities to effectively compete with its MNC rivals.

COUNTERATTACK

By building on a sound defensive position at home, some EMCs have counterattacked their MNC competitors in international markets. International expansion by an EMC is an expensive and risky proposition. Nevertheless, some EMCs have realized that the benefits of playing in international markets sometimes outweigh the costs. Bimbo, a large confectioner in Mexico, consolidated its hold on its vast domestic distribution network when it became evident that international competitors, including Pepsi, were about to enter the market. Its successful defense of the home market has emboldened it to launch an international expansion strategy that has led the company into Texas, where it has acquired the largest local bakery. Cemex, another Mexican firm, launched an international expansion initiative based on acquisitions that has made it the third largest cement manufacturer in the world. Arvind Mills, an Indian denim manufacturer, exports over half of its output making it the third largest, and fastest growing, denim supplier in the world. Jollibee, the Filipino fast-food company, now has over 25 stores outside its home market. Titan watches, an Indian watch maker, threatened by the entry of international brands, has launched a deliberate strategy to become a "world brand."

These expansion strategies have some interesting elements in common. A first step to international expansion for many EMC firms appears to be to enter analogous markets in which key success factors such as consumer preferences, or distribution requirements, are similar to those in their home markets. Thus, Titan's first international foray was into the Persian Gulf states, where a large expatriate Indian community was already familiar with the brand and was easily targeted using the same media as the domestic Indian market. For the same reasons, Jollibee's first international stores were located in the Persian Gulf and Hong Kong, where it found a large expatriate community which readily identified with its brand and appreciated its products. Cemex has chosen to expand first into markets in which cement is, as in Mexico, a branded product rather than a commodity. Analogous market expansion allows EMCs a stepping stone to international expansion.

Expansion into the major markets of the developed countries is a much larger step, requiring significant commitment of resources. Titan watches of India has in recent years launched a major brand-building campaign in Europe, positioning itself as a global brand. While, so far, Europe accounts for less than 10 percent of Titan's sales, the brand now enjoys a reputation in the Indian market as the only domestic watch brand capable of playing internationally. More importantly, its participation in the international markets would enable Titan to deny the MNCs entering the Indian market the option of exclusively leveraging their "internationalness" as a positioning platform (often a powerful platform for competing in emerging markets as this claim is inimitable by EMCs). Titan further claims to have learned about doing business and meeting stringent customer expectations by operating in Europe. Through a rotation of managers, this knowledge is fed back home where the firm is bracing to meet international competitors. Arvind Mills of India believes it has already benefited domestically from its international expansion. It has achieved standards of reliability in delivery and product quality that its local competitors cannot match.

The expense and risk of international expansion have kept most EMC firms at home. There are very few EMC international brands. However, they are expanding rapidly. Many of the firms we have discussed in this chapter are firms to watch in the coming years. While they may not achieve the ubiquity of MNC brands in the short term, they are certain to give their MNC competitors a run for their money in local markets. And with the internet rapidly eroding the value of complementary assets held by the MNCs (their distribution equity in particular), many EMCs now have lower costs of entry into international markets.

CONCLUSIONS

EMCs in liberalized markets face a very tough new competitive reality. However, the challenges of this new competitive landscape are not insurmountable. As we have seen, some firms are rapidly adapting to this new market environment and taking advantage of opportunities that derive from their specific competitive advantages. These firms are well poised to defend their turf, and even launch counterattacks into international markets.

Note

1. See Dawar and Frost 1999 for an exception.

References

Dawar, Niraj and Tony Frost. "Competing with Giants: Survival Strategies for Local Companies in Emerging Markets." *Harvard Business Review* 77, no. 2 (March–April 1999): 119–129.

15 BRANDING CHALLENGES FOR TRANSITIONAL ECONOMY FIRMS IN LOCAL MARKETS

Erich A. Joachimsthaler
University of Virginia and Prophet Brand Strategy
Jordi Garolera
University of Pompeu Fabra, Barcelona
Dana Pillsbury
Prophet Brand Strategy

Introduction

International brands are spreading across the globe, swallowing up markets that previously have been the turf of smaller, local brands. Sometimes local market share is acquired through the acquisition of local companies by global competitors. Global brands thus tend to quickly gain local market strengths. If the remaining local brands in transitional economies are to survive in face of such strong international competition, local brands must find a way to favorably differentiate themselves from larger rivals, to create customer connections, and to communicate this difference in a way that neutralizes the deep-pocket advantage of international players.

Local brands in transitional economies face unique and special challenges. Their markets are by definition in a state of rapid flux, making it doubly difficult to maintain a consistent, appealing brand positioning. In addition, there is often a preference for imports due to the perceived attractiveness of developed countries of origin.

This chapter considers how such brands can build their strength by "outlocalizing" global brands.

BACKGROUND

There are several relevant areas of scientific research that help to understand the challenges and opportunities of local brands in transitional economies. One area is the field of memory research in psychology, which has as its fundamental premise the idea that knowledge is organized and structured. According to this stream of research, a person's memory consists of links between related concepts or units and the activation of one concept activates or primes connected concepts. Various models have been developed (e.g., Anderson 1983) to describe the organization of memory and are generally referred to as association structures or associative networks.

An association structure or network can be described through a limited number of characteristics. Psychological research has focused mainly on the network size, that is the number of meaningfully related associations linked to a certain word. Research has shown that words with a smaller set of associations are more likely to be recalled than those with a larger set of associations. Another characteristic is the interconnectivity or linkages among the associations (Nelson *et al.* 1993). Empirical research has shown that smaller set size and higher interconnectivity relates positively to recall and recognition. Most recent research (e.g., Nelson *et al.* 1998; Nelson, McKinney and Bennett in press) has shed light on the process of how associations linked to familiar words are activated from memory and how new experiences and past experience influence memory retrieval. We believe that this research is crucial for understanding the nature of brands, and especially the strengths and opportunities of local brands over global brands.

Brands are often thought of as a network of associations in the mind of consumers. The association structure of a brand determines a brand's strength. For example, brands with smaller but focused set sizes should be easier to be recalled by consumers than brands with larger set sizes. Krishna (1996) studied four characteristics as it relates to brands: set size, valence, uniqueness and origin. Set size was defined as the number of associations evoked by a brand name. Valence was defined as the number of net positive associations (positive associations minus negative associations). A unique association is one that is not shared with other brands. And finally, origin was a variable that distinguished associations that were generated from direct experience and those that were linked to a brand in a consumer's memory through indirect experiences such as word-of-mouth communications. Krishna has shown in an empirical study that these characteristics of a brand meaningfully describe a consumers' association structure and that this association structure determines a brand's strength or equity.

Many other researchers have studied characteristics of association structures. For example, Farquhar (1989) discussed the directionality of associations in an association structure. Of particular interest for our research is the work by Aaker (1996) who distinguished between types of associations: functional associations that are directly related to a specific product, and emotional associations that create desirable emotions and feelings with the consumer. Strong brands often create value to customers based on emotional associations and benefits.

RESEARCH QUESTIONS

What then are the opportunities or strengths for local brands over global brands? Our experience in helping companies to build strong brands in many countries shows that strong local brands in general are well known among consumers. Strong local brands tend to be mature brands that from a consumer's point of view "have been around here forever." They often lack the energy, novelty and vitality of global brands. Our experience also shows that often strong local brands are functionally at least equivalent to global brands. In other words, they are functionally undifferentiated. Some are perceived as inferior, especially in transitional economies. We believe that changing perceptions about functional benefits is difficult.

Our experiences also show that strong local brands often have brand strengths/equity by invoking one of two key emotions, which could be called personal consumer connections and cultural consumer connections. Creating a personal consumer connection requires the brand strategist to focus on associations that link the brand with activities and interests or values and beliefs of the consumer's everyday life. This is one way local brands can become relevant for consumers. For example, when Adidas organizes 'streetball' competitions in Europe, or when it sponsors local clubs and leagues who run soccer clinics, little league competitions and summer camps, it connects in a personal way with young consumers. Children of all ages experience the passion of playing soccer, and the fun of participation in Adidas athletic wear, shoe wear and Adidas equipment.

Cultural consumer connections are created when a brand creates relevance with a specific consumer culture without appealing to patriotism or nationalistic sentiments. Local brands are better suited to exploit brand associations that link them with a specific culture. Consider, for example, the ice cream brand Freddo, a super premium ice-cream brand in Argentina. This brand has been built in just a few years by understanding the way people in Argentina like to eat ice cream, and by adapting its business accordingly. Its flagship stores around Buenos Aires are a key distribution channel and brand-building tool. Homes tend to have small freezers, if they do have one at all. Its flagship stores are key for serving the take-home market. Flavors are adapted to Argentinian tastes. The now very successful Argentinian dulce de leche flavor of Haagen-Dazs in America has been topping the list of Freddo's from its founding. Freddo's have personalized its business. Even for those who do not know the family, the name suggests the ice cream is made by a local. The look and feel of its parlors are unique and definitely suggest that super quality ice cream is served here. It is therefore not surprising that Haagen-Dazs that has been successful in many other countries, has had little impact on the Argentinian market, while Freddo's business has been thriving.

We were interested in exploring several ideas regarding building strong local brands in transitional economies. The first research question concerns the differences between strong local brands and strong global brands with regard to their association structures. The second research question concerns the impact of the differences in association structure on brand strengths/equity. Specifically, we formulated the following research hypotheses:

H1: Relative to strong global brands, strong local brands will have:

- The same association structures (as determined by its size, favorability and uniqueness) in terms of functional benefits.
- Different association structures in terms of emotional benefits that determine personal consumer connections.
- Different association structures in terms of emotional benefits that determine cultural consumer connections.

H2: The more favorable a brand is perceived on emotional benefits that determine personal and cultural consumer connections, the higher is its brand strength/equity.

THE STUDY

In-home semi-structured personal interviews were conducted with 300 homemakers in Madrid and Barcelona. Pretesting was conducted with student subjects. Spain is not exactly a transitional economy, even though it compares better to some transitional economies countries than with developed countries. Its GDP is US$14,200 compared to South Korea (US$9,500) and the Czech Republic (US$5,200). Average monthly wages are US$1,470 versus South Korea (US$2,300) and the Czech Republic (US$330). Unemployment is nearly 20 percent versus South Korea (6.5 percent) and Czech Republic (5.2 percent). We also feel that the brand-building challenges of local brands versus global brands is not specific to transitional economies but also observable in more developed countries.

The interviews focused on three consumer product categories: beer, soup and soluble chocolate. These categories were chosen because in each at least one strong local brand was being challenged by at least one aggressive global brand. The strongest local/global brands in each category based on sales were: Estrella/Heineken (beer), Avecrem/Maggi (soup), and Cola-Cao/Nesquick (soluble chocolate). In addition to the free association tasks for each of the brands, we also collected standard brand-specific information such as the relative performance and the importance of brands along key brand associations. A 7-point agree/disagree scale was employed (Table 1).

Specific metrics were developed for three association structure characteristics of size, favorability and uniqueness as follows:

(1) $Size_{brand j}$ = number of functional associations which the respondent rated "strongly agree," "agree" or "somewhat agree" for brand j

(2) $Favorability_{brand j}$ = average rating across functional associations for brand j

Table 1. Variable Definition and Operationalization

Construct	Operationalization
Functional benefits	Refreshing/nutritious
- benefits specific to the product	Good quality
	Good taste
Emotional benefits	
- Personal consumer connection	I like it
- the "fit" with activities, interests,	I can identify with it
values and beliefs of local consumers	Modern/up-to-date
- Cultural consumer connection	A "national" brand
- the "fit" with activities, interests,	Well adapted to local tastes
values and beliefs of a specific local culture	Sold mainly locally

$$(3)\ Uniqueness_{brand\,j} = \sum_{\text{functional benefits}} (\text{share of association})$$

where:
share of associations = 0 if the respondent did not rate brand j "strongly agree" on that benefit, and
share of association = 1/n, n = total number of brands rated "strongly agree" on that association, if the respondent rated brand j "strongly agree" on that association.

Brand strength/equity was measured independently for each product category via a standard conjoint choice exercise. Variables consisted of price and brand only. The competitive set consisted of the global brand in the category, the local brand in the category and a generic/private label brand. Results were analyzed using Sawtooth Software's CVA System Version 2.0. Brand strength/equity for each respondent and brand was defined as the normalized utility across respondents and brands:

$$(4)\ \text{Brand Strength/Equity}_{brand\ i,\ case\ j} = \frac{\text{Utility}_{brand\ i,\ case\ j} - \min(\text{Utility})_{cases,\ brands}}{\max(\text{Utility})_{cases,\ brands} - \min(\text{Utility})_{cases,\ brands}}$$

RESULTS

In each product category (beer, soup, etc.), a "simple factorial analysis of variance" was performed, with the size, favorability, etc. of associations (functional, emotional, etc.) as the dependent variables, the brands as the factors, and brand strength/equity as the covariate.

As shown in Table 2, this ANCOVA analysis revealed no consistent, statistically significant differences between global and strong local brands with two major exceptions: brand strength/equity and culturally relevant emotional benefits. There were statistically significant differences in terms of the association structure of global brands and local brands. The key question then is: do these differences translate into brand strength/equity? We explored this question in Figure 1.

The figure shows that the more an association structure is built on associations that create cultural consumer connections, the higher is the brand's equity. The only exception is the brand Maggi.

BUILDING STRONG LOCAL BRANDS

In this research we have explored some initial ideas about local brands and global brands. We believe that the study of association structures of local and global brands is an important area of inquiry for those who wish to understand the opportunities and strengths of local brands versus global brands.

The research suggests ways strong local brands can be built. First, the research shows that visibility or differentiation, the conventional brand-building objectives, do

Table 2. Local vs. Global Comparisons: ANCOVA Results

	Beer		Soup		Soluble Chocolate	
	Estrella (local)	Heineken (global)	Avecrem (local)	Maggi (global)	Cola Cao (local)	Nesquick (global)
Covariate (brand strength/equity)	0.61[a]	0.47	0.58[a]	0.45	0.56[a]	0.48
Functional benefits						
Size	2.88	2.79	2.76	2.66	2.97	2.93
Favorability	6.07	5.83	5.83	5.47	6.52[a]	6.28
Uniqueness	1.86	1.82	1.94[a]	1.68	2.13[a]	1.89
Emotional benefits						
- Personal connection						
Size	2.70	2.58	2.63	2.42	2.75	2.72
Favorability	5.65	5.23	5.56[a]	4.96	5.83	5.59
Uniqueness	1.89	1.74	1.94[a]	1.64	1.98[a]	1.80
- Cultural connection						
Size	2.48[a]	2.01	2.39[a]	2.07	2.37[a]	2.25
Favorability	5.41[a]	3.76	5.23[a]	4.45	5.14[a]	4.75
Uniqueness	1.83[a]	1.56	1.82[a]	1.59	1.85[a]	1.68

[a]$p < 0.01$ $0 \leq$ utility ≤ 1 $0 \leq$ size, uniqueness ≤ 3 $1 \leq$ favorability ≤ 7

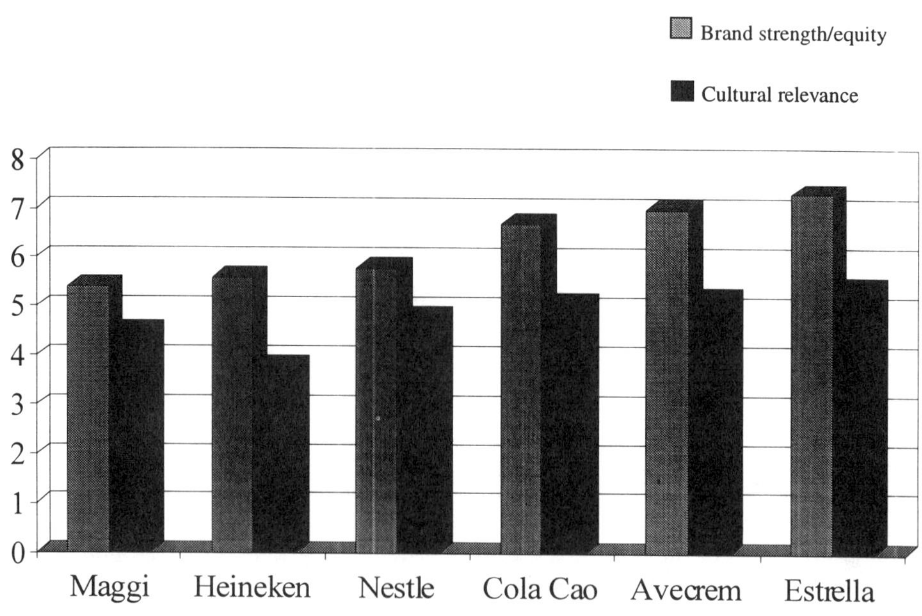

Figure 1. Cultural Consumer Connection and Brand Strength/Equity

not hold for local brands in transitional economies. Of course, both visibility and differentiation are important; however, these two key brand-building objectives are not sufficient. Strong local brands need to develop ways to create customer connections. Differentiation alone favors global brands. Customer connection favors local brands.

We have distinguished in this research between personal customer connection and cultural customer connection. As far as personal customer connection is concerned, strong local brands and strong global brands are not different. The real opportunity for local brands consists of building a brand identity based on associations that emphasize cultural customer connections. Brands that perform more favorably on customer connection associations generally tend to be stronger brands.

FUTURE RESEARCH

Our research is preliminary and really has the purpose to communicate a direction for future research. The notion of association structures of local versus global brands is central to understanding the differences between these types of brands. Brands are built by having a strong and clear brand identity. Building a brand identity requires understanding how to influence the association structure of consumers in transitional economies.

An understanding of the association structure can be gained by using qualitative brand research as we have conducted in our study. We believe that standard market research approaches that are used in developed economies tend to be inappropriate for use in transitional economies. Consumers are not used to many standard research approaches or are unwilling to participate. The research we have conducted framed the data collection process in a sort of dialog or discussion with a consumer rather than in a typical interviewer-respondent format. These methodological issues, we believe, are critical in data collection in transitional economies.

There are many opportunities for research into the association structures consumers in transitional economies have concerning brands. We know little about how past and present experiences with brands influence these association structures. Little is also known about the relative effectiveness of media advertising versus alternative brand-building approaches in shaping association structures. These are key research areas that will help us to learn about strategies through which local brands can "outfox" global brands in transitional economies.

Another important area of research is the documentation of 'best practices' in brand-building approaches in transitional economies that go beyond the one big annual advertising campaign. Few local brands can afford media advertising. Few local brands can or should spend limited resources on a major media campaign. The fragmentation of media and markets makes this issue even more important for future years. Joachimsthaler and Aaker (1997) have suggested ways of building brands beyond media advertising using a case study research approach. They studied over 200 brands in Europe and provided several 'best practice' cases of companies that have built brands "outside the box of" advertising. Similar research does not exist concerning brand building in transitional economies. We strongly believe that for research and marketing science to make a contribution for companies and brands in these economies, there is a need to do more discovery-oriented research, case studies and 'best-practice' research in transitional economies. This research will help to bridge theory, scientific research and actual brand-building practice in transitional economies.

References

Aaker, David A. *Building Strong Brands*. New York: The Free Press, 1996.

Anderson, J. R. *The Architecture of Cognition*. Cambridge, MA: Harvard University Press, 1983.

Farquhar, Peter H. "Managing Brand Equity." *Marketing Research* 1 (September 1989): 24–33.

Joachimsthaler, Erich A. and David A. Aaker. "Building Brands Without Mass Media." *Harvard Business Review* 75, no. 1 (January–February 1997): 39–50.

Krishna, H. S. "Characteristics of Memory Associations: A Consumer-Based Brand Equity Perspective." *International Journal of Research in Marketing* 13 (1996): 389–405.

Nelson, Douglas L., David L. Bennett, Nancy R. Gee, Thomas A. Schreiber and Vanesa M. McKinney. "Implicit Memory: Effects of Network Size and Interconnectivity on Cued Recall." *Journal of Experimental Psychology: Learning, Memory and Cognition* 19, no. 4 (1993): 747–764.

Nelson, Douglas L., Vanesa M. McKinney and David L. Bennett. (in press) "Conscious and Automatic Uses of Memory in Cued Recall and Recognition." In *Stratification of Consciousness and Cognition,* edited by B. H. Challis and B. M. Velichkovsky. Amsterdam: John Benjamins Publishing.

Nelson, Douglas L., Vanesa M. McKinney, Nancy R. Gee and Gerson A. Janczura. "Interpreting the Influence of Implicitly Activated Memories on Recall and Recognition." *Psychological Review* 105, no. 2 (April 1998): 299–324.

16 BRAND-BUILDING CHALLENGES IN OVERSEAS MARKETS FOR KOREAN COMPANIES

Rajeev Batra
University of Michigan
Youjae Yi
Seoul National University

Introduction

The challenges facing companies from Korea (South Korea, or the Republic of Korea) as they try to build their brands in the West (North America and Western Europe) are very important to Korea, given its export orientation. Korea derived 55 percent of its GNP from exports in 1997, 34 percent of that from exports to the West (North America and Western Europe). This success of the last 10 years (1988–97), in which Korean exports grew by 12 percent a year and GNP by 10 percent a year, is being threatened not only by the current currency and debt crisis, but by the longer-term challenge from countries with even lower cost structures, such as China (Lee 1994). If Korea is to avoid entering into ruinous price wars with these new competitors, and if it is to realize higher margins on its exports, it must have the ability to charge higher prices, by marketing stronger brands. Korean companies have historically focused on an OEM-supplier export strategy, relying on low costs as their competitive advantage, but this needs to change as their relative costs go up. They thus need to learn how to move beyond such an "OEM supplier strategy," but this will require new skills, because the success requirements for "own brand exporting" are different from those of successful OEM exporting (Lee and Son 1993). (A background note on the Korean economy and exports is attached to this chapter as an Appendix.)

Beyond their obvious relevance for Korean companies, however, the challenges that face Korea are of broader interest as well, and that is why they are studied in this chapter. The history of Korean export development contains important lessons for other newly industrialized countries (NICs), especially "transitional economies" (TEs) such as China, Vietnam, Russia and the other FSU countries, Czech Republic, Poland,

Hungary, etc. Like Korean companies, companies from other NICs and the TEs usually begin by serving as "private label" suppliers or as captive low-cost manufacturing sites for original equipment manufacturers (OEMs) in developed markets. Like Korean companies, these latter companies often produce goods in industries (such as automobiles and electronic goods) where consumers seek products that offer not only functional value but also psychological and symbolic benefits, of the kind offered by strong brands. And like Korean companies, these latter companies usually possess only limited financial and management resources to actually create such strong brands.

Indeed, this last resource constraint makes the brand-building challenges facing Korean companies important to the theoretical body of knowledge on brand-building itself. Almost all of the existing branding literature deals with companies having pockets deep enough to invest in many media and for many years to build up their brands.[1] While the large Korean companies that we also study (the Chaebols) are extremely big (several would qualify for the Global Fortune 500, when considered as Groups), their dollar resources are still small compared with those of the North American and West European competitors they must fight. In addition, the Korean companies must also contend with an image of Korean products overseas that in general is not too favorable, and they thus have to find a way to fight and refute this negative "country of origin" (CO) image. This is very dissimilar to the experience base described in the branding textbooks.

Thus there may be learnings from the Korean case for managers from other NIC and TE companies, for governments in these countries interested in export promotion and training, and for the body of academic knowledge on how brands can get built up even when the odds are against you.

A BRAND-BUILDING FRAMEWORK

It is important to very briefly review here some commonly accepted conceptualizations of "brand equity" and of brand-building, if for no other reason than to lay out the framework we will be using subsequently. We can find agreement in the literature (e.g., Aaker 1991, 1996; Keller 1993) on the following key ideas[2]:

1. The term "equity" suggests a financial value. This overall asset value, in turn, is usually based on the ability of the brand in question to extract higher prices and margins than competing brands of supposedly-equal "objective," functional value.
2. This "financial extra," of whatever kind, exists because the brand's customers (such as OEMs or distributors) and/or end-consumers feel some special affinity to this brand, that can be measured as higher attitude or liking scores, higher loyalty or repurchase-intent scores, or higher "goodwill" scores.
3. Current conceptualizations (e.g., Aaker 1991) argue that strong brands have
    a. high unaided awareness levels;
    b. strong reputations for product quality;
    c. other strong, focused, differentiating brand associations or imagery;
    d. loyal consumers or customers; and

e. other proprietary assets, such as a strong distribution network, patents, access to raw materials, etc.

In this chapter, we will not examine the issue of building strong distribution, but will focus on the challenges of building high awareness, strong quality reputations and strong brand associations and imagery (and, through these, strong emotional loyalty).

4. For a strong brand, the outcome of greater preference and loyalty exists not because it has a functionally superior product or service, objectively speaking, but because of "the brand" (the totality of the consumer purchase, including intangibles). This difference between the "tangible" and the "intangible," therefore, is the essence of a "brand," which exists only as a subjective, "imaginary" concept in the mind of the consumer, as a set of perceived facts and feelings. This knowledge and these feelings are evoked in the consumer's mind and heart by the brand's branding elements, such as its name, logo and symbols; its packaging size, color and shape; and the residues left in the consumer's mind and heart by the brand's various sponsored and non-sponsored communications (such as advertising and public relations, or spontaneous word-of-mouth and fashion influences).
5. The relative importance of these "subjective intangibles" in influencing brand choice varies, depending on the product category and the individual; it is higher when product quality is "ambiguous" or "hard-to-determine" for the consumer. Very high-tech product categories, where consumers lack product knowledge, are likely to be high in such ambiguity. In many business-to-business situations, where the choice of a supplier or product can often involve a high level of risk, the decision of which suppliers to consider further (the formation of the "consideration set" or "approved supplier list") is often based substantially on the level of intangible "confidence" the purchaser has in the supplier's trustworthiness and reliability.
6. Earlier research on the types of product categories where brand image appeared to be relatively more important also found that a product's "social conspicuousness" was an important variable. Such conspicuousness implies that the ownership or usage of the product or service be publicly visible (as in automobiles, or living-room audio-video equipment). This makes intuitive sense, because the symbolic aspects of brand and product choice should matter more when significant others can see us choose and use them, and the reactions of these significant others then shapes consumers' sense of their "identity."
7. Obviously, even for the same kind of product category, consumer segments vary in their susceptibility to being influenced by image-altering or image-emphasizing communication strategies. Teenagers, for example, are considered more susceptible.
8. The equity-forming knowledge and feelings can usefully be described by the catch-all term of "associations" or "meanings." The essence of a brand is thus the many associations that the brand's name, symbol, packaging color (etc.) evoke in the mind of the consumer. These associations can be about:

a. the brand's functional properties (what it does and how it does it);
b. its overall or attribute-specific level of quality and reliability;

c. the consumer benefits to be gained from those functional properties and that level of quality, e.g., "an airline with more planes has more flights so I lose less time traveling and become more productive and therefore more successful;"
d. the kinds of users and usage-contexts the brand is meant for (such as situations of individualistic independence versus social affiliation, people who are conformists versus individualists, etc.);
e. the company that makes the brand (its reputation for quality, innovativeness, community and environmental orientation, etc.);
f. the country from which that brand originates (e.g., if it comes from Italy, it must be stylish and fashionable);
g. various kinds of symbolic and cultural meanings and values (e.g., this is a "macho" brand for "aggressive" people, or a "fun" brand, or a brand that connotes "safety" or "nurturance");
h. various feelings and sensations evoked by the brand's non-verbal cues (such as symbols, packaging, colors, smells), leading to the transformation of the purchase or usage or consumption experience to include the experience of certain associated feelings and emotions (including feelings of pride of ownership or display, feelings of security or comfort, feelings of fun and excitement, of sophistication, of "sexiness," etc.);
i. the degree of "intimacy" and the kind of "relationship" or "distance" the consumer feels toward the brand.

9. These associations, by their very nature, can and do vary across consumers and segments. A "brand" can thus be said to consist of those associations that are widely shared and strongly held by its target segment.
10. These associations can be depicted in the form of an "association map," which can be created by either using judgment or research techniques.
11. Marketing communications (advertising, PR, packaging, brand name, logo, etc.), as well as other signals or cues (such as price, the types of distribution outlets used, the nature of service experiences, etc.) play a crucial role in shaping a brand's associations. They must be chosen or designed in such a way that they create or reinforce *target associations*, which must be selected because they are potentially *differentiating, credible* and *motivating* (relevant to how and why people choose a brand in that category).

PREVIOUS RESEARCH ON COUNTRY OF ORIGIN

As just mentioned, CO image can be one of a brand's major associations, and this has been shown to be a crucial product attribute used by consumers in evaluating product and brand quality. Reviews of the scores of articles that have appeared on the topic of CO effects can be found in Ozsomer and Cavusgil (1991), Baughn and Yaprak (1993) and Heslop and Papadopoulos (1993). In brief, a brand's CO serves as an "extrinsic" cue (along with price and brand name) that supplements the use of "intrinsic" cues (perceptions of design, performance, etc.) in helping consumers evaluate a product, based on economic, cultural and political perceptions of the CO in question. The effect of CO has been found to vary across product classes and consumer types, and to be larger when the consumer has lower knowledge and familiarity with the product category.

In general, consumers tend to be biased against buying products from a country with a poor or negative CO; as we shall show below, Korea clearly suffers from a less-than-positive CO among many developed country consumers, and successfully overcoming (and changing) this image is a key task facing Korean exporters. Companies from other countries with similarly negative or weakly-developed images thus have much to learn from the Korean situation.

Country of Origin Image of South Korea

Consistent with the literature, the CO imagery of Korea (relative to that of competitors from Japan, Germany, the United States, etc.) has been found to be an important determinant of brand preference by the Korean companies in many markets. This stereotypic country image plays a major role because the brand images are typically very weak or non-existent, so that consumers "fill in the gap" by drawing on the country stereotype.

According to a survey in the United States conducted in Fall 1996 jointly by the Federation of Korean Industries and The Korean Chamber of Commerce, Korean companies were perceived as being most competitive in the areas of electronics and high-tech products. Products related most to Korea were automobiles, consumer electronics, steel, ships and semiconductors. In addition, Korean companies were seen as being most competent in the functions of production, technology, pricing and financial status, *less so in reliability and product quality*, and even less in customer service, honesty and marketing. *Korean products were known more for price, improvement and value, than for product quality and reliability, and least for design, brand image and product service.*

According to Daewoo Motors' research, Korea evokes associations of a robot-like, somewhat cold and inhuman, highly organized and disciplined, ambitious and dynamic—but poorly-paid and exploited—workforce. This does evoke some admiration, but not much warmth and affection! *This research also suggests strongly that Korea is seen as a country with a "lack of innovation" and that it merely "copies other countries."* Another strong and frequent perception is that of *cheap, poor quality and less sophisticated products, much lower than Japanese products*, and similar to Chinese products (Daewoo Motors Research (DMR) 1997, Appendix). They also found that Korea is not perceived as a "car-making country," unlike Germany or Japan, and this undermines Daewoo Motors' perceived credibility and reliability.

Differences in CO exist across demographic consumer segments. Samsung reports that the image superiority of Japanese over Korean products is larger among higher-income consumers than among middle-income consumers—the gap is only 0.5 scale points out of 5, in the latter. According to Cheil Communications, Samsung's image is stronger among younger and more price sensitive consumers.

There are also regional and geographic differences. A clearer image of Korea apparently exists in the United States than in Western Europe, according to Samsung's research. Samsung has also found that esteem for Japan exceeds that for Korea in Latin

America, esteem for Germany exceeds Korea in Turkey, but that esteem for Korea is even greater than for Japan in countries such as Russia, India and Vietnam, because of the success of Daewoo cars in these countries and because investments in these countries by Korean companies have been larger or more visible than by Japanese companies. *However, further probing revealed that this admiration for Korea might be more on dimensions of "citizenship" and "admiration for the country" than on "quality of products."*

Given this vague or unfavorable CO of Korea, most of the companies studied are trying to not associate themselves with Korea. This is true especially of Samsung and of LG, which don't want to be seen merely as Korean brands but as powerful Global brands in their own right. This was part of the reasoning behind LG's transition from the GoldStar name to LG in 1995, where LG is intended to be a more 'upmarket' (high-end) brand.

OVERALL STRATEGIES FOLLOWED BY KOREAN COMPANIES IN DEVELOPED MARKETS

While this chapter obviously stresses the similarities in the strategies and tactics followed by the companies we studied, significant differences exist among them as well. For example, Daewoo Motors and Hyundai Motors have used very different distribution and branding strategies and tactics overseas, as will become apparent below. For this paper, we obtained information mostly from Samsung Electronics, LG Electronics, Daewoo Motors and Hyundai Motors. We believe the lessons from these companies' experiences apply broadly to most Korean companies.

It must be remembered, as background to understanding the Korean companies' overseas strategies, that the goal of many Korean companies is to "beat the Japanese" (Holstein and Nadkarni 1995); this goal is born both of the desire to learn from the experience and success story of the Japanese, and of the historical animosity towards Japan, which colonized Korea until 1945. This desire to learn from and beat the Japanese helps explain the choice of product categories in which Korean companies focus their overseas sales (automobiles, consumer electronics, electronic and computer components; see Appendix A).

Most Korean companies today have also made a strategic choice to focus on expanding their businesses in the emerging markets (51 percent of Korean exports in 1997 were to Asia). The logic for this choice is quite compelling. First, these markets have, until recently, had very high growth rates and growth potential (which may now decline with their recent currency crises). Second, marketing costs are lower here than in the developed markets. Third, consumers in these markets have lower incomes than in the developed market, and therefore place greater priority for "value" than for the "highest quality," playing to the strengths of the Korean companies. Fourth, such consumers have less of a negative CO of Korea than Western consumers have. Fifth, such consumers may not yet have formed loyalties to the (Japanese, American and European) brands that these Korean companies compete with. Sixth, they may have lower quality expectations (Schuman 1997; Brzezinski 1997). Managers from Daewoo Motors told us that, in their judgment, consumers in Western Europe are more conservative and less willing to try new brands than consumers in (e.g.) Latin America. Still, the developed markets accounted for almost 30 percent of Korean exports in 1996 (Schuman 1997), and with the recent economic slowdown in Asian and other developing markets, these developed markets are of even greater importance to the Korean companies.

Our focus in this chapter is the challenge faced by Korean companies in these developed, not the developing, markets. *The key element of the export marketing strategy used by Korean companies in such developed markets appears to be a focus on providing and stressing "greater value-for-the-money." This is elaborated on, and critiqued, below.*

Consumer Segments Targeted: Demographics and Psychographics

Given this "greater value-for-money" positioning, many of the Korean companies have, not surprisingly, gone after those consumer segments in developed markets which are either more value-driven, or less brand-loyal, or seeking greater functional value. Thus they often go after students, retirees, etc. Daewoo Motors, for instance, has explicitly chosen a "value positioning" and targeted the "price-conscious segment" in Western Europe, and has targeted college students in its 1998 launch in the United States, hiring 'campus representatives,' as well as young adults (Akre 1998). Samsung Electronics has, in many markets such as Japan, explicitly targeted 20 to 39-year olds, "whose loyalty for brands have not been established" (Samsung Electronics 1995 Advertisements' Collection). Daewoo Motors research shows it appeals mostly to buyers buying rationally, for functional reasons (DMR 1997, p. 55). Hyundai Motors is, in the United States, aiming at a group of buyers they call 'young sensibles,' described as "age 18 to 34, practical, interested in substance and wanting to make sensible decisions" (Simison 1998).

There are a few exceptions. Samsung Electronics has for many years run, in the U.S. market, a "fashion oriented" advertising campaign created by Peter Arnell Associates themed "Simply Samsung," aiming to build the brand's emotional associations and explicitly choosing not to talk about product features. Even this campaign, however, has been aimed at younger (age 18–34) and more technically-savvy consumers, in the belief that they are less loyal to established brands and more willing to try new brands. This campaign is described further below.

Product and Product-Line Strategies

This "greater value" strategy is also reflected in the product strategies followed. The Korean companies appear to follow, in many cases, a strategy of giving greater "value" to consumers by adding many more features in their products, when compared to competition. Goldstar, for instance, in one ad campaign used the phrase, "Expensive Electronics without the expense" (Verespej 1987). Daewoo Motors has followed a policy in Western Europe of providing value options, such as standard power steering, anti-lock brakes, power locks and air conditioning, free of charge (Daewoo Cars UK 1996 brochure).

We will raise questions about this strategy below, in terms of its impact on brand-building. Meanwhile, some of the companies have begun to question this strategy themselves, for other reasons. Thus Samsung Electronics is now seriously considering a "de-featuring" of many of its products, in an effort to lower the costs and complexity of its products, and to increase the mean time between failures (reliability).

On another product-line dimension, many of the products chosen (other than in the business-to-business categories) have tended to be "mass consumer goods." Such products, such as microwave ovens and VCRs, have really helped Samsung build brand awareness—it is now neck-and-neck with Sharp in being the world's #1 microwave oven producer, with almost a 20 percent market-share (*Korea Times* 1997).

Pricing Strategies

This "value strategy" obviously finds clearest expression in pricing decisions. In developed markets, Samsung typically prices its consumer electronics products 10–30 percent below SONY (Nadkarni 1995a), and has found it hard to command a brand premium. Daewoo has priced its cars 10–15 percent below comparable competition in Western Europe (Siler 1996). Hyundai Motors launched its cars in the United States in 1986 priced 20 percent below Japanese competitors, though the price differential today is only about 10 percent. Such a pricing strategy is crucial in communicating the "greater value" positioning discussed earlier, and the target consumer segments are correspondingly those of lower incomes.[3]

However, this strategy suffers from several potential brand-building negatives. For one, a lower price might serve to communicate lower quality in some cases.[4] This has apparently happened to Daewoo cars in Germany (Siler 1996). Secondly, pricing a product lower than competition might reduce its "aspirational" value, especially in symbolically-important product categories such as automobiles. We will comment on this in more depth later.

Advertising Strategies and Tactics

A history of how Korean companies' foreign advertising has evolved over the years is presented by Cho, Choi and Yi (1994). Especially noteworthy is the trend from corporate identity-building advertising, focusing on size and skills and high value for low cost, to product ads created by local subsidiaries focusing on low cost and higher quality, to globally-coordinated image differentiation strategies.

An examination of global advertising of the companies studied over the last few years reveals that in the past they have stressed themes of being (a) global companies, (b) offering greater value, (c) technology leaders, (c) diversified, integrated "chips-to-ships" manufacturers and (d) "humanizing," "empowering" or "socially responsible" companies. Examples of such campaigns appears below; many campaigns quite naturally combine several of these themes.

Global/Size Themes

In 1996, Samsung Group ran a global image advertising campaign during the Summer Olympics in Atlanta with the theme "The World Inspires Us," showcasing its diverse worldwide product line against wordwide settings such as Hong Kong, Utah, African plains and an arctic glacier, etc. (Lee 1996), spending about US$30 million worldwide.

Currently, Samsung is beginning a campaign to position itself as a major global corporation, in the company of other global giants such as IBM, Coca-Cola, Xerox and Panasonic, implying that it too is therefore a high quality, trustworthy company. This is being implemented primarily through an Olympics' sponsorship: Samsung paid $45 million to become one of only 11 worldwide Olympics' sponsors for the upcoming 2000 Sydney Olympics. Samsung also paid to become the official "wireless communications partner" for the Nagano Winter Olympics, and the official "white goods" sponsor for the Asian Games in 1998. The strategy is to run advertising that will make a connection between the features/technology of Samsung products and the benefits to the Olympics and its athletes.

In a similar vein, LG bought the rights to being the "official large home appliance" of the World Cup 1998 in France, for washing machines, refrigerators, air conditioners etc., attempting to create associations of "reliable" and "global." LG thus features the ball and logo of the World Cup in its ads. In addition, they themselves sponsor a low-cost LG soccer cup, which was played in Tunisia in 1997 featuring teams and coaches from Romania, Iran, Peru and Nicaragua.

Another way in which Samsung has pursued this "global corporation" theme is through a "world citizenship" campaign, making a linkage with the Nobel Foundation—this has allowed Samsung to use Nobel Laureates in its advertising, and link itself to themes such as world peace, literature, and the arts, in trying to connect with educated consumers worldwide (Matzer 1996). However, the implied connection between these Nobel laureates and Samsung appears to be weak.

The Value Theme

When Hyundai Motors launched its cars in the United States in 1986, the brand was positioned on its low price, with campaigns such as "cars that make sense" and "2 cars for the price of one." As a consequence, however, its image suffered, so the company has now changed its message, and begun to invest more in standardized national advertising.

The "Diversified/Integrated" Theme

According to Daewoo Motors research, there is some consumer knowledge that Daewoo is a company that also makes electronics and home appliances, but the group's manufacturing of ship-building, construction, etc. are not well-known (DMR 1997, p. 24). Would such knowledge help? The same research also showed that for some consumers, especially those from developing countries, knowing the scope of group activities would help reassure them and add perceived technological competence and thus build confidence; but for most others, especially those from developed countries, such scale and size was not that impressive, and even lead to a negative image of "non-specialization" (DMR 1997, p. 26). This research suggested, however, that knowledge of the scope and size of the group's activities would tend to increase consumer confidence and security, and reduce perceived risk (DMR 1997, p. 29).

Thus when Daewoo Motors launched its passenger cars into Western Europe, it followed the advertising strategy of introducing the company first, before talking about its passenger cars. The advertising talked about the fact that Daewoo was a 35-year-old huge corporation (US$50 billion in sales, Fortune #35), making 750,000 vehicles worldwide every year, among other products such as ships, electronics and heavy machinery (in a TV ad called "Transporter," Daewoo products including a satellite, a supertanker, a plane and a computer were lined up on a car transporter). The campaign was entitled "Daewoo. The Biggest Car Company You Never Heard Of." In addition, they decided to position Daewoo on the basis of "customer focus" (Koranteng 1996).

During 1993–96, Hyundai Motors used the ad strategy of pointing out that it was a very large Korean company, making everything "from chips to ships." However, their research showed them that this only helped in developing countries, because in the developed world consumers actually preferred the image of a specialized supplier (Source: Some conversations with Diamond Advertising managers). As a consequence, in 1996 Hyundai split up the world into two regions for advertising purposes, the developed and developing countries. In the former, the new imagery became one of an athlete, reaching higher, implying an emphasis on quality. In the former, different branding strategies were used in different parts of the world (Latin America, Europe, etc.). The advertising was aimed at global business opinion leaders, and appeared in media such as the *Wall Street Journal, Scientific American*, etc.

Technology/Quality Leadership

In South Africa, Samsung has been very successful in building brand equity with an ad campaign headlined "leadership through products," stressing the greater number of high-end features offered in Samsung products. After an initial phase of building dealer support, Samsung invested in this very high share-of-voice ad campaign, utilizing sub-brands, and an ad tonality that was sophisticated and product centered. Samsung, in 1995, also ran corporate advertising playing up its technology, and it ran ads in many countries for Samsung Electronics, playing up its global investments in R&D, its size and worldwide and product-line scope, as well as its leadership in display technology (such as no-curvature TV display tubes).

We will discuss Hyundai's problems with its quality image in the United States below. In 1996, Hyundai ran a global campaign that attempted to change Hyundai Motor's quality image, using the new Tiburon coupe as support, and employing a refutational tone, "where reality exceeds expectations." Meanwhile, Daewoo Motors' advertising strategy has been to differentiate itself on quality perceptions from other Korean competitors, notably Hyundai. Thus they have tried to claim that Daewoo Motors produces the best cars in Korea, priced higher than Hyundai, with higher quality.

The Humanizing/Empowering Theme

Samsung Electronics has since 1996 run, in the U.S. market, a "fashion-oriented" advertising campaign created by Peter Arnell Associates. Themed "Simply Samsung," it is aimed at younger (age 18–34) and more technically-savvy consumers, focusing on simplicity of usage, and using as support Samsung's attempts to create products that are ergonomically advanced and customized so that they can "humanize" technology and "empower" consumers. The proposition is "the most advanced technology in the simplest way." (cf., Samsung Electronics PowerBrand Manual, 1995). The goal is to make Samsung appear distinctive and contemporary, and to supplement the "rational" reasons for buying Samsung products with a "sensual and emotional" image. The look-and-feel of the advertising is thus very sophisticated and modern (Levine 1996). The campaign has reportedly increased Samsung's awareness and contemporary image ratings in the United States. However, some Samsung managers seem to think that the Arnell campaign was off-strategy, in that it did nothing to refute the poor quality perception.

In many other countries too (such as France, Portugal and the United States), Samsung Electronics has utilized this idea of "humanizing" technology, using themes such as "Technology that works for life" (Samsung Electronics 1995 Advertisements' Collection).

Events/Sponsorships

All the companies studied appear to be placing heavy emphasis on sports marketing, apparently following the lead of Nike in the United States and Dentsu in Japan. As mentioned, Samsung has an association with the Nobel Prize Committee (1996), and has become an official Sponsor of the Olympics; LG became the "official large home appliance" of the World Cup 1998 in France, and themselves sponsor a LG Soccer Cup. Hyundai Motors has been involved with the 1997 International Judo Federation, the qualifying rounds for the 1998 World Cup soccer competition and the FIFA All Star Game, the 1994 World Archery Competition and the Asia-Pacific Car Rally Championship series in Australia in 1995 and 1996 (Hyundai Motors Annual Report 1997).

Public Relations

Daewoo Motors, realizing the limitations of its small ad budget, is using PR heavily. They invited 400 journalists from around the world to Korea to witness the launch of their new small car (the Matiz), an effort which they estimate will cost only US$3–4 million, because current airfares to Korea are so cheap (due to the currency crisis). Samsung invited 180 dealers in telecommunications, from around the world, to Nagoya. LG is also doing some product placement, and featured its products in a recent "Sneakers" movie.

Promotions/Sampling/Trial

Daewoo Motors relied heavily on a "test drive" program in Western Europe. They reserved 10,000 high-end cars (e.g., they had leather seating, and lots of options) for this program, making them available for free rentals, for 1–2 to 12 weeks, even for long vacations, and offered them as sweepstakes prizes at the auto shows. In early 1998, Daewoo Motors ran a promotion in Western Europe offering, to those consumers who traded-in their cars purchased in 1994–95 for new ones, an expense-paid 6-day trip to Korea. This is a US$3000 value but costs Daewoo much less (because airfares to Korea on KAL have dropped significantly because of the won depreciation); the trip included plant tours, sightseeing, test-drives, etc.

Daewoo Motors has also attempted to organize "Pan-Korea" clubs among buyers in Western Europe, in which Daewoo car buyers who influenced their friends to buy Daewoo cars would get a credit.

Hyundai Motors is relying on a "test drive" claim to try to turn around its poor image: "driving is believing" is its advertising theme line in 1998 in the United States. As part of the program, Hyundai created a "learn and drive" test-drive program for numerous weekend basketball tournaments around the country, in which young adults and families could drive Hyundai cars while waiting between events.

Logos/Graphic Identity/Corporate Identity

Samsung has established a corporate identity (CI) program—reportedly the first among Korean companies—stressing its oval logo, with blue colors.

LG has its 3-year old "Face" logo, made up from the letters L and G (its "face of the future"), in "LG Red" (Pantone 207C) color, and its curved "LG wave." They are very strategic in the kinds of brand associations they want to build around their LG brand, according to the branding document prepared for them by their advertising agency, DMB&B. The "LG wave" is intended to communicate "active, emerging, moving," while the smile logo and corporate identity are intended to communicate "trustworthy, reliable, friendly, contribute to society, and technical leadership, innovative, inspiring, energetic and vital." Overall, LG is attempting to identify itself as being a "hi tech" + "hi touch" company that by combining these two philosophies "improves quality of life" and leads to "hi hope" at the top of the "image pyramid."

Hyundai seems to lack a coherent corporate identity effort; it has used different logos, beginning with a green triangle for Hyundai Construction, and today lacks a unified look.

ASSESSMENTS OF SUCCESS OF THESE STRATEGY AND TACTICS

Having reviewed the marketing and communications strategy and tactics followed to date by Korean companies in the developed countries, we turn to looking at what these tactics have yielded in terms of brand equity payoffs for these companies in Western markets.

Brand Equity of Korean Companies in Western Markets

Samsung claims to be one of the world's 100 leading brands, because they were cited as such in a book by Interbrand in 1996 (Kochan 1997), mostly for the "width" (extensiveness) of the brand. Samsung has collected brand equity data since 1994, among both end-users and dealers, and has tracked movements in its "positive opinion" (esteem) and "aided awareness" figures over the years, and compared themselves to the competition. (The survey is conducted by Research International, with a global sample size of 40,000). In these data, Samsung's overall scores on esteem have gone up from about 30 percent in 1994 to about 65 percent in 1997, almost equaling those for Sharp, but still below Toshiba's score of 80 percent. Aided awareness percentages, which were also around 30 percent in 1994, have since become higher (exact numbers were not revealed). (*Note that **unaided awareness** of Samsung, however, is still likely very low.*) However, Samsung admits that in most countries it is still seen as a "blue-collar" brand, and that *the high esteem and awareness numbers reported above are more true of developing countries than the developed markets.*

In the United States specifically, Samsung reports that its brand image is strong on dimensions of 'value for money,' and 'affordability,' and on 'ease of use' and 'simplicity,' but is not yet as strong on a purer 'quality' dimension. Similar results appear for Samsung from Western Europe: it has a strong image for 'value for money,' but not for 'quality.' These were confirmed by other sources (Cheil Communications), which also said that Samsung did not have many associations, other than its Asian and/or Korean country origin, even among buyers of its products. (Indeed, Samsung was apparently seen as #1 among the Korean companies by consumers, and thus had most claim to "Koreanness"—that could potentially be used to Samsung's advantage if positive associations could be attached to Korea and its companies, a strategy that Samsung is reportedly investigating, see below). Other than these country origins, the predominant associations for Samsung were 'value for money,' 'cheap,' 'product features' and 'copycat'. "Consumers today buy Samsung out of (financial) necessity, not out of choice," one executive remarked.

According to some brand image research we have seen, Daewoo Motors showed extremely low levels of unaided awareness in Western Europe, and higher but "almost last in category" levels of aided awareness. In terms of brand associations, the data suggest that very few associations exist, and the overall image is 'neutral' (p. 35); those that do exist are primarily associations with 'value,' 'low price' and 'lack of prestige' (DMR 1997, pp. 13–14). Data from a few countries hints at a more 'feminine' image (appendix), allegedly going with low-prestige! A few other associations appear in data from particular countries (e.g., in Australia Daewoo had a somewhat 'cheerful and bright' personality rating, in Belgium and the Netherlands a 'contemporary' and 'self-confident' rating, in Spain a 'fashionable' rating—but these were all still low, just a bit above neutral). There is some knowledge that Daewoo is a company that also makes electronics and home appliances, but the group's manufacturing of ships, construction, etc. are not well known (DMR 1997, p. 24). Overall, consumers have very low knowledge of, familiarity with, and trust in, the brand, which creates considerable fear and doubt about the product's long-term quality and reliability, so that most consumers are taking a "wait-and-see" attitude concerning Korean products (DMR 1997, p. 24). Their report states: "In most countries, the reasons for NOT buying Daewoo had to do with fear of the unknown, or the perceived risk in going with a little known brand" (DMR 1997, p. 55). Overall, these low levels of awareness imply a lack of familiarity, and thus of trust (DMR 1997, p. 22).

LG has undergone a brand transition from its Lucky and Goldstar names to LG, starting in 1995 in Korea, and as of today, almost complete worldwide. It reports conducting regular marketing research on its brand equity, but only in Eastern Europe and other developing countries. In general, they suspect that LG has a "poor perception" in North America and Western Europe, where they began marketing only in the mid-80s, much later than the Japanese companies. "We need more time and investment" was their opinion. They told us that a 'poor quality perception' was their main challenge, due (in their judgment) to a negative CO image for South Korea overall.

Hyundai Motors says that its brand image research shows that it has a poor image in the United States and Western Europe, where it has thus far only launched its "first generation" products, but is rated much better in Australia, where it has "second generation" products and has invested in better after-sales service and in developing a quality image. It concedes the need to improve its levels of brand awareness and image in the United States. (See below for a discussion of Hyundai's low quality image in the United States.)

Research conducted by the Korean Broadcasting and Advertising Company in 1996 found Samsung Electronics to be perceived as the most successful of the Korean companies in overseas marketing, followed by Hyundai Motors. Samsung Electronics and Daewoo Motors were seen as best on product quality, Hyundai Motor as best on price, and LG Electronics and Samsung Electronics as best in distribution. Awareness was perceived to be highest for Samsung Electronics, Hyundai Motor, Daewoo Motor, Korean Airlines and LG Electronics in that order.

It should be noted that, consistent with their geographical strategy, the brand image of Korean companies is much better in the developing world than in developed countries. Thus Samsung reports that its brand equity is much higher in countries such as Russia and India, where it is seen as one of the top brands, than in the West (e.g. a survey by the Indian *Economic Times* in December 1997 rated Samsung just a nudge higher than SONY on quality and reputation). Daewoo Motors has fairly high awareness levels in Latin America (Chile and Colombia), and reports several positive brand associations, such as vitality and self-confidence, in Hungary, Chile etc. (DMR 1997, pp. 35–37).

The Effects of Consumer Experiences with Hyundai

Samsung claims that it has found, in its brand equity data from the U.S. market, that the negative experiences that consumers have had with Hyundai and Kia cars have hurt the image of Korean products. There has apparently been a negative spillover from cars to electronics (and other categories). This poor rating of Hyundai and Kia in initial quality surveys and customer satisfaction in the United States is reported by others as well (Stanley 1995).

According to various reports and sources, Hyundai (which entered the U.S. car market in 1987) acquired a reputation for poor-quality and service in the United States with its earliest Excel model, which it is trying hard to change. Hyundai's U.S. sales peaked in 1988 at 264,282 vehicles; in 1996 it sold just 108,468 (Schuman 1997). (Sales in the last few years have fluctuated between 105,000 to 126,000, according to company sources.) Today, Hyundai still scores very low in the United States J. D. Powers quality surveys, and Kia today sells more cars in the US per month than Hyundai despite Hyundai's 10-year lead (Halliday 1998). In conversations with us, company managers asserted that real product quality today exceeds these perceptions. They complained to us that the J. D. Powers methodology was flawed—a car brand was given an equal one point knock for having a washer breakdown and an engine failure, which they considered unfair! More recently, however, Hyundai's redesigned models, and its new warranty program (discussed later) led to a resurgence in sales in early 1999 (Krebs 1999).

In Western Europe, however, Hyundai has done well, selling about 130,000 cars a year, more than Chrysler. According to Daewoo Motors, Hyundai has not had the same negative image effect in Western Europe, and so this issue of "negative spillover" is not as severe there. (They believe this could be because Hyundai sells in lower volumes, and has a lower profile in Western Europe, as well as the fact that news about products flows less readily around Europe than within the United States.) However, Samsung claims that the fact that Daewoo cars sold in Western Europe have appealed mostly to lower-income segments has led to a "downscale" image for all Korean products. Daewoo Motors, too, finds that consumers do not really distinguish between Daewoo and Hyundai, and lump them together as "Korean" companies.

Conclusions Regarding Brand-Building Strategies Followed

A one-line summary assessment of the brand-building experience of the Korean companies studied could thus be that, in developed country overseas markets, they have (overall) succeeded in building brand associations of 'high value for the money,' but not yet for 'high quality,' nor yet of other brand-enhancing associations. In addition, further work remains to be done on the awareness-building front.

Is a reputation for high value as good as a reputation for high quality, for brand-building purposes? Aaker's branding framework (1991) talks about a perception of quality as being a crucial determinant of a brand's success. While he is silent on the issue of whether a reputation for value is equivalent (or better) than a reputation for quality, other authors (such as Gale 1994) have argued that it is value (which is quality adjusted for price), not "raw" quality, that determines a brand's attractiveness to consumers. It might also be argued that reputations for Quality and Value are interchangeable, from a brand-building standpoint.

However, further thought suggests that a 'value message' could actually subtly communicate a message of 'decent, but not the best, quality." Samsung apparently found in its research that "value for money" perceptions were *negatively* related to perceptions of "quality." Further, in Daewoo Motors' consumer research, we find reports of some consumers saying that, "The only thing I think with Daewoo is good value for money . . . but what's good value for money against reliability?" (DMR 1997, p. 19), and that its "low price evokes suspicions about its perceived quality" (DMR 1997, p. 20). In addition, a publicly-known "cheap price" can also hurt a brand from a "social visibility" standpoint, especially in cars, TV sets, etc. Daewoo Motors' research found that many people report a lack of pride in owning a Daewoo, because of its lower price (DMR 1997, p. 21).

We believe, therefore, that while both perceived "raw" quality, and value, are important in shaping a brand's attractiveness, it is the perception of high "raw" quality that is the more important. Strong brands, we would argue, have an 'aspirational' quality to them; consumers have a desire to own them because owning them gives them the satisfaction of owning 'the best,' and 'the most admired and widely wanted,' and thus enhances their self-esteem. (Think, for example, of the SONY advertising line, "It's a SONY," implying unique, unequaled quality.) If a brand is suspected to be of only mediocre quality, but of high value because it is priced low, a consumer is unlikely to feel attracted to it; while it may be rationally appealing, it is likely to be emotionally unsatisfying. In addition, as mentioned before, there is the additional problem of a low price signaling a lower quality, even if the brand is objectively of high product quality.

This is especially important when the brand is one that comes from a country with a poor or negative CO image, as Korea does: if not much else is known about the brand (the case with most of the Korean companies studied here), the country's CO image becomes a crucial brand association. If the CO image is one of low quality, copycat products, as Korea's CO image unfortunately seems to be, then this will be the consumer expectation of almost every Korean-made brand. A low price merely reinforces this expectation of relatively lower quality, given the signaling value of price in product categories where consumers associate higher prices with higher quality. Low prices are obviously a competitive advantage in 'private label' sales to OEMs, which is where Korean exporters have historically done much of their business. But in marketing automobiles and consumer electronics to consumers—which are socially visible, high risk categories—and even in many business-to-business situations, this may not be the smartest brand-building message to be sending out. Indeed, given these prior consumer expectations of low quality, born of the poor/negative CO image, it becomes even more important for Korean brands to create an impression of the highest possible quality.

It could be argued in response that the Korean brands have no choice but to single-mindedly communicate greater value for the money, in competing with the Japanese and other global brands that possess greater brand equity and are priced higher. We will assert below that, while the Korean brands do in fact need to set product pricing and features/functionality that deliver greater competitive value, their marketing communications should be setting up the expectation of the highest possible quality. Consumers will then feel an aspirational urge to buy these brands, and expect to pay high prices for them; the actual, lower prices will then come as a pleasant surprise, encouraging a purchase.

In sum, we would argue that a marketing and communications strategy that focuses on communicating "high value," instead of "high (raw) quality," is not optimal from a brand-building standpoint, given the prior negative CO image of Korean products.

HOW TO COMMUNICATE QUALITY/REFUTE POOR QUALITY

If the previous argument is accepted, the question then becomes: Given the overall current reputation for only medium quality discussed above, how can the Korean companies specifically and explicitly try to refute this current consumer perception?

There are well-known cases of brands refuting or turning around poor quality expectations. In the United States, Saturn (the automobile brand) faced low-quality product expectations when the cars were launched in 1990, but turned the expectations around through delivering superior service quality, and through a marketing communications strategy focusing on the quality of the company's *people*, rather than its cars.[5] Also potentially relevant is learning from the Japanese experience of the 1960s and 70s, when Japanese companies succeeded in turning around poor quality perceptions in the United States and Western Europe; these are discussed briefly later in this paper.

There are clearly many problems for a brand perceived to have lower quality in trying to raise its quality image in a bid to charge higher prices—going "upmarket," to use a marketing phrase. Some of these problems have been discussed by Aaker (1997), in the context of brand extension strategy. He argues that, in attempting such moves, a brand with an existing lower-quality image should:

1. Try to make only a "reasonable" upward move, by aiming for the 'low end' ofthe upscale market;
2. Differentiate the new higher-quality offering from the current one through real product quality, product design, added services and communications;
3. Use the new high-end brand in a 'silver bullet' role, to raise the image of the entire line;
4. Use a new brand name (as Toyota did with Lexus), or create a clearly-marked sub-brand, because it is extremely hard to try to raise the quality perceptions of a perceivedly-low-quality brand.

It thus seems appropriate, before we examine the potential role of differing marketing instruments (such as product design, warranties, PR, pricing, etc.) in raising brand quality perceptions, to discuss the policy of many of these Korean companies toward using multiple brands and/or sub-brands.

Need for New Brand Names/Sub-brands

Most of the Korean companies we spoke to reported corporate philosophies and tradition that compelled reliance on the (one, single) corporate name, often because of the pride the chairman took in the family name.

However, some use of sub-brands is beginning. Samsung has built a very successful sub-brand in its computer monitor line, SYNCMASTER; it has also used a "World Best" sub-brand in various markets, including South Korea itself, and Singapore, Indonesia and Latin America, and a lower-end "GPM" sub-brand in a few markets. Sub-branding has also reportedly been used by Samsung in South Africa (Samsung MegaView TVs, Samsung Liitle Big Max Hi-Fi Sets, Samsung ColorView Camcorders, DiamondHead VCR, Touch-N-Think microwave ovens) and in Peru (Cheff Samsung for microwave ovens, Lavasoft Samsung Washing Machines).

Daewoo Motors is planning to keep its Ssangyong Sports Utility Vehicle product under a sub-brand name in Western Europe, and has even considered launching its best new car, the Leganza, under that new sub-brand. LG killed its Goldstar brand in the United States and Western Europe; it thought that while this brand had awareness (which they have therefore lost), it did not have a reputation for quality, or other positive associations, or loyalty. LG's plan is to attach higher-quality associations to its newer LG name. Goldstar however is still being used as the name for its 14″ and 15″ PC monitors in the United States, but this will be changed to the LG name when higher quality and bigger monitors are launched. LG today is using the Zenith brand name for TVs and VCRs, and intends to use it for other hi-tech products. It uses the LG name for CD-ROMs.

It should also be noted that, apart from the obvious problem a 'one-brand' policy creates for new up-market moves, it also makes it hard for a brand to acquire unique, differentiating associations. If the same brand (corporate) name is used on scores of different businesses and thousands of individual products, it becomes hard for that name to stand for anything distinct. This is borne out by the Japanese experience, where the two arguably strongest brands are SONY and Honda, known for consumer electronics and autos respectively, unlike Toshiba, Mitsubishi, Fujitsu, etc., which, though, known for quality products, are less clear in terms of what they stand for. As a result, though their scale and scope arguably give each of these large Chaebol names an image of trust, there is perhaps no unique perceived competence for each.

In summary, it would appear that a pre-requisite for Korean brands to raise their overall quality reputations would be to launch newer sub-brands that are used on higher-quality, higher-priced, products. We note here that Samsung has found a reluctance among dealers in developed country markets to carry its higher-end sub-brands; the dealers apparently do not believe that consumers will buy these higher-priced brands. Thus gaining dealer buy-in for the newer sub-brands will be a crucial implementation challenge.

An alternative would be to launch totally new brands. These have the disadvantages of requiring greater marketing dollars (the consulting firm McKinsey apparently told LG it costs a billion dollars to launch a new global brand), and possibly having less of an image-lifting spillover effect on the rest of the line (which carries the current brand name), though they might be unencumbered with any existing negative imagery possessed by the existing brand name. One way to use a totally-new brand is to build one from scratch; another is to acquire or license one. Korean companies have tried to acquire new brands; their experience in such brand acquisitions has not been totally satisfactory, as is now discussed.

Brand Acquisition Strategies and Results

Perhaps the best-known example of such an acquisition of an existing brand is that of AST Computers by Samsung. Samsung gained control over AST Computers in the United States by investing US$720 million for 40 percent of the company in July 1995; this took advantage of Samsung's ability to provide component supplies, and gave Samsung access to AST's brand name, distribution (including a deal with retailing giant WalMart), and its service network. But AST's brand equity was never very strong, and AST has been losing money since 1994 (Kraar 1996). Samsung managers now agree that the AST acquisition was not a great experience for them: the acquisition was made mostly on technical criteria, and AST's (lack of) "brand power" did not get adequate attention. Samsung finally sold AST in 1999 for about US$200 million (Carlton 1999).

The other major 'case' is that of LG and Zenith. LG acquired control (bought 55 percent) of 80-year old Zenith TV in the United States, one of the top 3 brands in the category, in 1995 by spending US$351 million. LG wanted to bring capital and manufacturing expertise, and get Zenith's HDTV and multimedia technology (it had several HDTV patents), and its supposedly-strong brand name and distribution, in return (Nadkarni 1995b). Thus LG-made VCRs were sold under the Zenith name to Sears and Circuit City (Kraar 1996). Zenith is the number two U.S. brand of color TVs, behind the RCA label of Thomson SA of France. But Zenith has been doing very poorly financially; it has had only one profitable quarter since 1985. Due to various operational problems, it lost US$300 million in 1997–98, and on May 22, 1998 it announced it would file for bankruptcy and become a closely-held unit of LG Electronics in exchange for about US$200 million that it owes LG. It plans to simply leverage its brand name and outsource manufacturing.

Hyundai and Daewoo have also pursued this strategy. Hyundai purchased Maxtor (a disk drive maker) in 1995 for US$150 million, as well as Symbios Logic, a semiconductor maker. (Kraar 1996; Lee 1994). Daewoo tried to acquire RCA (Thompson Multimedia) in France but failed because of governmental concerns.

The summary learning from these experiences seems to be that while acquiring existing brands should remain an image-raising option, the brands being acquired need to be carefully studied for their existing (not historical) brand strength. In the case of both AST and Zenith, the brands acquired were not really that strong.

Obviously, buying really strong brands is going to be more expensive, and might make such a strategy out of reach. We are left then with the issue of how existing brands might receive an 'image upgrade,' through higher quality, higher-priced sub-brands marketed as 'flagship' or 'silver bullet' brands in a way to raise the image of the entire line. We examine below the role of the different marketing instruments in implementing such a strategy.

Product/Line Changes

The data on the 'real' or 'objective' product quality of Korean products seems to be mixed. Many of Samsung's products do seem to have excellent quality. This is manifested in the U.S. magazine *Consumer Reports* ratings of its TV sets; in ratings by the British consumer magazine *Which?* of the reliability ratings of its camcorders, VCRs and TV sets (*Which?* 1998); and in the low failure rates of its products (e.g. in South Africa its TV sets failed under 2 percent while the average was 5–8 percent: Koenderman 1997). On the other hand, real defect ratios in Korean cars are still higher than in Japanese cars, supposedly due to less control by Korean companies over subcontractors (Lee *et al.* 1996).

Korean companies have made major attempts in recent years to upgrade the technology base for their products. Daewoo has technology tie-ups in its car business with GM, Honda, Suzuki and (through its acquired Ssangyong business) with Benz. It has also invested huge sums in developing its own engineering and technical capabilities in the automotive business, and in improving the reliability of its color TV sets (Schuman 1997). Hyundai has technology tie-ups with Ford and Mitsubishi. LG has had tie-ups with AMD, Hitachi, etc, and is attempting to get R&D leadership in TFT displays and multimedia, with the help of Zenith.

This impressive record of investments and tie-ups may not be enough. The danger in playing up these technology partnerships is that, while they may show the Korean companies as having access to world-class technology, they may still communicate that Korean companies are playing catch-up, and are "copycats." What they may need to communicate is *technology leadership*—even higher technology, in a few, targeted symbolically and strategically-vital areas, than the Japanese, Germans and Americans. Samsung has sought a leadership position in some of its product lines: in memory technology (64 and 256 Meg, and 1 Gigabyte, DRAMS), thin/flat screen displays, and digital CDMA cell technology (Samsung Electronics Annual Report 1996). To obtain and support this leadership, it has technological joint venture agreements with several

U.S. (e.g., AT&T, Motorola, Sun, Digital, General Instrument) and Japanese companies (including NEC, Toshiba, Fujitsu). They also have relationships with Nissan in cars, and spend heavily—billions of dollars—on R&D (US$8 billion on semiconductors, US$3 billion on multimedia and telecom, by 1997) (Holstein and Nadkarni 1995). Though impressive, these amounts in some cases are still small relative to what may needed in those industries and relative to other global competitors. For example, it takes US$2 billion to develop a new automobile engine, and the top 5 Korean automakers' R&D is still only 12 percent of that of General Motors, according to Lee *et al.* (1996).

Despite these efforts, it could fairly be concluded that *perceptions* of product quality have not gone up enough. Thus more than injections of technology are necessary: attention needs to be paid to how product line and product features can be used to *signal* high product quality to consumers. Do consumers really make overall product quality inferences from the leadership position of the company in semiconductor technology?

Perhaps the most relevant question here is: Do developed country consumers equate quality with a larger number of features? The latter seems to be the understanding with which many Korean products and ads are currently designed. Yet it could be argued that what is needed is a credible communication of greater *reliability* and *durability* and *worksmanship*, not of 'more features,' which is really the same 'greater value for money' theme we have argued is insufficient to create/change quality perceptions. Samsung has performed regression analyses on consumer data in South Africa, and found brand attitudes to depend most significantly on perceptions about "quality," "reliability," and "ease-of-use," with value being relatively less important. In Daewoo Motors' global research (DMR 1997, Appendix), analyses on criteria for car purchases found "quality" and "reliability" to usually act together in a combined fashion on the first, most important for purchase, factor. Note this consumer comment to Daewoo: "The only thing I think with Daewoo is good value for money . . . but what's good value for money against reliability?" (DMR 1997, p. 19). Honda and Toyota have built their quality reputation in the U.S. car market not by offering more features, but by single-minded focus on reliability and durability; there is much to be learned from their experience.

It may also be important to convey technology leadership through pioneering in the latest 'gee-whiz' area of the relevant market-space. LG seems to understand this. It believes that quality perceptions will eventually be shaped by technical leadership, being first-in-market. LG Electronics has the official goal of "leading the electronics market as an innovator, not a mere trend-follower, with a global, future-oriented mindset." It has decided to follow a policy of "star products" to bolster its product quality image. Thus, for example, it is pursuing the PDA/HPC market, with its new "Phenom" product, which—in addition to being price competitive—has a color screen option and other advanced features, and its new hybrid PDA, which also has cell-phone capabilities (all advanced features). (Ironically, however, LG was forced to private-brand their PDA in the United States!). Similarly, LG is pursuing multimedia products, and has decided not to market appliances in the United States. Similarly, Samsung has had great success in China with its Video Compact Disk player (VCD), where it was the first in the market with the product, at a price about half that of SONY's equivalent high-end player.

Obviously, real product innovation in features and functionality can also help a lot. A few cases came to our attention. In creating TV sets for Indonesia, where electricity voltages fluctuate unreliably, Samsung added a "soft start" feature that reduced the electricity surge at boot-up (in addition to other features); these apparently really raised its quality perceptions there. In Russia, its "BioTV" TV sets, that emit far-infrared rays, apparently gained an (undeserved) reputation for being "good for building stamina"! Thus obtaining a reputation for quality leadership is not so much a question of incorporating the latest technology, but can depend much on a better understanding of consumer needs that competitors are slow to catch on to.

There is some evidence that Korean companies need to pay much greater attention to the "cues" and "signals" used by consumers to gauge quality, such as product fit-and-finish, and materials. Data from Daewoo Motors' global consumer research (DMR 1997, Appendix) showed numerous instances of consumers concluding that its cars were not of high quality because they had cheap-looking and broken/fragile parts, ugly dashboards, poor paintwork, loud engine noise, non-working electrical systems (e.g. locking systems and electric window openers), and generally poor "finish." One wonders whether the fact that Korean manufacturers do not face much competition from imports in their home (Korean) market contributes to this under-appreciation of product quality cues and signals. Riding in Korean cars one often gets the impression that though they have many or most of the features of more expensive Japanese cars, the quality of materials (such as the types of plastics used) and worksmanship (such as the stitching of leather) is not as good. One wonders if the Korean companies do as much research on the quality "signaling" and "emotional satisfaction," "human touch" implications of product features as the Japanese do. In addition, one wonders if the low-price nature of the local market (which may force the companies to use lower-quality materials to keep costs down) hurts them in the need to create higher-cost, higher-quality products for developed overseas markets. This is again a difference from the case of Japanese manufacturers, who face a domestic market that is arguably the most quality-conscious in the world! Since the local market is protected from imports, local consumers in Korea are perhaps less demanding of world-class fit-and-finish, giving local managers the impression (false confidence) that their existing standards will also suffice in the overseas markets of the West.

Product Design

In communicating product quality, the role of *product design* cannot be underestimated. Daewoo Motors, in selling cars in Western Europe, has suffered from selling only two older models (the Wexia and Asparo), designed several years ago on Opel-based platforms (somewhat similar to the Opel Astra), when Daewoo manufactured cars for General Motors (Pontiac Le Mans) and Opel (the Opel Kadett). Newer models have been recently introduced, however, and Daewoo is relying on its new top-end car, the Leganza, to help build its image. Hyundai Motors, too, has relied a lot for image-changing on its stylish Tiburon coupe, its luxurious Dynasty (in Korea), its new versions of the Sonata, etc.

Samsung, probably more than any of the other Korean companies, has for many years placed a high emphasis on product design to distinguish its products. It has supposedly consulted with Tom Hardy, an ex-IBM designer. Samsung also uses other European and American designers for many of its products (such as Porsche Design for its cordless phones), and often wins awards in design competitions such as the IDEA awards (Nadkarni 1995a). Similarly, Daewoo Motors has found that the "old-fashioned styling" of its old cars models has hurt them (DMR 1997, p. 32). Currently, however, they have contracted with Giorgetto Giugiaro's Italdesign to design its new cars (such as the Lanos and Leganza), has used Porsche for some design work, and has a controlling interest in a UK design firm (International Automotive Design). Thus they have a "design partnership" that includes partners from the United Kingdom, Germany and Korea.

Pricing

As discussed previously, Korean companies have in most cases positioned themselves as being "middle quality and low price" compared to the Japanese, who are "higher quality and higher priced." We would suggest that perhaps the Korean companies need to re-position themselves as "equally high quality but lower priced," focusing on quality rather than price in their communications—and communicating the message of quality not through "more features," but through credible evidence of reliability, durability, etc.

This would clearly be a fundamental and controversial shift in marketing strategy. Valid questions can be raised: Will the Japanese be willing to cede share in the higher-priced segments? Aren't the existing Japanese brands already too strong there? (Verespej 1987). Why shouldn't Korean companies just stay in their existing lower-price niche? Samsung, for example, feels that its current pricing strategy in the United States is correct, because it is consistent with Samsung's current brand equity—in other words, Samsung's current brand equity would probably not allow it to charge a higher price. However, Samsung feels that it does have the potential to charge higher prices in other countries, and possibly even within the United States in the microwave category; but they recognize they may need to create a higher-end sub-brand before attempting to do so. Samsung's goal is to lower its price differential from premium brands to less than 10 percent, after making sure such a move would meet with support from its distribution channels.

Given that the Korean companies do need to offer greater value than SONY, Panasonic, etc., one way out of this dilemma might be to price the bulk of their product-line lower than competition, but to also have a few higher-end "silver bullet" products that imbue the entire brand and product-line with a brand-building aspirational quality. As discussed earlier, this might be possible by creating higher-quality and higher-priced sub-brands.

Marketing Communications

The issue here is: What types of marketing communications are most likely to help create a higher-quality (or other positive) brand image for these Korean brands, given the present perceptions of good value-for-money, but not the best quality? We will discuss here not only possible changes in advertising strategy and tactics but also in other communication tools, such as public relations, sponsorships, etc.

Subsequently, we will discuss the challenge faced by these companies in raising the levels of brand awareness, given the constraint of (comparatively) small budgets.

Advertising Message Strategies to Change Quality Perceptions

In our review of advertising themes used by the Korean companies up to this point, we pointed out that the following themes were evident:

(a) being global companies,
(b) offering greater value,
(c) becoming technology leaders,
(d) being diversified, integrated "chips-to-ships" manufacturers, and
(e) "humanizing," "empowering" or being "socially responsible" companies.

On the face of it, it would appear that of all of these the "technology leader" theme might have the most potential in altering quality perceptions. This was supported in a small-scale pilot test among students in the U.S. Midwest, conducted by one of the co-authors (with Zeynep Gurhan). In this test, students were asked which of six possible ad messages was the strongest and most powerful/convincing/effective in convincing them of the high quality of a Korean-made, SAMSUNG-branded TV set. The six messages tested were:

(1) the company is one of the world's 20 largest companies, operating in over 100 countries;
(2) the product cost the same as another SONY TV set but had 20 percent more useful features;
(3) the product had the same features as a similar SONY set but costs 20 percent less;
(4) the company was a technology leader in display, multimedia and semiconductor technologies;
(5) the product had the same price as a similar SONY TV but came with a longer warranty (3 years instead of 1); and
(6) the company was one of the world's largest companies, manufacturing products ranging from electronics to chemicals to ships to polyester.

It can be seen that these tested messages follow the studied themes of (1) global, (2) and (3) value, (4) and (5) technology and (6) large diversified manufacturer. Of the six messages tested, the strongest in self-reported effectiveness was the (4) technology leader claim, followed by the (5) longer warranty message. The least effective messages were (6) large diversified manufacturer and (2) more features for the same price. Though these results obviously need valid large-scale testing for confirmation, they do suggest that the advertising themes currently favored might not be potentially the most effective in creating higher quality perceptions.

Not everyone agrees that a "better technology" message is the right one, however. There is doubt among some key players we spoke to (at Cheil Communications, Samsung's agency) that technology can really be used today as a brand differentiator. Various arguments were provided. First, there is equality among the leading companies on technology—or, Samsung cannot really claim leadership. Second, a "highest technology" positioning would only appeal to the "early adopters" in a market, not the mass majority market. Third, Samsung's leadership in, for example, DRAM memory chips, would only be useful in business-to-business sales, because these components are not used in most of its consumer products, so it would be hard to make a linkage between such corporate leadership and consumer benefits from its products. Cheil argued instead that the appropriate message was not "best technology" but "right technology for you" focusing on the consumer *benefit* gained from some "core competence" of Samsung, such as its leadership in "optical science," exemplified in areas such as TFT LCDs, allowing "wide screen" benefits to consumers. This logic seems correct: a linkage has to be made between technology and consumer benefits.

It is also self-evident that some part of the advertising message does indeed need to reduce the consumer's level of perceived risk by highlighting the company's global size and broad product scope. Based on its European consumer research, Daewoo Motor's agency (Korad) has suggested to the company to play up Daewoo's decades of experience in car-making, and its connections with GM/Opel (DMR 1997, pp. 59–60). Note that such a message strategy still focuses on highlighting relevant, specialized product experience, instead of unrelated product lines. Perceived risk can also be reduced by a marketing communications strategy that uses familiar and consistent themes, to create a greater sense of familiarity and therefore trust in the consumer. It also seems sensible to target those consumer segments who are more willing to try out non-traditional and lesser-known brands, a strategy that these companies already follow. In Daewoo Motor's case, for instance, its ad agency (Korad) defined its target consumer as: "people who follow (their) own path," individualistic, intelligent, and creative (DMR 1997, p. 71).

In addition, we would repeat once again that credible messages of proven reliability and durability appear to be very important. Credible ways of communicating these would seem to include longer warranties and third-party endorsements.

Longer Warranties and Better Customer Service

We saw that in the pilot consumer test a longer warranty message proved quite effective in conveying product quality. This is consistent with the literature on how warranty length can signal high quality.

A longer warranty has in fact proved very helpful to Daewoo Motors, in overcoming consumer scepticism. They offered a 3-year warranty in Western Europe, higher than the usual 1-year warranty offered by competitors. In March 1998, Hyundai Motors conceded to us that offering a longer warranty might be helpful in refuting its poor quality image, but said the cost—$500/car right now—would be too high. In late 1998 however, just as this chapter was being written, they announced a much longer warranty in the United States, of five years or 60,000 miles on all parts, up to 10 years or 10,000 miles on the engine and transmission (Krebs 1998). The goal is to help overcome negative quality perceptions flowing from Hyundai's history in the United States (as discussed earlier).

LG apparently varies its warranty by region, offering 2-year warranties in some European countries. Their market research has told them a longer warranty is helpful in some markets (e.g. China), but not in all. Clearly, a longer warranty could be tested on a case-by-case basis for its potential sales and profit impact, using market research techniques such as conjoint analysis.

Related to longer warranties is the issue of providing superior after-sales service (by the company and its dealers), for the perceived absence of good after-sales service can increase perceived purchase risk and negate the effect of a longer warranty. It is not clear that the Korean companies have focused enough on this attribute. In fact, Daewoo Motor's global consumer research (DMR 1997, Appendix) showed that its service satisfaction levels still need improvement in many countries, including Australia, Chile, France, etc. However, Daewoo Motors has had a very successful payback from superior customer service in its car operations in the United Kingdom, similar to (and possibly modeled after) Saturn's strategy in the United States. After studying consumer research, they offered free service for three years (including free oil changes and tune-ups); pickup and delivery of vehicles that need servicing, free liability and collision insurance; free roadside assistance; and a 3-year warranty, longer than that offered by most competitive brands (Daewoo Cars UK Brochure 1996; Schuman 1997). In addition, they sold their cars at fixed prices, with no haggling; the cars were sold by Daewoo-employed salesmen in Daewoo-owned outlets, compensated mostly on straight salaries (and a small group incentive). They also offered a 30 days/1,000 miles exchange or refund commitment! As a result, they were rated #1 in customer service reputation in the United Kingdom, and built up very high (90 percent) awareness through favorable media coverage. (In the rest of Western Europe, they still offer a 3-year or 100,000 km warranty, and their free-maintenance deals are modified according to local market conditions.) A similar stress on good quality service is planned for their upcoming U.S. launch.

Samsung Electronics has a high reputation for good service in Korea, and has supposedly placed great importance on providing good service (such as 24-hour support) in world markets as well. However, this does not appear to have been implemented well or at all because, at least in the United States, Samsung's customer satisfaction scores are still not very high, and Samsung's consumer research does not show it as having a high reputation for customer service. In addition, this policy imposes high overhead costs on Samsung, which are apparently becoming an issue as margins get squeezed.

LG makes "happy calls" in some markets (customer service follow-up calls as a follow-up to purchase), but only where they have their own sales network, not where they only sell through a sales agent. LG has also placed a lot of emphasis on customer service in Western Europe and other markets; it offers 24-hour service (Express Service) in Mexico and loaner products in Brazil (zero-hour sevice).

Endorsements/Reviews/Public Relations

As mentioned, credible third-party endorsements are clearly very helpful in building trust in a brand's quality, when the brand itself is not well-known and/or does not have a long history. Several of the companies have sometimes used this tactic, though there does not seem to be a clear, explicit strategy to do so.

Samsung has used computer magazine reviews of its award-winning computer monitor line (SYNCMASTER) in its very successful advertising for these products, which therefore does not simply talk about features. Samsung also believes that its image for quality in the United States is going up because of favorable reviews in *Consumer Reports* (e.g., rated #1 for 19 and 20-inch TV sets, #2 in big-screen sets). Similarly, the British consumer magazine *Which?* Rated it best for reliability for its camcorders, VCRs and microwave ovens (*Which?* 1998).

Daewoo Motors received favorable reviews for its cars and sales/service arrangements in the United Kingdom from, among others, *BBC Top Gear Magazine, Auto Express, Parents,* etc., and featured these in its 1996 and 1997 brochures. In addition, they received *What Car? Magazine*'s Best Warranty and after-sales Award in February 1998. It also ranked second in a customer satisfaction survey in the United Kingdom run jointly by J. D. Powers and BBC TV. Daewoo Motors also received very favorable reviews in Germany for its new Leganza; a car magazine there rated it very close to the Camry. This fact has not been played up in advertising, however. Hyundai Motors cars have also received awards at auto shows (1996 Moscow, Bulgaria, etc.)—though it is not clear how much weight these auto shows carry with Western consumers!

LG too uses PR heavily to boost awareness and create a quality image, especially press tours of journalists from *PC Magazine, BYTE*, and *Mobile*; it invites them to Korea, in addition to itself conducting media tours in the United States. LG monitors have suposedly received good reviews and have a good reputation in Western Europe. LG says it tries very hard to use good press reviews and endorsements in its advertising, such as award icons, etc.

In general, we would strongly encourage more, systematic, strategic garnering and usage of credible third-party reviews, ratings, and awards. In fact, it might be worthwhile (where facts permit this) for Korean companies to mount a "comparative advertising" attack on higher-reputation brands, using such third-party reviews as support. Such comparative advertising has often proved very effective in re-positioning weaker challenger brands and making them appear to be in the same quality league as the leader brands compared to in the advertising.[6]

Co-Branding and "Linking"

Another way of obtaining an implicit "endorsement" from a higher-quality brand is by developing "co-branding" campaigns with better-known and more-trusted brands. Samsung has run co-branded advertising for its digital cellular telephone products with Sprint PCS and AT&T in the United States, and has also run co-promotions with NTT in Japan. However, Cheil does not feel it has obtained enough benefit regarding enhanced visibility for Samsung from these efforts. One can only wonder why these results were unsatisfactory: perhaps not enough advantage was taken of this linkage, in media campaigns (for an example of successful leveraging of co-branding, see the Summer 1998 Iberia Airlines campaign in the United States, taking advantage of its frequent flyer alliance with American Airlines). LG also co-brands its products in some cases: in China, it has LG-Panda and LG-Chulan (for refrigerators); in Korea, it uses LG-IBM for PCs and laptops (the venture is owned 51 percent by IBM), which uses LG's distribution channels; and LG-EDS for a software database venture.

Daewoo Motors ran a promotion with a high-end hotel chain in Europe, Steinberger Hotels, where guests staying at the hotel had free use of Daewoo cars. Daewoo Motors has also contracted with Giorgetto Giugiaro's Italdesign to design its new cars (such as the Lanos and Leganza), and plays this up in its sales materials, as well as the fact that it uses Bosch ABS and German-designed ZF transmissions (Daewoo Cars UK Brochure 1997). Such "ingredient" branding has helped many smaller PC manufacturers in the United States and elsewhere, who use Intel's strongly-branded microprocessors. However, when Daewoo Motors researched whether its association with Opel and General Motors (and the use of Opel engines in its cars) would help or hurt them, they found that though for many consumers the fact that these cars had Opel engines would indeed add a significant degree of security and reliability, there is the counter-argument that it might also add to the perception that Daewoo were "imitators, not innovators" (DMR 1997, p. 30), a negative. Therefore, co-branding opportunities must be carefully managed to not create such perceptions of imitation.

Sponsorships

As mentioned, in the past almost all these leading Korean companies have been major users of sports and events marketing, and sponsorships, including tie-ups with the Olympics, World Cup, etc. Sponsorships are no doubt a potentially effective way to transfer associations to a brand. One wonders, however, whether the kinds of sponsorships paid for so far—or the marketing use of them—have really enhanced the "higher quality" association we have argued needs development. While building a reputation as a "large, global, diversified" corporation, or as a munificent sports sponsor is certainly helpful, one wonders if it might be more productive to *more directly* attempt to create a "highest quality, technical leader" reputation/image by sponsoring events or organizations or people that are more explicitly identified with quality leadership. It is not at all clear that the Korean companies' investments in sports' sponsorships is really that relevant to such a task. While identifying such relevant sponsorship opportunities remains a creative challenge for the companies' PR and advertising agencies, some relevant ideas might include the sponsorship of best-in-class contests in relevant fields, linking up with quality (e.g., Deming or Juran) awards, and events designed to highlight reliability, durability and quality (e.g., car endurance rallies, such as the Asia-Pacific Car Rally Championship series Hyundai Motors is already sponsoring in Australia (Hyundai Motors Annual Report 1997)).

Creating Other/New Brand Associations

It could also be argued that one way for the Korean brands to reduce the effect of the Korean CO image on purchase decisions might be to create some entirely new brand associations that would then supplement (and hopefully replace) the current 'poor quality' associations. (Theoretically, this could be interpreted as attempting to reduce the 'relative accessibility' of this stereotype image in the consumer's mind, and/or reduce the use of a "price→quality schema" by consumers, which would otherwise imply low quality for a low-priced product.)

Two efforts to create such "different" brand associations emerged in our research. One is LG's effort to shape its new brand or corporate identity. Its "LG wave" is intended to communicate "active, emerging, moving," the smile logo and corporate identity are intended to communicate "trustworthy, reliable, friendly, contribute to society, and technical leadership, innovative, inspiring, energetic and vital." Overall, LG is attempting to identify itself as being a "hi tech" + "hi touch" company that by combining these two philosophies "improves quality of life" and leads to "hi hope" at the top of the image pyramid. Possible problems with this strategy are that it is (a) not unique, being too much like that of all other Korean companies, and (b) it is not consistent and focused, being too broad and all-encompassing. LG admits it doesn't really deliver on this imagery right now, but says it is trying to create products and communications so that it does.

The second effort, discussed earlier, is that of Arnell's U.S. campaign for Samsung Electronics. The goal is to make Samsung appear distinctive and contemporary, and to supplement the "rational" reasons for buying Samsung products with a "sensual and emotional" image. The look-and-feel of the advertising is thus very sophisticated and modern (Levine 1996).

Clearly, research is needed on whether such additional/alternate associations help, and on what such associations need to be. An interesting direction here is that of creating or reinforcing different associations not for any one company, but for Korea itself.

Attempting to Alter Korea's CO Image Itself

Samsung has apparently been examining an advertising strategy that would look for positive things that could be said about Korea itself, which could then be used to draw the implication that Korean products in the electronics and automotive and other categories should therefore be of high quality. The analogy given to us by Cheil Communications was that Japanese companies, in the 1960s, drew on the Japanese reputation for making small/miniature products well to refute the reputation for poor quality that Japanese products had at that time, and that Korea might be able to do something similar.

Though Samsung and Cheil did not reveal to us what this possible message was, it is possible it is one of a Korean sense of simplicity and harmony with nature. This (or any other such message) would represent an interesting line of attack and certainly warrants much thought. Obviously, such image-changing efforts would benefit if the Korean government coordinated and/or helped fund such efforts. We understand that while the Korean government does currently conduct research on Korea's overall CO image, it only has a weak co-op advertising effort regarding the quality of Korean products.

THE AWARENESS-BUILDING CHALLENGE

While we have focused most of this chapter on association-building, creating high unaided awareness is also a vitally important part of brand-building. High awareness puts brands in consumers' "consideration sets" and creates a sense of trust and familiarity. It clearly takes a lot of money to build a brand in the West—Hyundai spent

US$100 million to launch its Accent car in the United States in 1986, Kia spent US$30 million in advertising in 1994 (Stanley 1995). In 1998, Hyundai Motors' ad budget in the United States was about US$65 million, and Kia's was about US$40 million (Halliday 1998). According to published reports, SAMSUNG had a total worldwide ad budget of US$775 million in 1996 (Lee 1996), with an ad budget in the United States of US$25–30 million (up to US$60 million in 1996, according to Levine 1996) and possibly US$20–30 million in Europe. Daewoo Motors reports a very small, and declining, advertising budget for Western Europe. LG Electronics is planning to spend US$30 million in Europe in 1998. Hyundai Motors is planning to spend US$20 million for a pan-Europe image-building ad campaign in 1998.

These amounts are large—but are they large enough? McKinsey consultants reportedly told LG that it would cost them US$1 billion and many years of effort to build a Global brand (Kraar 1996) and to build a national car brand in the United States might require US$500 million, including US$100 million in advertising alone (Stanley 1995). Given this supposed need, the Korean companies budgets look small. These resources have become even lower in recent years, with the currency decline of the won (which declined from 900 won per U.S. dollar in November 1997 to 1800 won per dollar in December 1998), the decline in semiconductor prices and in the domestic car market in 1998 (which has declined by almost 50 percent over 1997 with the currency crisis).

Given small budgets, the Korean companies need to build brands in ways that use up smaller budgetary resources. Research conducted by the Korean Broadcasting and Advertising Company in 1996 showed that the Korean companies used TV, newspapers and magazines most heavily; outdoor and neon signs next (especially Samsung Electronics, Daewoo Electronics and Daewoo Motors); and airport carts (Samsung, LG and Daewoo Electronics). Most of Samsung's global image campaigns have been in major global media, such as *Business Week, Fortune, Forbes, Newsweek, USA Today, the Financial Times, The Economist, CNN International, Eurosport,* etc. In many parts of the world, especially in the emerging markets, Samsung and the others have built up brand awareness among key elites by sponsoring airport baggage carts, and by heavy use of outdoor advertising.

Given this resource challenge, how can the allocation of media be made more efficient? Ideas here include

(a) more efficient media buying, and
(b) re-allocation away from TV and print advertising to cheaper advertising, PR and direct marketing vehicles.

Some of the companies are already paying attention to the first: Hyundai Motors has used media-buyer Western International Media in New York City for its buys of global business media e.g. the *Wall Street Journal* and *Scientific American.* Concerning the second, LG uses a lot of radio to build awareness, and in some markets has used 5 to 10-second radio billboard time announcements to build an image of precision and reliability and credibility—called "GoldStar time." Daewoo Motors apparently also relied heavily on cheap radio media to launch its cars in the United States in 1998 (Halliday 1998).

Surprisingly, however, not much attention has been given to exploiting the powers and cost efficiencies of direct and database marketing. Direct (including Internet) marketing makes a lot of sense because of its low costs (Wadia 1997), its ability to target narrow consumer segments, its ability to foster loyalty, its ability to promote cross-selling and up-selling of products such as appliances and consumer electronics—and because it allows bypassing traditional distribution channels, a key problem area for some of these companies. There are a few exceptions to this relative lack of use of database marketing. Daewoo Motors did use database marketing in its U.K. car business to target car-buying prospects: a car giveaway was used to generate leads (Lee 1996) as was an ad campaign that invited consumers to telephone a toll-free number to voice their dislikes about buying a car (Koranteng 1996). Daewoo Motors however says that though database marketing is used by some of its distributors and ad agencies in Western Europe, it does not use it systematically itself. LG does, in some countries, attempt database marketing, where it asks consumers to send in a registration postcard placed in the product carton, with a sweepstakes incentive.

Overall, though, more money needs to be moved into this area. Samsung/Cheil report wanting to do more resource shifting into direct marketing, but haven't yet done so, and say they are building up their capabilities to do so. The Korean companies could also benefit from studying the experiences of other companies in Europe (such as Swatch and Adidas) that have used non-advertising media for brand-building, such as retail outlets and merchandising, strategically-relevant sponsorships, product sampling, etc.[7]

SUMMARY AND RECOMMENDATIONS

It could be said that in the mid 1980s, in "Phase I," Korean companies made the transition from being OEM brands to launching their own brands. Next, in "Phase II," they succeeded in raising the levels of technology and productivity and in positioning themselves as "Value Brands." We are arguably now in "Phase III," when the potential exists for many of them to become "Power Global Brands."

The competency needs for being "own brand" exporters are very different from those of "OEM suppliers": for the former, a company needs better R&D and product design capability, and better marketing skills and brand-building ability and resources. As Lee and Son (1993) discuss, the transition from the latter to the former requires moving from a strategy of focused-cost leadership to one of differentiation; from making low-priced goods in large quantity to making high-price, high-quality goods; and from process-related R&D leadership to product-design and development R&D leadership.

However, this will not happen on its own, by default, through some automatic process. These Korean companies have, in recent years, spent enormous amounts of money and time in becoming world-class *manufacturers*, by acquiring and developing the skills and technologies to produce the products themselves. They assumed that if they made the necessary high-quality and higher-value products, world sales and success would follow. But they do not appear to have realized that consumer perceptions need to be changed as well, and that a brand-building strategy needs to be consciously and explicitly implemented with the same intensity that went into their product-design and manufacturing strategies.

Such brand-building is essential today because, if the Koreans continue to compete only on low price and added features and value, they are making themselves vulnerable to attack from the even lower-cost economies of China, Eastern Europe, etc. Thus, brand-building is necessary not only from an *offensive* (market-gaining) standpoint, but also from a *defensive* (market-protection) perspective.

In their brand-building marketing communication efforts, the Korean companies appear to have focused to date on building *awareness* (e.g., via outdoor advertising and sports' sponsorships) and communicating a message of greater *value* (through product feature proliferation and below-market pricing). We have made the case here that, in order to realize their potential to become Global Power Brands, the emphasis needs to shift to *building an image of very high quality*, through changes in advertising themes, the nature of sponsorships and product and pricing policy. We have argued that this is essential if the real quality of these brands is not to be obscured by the inadequate quality image of their country of origin, Korea, which creates a situation where low price is inferred by consumers to imply inadequate quality and status. Given this Korean CO image, a message of greater value and of lower prices is easily interpretable by consumers as implying quality that is "not the best."

Though this may seem obvious, research conducted by the Korean Broadcasting and Advertising Company in 1996 showed a great felt need among Korean companies to increase advertising exposure (21 percent), but much less of the need to better establish a consumer reliability and quality image (7–9 percent). This mindset needs to change dramatically. Building strong global Korean brands is not simply a question of more resources and more time. It also calls for a fundamental shift in brand-building strategy and tactics.

Notes

The authors would like to thank the many managers from Cheil Communications, Daewoo Motors, Diamond Advertising, Hyundai Motors, the Hyundai Research Institute, Samsung Electronics, and LG Electronics, who graciously allowed us to interview them to compile data for this chapter. Thanks also to The Davidson Institute for funding this research.

1. For an exception, see Joachimsthaler and Aaker 1997.

2. The section below is taken from Batra (1998). For additional frameworks, see Aaker (1991, 1996), and Keller (1993).

3. In some developing markets, however, the Korean companies do manage to get market-leader pricing: LG claims it gets high prices in markets such as Uruguay, the Caribbean, etc., markets that it says SONY neglects. Samsung microwaves apparently sell for 2–5 percent higher than Sharp in Latin America.

4. See Nagle and Holden 1995 for a discussion.

5. See Aaker 1994 for details.

6. See Batra, Myers and Aaker (1997), pp. 390–400 for a review.

7. See Joachimsthaler and Aaker 1997 for details.

References

Aaker, David A. *Managing Brand Equity*. New York: The Free Press, 1991.

_____. "Building a Brand: The Saturn Story." *California Management Review* 36, no. 2 (Winter 1994): 114–133.

_____. *Building Strong Brands*. New York: The Free Press, 1996.

_____. "Should You Take Your Brand to Where the Action Is?" *Harvard Business Review* 75, no. 5 (September–October 1997): 135–143.

Akre, Brian S. "Korean Carmaker Targets U.S. College Students." *Ann Arbor News* (October 5, 1998): A5.

"Avoiding a Breakdown." *Which?* (UK) (February 1998): 8–12.

Batra, Rajeev. "Building Brand Equity Through Advertising." Unpublished Working Paper, University of Michigan Business School, Ann Arbor, MI, 1998.

Batra, Rajeev, John G. Myers and David A. Aaker. *Advertising Management*. 5th ed. Upper Saddle River, NJ: Prentice-Hall, 1996.

Baughn, C. C. and A. Yaprak. "Mapping Country-of-Origin Research: Recent Developments and Emerging Avenues." In *Product-Country Images: Impact and Role in International Marketing*, edited by Nicolas Papadopoulos and Louise Heslop, 89–116. New York: International Business Press (Haworth), 1993.

Brzezinski, Matthew. "Daewoo Boldly Invades Old Soviet Bloc." *Wall Street Journal* (May 7, 1997): A14.

Carlton, Jim. "Ex-Packard Bell CEO Agrees to Buy Samsung Group's AST Computer Unit." *Wall Street Journal* (January 11, 1999): A30.

Cho, Dong-Sung, Jinah Choi and Youjae Yi. "International Advertising Strategies by NIC Multinationals: The Case of a Korean Firm." *International Journal of Advertising* 1, no. 13 (Winter 1994): 77–92.

Daewoo Cars Brochure (UK). *Why Settle for a Car When You Can Have a Daewoo*. Daewoo Motors, 1996.

_____. *Welcome to a New Generation*. Daewoo Motors, 1997.

Daewoo Motors Research (DMR). "Brand Image Research: Final Recommendations." (Covering Australia, Belgium, Chile, Colombia, France, Germany, Hungary, Israel, The Netherlands, Spain and the United Kingdom). Report by Korad, Ogilvy and Mather, February, 1997.

Gale, Bradley T. *Managing Customer Value*. New York: The Free Press, 1994.

Halliday, Jean. "South Korean Auto Importers Duel for Market Share." *Advertising Age* (February 23, 1998): 14.

_____. "Finally Making U.S. Entry, Daewoo Relies on Radio." *Advertising Age* (August 31, 1998): 33.

Heslop, Louise A. and Nicolas Papadopoulos. "But Who Knows Where or When: Reflections on the Images of Countries and their Products." In *Product-Country Images: Impact and Role in International Marketing*, edited by Nicolas Papadopoulos and Louise Heslop, 39–75. New York: International Business Press (Haworth), 1993.

Holstein, William and Laxmi Nadkarni. "Korea." *Business Week*, no. 3435 (July 31, 1995): 56–64.

Hyundai Motors. *Hyundai Motors Annual Report 1997*. Seoul, South Korea: Hyundai Motors, 1997.

Hyundai Research Institute. Federation of Korean Industries (NY Office) and U.S.-Korean Chamber of Commerce. *Research on American Perceptions of Korean Companies and Brands*. Seoul, South Korea: Hyundai Research Institute, July–December 1996.

Ihlwan, Moon and Brian Bemmer. "Samsung: A Korean Giant Confronts the Crisis." *Business Week* (Asian Edition) (March 23, 1998): 14–18.

Joachimsthaler, Erich and David A. Aaker. "Building Brands Without Mass Media." *Harvard Business Review* 75, no. 1 (January–February 1997): 39–47.

Keller, Kevin L. "Conceptualizing, Measuring, and Managing Customer-Based Brand Equity." *Journal of Marketing* 57, no. 1 (January 1993): 1–22.

Kochan, Nicholas, ed. *The World's Greatest Brands*. New York: New York University Press, 1997.

Koenderman, Terry. "How Samsung Captured South Africa." *Financial Mail* (South Africa) (July 11, 1997): 87.

Koranteng, Juliana. "Daewoo Cars." *Advertising Age International* (December 1996): I22.

Korean Broadcasting and Advertising Company (KOBACO). "Research on Image of Korea and Overseas Advertising." Conducted during the 35th IAA Seoul Advertising Congress Meeting. Seoul, South Korea: Hyundai Research Institute, 1996.

Krebs, Michelle. "To Counter Stigma, Hyundai Bolsters Warranty." *New York Times* (November 8, 1998): 42.

_____. "An Economical Vehicle For the Comeback Trail." *New York Times* (February 28, 1999): 34.

Kraar, Louis. "Guess Who's Betting on America's High-Tech Losers." *Fortune* 134, no. 8 (October 28, 1996): 151–158.

_____. "Korea's Comeback . . . Don't Expect a Miracle." *Fortune* 137, no. 10 (May 25, 1998): 120–126.

Lee, Byung-Jong. "New Whiz Kids on the Bloc." *Business Korea* 11, no. 9 (March 1994): 24–26.

Lee, Dong-Ok, Keunchul Lee, Jae-Jin Kim and Gill-Chin Lim. "The Korean Automobile Industry-Challenges and Strategies in the Global Market." *Journal of International Marketing* 4, no. 4 (Winter 1996): 85–96.

Lee, Mushin and Byungho Son. "Korean Strategies for Export Markets." *Long Range Planning* 26, no. 6 (December 1993): 99–106.

Lee, Yoo-Lim. "Samsung's Plan: Make a Name in Auto Industry." *Advertising Age International* (October 1996): I4.

Levine, Joshua. "You've Got Just Two Seconds." *Forbes* 158, no. 1 (July 1, 1996): 74.

Magaziner, Ira C. and Mark Patinkin. "Fast Heat: How Korea Won the Microwave War." *Harvard Business Review* 67, no. 1 (January–February 1989): 83–92.

Matzer, Marla. "Samsung Hitches onto Nobel's Global Halo." *BrandWeek* 37, no. 23 (July 3, 1996): 3.

Nadkarni, Laxmi. "Look Out, World—Samsung is Coming." *Business Week,* no. 3432 (July 10, 1995a): 52–53.

_____. "Will Lucky GoldStar Reach Its Peak With Zenith?" *Business Week,* no. 3436 (August 7, 1995b): 40.

Nagle, Thomas T. and Reed K. Holden. *The Strategy and Tactics of Pricing.* 2d ed. Englewood Cliffs, NJ: Prentice-Hall, 1995.

Ozsomer, A. and S. T. Cavusgil. "Country-of-Origin Effects on Product Evaluations: A Sequel to the Bilkey and Nes Review." In *Enhancing Knowledge Development in Marketing,* edited by M.Gilly *et al.*, 269–277. Proceedings of the 1991 AMA Educators' Conference, Vol. 2. Chicago: American Marketing Association, 1991.

Samsung Electronics. *1995 Advertisements' Collection.* Seoul, South Korea: Samsung Electronics, 1995.

Samsung Electronics. *Samsung Electronics Annual Report, 1996*. Seoul, South Korea: Samsung Electronics, 1996.

Samsung Electronics Power Brand Manual. "Guide to a New Logic: Power Brand." The Arnell Group, 1995.

"Samsung Microwave to Top World Market." *Korea Times* (November 29 1997).

Schuman, Michael. "Daewoo Lifts its Sights to US and Europe." *Wall Street Journal* (March 4, 1997): A15.

Siler, Charles. "Daewoo Drives Growth in New Global Markets." *Advertising Age International* (January 15, 1996): I14.

Stanley, T. L. "Who the Heck is Daewoo?" *BrandWeek* 36, no. 36 (September 25, 1995): 24–25.

Simison, Robert L. "Hyundai Plans Turbo-Charged Warranty To Beat Rap of Problems With Quality." *Wall Street Journal* (September 23, 1998): A4.

Verespej, Michael. "Can Goldstar Earn Its Gold Star?" *Industry Week* 235, no. 5 (November 30, 1987): 33, 36.

Wadia, Kris. "The Future of Brand Marketing in Asia." *Journal of Direct Marketing* 11, no. 3 (Summer 1997): 58–63.

APPENDIX

Background on Korean Economy/Exports/Technology/Competencies

South Korea's own domestic per capita income was US$9,511/year in 1997 (down from a high of US$10,548 in 1996), the 26th highest per capita income in the world, making its GDP that year the world's 11th biggest. The growth rate over the period 1970–1995 was 8.1 percent per annum. Korea claims the largest number of Ph.D.s per capita in the world (Holstein and Nadkarni 1995). College graduates make up 19.7 percent of the population.

The domestic market in Korea consists of 46 million consumers, a large market. As one result, Korean automobile manufacturers get the bulk of their sales from Korea's own huge domestic economy—its own automotive market was US$27 billion in 1996. Nonetheless, the Korean economy depends heavily on exports. While Korean exports in the 1960s used to be mainly raw materials (such as tungsten, anthracite and raw silk), they had evolved by the 1970s to light industrial goods and by the 1980s to heavy industrial goods such as steel, shipbuilding, electronic goods, and textiles. By 1995, semiconductors were the single biggest export category (17 percent) followed by automobiles (7 percent) and petrochemicals (5 percent) (Hyundai Research Institute report citing statistics from KWTA Annual Trade Reports).

The electronics industry (semiconductors, VCRs, microwave ovens, stereos, computer monitors, etc.) accounted for 30 percent of Korea's total exports in 1994, at US$23 billion (Lee 1994). Korea is also now the world's fifth-largest auto maker (Holstein and Nadkarni 1995). The auto industry is a major sector: the Korean car companies had a domestic capacity of over 3 million automobiles in 1997, targeted to grow to 4 million by 2002, plus capacity outside Korea of 0.6 million in 1997, targeted to over 2 million by 2002 (Brzezinski 1997). Car exports were 730,000 units in 1996. In 1997, it manufactured 2.8 million cars, up from 100 cars in 1965. There are now over 10 million registered cars in Korea.

In 1997, 34.1 percent of South Korea's exports went to the North America (17.6 percent) and European Union (16.5 percent), down from 43.4 percent in 1990 (Schuman 1997). Most Korean companies still export to these markets largely as OEM suppliers, not under their own brand names. There are many good reasons why Korean companies initially focused on an OEM-supplier strategy, including technological and market learning, capability building, low marketing expenses, volume stability, cost reduction and avoidance of import restrictions—at the expense of lower margins and loss of self-reliance (Lee and Son 1993). Thus Samsung has for long been a "private label" supplier in the areas of microwave ovens (e.g., to GE and JC Penney), VCRs, etc; it has a 21 percent share of the world market and exports over 5 million units (Samsung Electronics Annual Report 1996). (For a fascinating look at how Samsung learned and eventually dominated this business and became the supplier to GE, see Magaziner and Patinkin 1989.) It currently sources consumer electronics products to SONY, Panasonic and Aiwa in specific markets (such as South America), and also supplies products to GE and Hewlett Packard. Daewoo Motors manufactured cars for General Motors and Opel until 1992, which were sold in the United States as the Pontiac LeMans. LG (as Goldstar) has been a private-label supplier since the 1960s, and even in 1987 over half its video sales in the United States came from PL products (Verespej 1987).

For most large Korean companies, the export marketing effort has evolved independently of the domestic effort because of the latter's large size (see Cho, Choi and Yi 1994), which also has a good discussion of the evolution of marketing strategies by Korean firms). Many Korean companies are doing more of their manufacturing overseas these days, both to improve decision-making and to avoid charges of dumping.

Much of the growth in Korean exports in high-technology businesses such as semiconductors and automobiles has benefited from a conscious program to assimilate foreign technology, through joint ventures and alliances, and applying low-cost labor and production skills to it. Korean companies have made huge investments in new technology: they spent US$48 billion in capital investment in 1995 (Holstein and Nadkarni 1995). Because of this reliance on foreign technology, however, the semiconductor business (as one example) still relies on foreign suppliers for three quarters of the material and equipment it needs to produce semiconductors (Lee 1994). The focus in recent years is supposedly less on foreign technology and more on home-grown innovation and technical leadership, going beyond the gaining of technology from U.S., Japanese and West European firms (Holstein and Nadkarni 1995).

Korea's total exports in 1997 were US$136 billion, accounting for 2.4 percent of world trade. Given the importance of their export marketing efforts, Korean companies are keenly interested in finding ways to improve their export sales. According to a report by KOTRA (the Korea Trade-Investment Promotion Agency) cited by the Hyundai Research Institute, Korean companies' strategies in the EC market suffer from poor brand image, poor country image, insufficient local physical distribution and an inadequate after-sales system. Thus, our study, seeking to find ways in which Korean companies can improve their brand and country image, is clearly important.

The Chaebols (large business groups) account for 40 percent of Korea's GNP (Kraar 1996).

CONTRIBUTORS

CARMEN BALAN

She can be reached at balanc@isp.acorp.ro.

Carmen Balan has been involved in teaching within the Faculty of Trade, Marketing Department, of the Academy of Economic Studies, ASEBUSS Business School, Bucharest, Romania, and a PHARE training project for Romania. As Assistant Professor, she teaches both in undergraduate and graduate programs, applying the knowledge and skills acquired in specialized programs attended in the 90s in Europe (Austria, France, United Kingdom), as well as in the United States. As free lance consultant, Professor Balan has carried out marketing research activities for local and foreign companies, including research commissioned by the British Know-How Fund.

RAJEEV BATRA

He can be reached at rajeevba@umich.edu.

Rajeev Batra is Area Director for Marketing at the William Davidson Institute and Professor of Marketing at the University of Michigan Business School. He received his Ph.D. from Stanford University. His research interests include international marketing (especially in the transitional economies), branding (including global brands) and advertising productivity and processes (including emotional advertising, repetition and budgeting). Professor Batra has published over thirty articles and book chapters in leading journals and books on these topics. He serves on the Editorial Board of the *Journal of Marketing Research* and four other journals. He has been at the University of Michigan since 1989; prior to that he was on the faculty of the Columbia University Business School, New York. He was a Brand Manager with Chesebrough-Pond's before becoming an academic, and he has consulted and done executive teaching with various major corporations.

RUSSELL W. BELK

He can be reached at mktrwb@business.utah.edu.

Russell W. Belk is N. Eldon Tanner Professor in the David Eccles School of Business at the University of Utah. He has taught there since 1979 and has had previous appointments at the University of Illinois, Temple University, the University of British Columbia, the University of Craiova, Romania and Edith Cowan University, Perth, Australia. His Ph.D. is from the University of Minnesota. He is past president of the Association for Consumer Research, and is a fellow in the American Psychological

Association, the Society for Consumer Psychology, and the Association for Consumer Research. He is past recipient of the University of Utah Distinguished Research Professorship and two Fulbright Fellowships. He currently edits *Research in Consumer Behavior*, and has been an advisory editor for the *Journal of Consumer Research* and is associate editor for the *Journal of Economic Psychology* and *Visual Sociology*. He has also served on the editorial review boards of 25 journals, has written or edited 17 books or monographs, and has published over 225 articles and papers. His research primarily involves the meaning of possessions, materialism, collecting, and gift giving and his recent research has been qualitative and cross-cultural.

STEVEN M. BURGESS

Steven M. Burgess is Professor of Marketing at the University of Witwatersrand, where he holds the Association of Marketers Chair and is a Faculty Affiliate of the William Davidson Institute at the University of Michigan Business School. He received his Ph.D. from the University of Witwatersrand. His research focuses on the strategic implications of behavior in emerging consumer markets, especially concerning the influence of individual differences (values, traits and identity) and consumer behavior (brand loyalty, innovation and information processing). Professor Burgess is an *International Journal of Advertising* editorial review board member and his research has appeared in *Research in Marketing, Advances in Consumer Research* and a number of South African journals. He has authored two books and has extensive senior management experience with Johnson & Johnson, the Altron Group and others.

DEBRA J. DAHAB

She can be reached at ddahab@dtn.com.

Debra J. Dahab is currently in market research and product development with Data Transmission Network, a global provider of market and weather information to agriculture, financial services and media industries. Her research studies cross-cultural marketing relationships. She has published articles on emerging retail formats in Albania and supply-chain relationships in transition economies. Professor Dahab received her Ph.D. in Business (Marketing) from the University of Nebraska-Lincoln in 1996 and was a Visiting Assistant Professor at the University of Wisconsin-Madison.

NIRAJ DAWAR

Niraj Dawar is Associate Professor of Marketing and Walter A. Thompson Faculty Fellow at the Richard Ivey School of Business, University of Western Ontario, Canada. His research is in the areas of international marketing and branding, and strategies for emerging market firms, and has been published in academic as well as managerial journals in the field.

ROHIT DESHPANDÉ

Rohit Deshpandé is Professor of Business Administration at the Havard Business School and Executive Director of the Marketing Science Institute in Cambridge, MA. His research expertise is in global marketing strategy with specific focus on issues of branding, knowledge use, and implementing a market orientation. He serves on the editorial boards of the *Journal of Marketing*, *Journal of Business Research*, *Science Communications* and *International Journal for Research in Marketing*. Prior to Harvard, he taught on the faculties of Dartmouth College and the University of Texas.

JOHN U. FARLEY

Besides the Henkel Professor of Industrial Marketing at the China Europe International Business School, John U. Farley is also the C.V. Starr Distinguished Research Fellow in International Business at the Amos Tuck School, and Ira A. Lipman Professor Emeritus at the Wharton School, University of Pennsylvania. He was Director of the Joseph H. Lauder Institute of Management and International Studies at the University of Pennsylvania, and he earlier served on the faculties of the Columbia Business School and Carnegie-Mellon University. He has served as a visiting faculty member at Sloan School of MIT, Handelshogskolan in Gothenburg, Sweden, INSEAD, the London Business School, the Harvard Business School, the International University of Japan, the Hong Kong University of Science and Technology and the National University of Singapore. He received his Ph.D. from the University of Chicago. His research concentrates on modeling and empirical generalizations on problems in global marketing and management. He is co-author of six books and has published articles in a variety of journals in marketing, statistics, management and management science, and the behavioral sciences.

JORDI GAROLERA

Jordi Garolera is Associate Professor of Economics and Business at the University of Pompeu Fabra, Barcelona, Spain. He received his Ph.D. from the Instituto de Estudios Superiores de la Empresea, Graduate School of Management, Universidad de Navarra, Barcelona. Professor Garolera's research includes interests in international work on Brand Personality and the future of brands. He has had external collaborations with other universities including Universitat de Girona, Portland State University, Universitat Oberta de Catalunya and Instituto Europeo de Derecho y Economia. He has consulted with numerous businesses such as U.S. Braiding, Inc. and the American Braiding Company.

JAMES W. GENTRY

James W. Gentry is Professor of Marketing at the University of Nebraska-Lincoln. His research interests focus on cross-cultural family issues and on retail evolution processes in countries undergoing economic transition. Professor Gentry received his doctorate from Indiana University and has been on the faculties of Kansas State University, Oklahoma State University and the University of Wisconsin-Madison.

MRINAL GHOSH

Mrinal Ghosh is Assistant Professor of Marketing at the University of Michigan, Ann Arbor. He received his Ph.D. in Marketing from the University of Minnesota – Twin Cities. His research interests lie in understanding the strategic implications of inter-firm coordination in the context of industrial markets, distribution channels and salesforce management. Specific topics include the design of cooperative inter-firm relationships and their contractual structures, pricing contracts, issues relating to channel design and structure, issues of measurability and their impact on contractual structures, component branding, product design and marketing–manufacturing interface and salesforce compensation. Professor Ghosh has worked as a marketing engineer at TELCO, Bombay and Thermax Ltd., Bombay.

LINDA K. GOOD

Linda K. Good is Associate Professor of Merchandising Management at Michigan State University. She received her Ph.D. from Oklahoma State University. Her research interests in Central and Eastern Europe include consumer distribution systems, employee motivation and retail structures. Professor Good's domestic research interests are retail turnover, socialization of entry-level management trainees and the role of social support in reducing employee stress. Her articles have appeared in the *Journal of Retailing, Academy of Marketing Science, International Marketing Review, International Review of Retail, Distribution and Consumer Research, Management Case Quarterly* and the *International Journal of Retail and Distribution Management.*

LOUISA HA

She can be reached at louisa_ha@gallup.com.

Louisa Ha received her Ph.D. from Michigan State University. She is currently a Research Director of the Gallup Organization responsible for clients such as Sears, Roebuck & Company, IBM and General Motors. She is the webmaster of the International Advertising Resource Center (http://www.getbiz.com/~louisaha/home.htm), a web site updated every month with comprehensive links to international marketing, communication and advertising sites. Professor Ha's research interests are international marketing and advertising with special interest in Asia, integrated marketing communication, Internet marketing and advertising media. She has published articles in many marketing and advertising journals such as the *Journal of Advertising Research, Journal of Advertising, Journal of Services Marketing, International Journal of Advertising* and *Current Issues and Research in Advertising.*

PATRICIA HUDDLESTON

She can be reached at huddles2@pilot.msu.edu.

Patricia Huddleston, Associate Professor, has been on the Merchandising Management faculty at Michigan State University since 1987. She has been conducting research on retail distribution and consumer behavior in Eastern Europe since 1991. She has collaborated with Professor Linda Good on several projects. One project examined the influence of country of origin on perceived quality and price of products for Russian and Polish consumers; another project surveyed Russian and Polish retail salespeoples' job satisfaction, perceived job motivators, organizational commitment and Protestant work ethic. Most recently, Professors Good and Huddleston have explored the concept of marketing orientation in the retail sectors of Russia, Poland and the United States. Professor Huddleston was present in Moscow in August 1991 and witnessed the coup firsthand.

ERICH JOACHIMSTHALER

He can be reached at eaj7f@virginia.edu.

Erich Joachimsthaler is a Visiting Professor of Business Administration at the Darden Graduate School of Business Administration, University of Virginia. He received his Ph.D. in Business Administration from the University of Kansas. He then joined the Harvard Business School as a Post-Doctoral Fellow. He is the author of more than 40 articles in leading academic journals including the *Journal of Marketing Research, Journal of Marketing, Journal of Consumer Research, Sloan Management Review, European Journal of Operational Research, Multivariate Behavioral Research, Harvard Business Review* and *MIS Quarterly*. Together with David Aaker, he wrote the book entitled *Implementing Brand Strategy in the Global Village,* which was published in 1998 by the Free Press.

DANA-NICOLETA LASCU

Dana-Nicoleta Lascu is Associate Professor of Marketing at the University of Richmond, where she teaches Global Marketing Management and Advertising. She has a Ph.D. from the University of South Carolina, and her areas of interest are cross-cultural consumer behavior, scale comparisons and international marketing strategy. She has published in the *Multinational Business Review, European Journal of Marketing, Psychology & Marketing, Journal of Global Marketing, Journal of Business Research*, among others.

XIAOLIAN LI

Xiaolian Li is a graduate research student at the School of Business of the University of Hong Kong. She holds a B.A. in Economics from the University of International Business and Economics in Beijing and an M.A. in Economics from the City University of New York. Ms. Li's areas of research include foreign investment in China, brand equity in the Asia-Pacific region and international marketing. Her research has appeared in *International Business Review, Journal of Global Marketing* and others.

AJAY K. MANRAI

Ajay K. Manrai is Professor of Marketing at the University of Delaware. He was previously on the faculty at the Wharton School of the University of Pennsylvania. He received his Ph.D. from Northwestern University. Professor Manrai's research is in the area of consumer perceptions, preference, consideration and choice models. His research publications have appeared in *Marketing Science, Journal of Marketing Research* and others. He serves on the Editorial Boards of four journals, and is a recipient of numerous teaching awards.

LALITA A. MANRAI

She can be reached at manrail@college.be.udel.edu.

Lalita A. Manrai is Associate Professor of Marketing at the University of Delaware. Professor Manrai received her Ph.D. from Northwestern University. Her research specialization is cross-cultural consumer behavior and strategic international marketing, with a focus on Eastern and Central Europe. Her publications have appeared in the *Journal of Business Research, European Journal of Marketing, Journal of Public Policy and Marketing* and others.

YIGANG PAN

He can be reached at ypan@oregon.uoregon.edu.

Yigang Pan is Associate Professor of Marketing, Lundquist College of Business, University of Oregon, Eugene. He has a Ph.D. in Marketing from Columbia University. His area of research is on brand and market entry strategies. In the past several years, he has published more than twenty articles in this area, several of which are about China. Currently, he is an active participant of several large-scale research projects about marketing in China, including business strategies and consumers in China. He teaches at the China Europe International Business School in Shanghai and is a Visiting Professor at Hong Kong University and City University of Hong Kong.

DANA PILLSBURY

Dana Pillsbury is an Associate at Prophet Brand Strategy in New York. She graduated from the California Institute of Technology in 1988 with a B.S. in General Engineering. Following six years as a translator and public relations associate in Bonn, Germany, she joined Aaker-Joachmisthaler & Partners as a Research Assistant in 1997.

J. RAMACHANDRAN

J. Ramachandran is BOC Professor of Business Policy at the Indian Institute of Management, Bangalore. He received his doctorate from the Indian Institute of Management, Ahmedabad. His major research interests are in the areas of corporate transformation and competitive strategy. Prior to joining the faculty at IIM, Bangalore, he was Vice President (Management Services) at Reliance Industries Limited, one of India's largest private sector firms. Professor Ramachandran has been the Harry Reynolds Visiting International Professor at the Wharton School of the University of Pennsylvania, the European Community Visiting Professor at INSEAD, Fountainebleau, France and a Visiting Professor at the Carlson School of Management, University of Minnesota. His research focuses on the strategic and organizational changes Indian firms must make in order to be globally competitive. He has a number of publications to his credit and has presented papers in both national and international conferences. He has also served as a consultant to various Indian and multinational companies.

RONALD SAVITT

He can be reached at rsavitt@bsadpo.emba.uvm.edu.

Ronald Savitt has been the John L. Beckley Professor of American Business at the School of Business Administration at The University of Vermont since 1985. He received a Ph.D. in Economics from the University of Pennsylvania. During the past eight years, his work has focused on the development of marketing organization and practices in the economic transformation in Central and Eastern Europe, primarily the Czech Republic and Hungary. His current research examines the extent to which old state enterprises in the Czech Republic are becoming market oriented. His work has been published in the *Journal of Marketing, Journal of Retailing, Journal of Business Research, European Journal of Marketing*, and other domestic and international journals. Besides the University of Vermont, he has taught at several institutions including Michigan State University, Czech Management Center, Wirtschaftsuniversitat, Vienna, International Management Center, Budapest, the University of Edinburgh and Stirling University.

BERND H. SCHMITT

He can be reached at bhs1@columbia.edu.

Bernd H. Schmitt is an expert on international strategy, brand management, corporate identity and communications. He received his Ph.D. from Cornell University. He has taught executive programs and seminars for international corporations in the United States, Europe and all over Asia. He joined the Marketing faculty of the Columbia University Business School, New York, in 1988 and has been a Visiting Professor at MIT, in Germany, Poland and Hong Kong. In 1996, he accepted the Marketing Chair at CEIBS – China's leading business school – located in Shanghai. Professor Schmitt has contributed more than thirty articles to academic and management journals (such as the *Journal of Consumer Research, the Journal of Marketing Research, California Management Review* and *Long Range Planning*). His book on *Marketing Aesthetics: The Strategic Management of Brands, Image, and Identity*, co-authored with Alex Simonson, was published in July 1997 by The Free Press. He is currently completing two new books entitled *Experiential Marketing* and *Capitalizing on the Chinese Consumer Revolution.*

LEO Y. M. SIN

Leo Y. M. Sin is Associate Professor of Marketing at the Chinese University of Hong Kong. He received his Ph.D. in Marketing from the University of British Columbia.

His research interests include consumer affective processes, Chinese consumer behavior and marketing in mainland China. Professor Sin's papers have appeared in the *Journal of Business Research, International Journal of Advertising* and others.

JAN-BENEDICT E. M. STEENKAMP

Jan-Benedict E. M. Steenkamp is Professor of Marketing and Marketing Area Coordinator at the Catholic University of Leuven, Belgium and the GfK Professor of International Marketing Research at Wageningen University, the Netherlands. He is also Honorary Professor at the European Institute for Advanced Studies in Management and a William Davidson Institute Research Fellow. Professor Steenkamp received his Ph.D. from Wageningen University. He was a Visiting Professor at the Pennsylvania State University, the University of Innsbruck, Austria and the University of Murcia, Spain. His research interests include international marketing, (international) marketing research methods and techniques, and stability (e.g., brand loyalty, trust and satisfaction) versus change (e.g., optimum stimulation level, innovativeness and conflict) in consumer and business-to-business relationships. He has written or edited four books and over seventy journal articles and book chapters, which have appeared, among others, in the *Journal of Marketing Research*, *Journal of Consumer Research*, *International Journal of Research in Marketing*, *Journal of Classification*, *Educational and Psychological Measurement* and *Marketing Letters*. He is the editor of the *International Journal of Research in Marketing*, and serves on the editorial boards of the *Journal of Consumer Research* and *Journal of Business Research*. He consults and does executive teaching in the areas of branding, product development and strategy for a number of companies and in Wageningen University's Executive Program.

DAVID K. TSE

He can be reached at davidtse@hkusua.hku.hk.

David K. Tse is Professor, as well as Chair, of International Marketing at the Business School of the University of Hong Kong. He received his Ph.D. from the University of California, Berkeley. Professor Tse's research interests include international marketing, marketing in Chinese economies and consumer satisfaction. His papers have appeared in the *Journal of Marketing, Journal of Marketing Research, Journal of Consumer Research, Journal of International Business* and other journals.

OLIVER H. YAU

Oliver H. Yau is the Associate Dean of Graduate Programs and Professor, as well as Chair, of Marketing at the City University of Hong Kong. He received his Ph.D. from Bradford University. His research interests include Chinese management, Chinese cultural values and marketing strategy. Professor Yau's papers have appeared in the *European Journal of Marketing, Journal of Business Research* and others.

YOUJAE YI

Youjae Yi teaches marketing at Seoul National University in Seoul, Korea. His current research interests include customer satisfaction, brand equity, persuasion and service quality. Professor Yi has authored about seventy articles in journals such as the *Journal of Marketing Research, Journal of Consumer Research, Journal of Applied Psychology* and *Korean Management Review.*

C. JOSEPH YU

C. Joseph Yu is Professor of International Business at National Chengchi University, Taiwan. He received his Ph.D. from the University of Michigan. His research interests include foreign direct investment, strategy of multinational firms and international business. Professor Yu's papers have appeared in the *Journal of International Business* and others.

JIE HAI ZHANG

Jie Hai Zhang is Assistant Professor at the Institute of Sociology of the Shanghai Academy of Social Sciences. He received his Ph.D. from East China Normal University, Shanghai, P. R. China. Professor Zhang's papers have appeared in *Economic Psychology, China Advertising* and *Business News.*